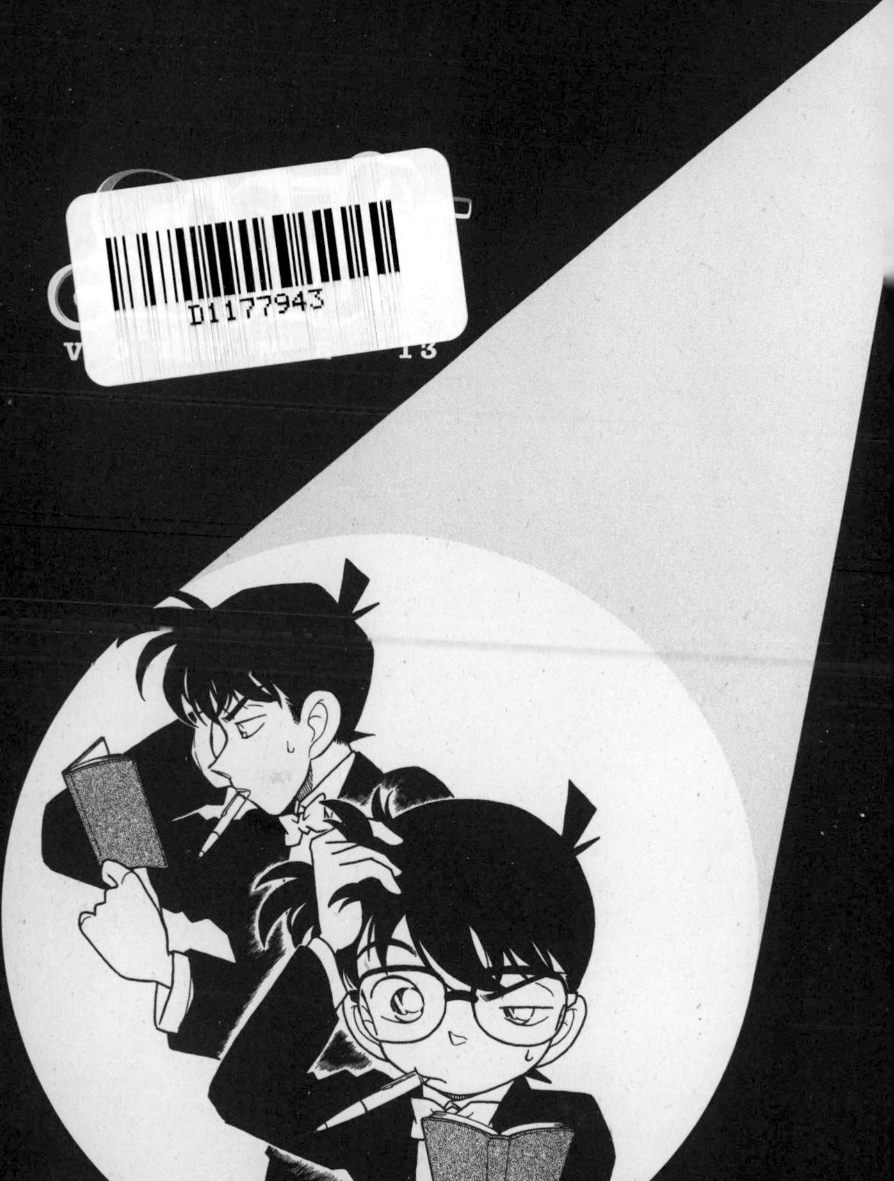

Gosho Aoyama

Case Briefing:

Subject: Jimmy Kudo, a.k.a. Conan Edogawa
Occupation: High School Student/Detective
Special Skills: Analytical thinking and deductive reasoning, Soccer
Equipment: Bow Tie Voice Transmitter, Super Sneakers, Homing Glasses, Stretchy Suspenders

The subject is hot on the trail of a pair of suspicious men in black when he is attacked from behind and administered a strange substance which physically transforms him into a first grader. When the subject confides in the eccentric inventor Dr. Agasa, they decide to keep the subject's true identity a secret for the safety of everyone around him. Assuming the new identity of first-grader Conan Edogawa, the subject continues to assist the police force on their most baffling cases. The only problem is that most crime-solving professionals won't take a little kid's advice!

Table of Contents

CONFIDEN

CASE CLOSED

Volume 13 • VIZ Media Edition

GOSHO AOYAMA

Translation & English Adaptation
Naoko Amemiya

Touch-up & Lettering
Walden Wong

Cover & Graphics Design
Andrea Rice

Editor
Urian Brown

Editor in Chief, Books **Alvin Lu**
Editor in Chief, Magazines **Marc Weidenbaum**
VP of Publishing Licensing **Rika Inouye**
VP of Sales **Gonzalo Ferreyra**
Sr. VP of Marketing **Liza Coppola**
Publisher **Hyoe Narita**

store.viz.com

PARENTAL ADVISORY
CASE CLOSED is rated T+ for Older Teen and
is recommended for ages 16 and up. This vol-
ume contains realistic and graphic violence.
ratings.viz.com

www.viz.com

Printed in the U.S.A.
Published by VIZ Media, LLC
P.O. Box 77010
San Francisco, CA 94107

10 9 8 7 6 5 4 3 2
First printing, September 2006
Second printing, March 2008

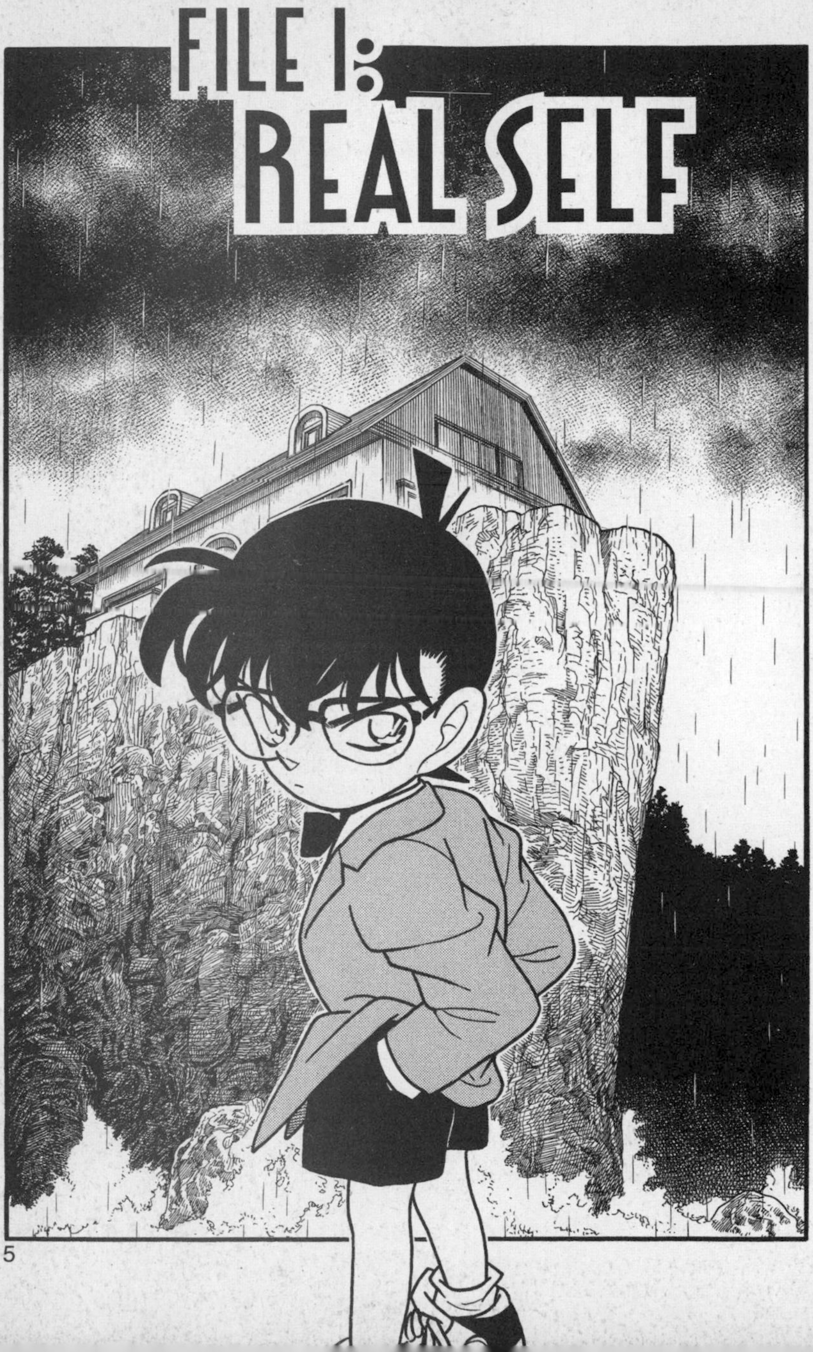
FILE 1:
REAL SELF

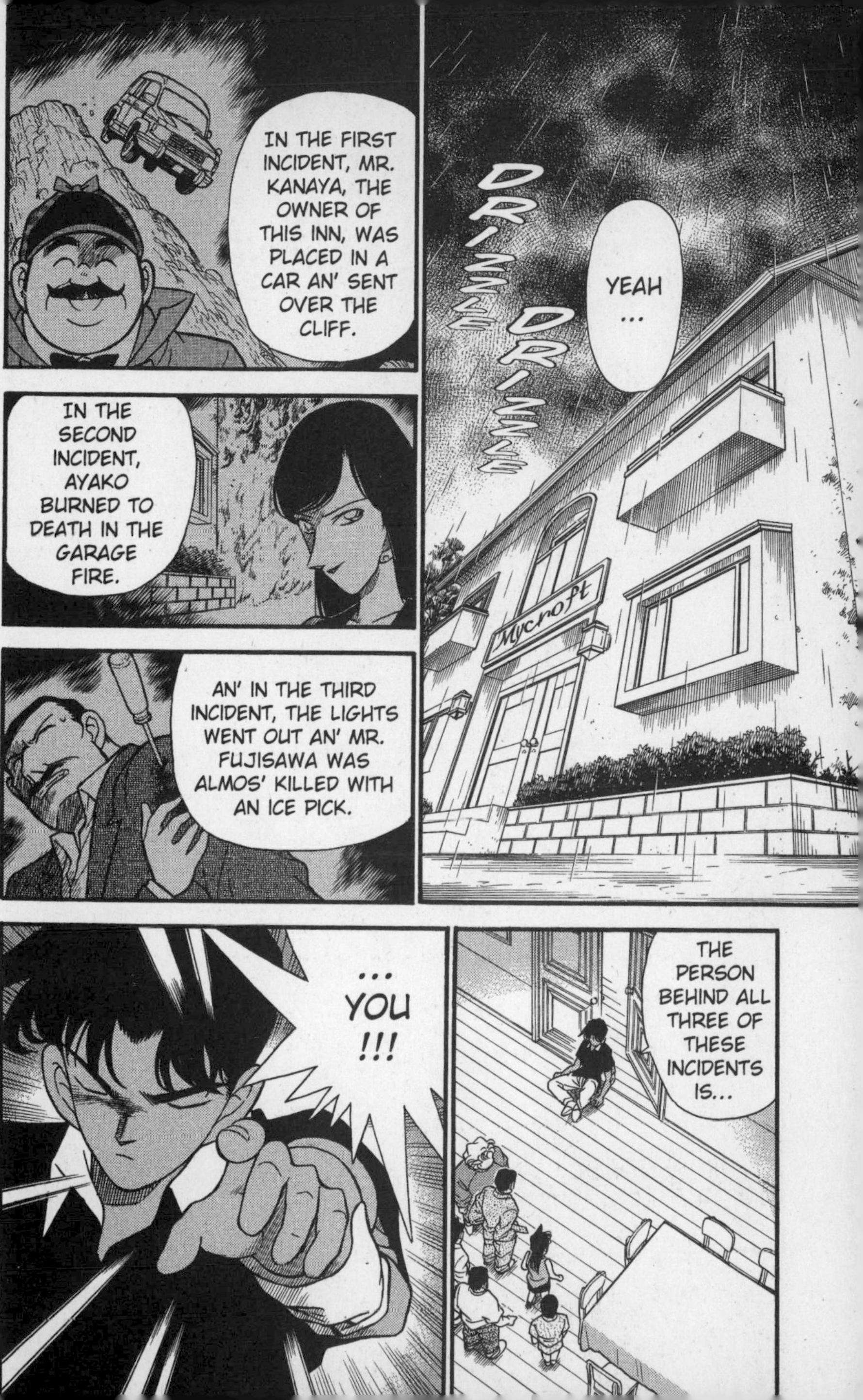
YEAH ...
DRIZZLE DRIZZLE
Mycroft
IN THE FIRST INCIDENT, MR. KANAYA, THE OWNER OF THIS INN, WAS PLACED IN A CAR AN' SENT OVER THE CLIFF.
IN THE SECOND INCIDENT, AYAKO BURNED TO DEATH IN THE GARAGE FIRE.
AN' IN THE THIRD INCIDENT, THE LIGHTS WENT OUT AN' MR. FUJISAWA WAS ALMOS' KILLED WITH AN ICE PICK.
THE PERSON BEHIND ALL THREE OF THESE INCIDENTS IS...
... YOU !!!

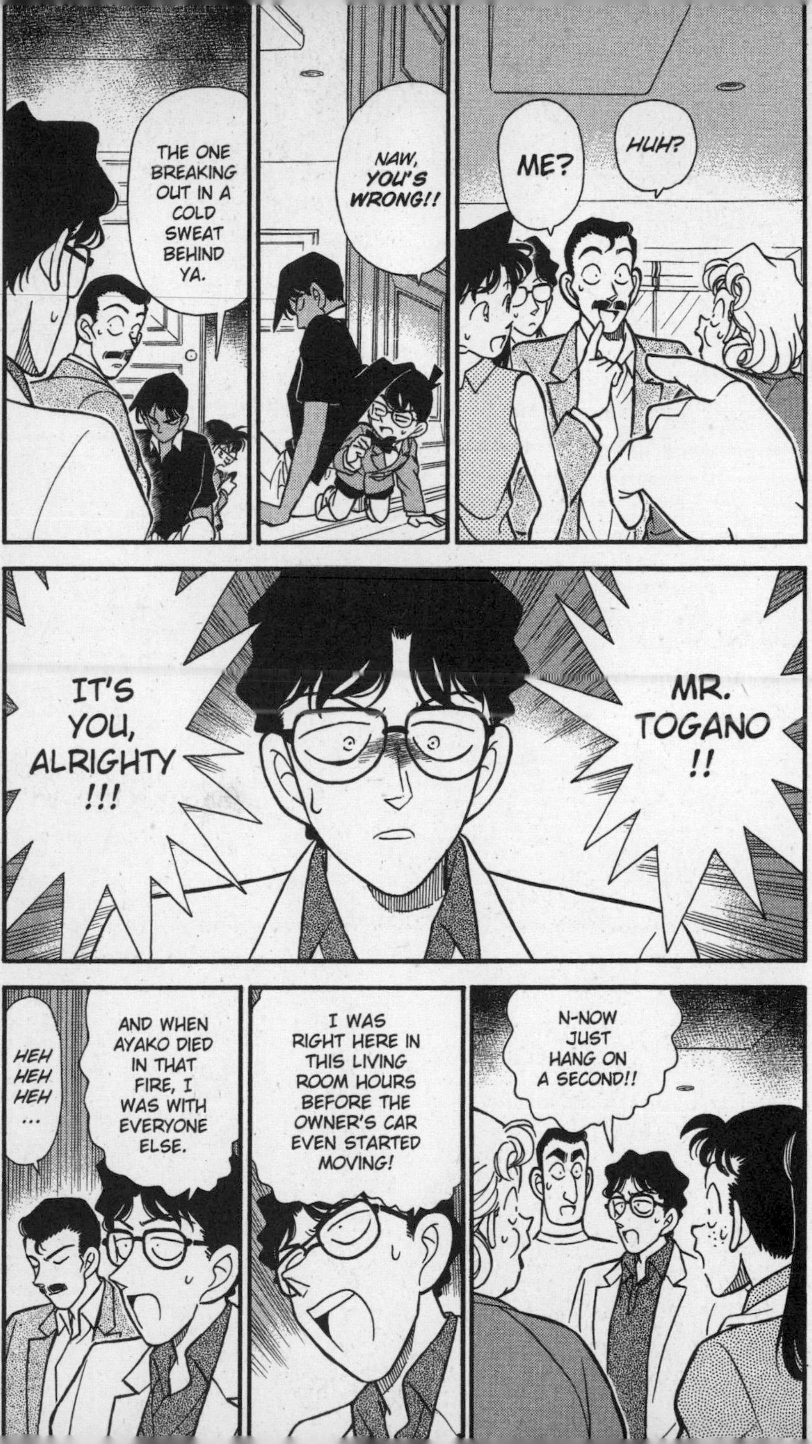
HUH?
ME?
NAW, YOU'S WRONG!!
THE ONE BREAKING OUT IN A COLD SWEAT BEHIND YA.
MR. TOGANO!!
IT'S YOU, ALRIGHTY!!!
N-NOW JUST HANG ON A SECOND!!
I WAS RIGHT HERE IN THIS LIVING ROOM HOURS BEFORE THE OWNER'S CAR EVEN STARTED MOVING!
AND WHEN AYAKO DIED IN THAT FIRE, I WAS WITH EVERYONE ELSE.
HEH HEH HEH ...

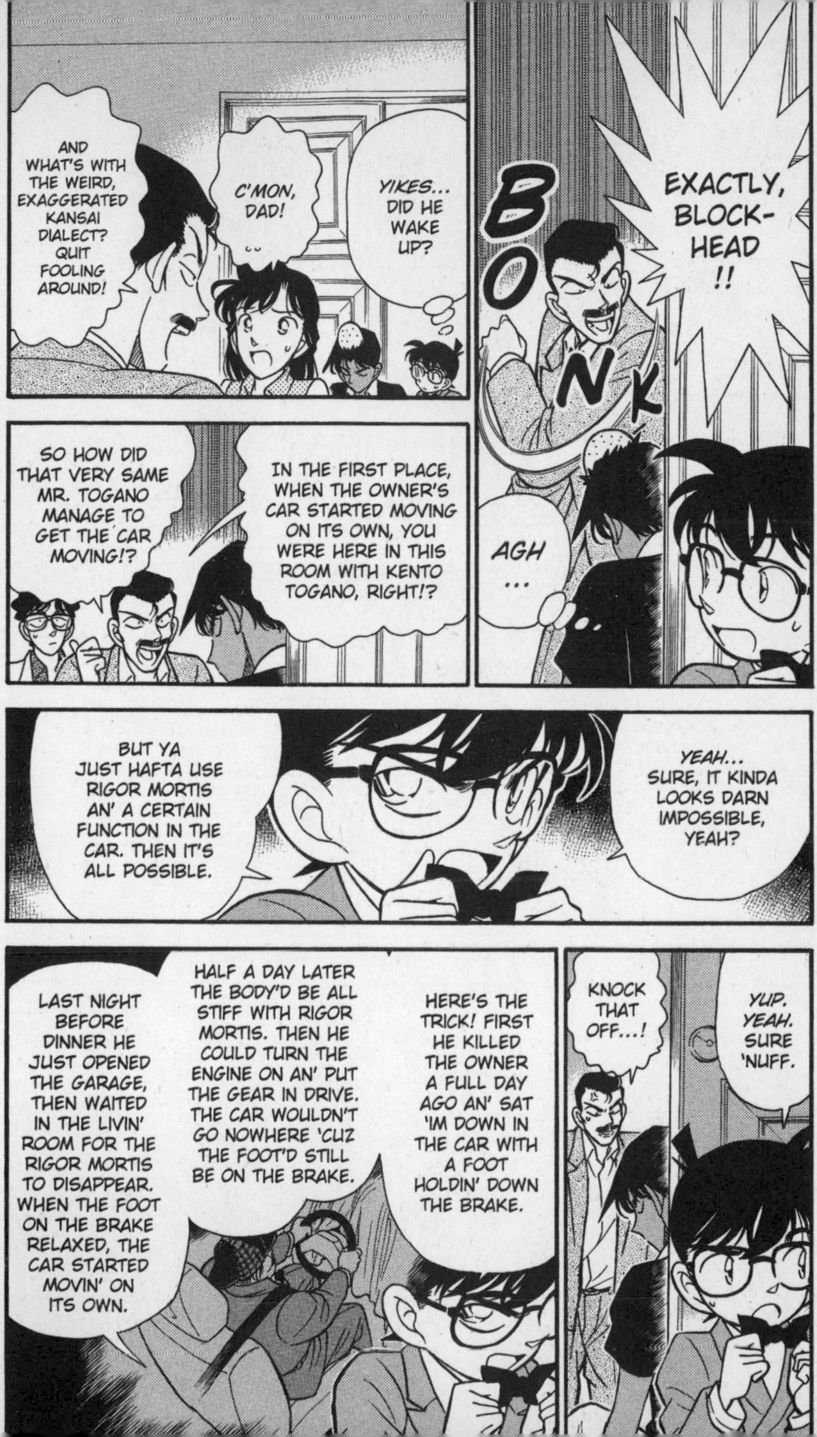
EXACTLY, BLOCK-HEAD!!
BONK
AGH ...
YIKES... DID HE WAKE UP?
C'MON, DAD!
AND WHAT'S WITH THE WEIRD, EXAGGERATED KANSAI DIALECT? QUIT FOOLING AROUND!
IN THE FIRST PLACE, WHEN THE OWNER'S CAR STARTED MOVING ON ITS OWN, YOU WERE HERE IN THIS ROOM WITH KENTO TOGANO, RIGHT!?
SO HOW DID THAT VERY SAME MR. TOGANO MANAGE TO GET THE CAR MOVING!?
YEAH... SURE, IT KINDA LOOKS DARN IMPOSSIBLE, YEAH?
BUT YA JUST HAFTA USE RIGOR MORTIS AN' A CERTAIN FUNCTION IN THE CAR. THEN IT'S ALL POSSIBLE.
YUP. YEAH. SURE 'NUFF.
KNOCK THAT OFF...!
HERE'S THE TRICK! FIRST HE KILLED THE OWNER A FULL DAY AGO AN' SAT 'IM DOWN IN THE CAR WITH A FOOT HOLDIN' DOWN THE BRAKE.
HALF A DAY LATER THE BODY'D BE ALL STIFF WITH RIGOR MORTIS. THEN HE COULD TURN THE ENGINE ON AN' PUT THE GEAR IN DRIVE. THE CAR WOULDN'T GO NOWHERE 'CUZ THE FOOT'D STILL BE ON THE BRAKE.
LAST NIGHT BEFORE DINNER HE JUST OPENED THE GARAGE, THEN WAITED IN THE LIVIN' ROOM FOR THE RIGOR MORTIS TO DISAPPEAR. WHEN THE FOOT ON THE BRAKE RELAXED, THE CAR STARTED MOVIN' ON ITS OWN.

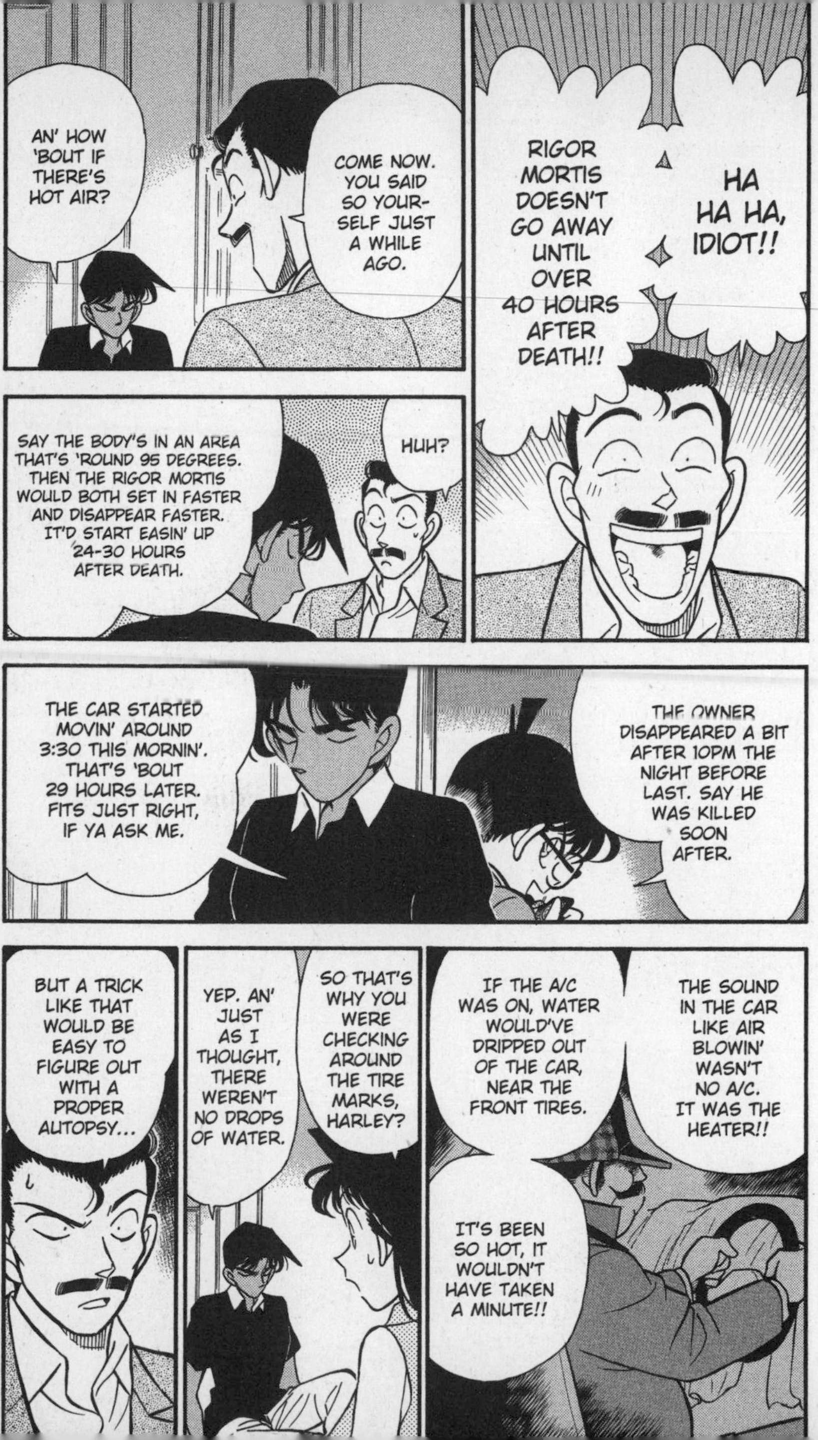
HA HA HA, IDIOT!!
RIGOR MORTIS DOESN'T GO AWAY UNTIL OVER 40 HOURS AFTER DEATH!!
COME NOW. YOU SAID SO YOURSELF JUST A WHILE AGO.
AN' HOW 'BOUT IF THERE'S HOT AIR?
HUH?
SAY THE BODY'S IN AN AREA THAT'S 'ROUND 95 DEGREES. THEN THE RIGOR MORTIS WOULD BOTH SET IN FASTER AND DISAPPEAR FASTER. IT'D START EASIN' UP 24-30 HOURS AFTER DEATH.
THE OWNER DISAPPEARED A BIT AFTER 10PM THE NIGHT BEFORE LAST. SAY HE WAS KILLED SOON AFTER.
THE CAR STARTED MOVIN' AROUND 3:30 THIS MORNIN'. THAT'S 'BOUT 29 HOURS LATER. FITS JUST RIGHT, IF YA ASK ME.
THE SOUND IN THE CAR LIKE AIR BLOWIN' WASN'T NO A/C. IT WAS THE HEATER!!
IF THE A/C WAS ON, WATER WOULD'VE DRIPPED OUT OF THE CAR, NEAR THE FRONT TIRES.
IT'S BEEN SO HOT, IT WOULDN'T HAVE TAKEN A MINUTE!!
SO THAT'S WHY YOU WERE CHECKING AROUND THE TIRE MARKS, HARLEY?
YEP. AN' JUST AS I THOUGHT, THERE WEREN'T NO DROPS OF WATER.
BUT A TRICK LIKE THAT WOULD BE EASY TO FIGURE OUT WITH A PROPER AUTOPSY...

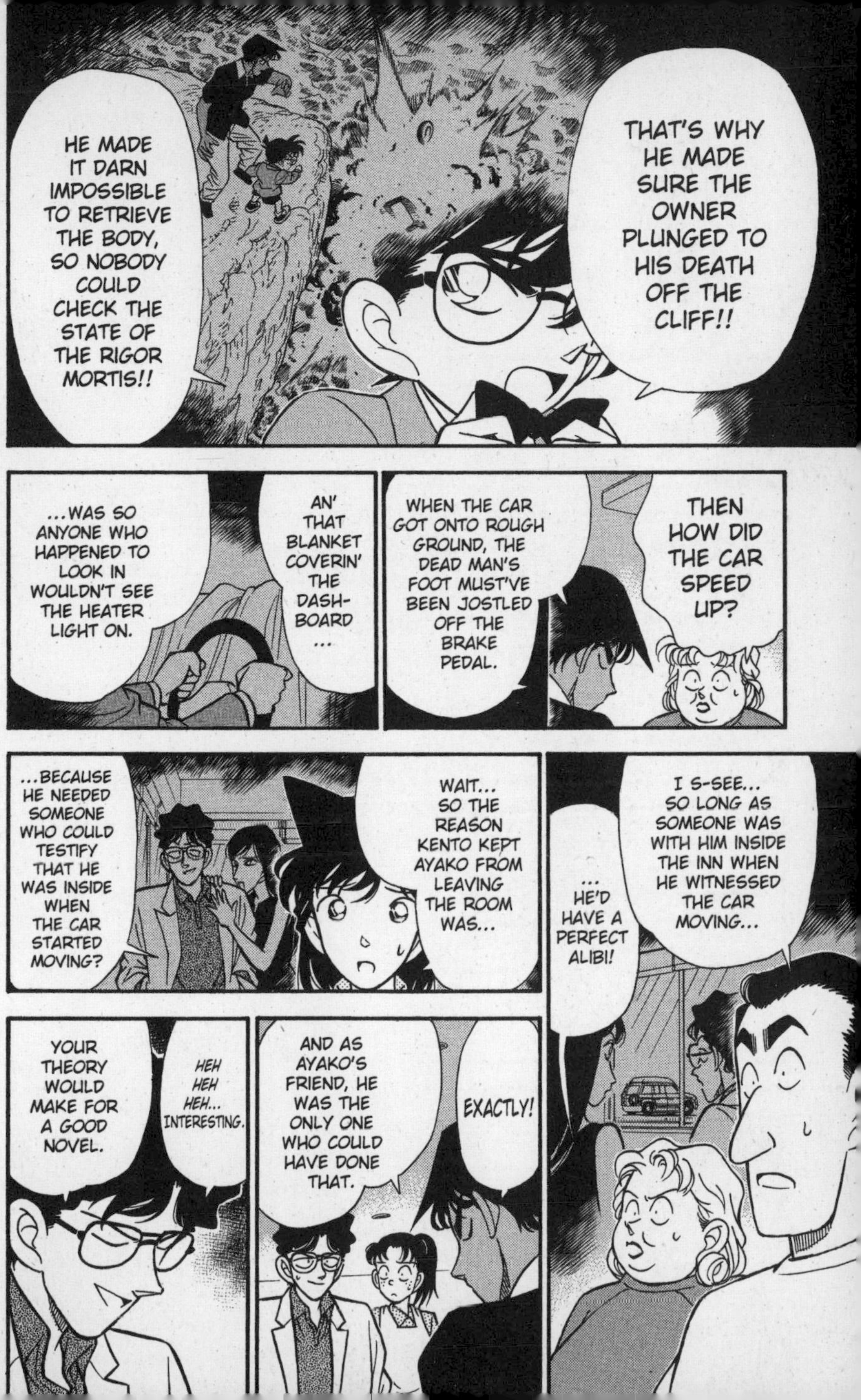
THAT'S WHY HE MADE SURE THE OWNER PLUNGED TO HIS DEATH OFF THE CLIFF!!
HE MADE IT DARN IMPOSSIBLE TO RETRIEVE THE BODY, SO NOBODY COULD CHECK THE STATE OF THE RIGOR MORTIS!!
THEN HOW DID THE CAR SPEED UP?
WHEN THE CAR GOT ONTO ROUGH GROUND, THE DEAD MAN'S FOOT MUST'VE BEEN JOSTLED OFF THE BRAKE PEDAL.
AN' THAT BLANKET COVERIN' THE DASH-BOARD ...
...WAS SO ANYONE WHO HAPPENED TO LOOK IN WOULDN'T SEE THE HEATER LIGHT ON.
I S-SEE... SO LONG AS SOMEONE WAS WITH HIM INSIDE THE INN WHEN HE WITNESSED THE CAR MOVING...
...HE'D HAVE A PERFECT ALIBI!
WAIT... SO THE REASON KENTO KEPT AYAKO FROM LEAVING THE ROOM WAS...
...BECAUSE HE NEEDED SOMEONE WHO COULD TESTIFY THAT HE WAS INSIDE WHEN THE CAR STARTED MOVING?
EXACTLY!
AND AS AYAKO'S FRIEND, HE WAS THE ONLY ONE WHO COULD HAVE DONE THAT.
HEH HEH HEH... INTERESTING.
YOUR THEORY WOULD MAKE FOR A GOOD NOVEL.

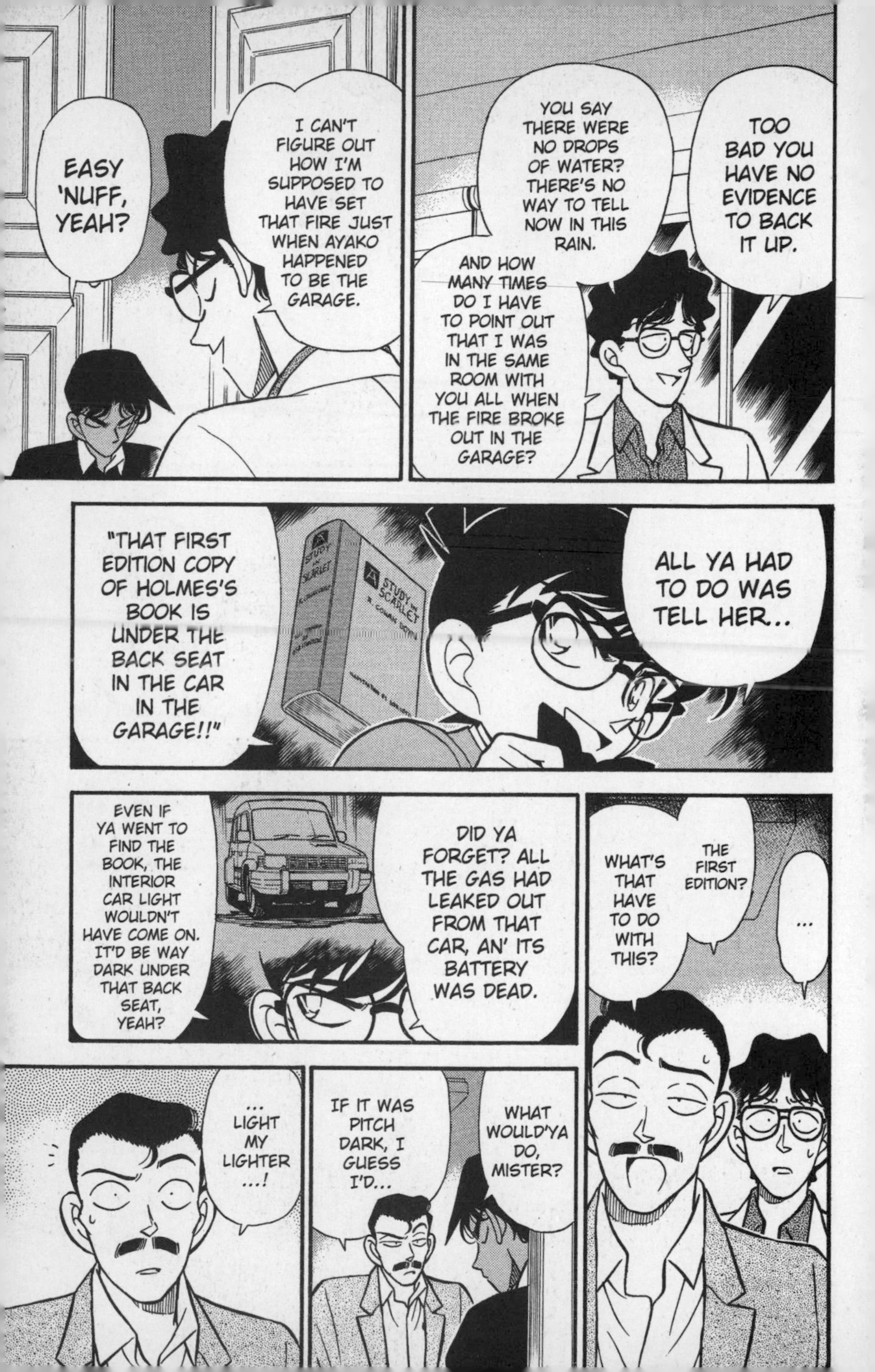
TOO BAD YOU HAVE NO EVIDENCE TO BACK IT UP.
YOU SAY THERE WERE NO DROPS OF WATER? THERE'S NO WAY TO TELL NOW IN THIS RAIN.
AND HOW MANY TIMES DO I HAVE TO POINT OUT THAT I WAS IN THE SAME ROOM WITH YOU ALL WHEN THE FIRE BROKE OUT IN THE GARAGE?
I CAN'T FIGURE OUT HOW I'M SUPPOSED TO HAVE SET THAT FIRE JUST WHEN AYAKO HAPPENED TO BE THE GARAGE.
EASY 'NUFF, YEAH?
ALL YA HAD TO DO WAS TELL HER...
"THAT FIRST EDITION COPY OF HOLMES'S BOOK IS UNDER THE BACK SEAT IN THE CAR IN THE GARAGE!!"
...
THE FIRST EDITION?
WHAT'S THAT HAVE TO DO WITH THIS?
DID YA FORGET? ALL THE GAS HAD LEAKED OUT FROM THAT CAR, AN' ITS BATTERY WAS DEAD.
EVEN IF YA WENT TO FIND THE BOOK, THE INTERIOR CAR LIGHT WOULDN'T HAVE COME ON. IT'D BE WAY DARK UNDER THAT BACK SEAT, YEAH?
WHAT WOULD'YA DO, MISTER?
IF IT WAS PITCH DARK, I GUESS I'D...
...LIGHT MY LIGHTER...!

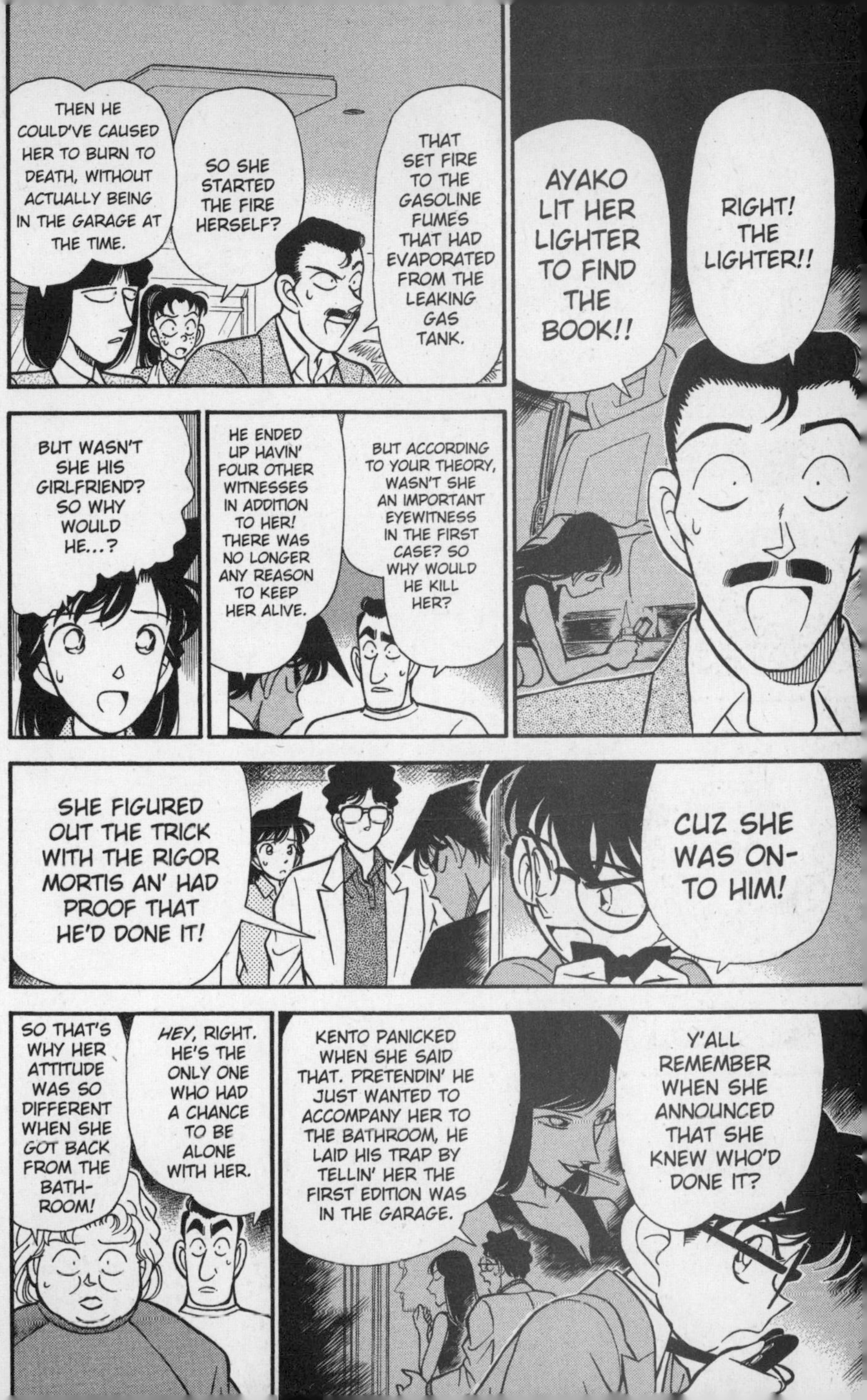
RIGHT! THE LIGHTER!!
AYAKO LIT HER LIGHTER TO FIND THE BOOK!!
THAT SET FIRE TO THE GASOLINE FUMES THAT HAD EVAPORATED FROM THE LEAKING GAS TANK.
SO SHE STARTED THE FIRE HERSELF?
THEN HE COULD'VE CAUSED HER TO BURN TO DEATH, WITHOUT ACTUALLY BEING IN THE GARAGE AT THE TIME.
BUT ACCORDING TO YOUR THEORY, WASN'T SHE AN IMPORTANT EYEWITNESS IN THE FIRST CASE? SO WHY WOULD HE KILL HER?
HE ENDED UP HAVIN' FOUR OTHER WITNESSES IN ADDITION TO HER! THERE WAS NO LONGER ANY REASON TO KEEP HER ALIVE.
BUT WASN'T SHE HIS GIRLFRIEND? SO WHY WOULD HE...?
CUZ SHE WAS ON-TO HIM!
SHE FIGURED OUT THE TRICK WITH THE RIGOR MORTIS AN' HAD PROOF THAT HE'D DONE IT!
Y'ALL REMEMBER WHEN SHE ANNOUNCED THAT SHE KNEW WHO'D DONE IT?
KENTO PANICKED WHEN SHE SAID THAT. PRETENDIN' HE JUST WANTED TO ACCOMPANY HER TO THE BATHROOM, HE LAID HIS TRAP BY TELLIN' HER THE FIRST EDITION WAS IN THE GARAGE.
HEY, RIGHT. HE'S THE ONLY ONE WHO HAD A CHANCE TO BE ALONE WITH HER.
SO THAT'S WHY HER ATTITUDE WAS SO DIFFERENT WHEN SHE GOT BACK FROM THE BATH-ROOM!

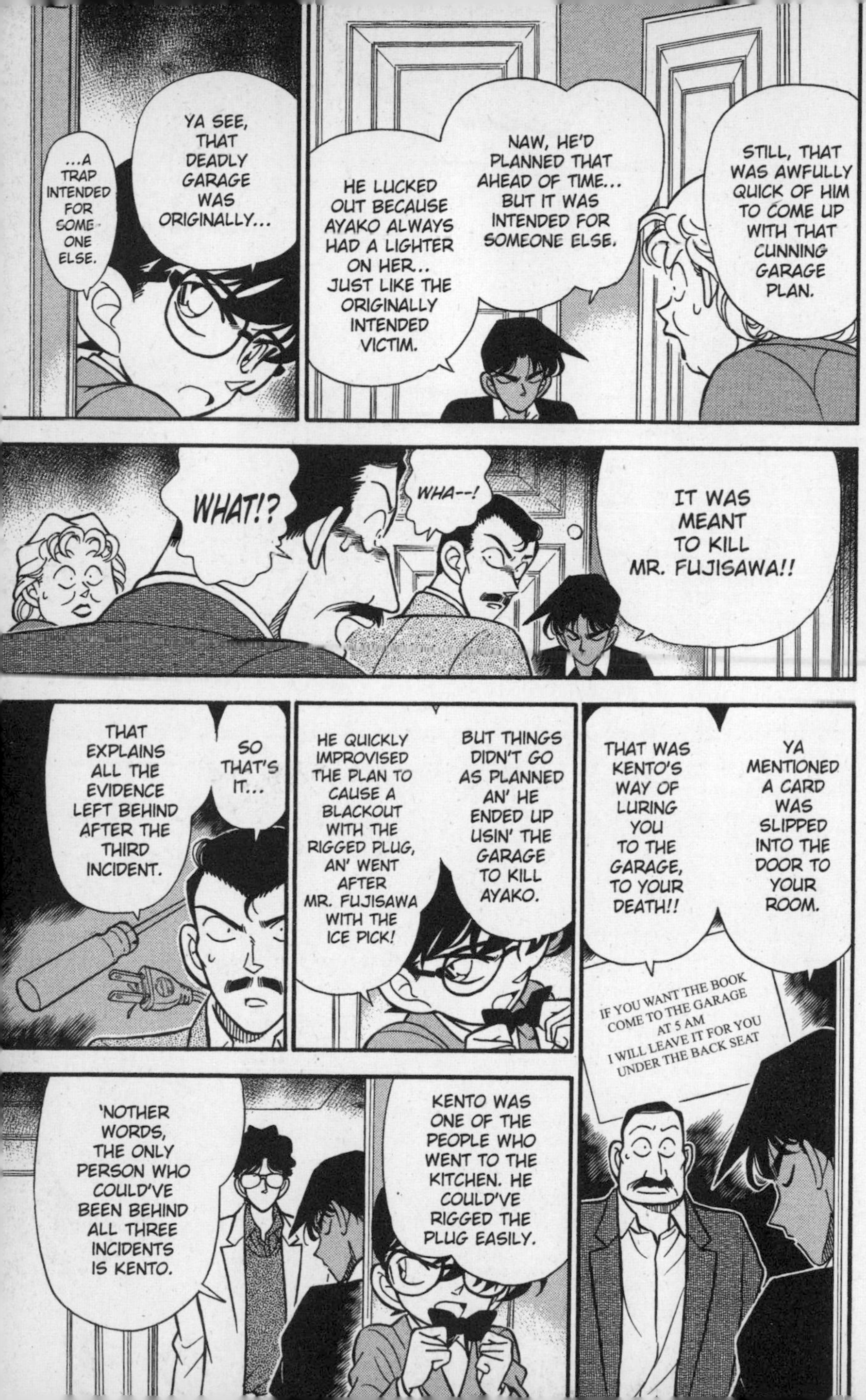
STILL, THAT WAS AWFULLY QUICK OF HIM TO COME UP WITH THAT CUNNING GARAGE PLAN.
NAW, HE'D PLANNED THAT AHEAD OF TIME... BUT IT WAS INTENDED FOR SOMEONE ELSE.
HE LUCKED OUT BECAUSE AYAKO ALWAYS HAD A LIGHTER ON HER... JUST LIKE THE ORIGINALLY INTENDED VICTIM.
YA SEE, THAT DEADLY GARAGE WAS ORIGINALLY...
...A TRAP INTENDED FOR SOME-ONE ELSE.
IT WAS MEANT TO KILL MR. FUJISAWA!!
WHA--!
WHAT!?
YA MENTIONED A CARD WAS SLIPPED INTO THE DOOR TO YOUR ROOM.
THAT WAS KENTO'S WAY OF LURING YOU TO THE GARAGE, TO YOUR DEATH!!
IF YOU WANT THE BOOK COME TO THE GARAGE AT 5 AM I WILL LEAVE IT FOR YOU UNDER THE BACK SEAT
BUT THINGS DIDN'T GO AS PLANNED AN' HE ENDED UP USIN' THE GARAGE TO KILL AYAKO.
HE QUICKLY IMPROVISED THE PLAN TO CAUSE A BLACKOUT WITH THE RIGGED PLUG, AN' WENT AFTER MR. FUJISAWA WITH THE ICE PICK!
SO THAT'S IT...
THAT EXPLAINS ALL THE EVIDENCE LEFT BEHIND AFTER THE THIRD INCIDENT.
KENTO WAS ONE OF THE PEOPLE WHO WENT TO THE KITCHEN. HE COULD'VE RIGGED THE PLUG EASILY.
'NOTHER WORDS, THE ONLY PERSON WHO COULD'VE BEEN BEHIND ALL THREE INCIDENTS IS KENTO.

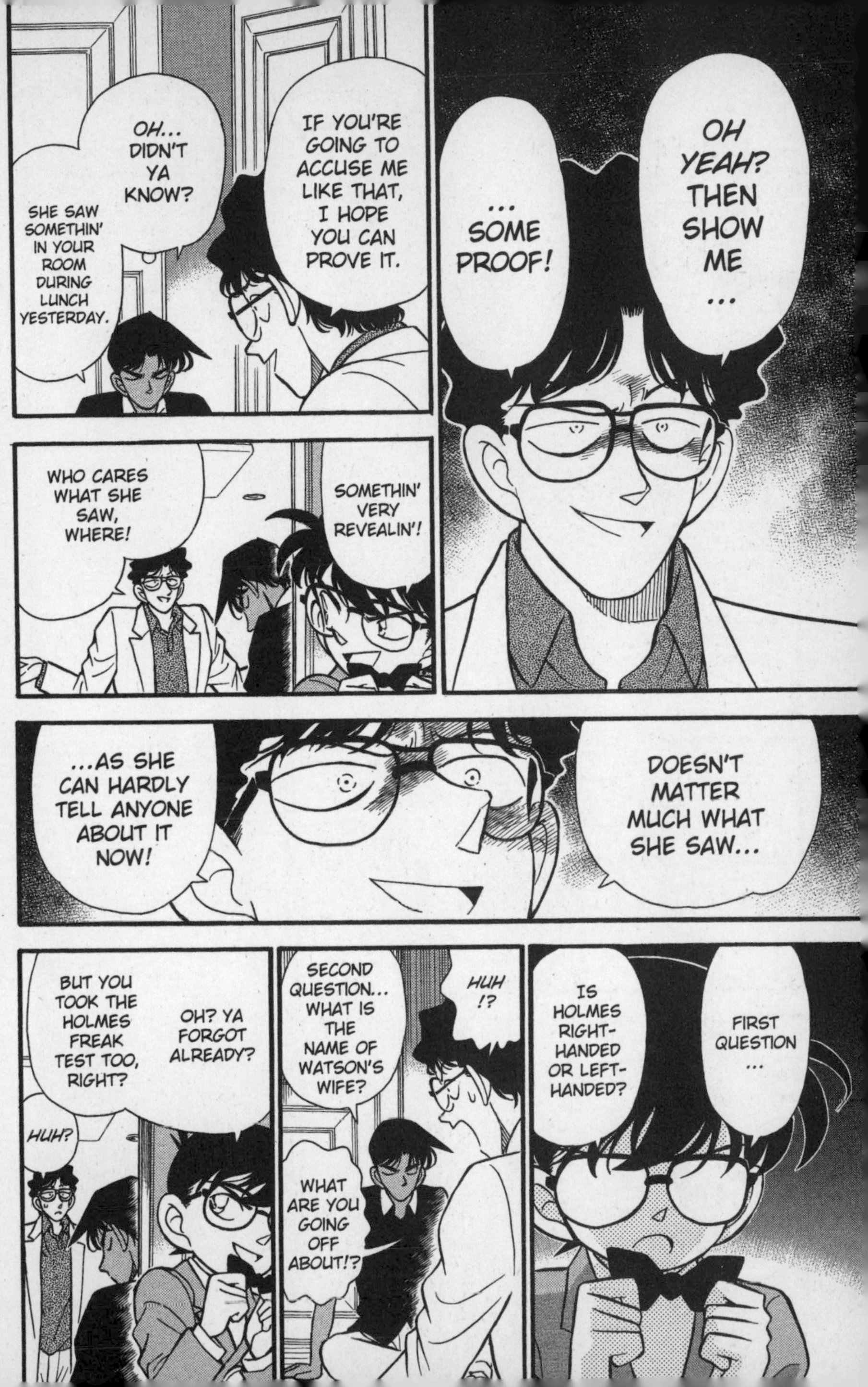
OH YEAH? THEN SHOW ME ...
... SOME PROOF!
IF YOU'RE GOING TO ACCUSE ME LIKE THAT, I HOPE YOU CAN PROVE IT.
OH... DIDN'T YA KNOW?
SHE SAW SOMETHIN' IN YOUR ROOM DURING LUNCH YESTERDAY.
SOMETHIN' VERY REVEALIN'!
WHO CARES WHAT SHE SAW, WHERE!
DOESN'T MATTER MUCH WHAT SHE SAW...
...AS SHE CAN HARDLY TELL ANYONE ABOUT IT NOW!
FIRST QUESTION ...
IS HOLMES RIGHT-HANDED OR LEFT-HANDED?
HUH !?
SECOND QUESTION... WHAT IS THE NAME OF WATSON'S WIFE?
WHAT ARE YOU GOING OFF ABOUT!?
OH? YA FORGOT ALREADY?
BUT YOU TOOK THE HOLMES FREAK TEST TOO, RIGHT?
HUH?

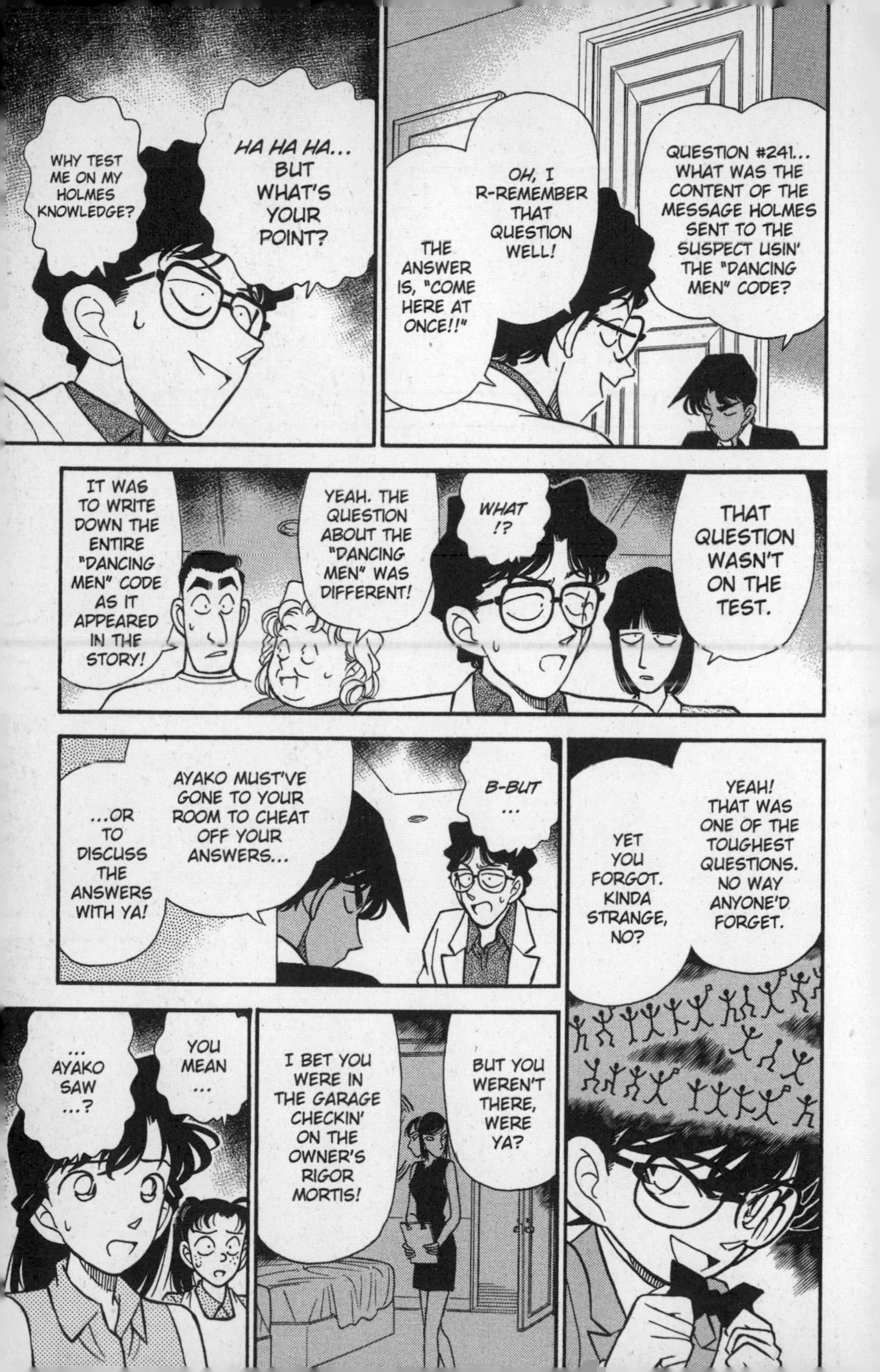
QUESTION #241... WHAT WAS THE CONTENT OF THE MESSAGE HOLMES SENT TO THE SUSPECT USIN' THE "DANCING MEN" CODE?
OH, I R-REMEMBER THAT QUESTION WELL!
THE ANSWER IS, "COME HERE AT ONCE!!"
HA HA HA... BUT WHAT'S YOUR POINT?
WHY TEST ME ON MY HOLMES KNOWLEDGE?
THAT QUESTION WASN'T ON THE TEST.
WHAT!?
YEAH. THE QUESTION ABOUT THE "DANCING MEN" WAS DIFFERENT!
IT WAS TO WRITE DOWN THE ENTIRE "DANCING MEN" CODE AS IT APPEARED IN THE STORY!
YEAH! THAT WAS ONE OF THE TOUGHEST QUESTIONS. NO WAY ANYONE'D FORGET.
YET YOU FORGOT. KINDA STRANGE, NO?
B-BUT...
AYAKO MUST'VE GONE TO YOUR ROOM TO CHEAT OFF YOUR ANSWERS...
...OR TO DISCUSS THE ANSWERS WITH YA!
BUT YOU WEREN'T THERE, WERE YA?
I BET YOU WERE IN THE GARAGE CHECKIN' ON THE OWNER'S RIGOR MORTIS!
YOU MEAN...
...AYAKO SAW...?

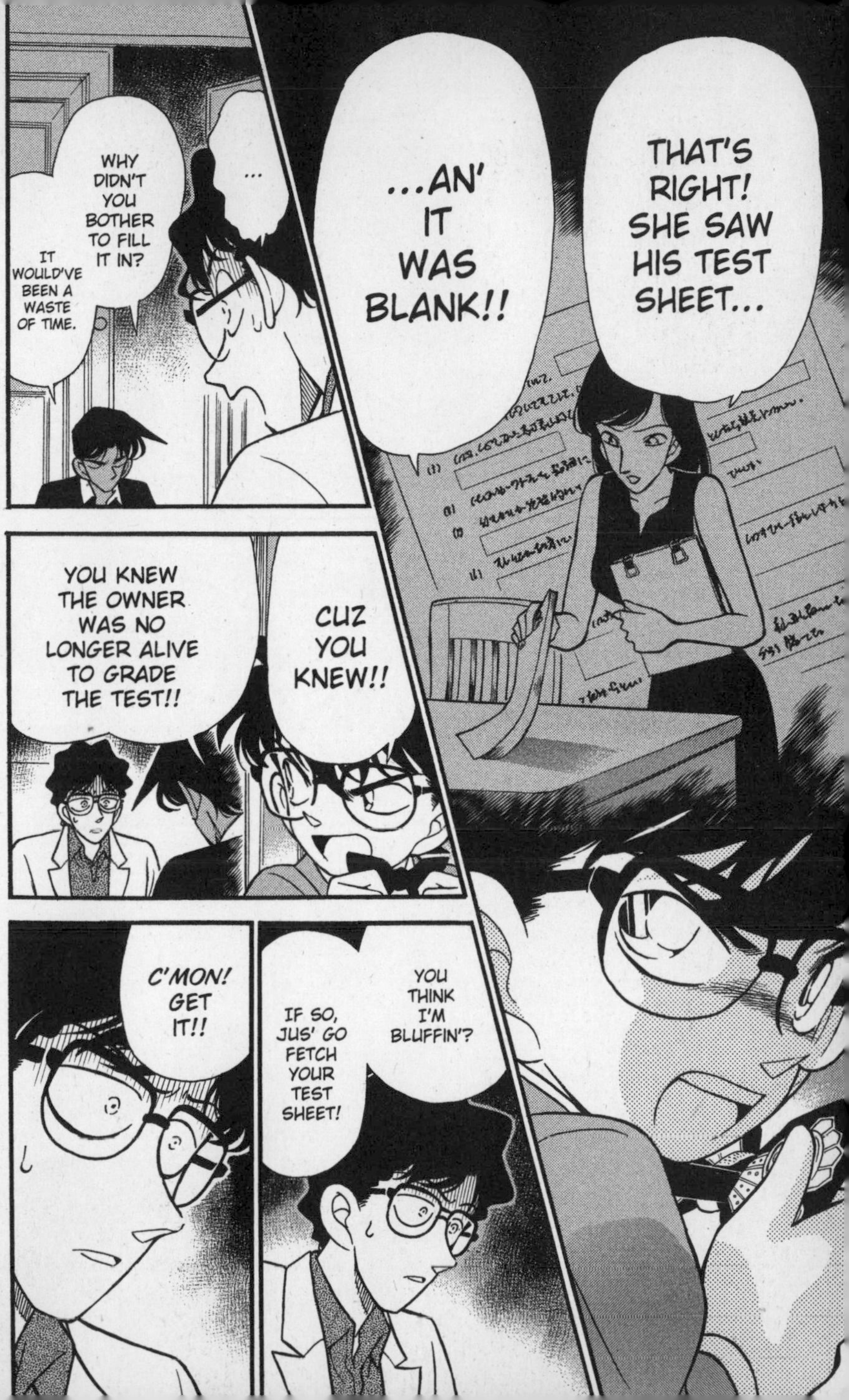
THAT'S RIGHT! SHE SAW HIS TEST SHEET...
...AN' IT WAS BLANK!!
...
WHY DIDN'T YOU BOTHER TO FILL IT IN?
IT WOULD'VE BEEN A WASTE OF TIME.
CUZ YOU KNEW!!
YOU KNEW THE OWNER WAS NO LONGER ALIVE TO GRADE THE TEST!!
YOU THINK I'M BLUFFIN'?
IF SO, JUS' GO FETCH YOUR TEST SHEET!
C'MON! GET IT!!

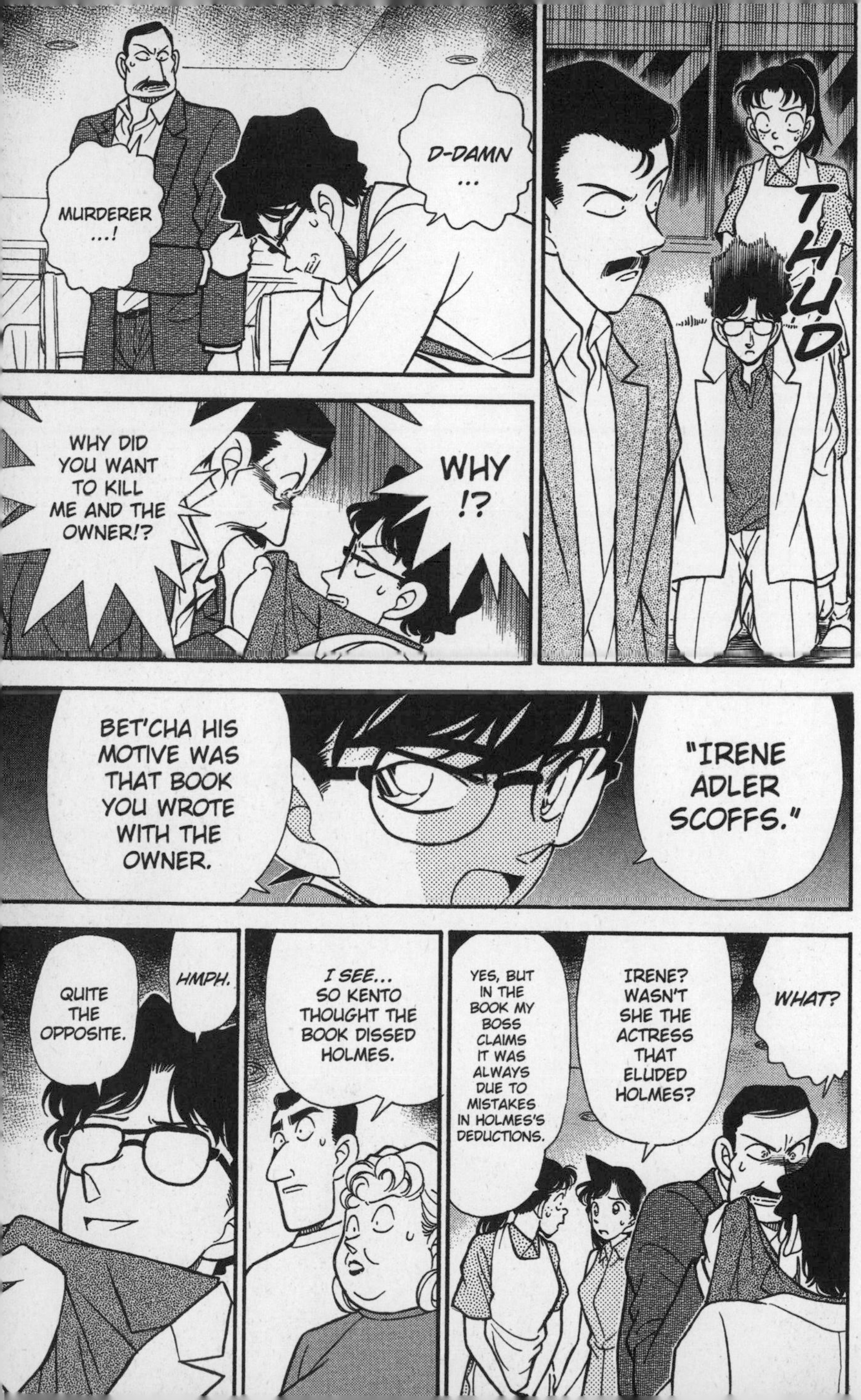
THUD
D-DAMN ...
MURDERER ...!
WHY !?
WHY DID YOU WANT TO KILL ME AND THE OWNER!?
"IRENE ADLER SCOFFS."
BET'CHA HIS MOTIVE WAS THAT BOOK YOU WROTE WITH THE OWNER.
WHAT?
IRENE? WASN'T SHE THE ACTRESS THAT ELUDED HOLMES?
YES, BUT IN THE BOOK MY BOSS CLAIMS IT WAS ALWAYS DUE TO MISTAKES IN HOLMES'S DEDUCTIONS.
I SEE... SO KENTO THOUGHT THE BOOK DISSED HOLMES.
HMPH.
QUITE THE OPPOSITE.

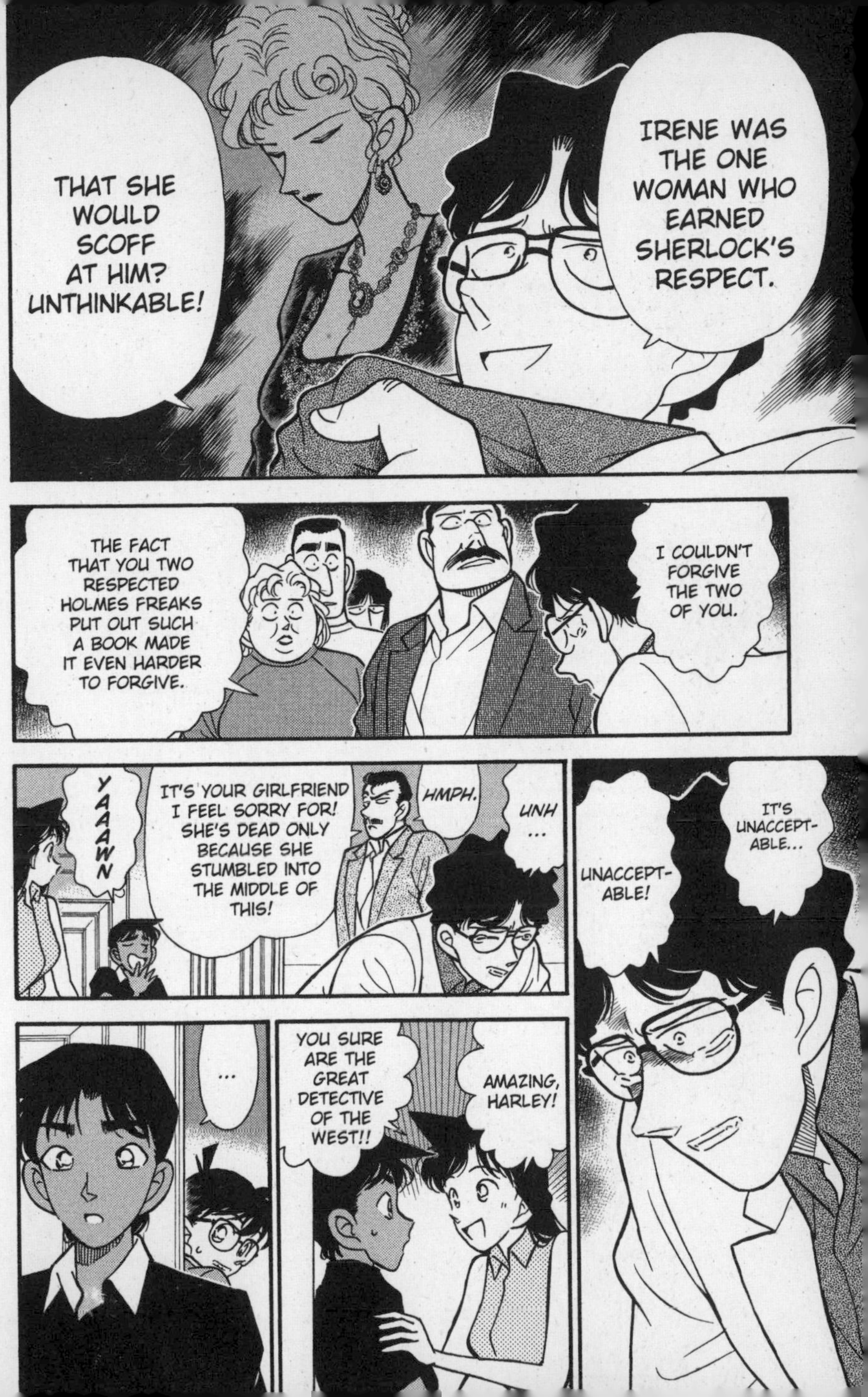
IRENE WAS THE ONE WOMAN WHO EARNED SHERLOCK'S RESPECT.
THAT SHE WOULD SCOFF AT HIM? UNTHINKABLE!
I COULDN'T FORGIVE THE TWO OF YOU.
THE FACT THAT YOU TWO RESPECTED HOLMES FREAKS PUT OUT SUCH A BOOK MADE IT EVEN HARDER TO FORGIVE.
IT'S UNACCEPTABLE...
UNACCEPTABLE!
UNH ...
HMPH.
IT'S YOUR GIRLFRIEND I FEEL SORRY FOR! SHE'S DEAD ONLY BECAUSE SHE STUMBLED INTO THE MIDDLE OF THIS!
YAAAAWN
AMAZING, HARLEY!
YOU SURE ARE THE GREAT DETECTIVE OF THE WEST!!
...

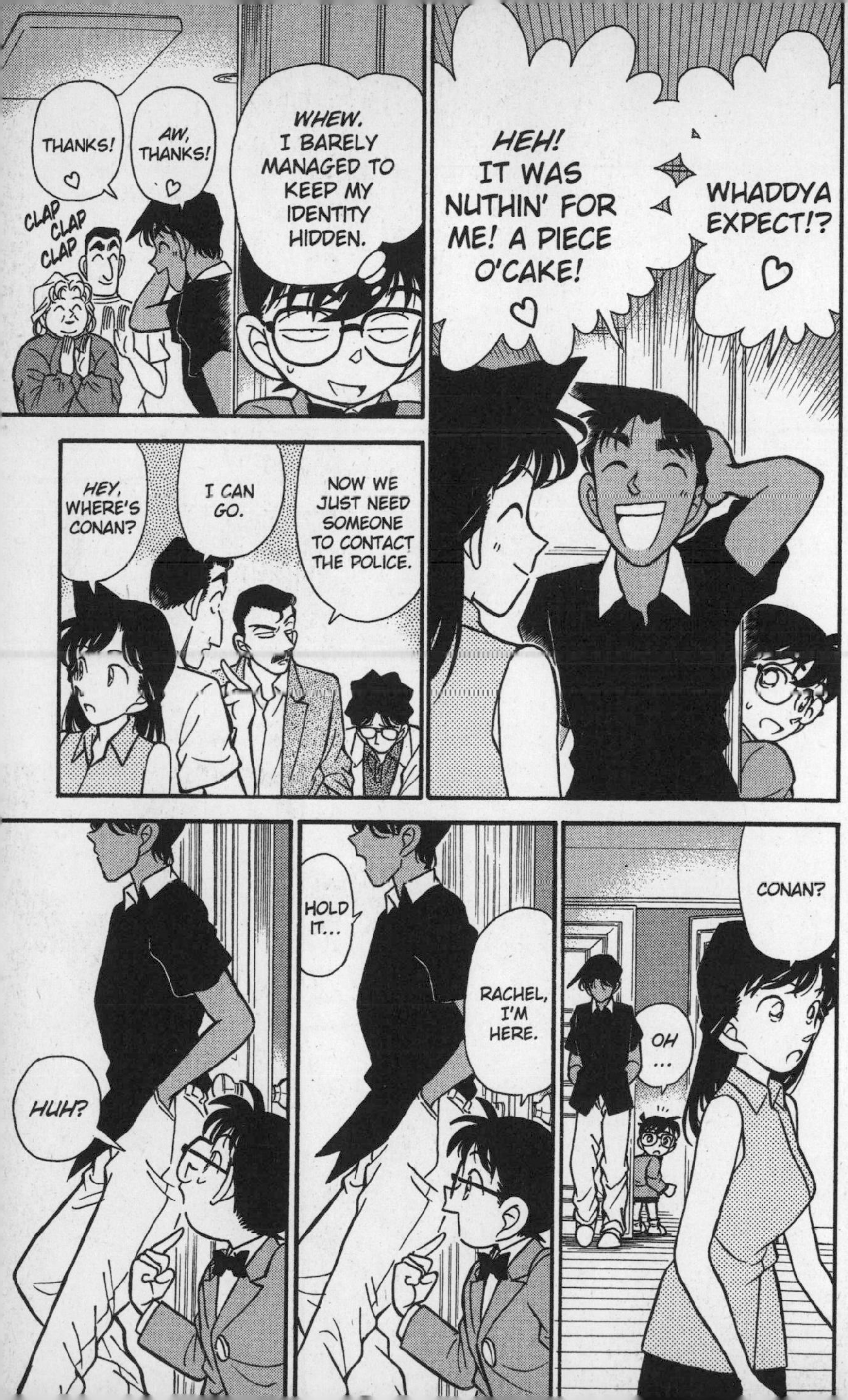
HEH! IT WAS NUTHIN' FOR ME! A PIECE O'CAKE!
WHADDYA EXPECT!?
WHEW. I BARELY MANAGED TO KEEP MY IDENTITY HIDDEN.
AW, THANKS!
THANKS!
CLAP CLAP CLAP
NOW WE JUST NEED SOMEONE TO CONTACT THE POLICE.
I CAN GO.
HEY, WHERE'S CONAN?
CONAN?
OH ...
RACHEL, I'M HERE.
HOLD IT...
HUH?

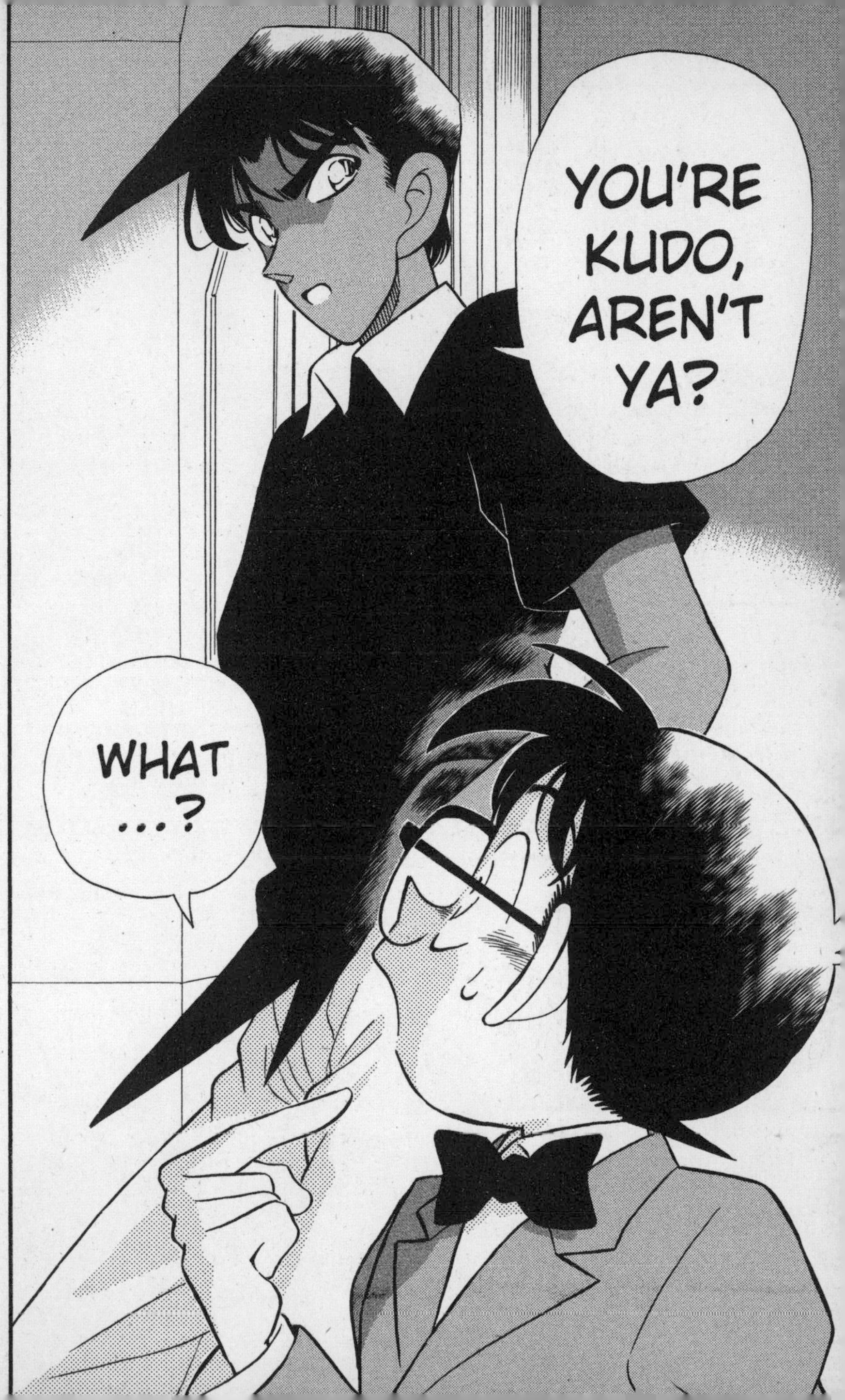
YOU'RE KUDO, AREN'T YA?
WHAT ...?

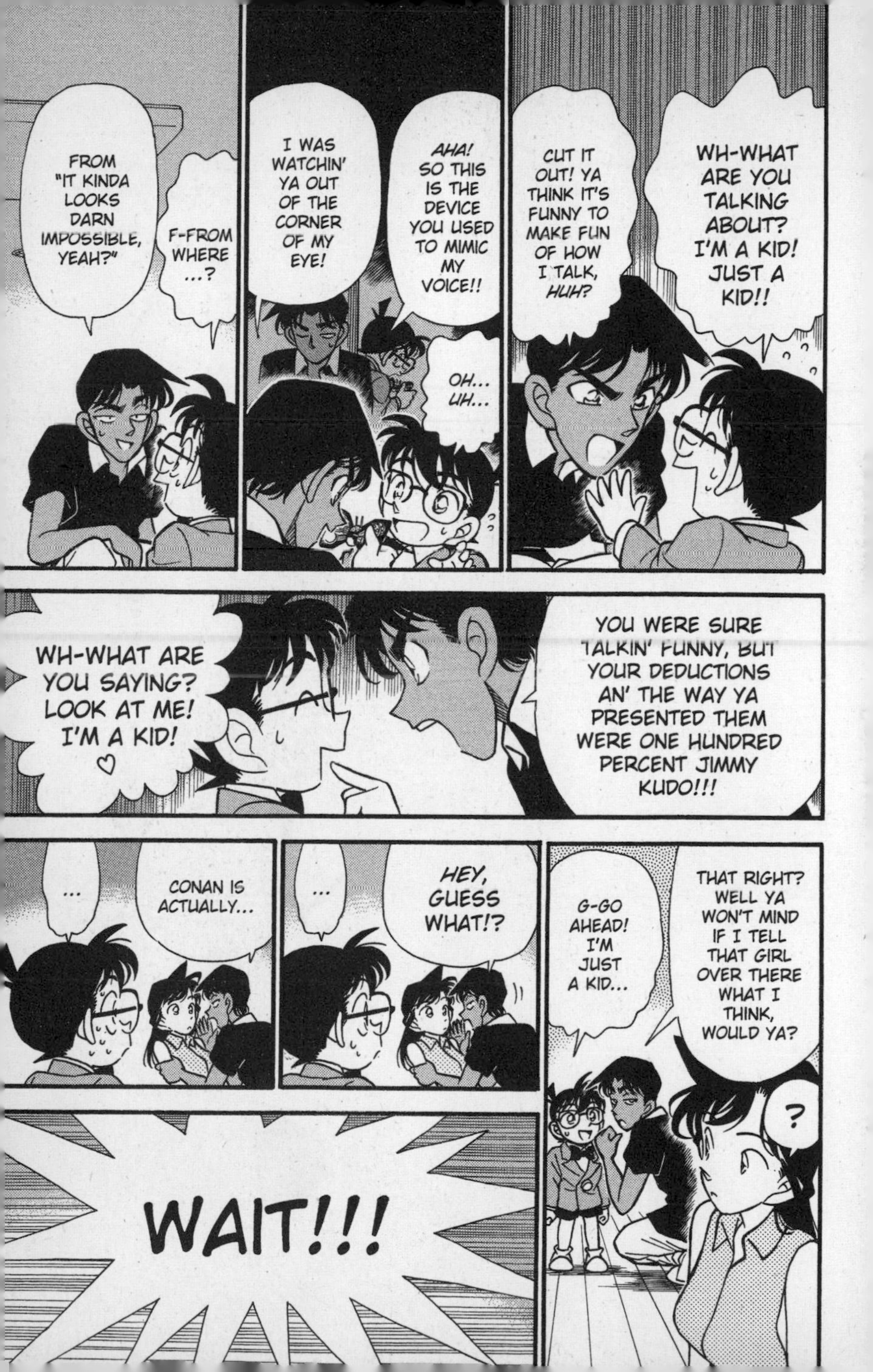
WH-WHAT ARE YOU TALKING ABOUT? I'M A KID! JUST A KID!!
CUT IT OUT! YA THINK IT'S FUNNY TO MAKE FUN OF HOW I TALK, *HUH?*
AHA! SO THIS IS THE DEVICE YOU USED TO MIMIC MY VOICE!!
I WAS WATCHIN' YA OUT OF THE CORNER OF MY EYE!
OH... UH...
F-FROM WHERE ...?
FROM "IT KINDA LOOKS DARN IMPOSSIBLE, YEAH?"
YOU WERE SURE TALKIN' FUNNY, BUT YOUR DEDUCTIONS AN' THE WAY YA PRESENTED THEM WERE ONE HUNDRED PERCENT JIMMY KUDO!!!
WH-WHAT ARE YOU SAYING? LOOK AT ME! I'M A KID! ♡
THAT RIGHT? WELL YA WON'T MIND IF I TELL THAT GIRL OVER THERE WHAT I THINK, WOULD YA?
G-GO AHEAD! I'M JUST A KID...
?
HEY, GUESS WHAT!?
...
CONAN IS ACTUALLY...
...
WAIT!!!

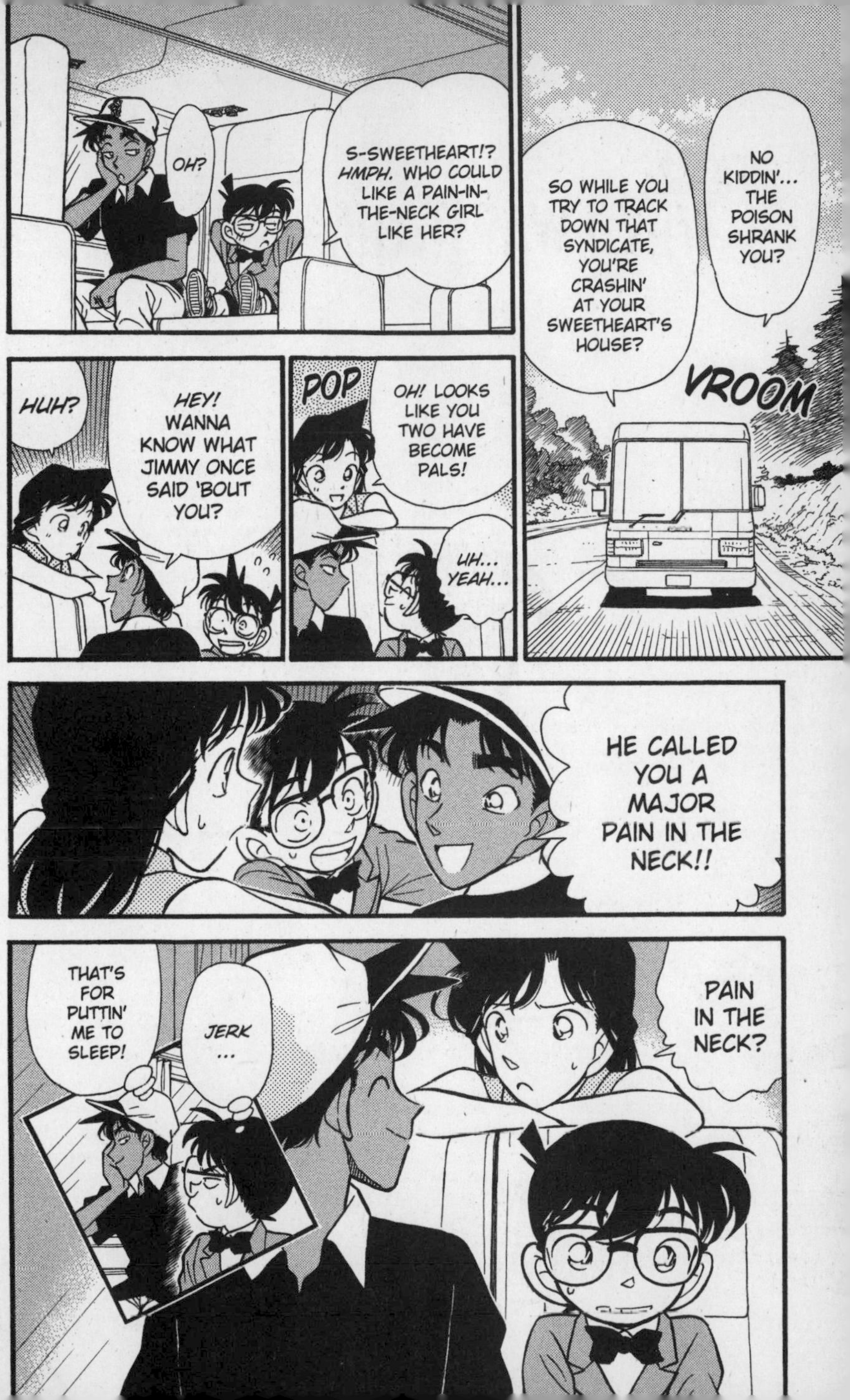
NO KIDDIN'... THE POISON SHRANK YOU?
SO WHILE YOU TRY TO TRACK DOWN THAT SYNDICATE, YOU'RE CRASHIN' AT YOUR SWEETHEART'S HOUSE?
VROOM
S-SWEETHEART!? HMPH. WHO COULD LIKE A PAIN-IN-THE-NECK GIRL LIKE HER?
OH?
POP
OH! LOOKS LIKE YOU TWO HAVE BECOME PALS!
UH... YEAH...
HEY! WANNA KNOW WHAT JIMMY ONCE SAID 'BOUT YOU?
HUH?
HE CALLED YOU A MAJOR PAIN IN THE NECK!!
PAIN IN THE NECK?
JERK ...
THAT'S FOR PUTTIN' ME TO SLEEP!

FILE 2:
WHO WAS IT THEY WITNESSED!?

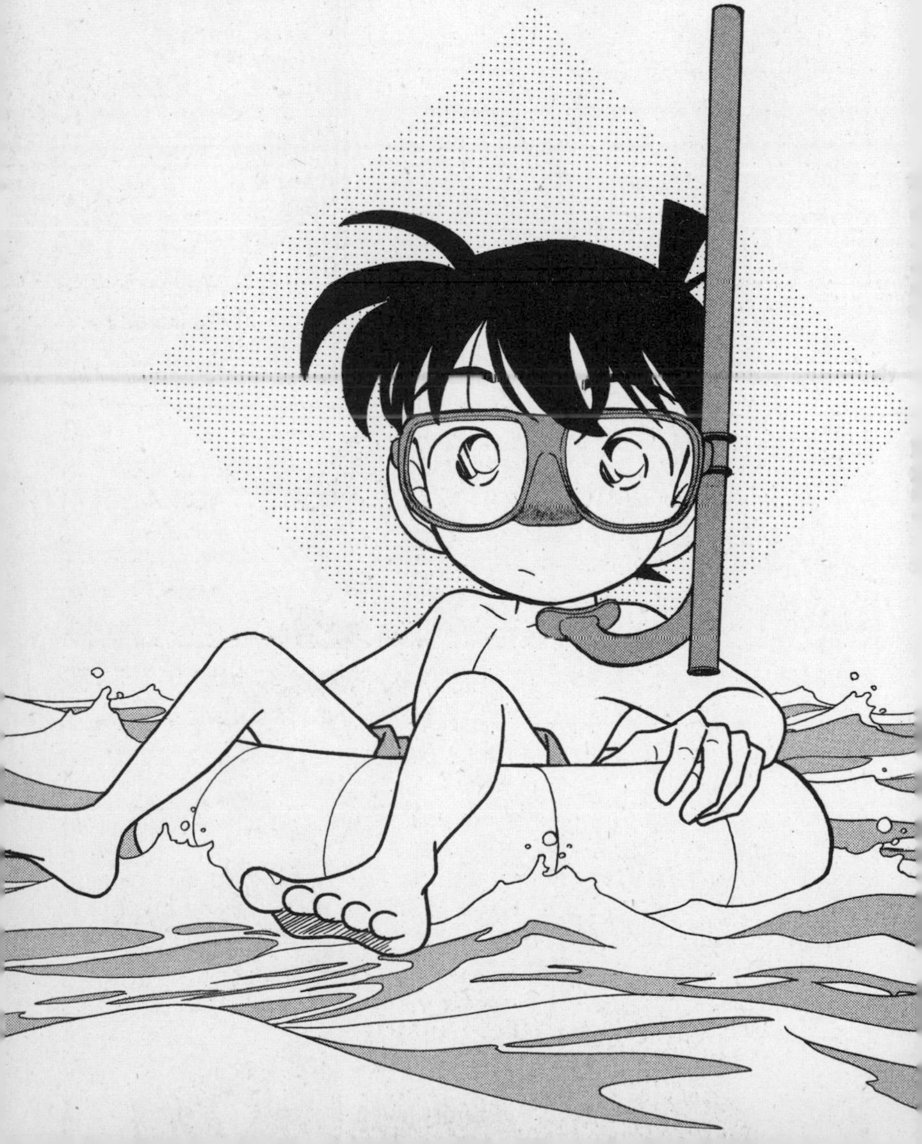

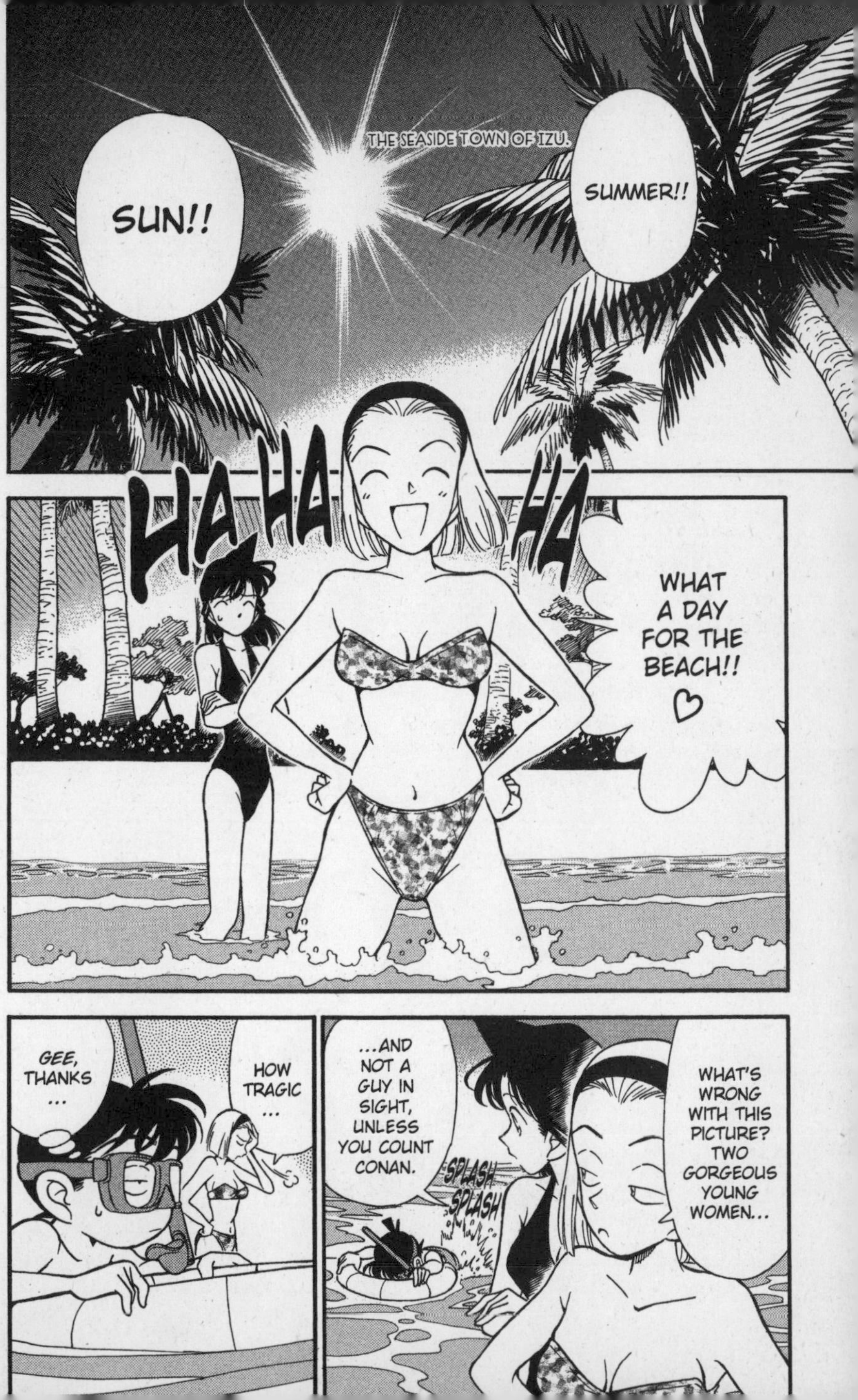
THE SEASIDE TOWN OF IZU.
SUMMER!!
SUN!!
HA HA HA
WHAT A DAY FOR THE BEACH!! ♡
WHAT'S WRONG WITH THIS PICTURE? TWO GORGEOUS YOUNG WOMEN...
...AND NOT A GUY IN SIGHT, UNLESS YOU COUNT CONAN.
SPLASH SPLASH
HOW TRAGIC...
GEE, THANKS...

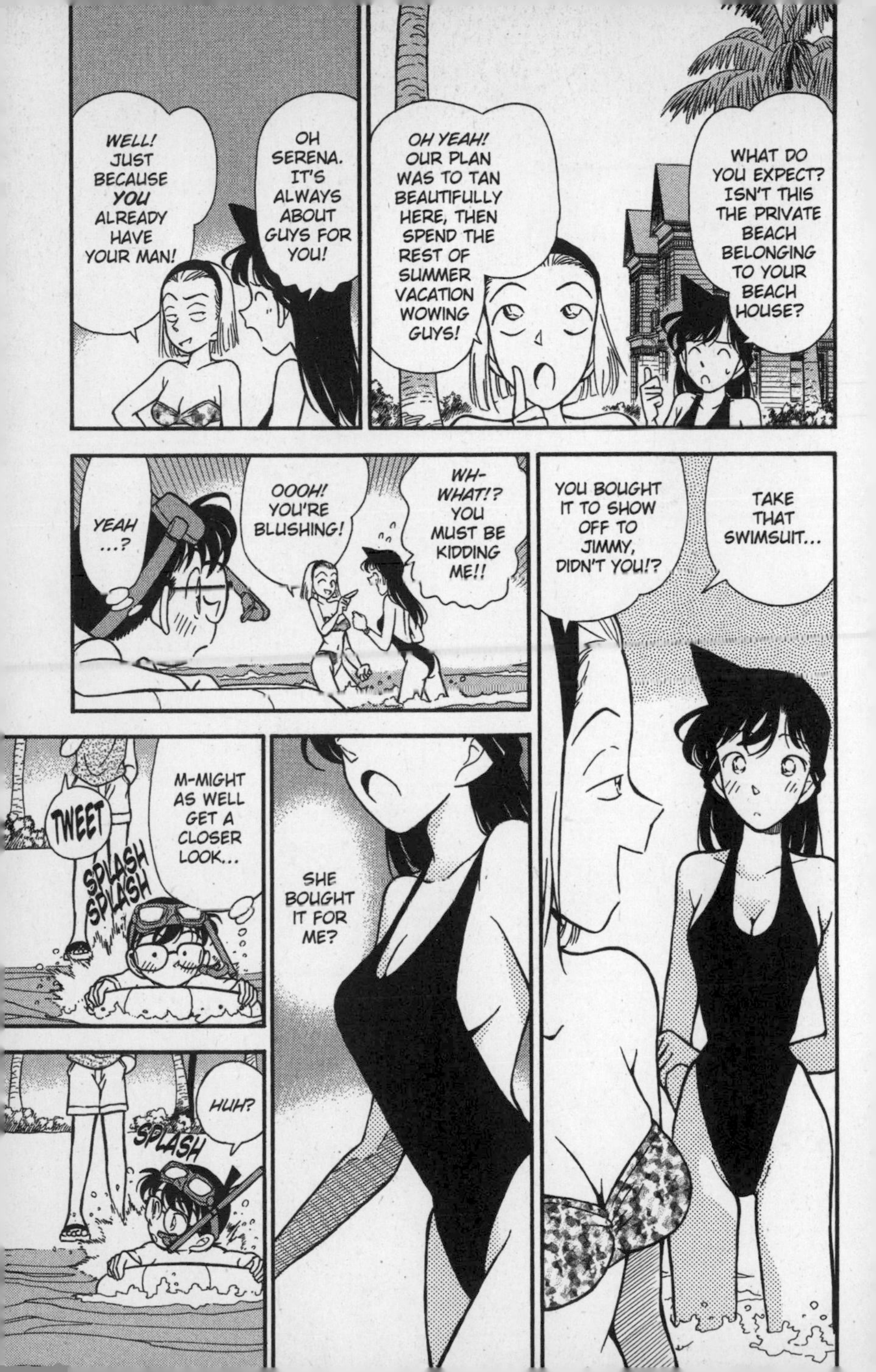
WHAT DO YOU EXPECT? ISN'T THIS THE PRIVATE BEACH BELONGING TO YOUR BEACH HOUSE?
OH YEAH! OUR PLAN WAS TO TAN BEAUTIFULLY HERE, THEN SPEND THE REST OF SUMMER VACATION WOWING GUYS!
OH SERENA. IT'S ALWAYS ABOUT GUYS FOR YOU!
WELL! JUST BECAUSE YOU ALREADY HAVE YOUR MAN!
TAKE THAT SWIMSUIT...
YOU BOUGHT IT TO SHOW OFF TO JIMMY, DIDN'T YOU!?
WH-WHAT!? YOU MUST BE KIDDING ME!!
OOOH! YOU'RE BLUSHING!
YEAH ...?
SHE BOUGHT IT FOR ME?
M-MIGHT AS WELL GET A CLOSER LOOK...
TWEET
SPLASH SPLASH
HUH?
SPLASH

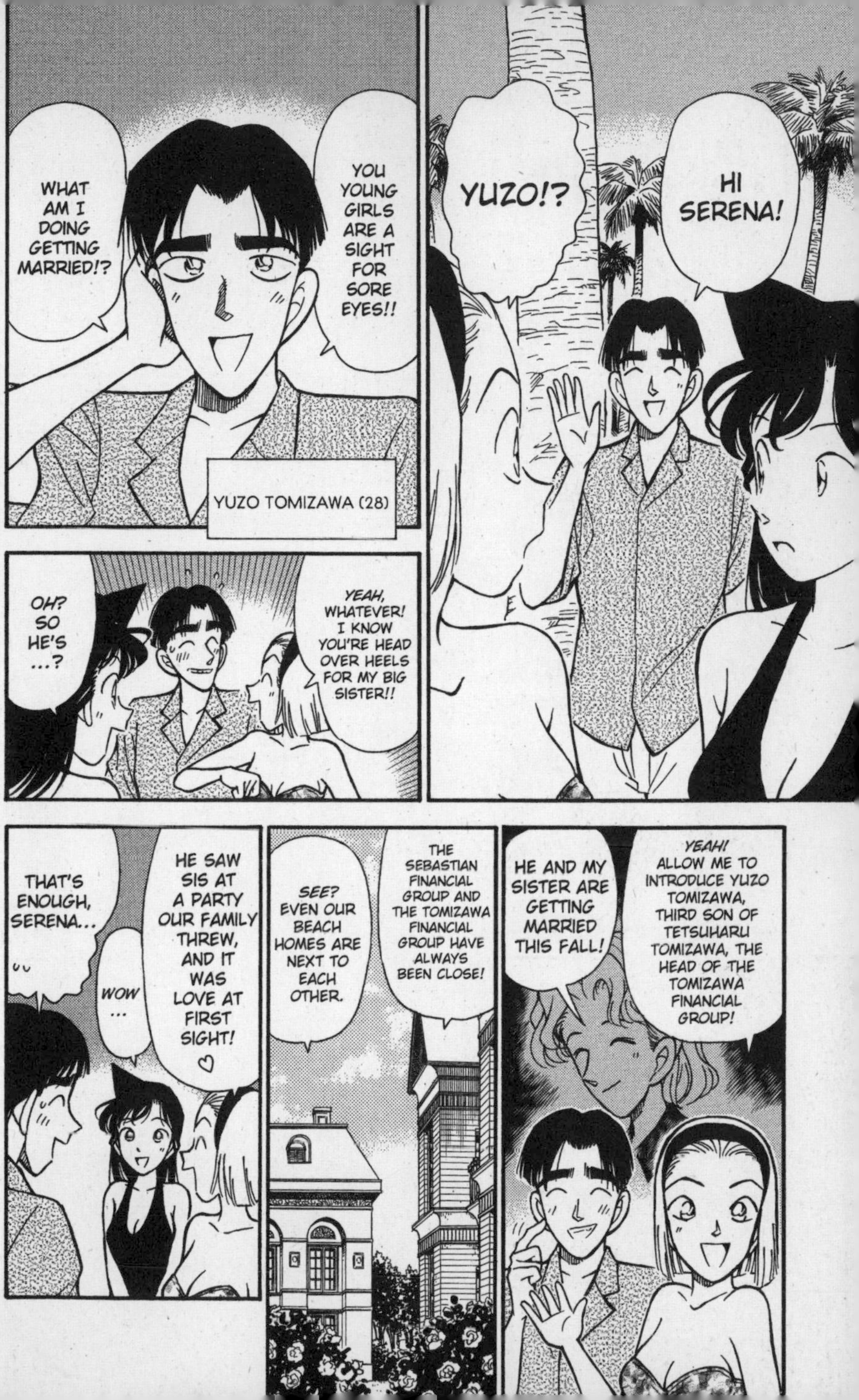
HI SERENA!
YUZO!?
YOU YOUNG GIRLS ARE A SIGHT FOR SORE EYES!!
WHAT AM I DOING GETTING MARRIED!?
YUZO TOMIZAWA (28)
YEAH, WHATEVER! I KNOW YOU'RE HEAD OVER HEELS FOR MY BIG SISTER!!
OH? SO HE'S ...?
YEAH! ALLOW ME TO INTRODUCE YUZO TOMIZAWA, THIRD SON OF TETSUHARU TOMIZAWA, THE HEAD OF THE TOMIZAWA FINANCIAL GROUP!
HE AND MY SISTER ARE GETTING MARRIED THIS FALL!
THE SEBASTIAN FINANCIAL GROUP AND THE TOMIZAWA FINANCIAL GROUP HAVE ALWAYS BEEN CLOSE!
SEE? EVEN OUR BEACH HOMES ARE NEXT TO EACH OTHER.
HE SAW SIS AT A PARTY OUR FAMILY THREW, AND IT WAS LOVE AT FIRST SIGHT! ♡
WOW ...
THAT'S ENOUGH, SERENA...

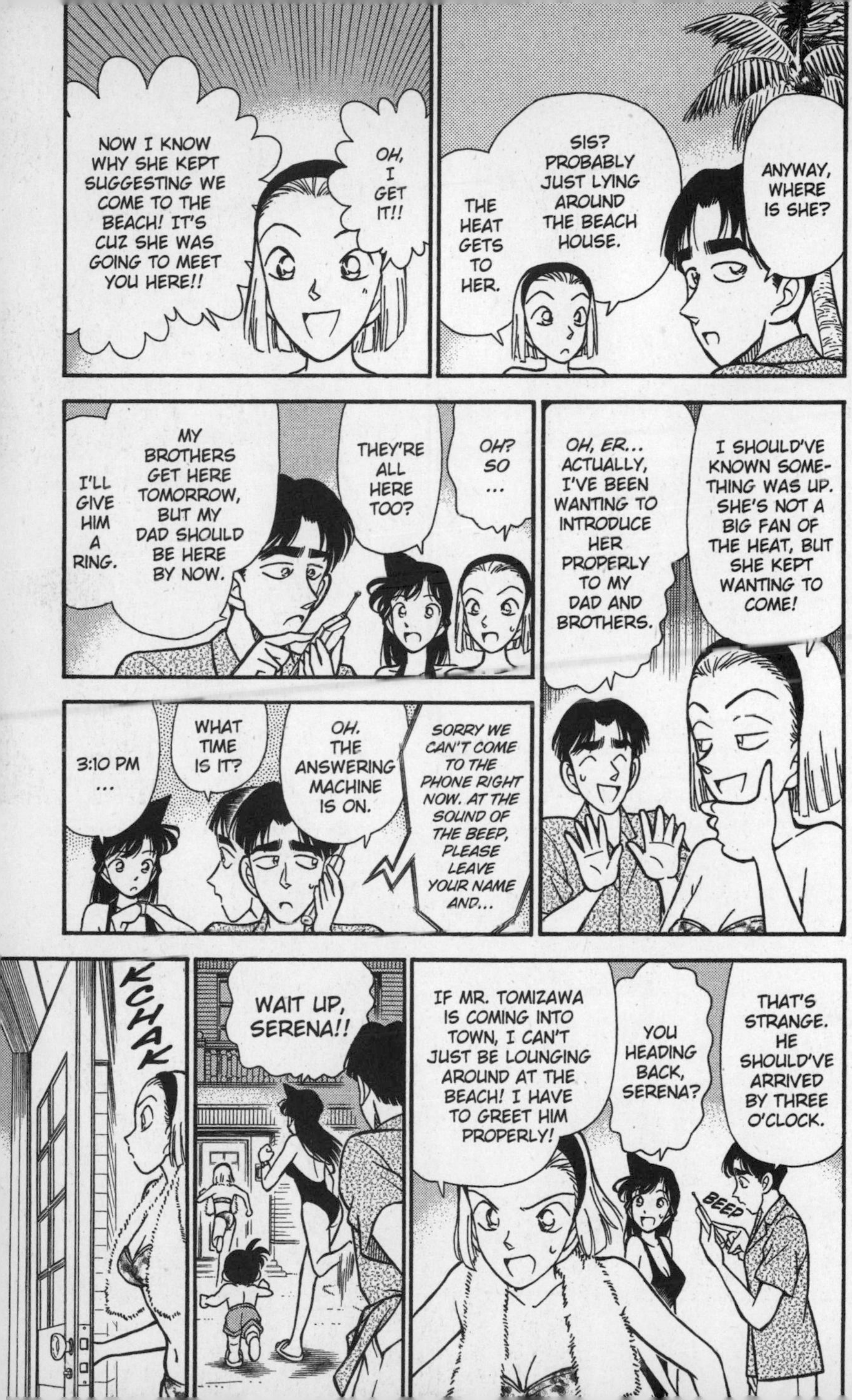
ANYWAY, WHERE IS SHE?
SIS? PROBABLY JUST LYING AROUND THE BEACH HOUSE.
THE HEAT GETS TO HER.
OH, I GET IT!!
NOW I KNOW WHY SHE KEPT SUGGESTING WE COME TO THE BEACH! IT'S CUZ SHE WAS GOING TO MEET YOU HERE!!
I SHOULD'VE KNOWN SOME-THING WAS UP. SHE'S NOT A BIG FAN OF THE HEAT, BUT SHE KEPT WANTING TO COME!
OH, ER... ACTUALLY, I'VE BEEN WANTING TO INTRODUCE HER PROPERLY TO MY DAD AND BROTHERS.
OH? SO ...
THEY'RE ALL HERE TOO?
MY BROTHERS GET HERE TOMORROW, BUT MY DAD SHOULD BE HERE BY NOW.
I'LL GIVE HIM A RING.
SORRY WE CAN'T COME TO THE PHONE RIGHT NOW. AT THE SOUND OF THE BEEP, PLEASE LEAVE YOUR NAME AND...
OH. THE ANSWERING MACHINE IS ON.
WHAT TIME IS IT?
3:10 PM ...
THAT'S STRANGE. HE SHOULD'VE ARRIVED BY THREE O'CLOCK.
BEEP
YOU HEADING BACK, SERENA?
IF MR. TOMIZAWA IS COMING INTO TOWN, I CAN'T JUST BE LOUNGING AROUND AT THE BEACH! I HAVE TO GREET HIM PROPERLY!
WAIT UP, SERENA!!
KCHAK

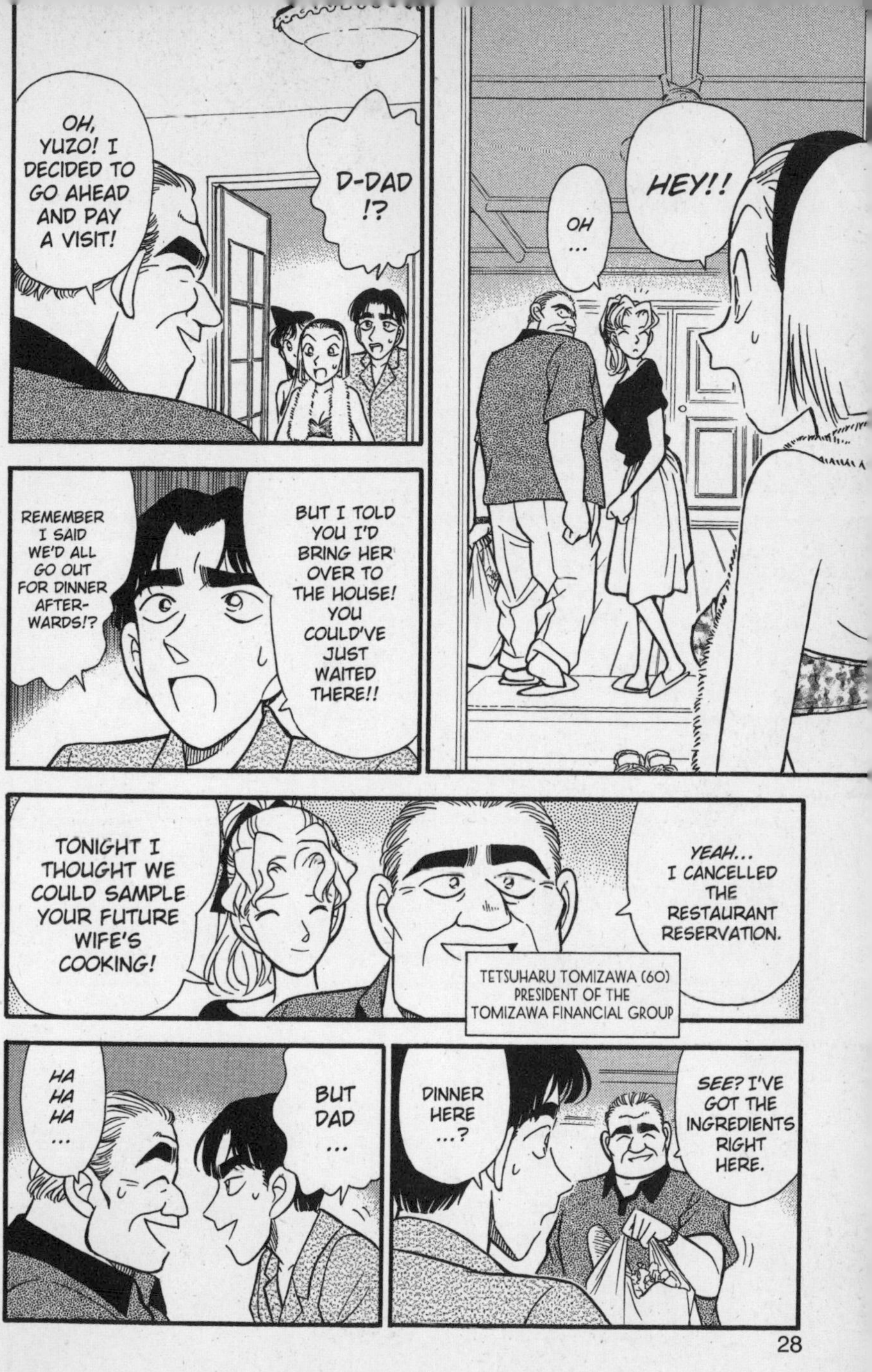
HEY!!
OH ...
D-DAD !?
OH, YUZO! I DECIDED TO GO AHEAD AND PAY A VISIT!
BUT I TOLD YOU I'D BRING HER OVER TO THE HOUSE! YOU COULD'VE JUST WAITED THERE!!
REMEMBER I SAID WE'D ALL GO OUT FOR DINNER AFTER-WARDS!?
YEAH... I CANCELLED THE RESTAURANT RESERVATION.
TETSUHARU TOMIZAWA (60) PRESIDENT OF THE TOMIZAWA FINANCIAL GROUP
TONIGHT I THOUGHT WE COULD SAMPLE YOUR FUTURE WIFE'S COOKING!
SEE? I'VE GOT THE INGREDIENTS RIGHT HERE.
DINNER HERE ...?
BUT DAD ...
HA HA HA ...

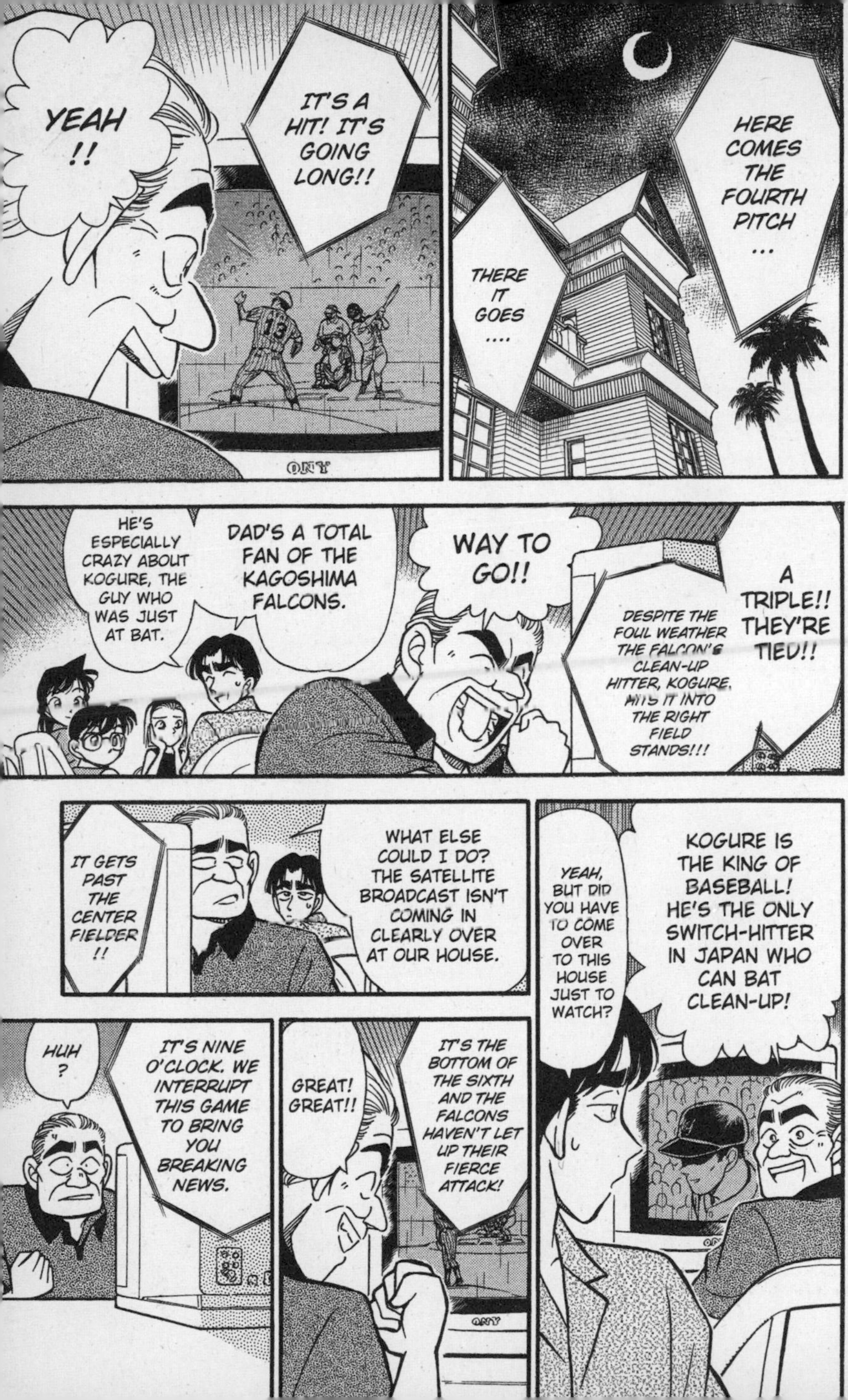
HERE COMES THE FOURTH PITCH ...
THERE IT GOES ....
IT'S A HIT! IT'S GOING LONG!!
YEAH !!
A TRIPLE!! THEY'RE TIED!!
DESPITE THE FOUL WEATHER THE FALCON'S CLEAN-UP HITTER, KOGURE, HITS IT INTO THE RIGHT FIELD STANDS!!!
WAY TO GO!!
DAD'S A TOTAL FAN OF THE KAGOSHIMA FALCONS.
HE'S ESPECIALLY CRAZY ABOUT KOGURE, THE GUY WHO WAS JUST AT BAT.
KOGURE IS THE KING OF BASEBALL! HE'S THE ONLY SWITCH-HITTER IN JAPAN WHO CAN BAT CLEAN-UP!
YEAH, BUT DID YOU HAVE TO COME OVER TO THIS HOUSE JUST TO WATCH?
WHAT ELSE COULD I DO? THE SATELLITE BROADCAST ISN'T COMING IN CLEARLY OVER AT OUR HOUSE.
IT GETS PAST THE CENTER FIELDER !!
IT'S THE BOTTOM OF THE SIXTH AND THE FALCONS HAVEN'T LET UP THEIR FIERCE ATTACK!
GREAT! GREAT!!
IT'S NINE O'CLOCK. WE INTERRUPT THIS GAME TO BRING YOU BREAKING NEWS.
HUH ?

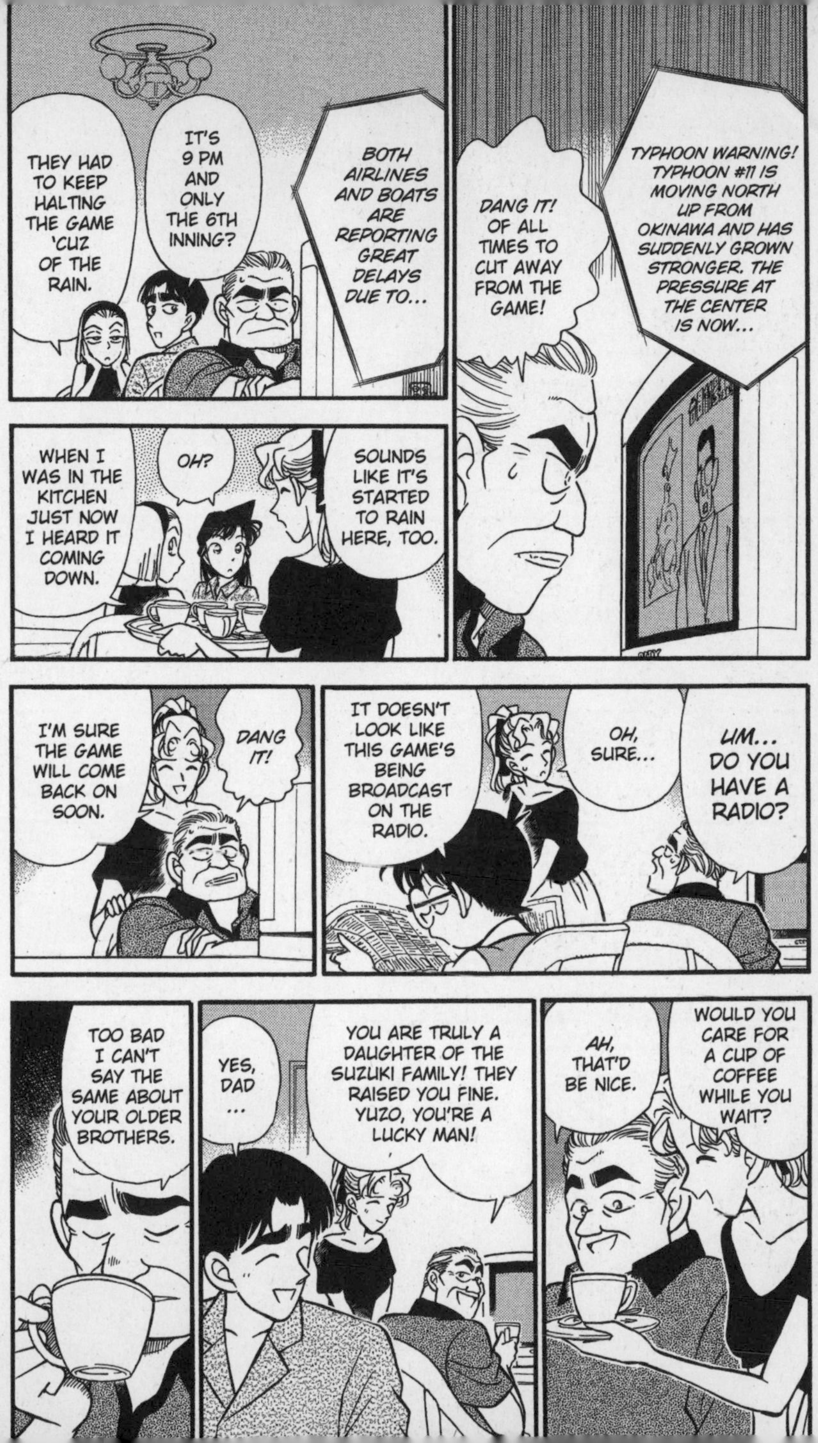
TYPHOON WARNING! TYPHOON #11 IS MOVING NORTH UP FROM OKINAWA AND HAS SUDDENLY GROWN STRONGER. THE PRESSURE AT THE CENTER IS NOW...
DANG IT! OF ALL TIMES TO CUT AWAY FROM THE GAME!
BOTH AIRLINES AND BOATS ARE REPORTING GREAT DELAYS DUE TO...
IT'S 9 PM AND ONLY THE 6TH INNING?
THEY HAD TO KEEP HALTING THE GAME 'CUZ OF THE RAIN.
SOUNDS LIKE IT'S STARTED TO RAIN HERE, TOO.
OH?
WHEN I WAS IN THE KITCHEN JUST NOW I HEARD IT COMING DOWN.
UM... DO YOU HAVE A RADIO?
OH, SURE...
IT DOESN'T LOOK LIKE THIS GAME'S BEING BROADCAST ON THE RADIO.
DANG IT!
I'M SURE THE GAME WILL COME BACK ON SOON.
WOULD YOU CARE FOR A CUP OF COFFEE WHILE YOU WAIT?
AH, THAT'D BE NICE.
YOU ARE TRULY A DAUGHTER OF THE SUZUKI FAMILY! THEY RAISED YOU FINE. YUZO, YOU'RE A LUCKY MAN!
YES, DAD ...
TOO BAD I CAN'T SAY THE SAME ABOUT YOUR OLDER BROTHERS.

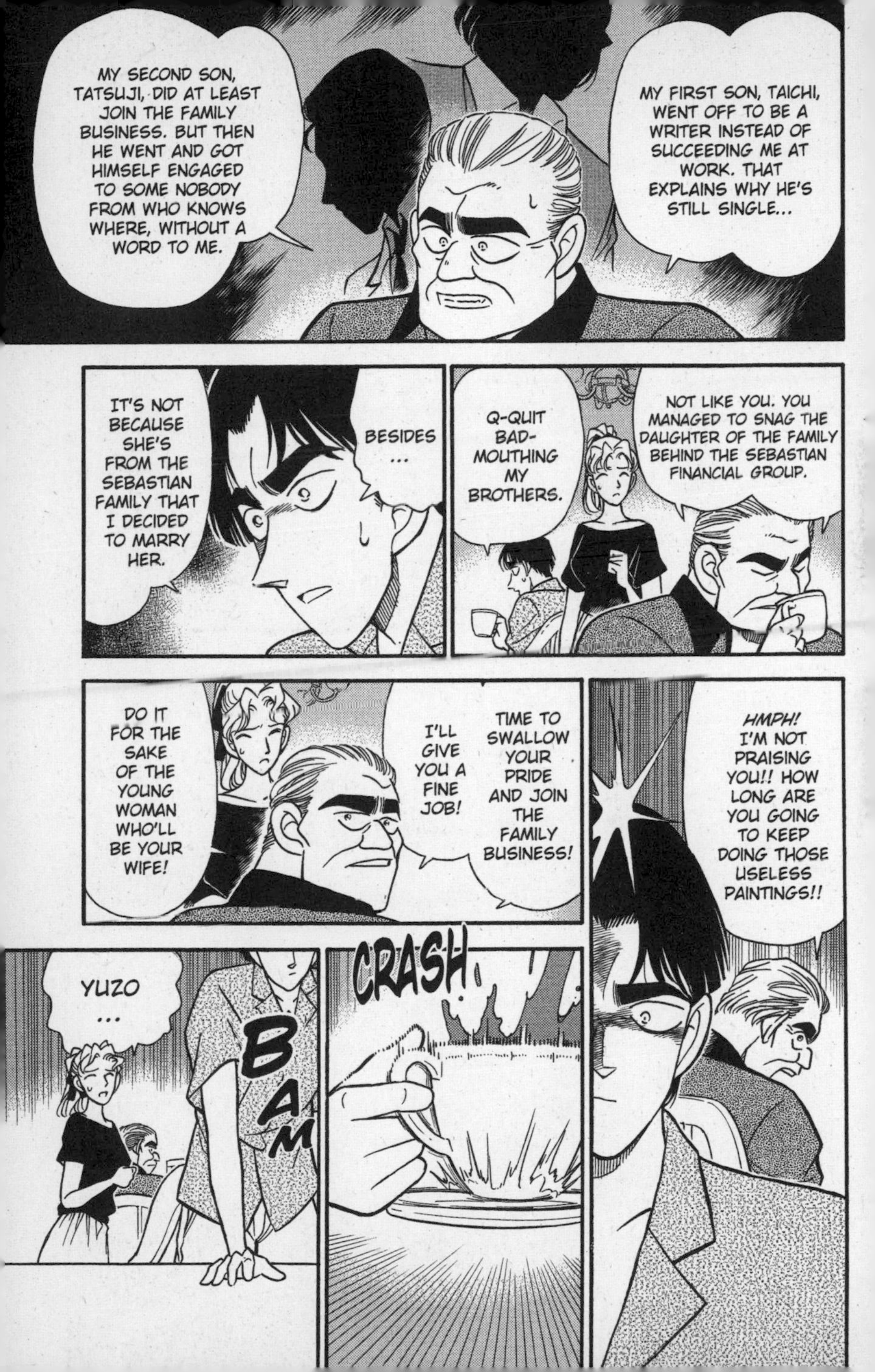
MY FIRST SON, TAICHI, WENT OFF TO BE A WRITER INSTEAD OF SUCCEEDING ME AT WORK. THAT EXPLAINS WHY HE'S STILL SINGLE...
MY SECOND SON, TATSUJI, DID AT LEAST JOIN THE FAMILY BUSINESS. BUT THEN HE WENT AND GOT HIMSELF ENGAGED TO SOME NOBODY FROM WHO KNOWS WHERE, WITHOUT A WORD TO ME.
NOT LIKE YOU. YOU MANAGED TO SNAG THE DAUGHTER OF THE FAMILY BEHIND THE SEBASTIAN FINANCIAL GROUP.
Q-QUIT BAD-MOUTHING MY BROTHERS.
BESIDES ...
IT'S NOT BECAUSE SHE'S FROM THE SEBASTIAN FAMILY THAT I DECIDED TO MARRY HER.
HMPH! I'M NOT PRAISING YOU!! HOW LONG ARE YOU GOING TO KEEP DOING THOSE USELESS PAINTINGS!!
TIME TO SWALLOW YOUR PRIDE AND JOIN THE FAMILY BUSINESS!
I'LL GIVE YOU A FINE JOB!
DO IT FOR THE SAKE OF THE YOUNG WOMAN WHO'LL BE YOUR WIFE!
CRASH
BAM
YUZO ...

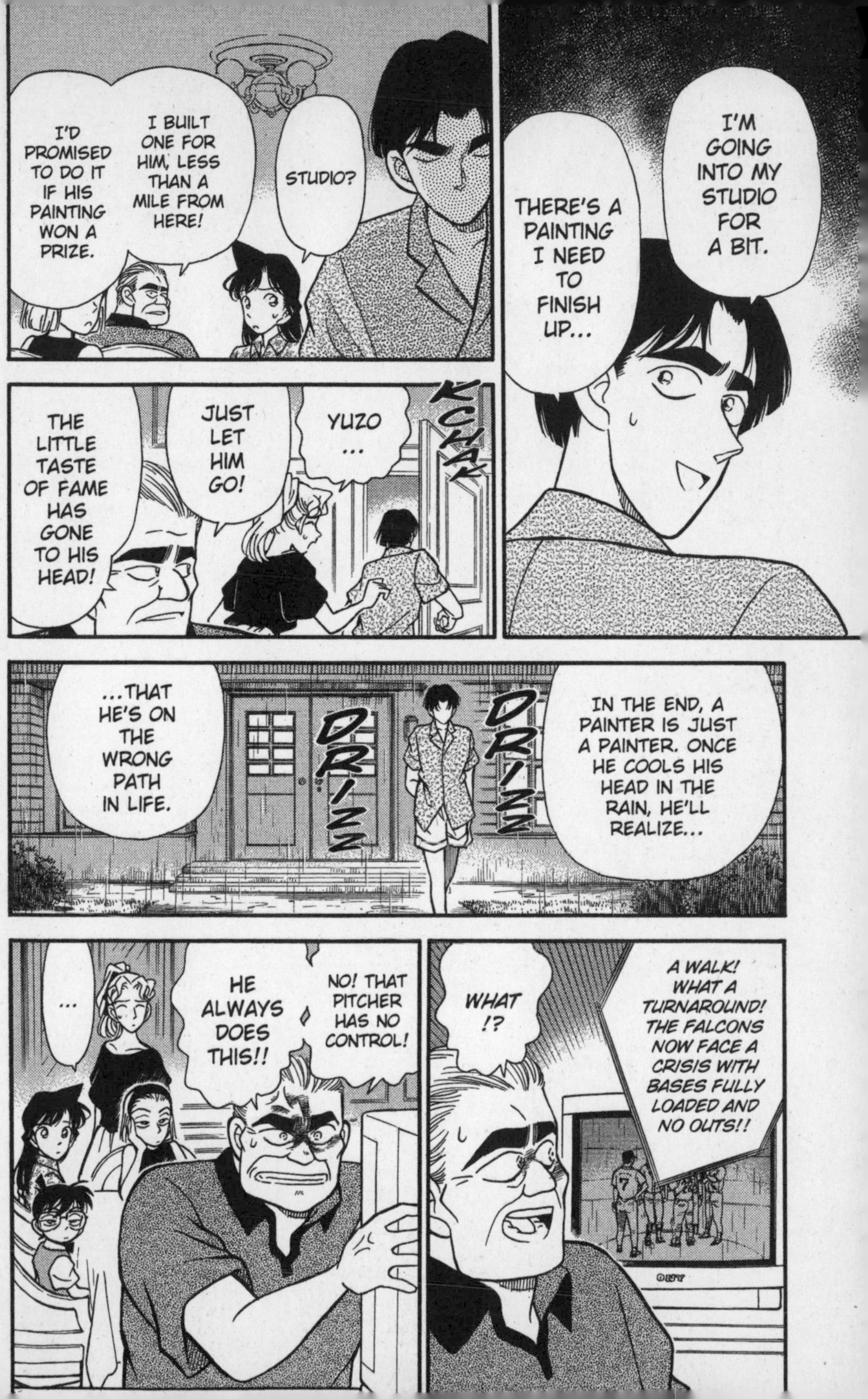
I'M GOING INTO MY STUDIO FOR A BIT.
THERE'S A PAINTING I NEED TO FINISH UP...
STUDIO?
I BUILT ONE FOR HIM, LESS THAN A MILE FROM HERE!
I'D PROMISED TO DO IT IF HIS PAINTING WON A PRIZE.
KCHAK
YUZO ...
JUST LET HIM GO!
THE LITTLE TASTE OF FAME HAS GONE TO HIS HEAD!
IN THE END, A PAINTER IS JUST A PAINTER. ONCE HE COOLS HIS HEAD IN THE RAIN, HE'LL REALIZE...
DRIZZ
DRIZZ
...THAT HE'S ON THE WRONG PATH IN LIFE.
A WALK! WHAT A TURNAROUND! THE FALCONS NOW FACE A CRISIS WITH BASES FULLY LOADED AND NO OUTS!!
WHAT !?
NO! THAT PITCHER HAS NO CONTROL!
HE ALWAYS DOES THIS!!
...

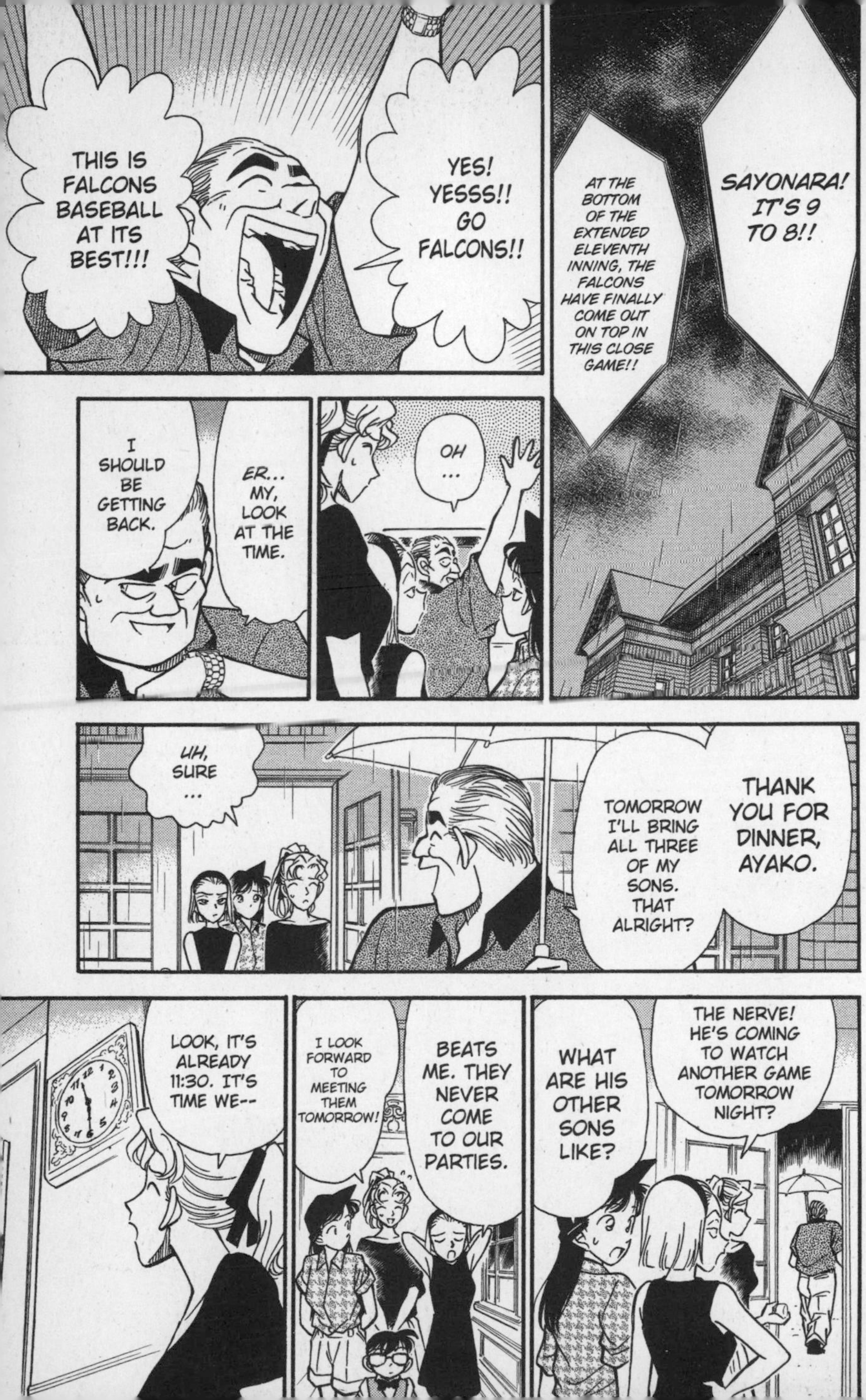

SAYONARA! IT'S 9 TO 8!!
AT THE BOTTOM OF THE EXTENDED ELEVENTH INNING, THE FALCONS HAVE FINALLY COME OUT ON TOP IN THIS CLOSE GAME!!
YES! YESSS!! GO FALCONS!!
THIS IS FALCONS BASEBALL AT ITS BEST!!!
OH ...
ER... MY, LOOK AT THE TIME.
I SHOULD BE GETTING BACK.
THANK YOU FOR DINNER, AYAKO.
TOMORROW I'LL BRING ALL THREE OF MY SONS. THAT ALRIGHT?
UH, SURE ...
THE NERVE! HE'S COMING TO WATCH ANOTHER GAME TOMORROW NIGHT?
WHAT ARE HIS OTHER SONS LIKE?
BEATS ME. THEY NEVER COME TO OUR PARTIES.
I LOOK FORWARD TO MEETING THEM TOMORROW!
LOOK, IT'S ALREADY 11:30. IT'S TIME WE--

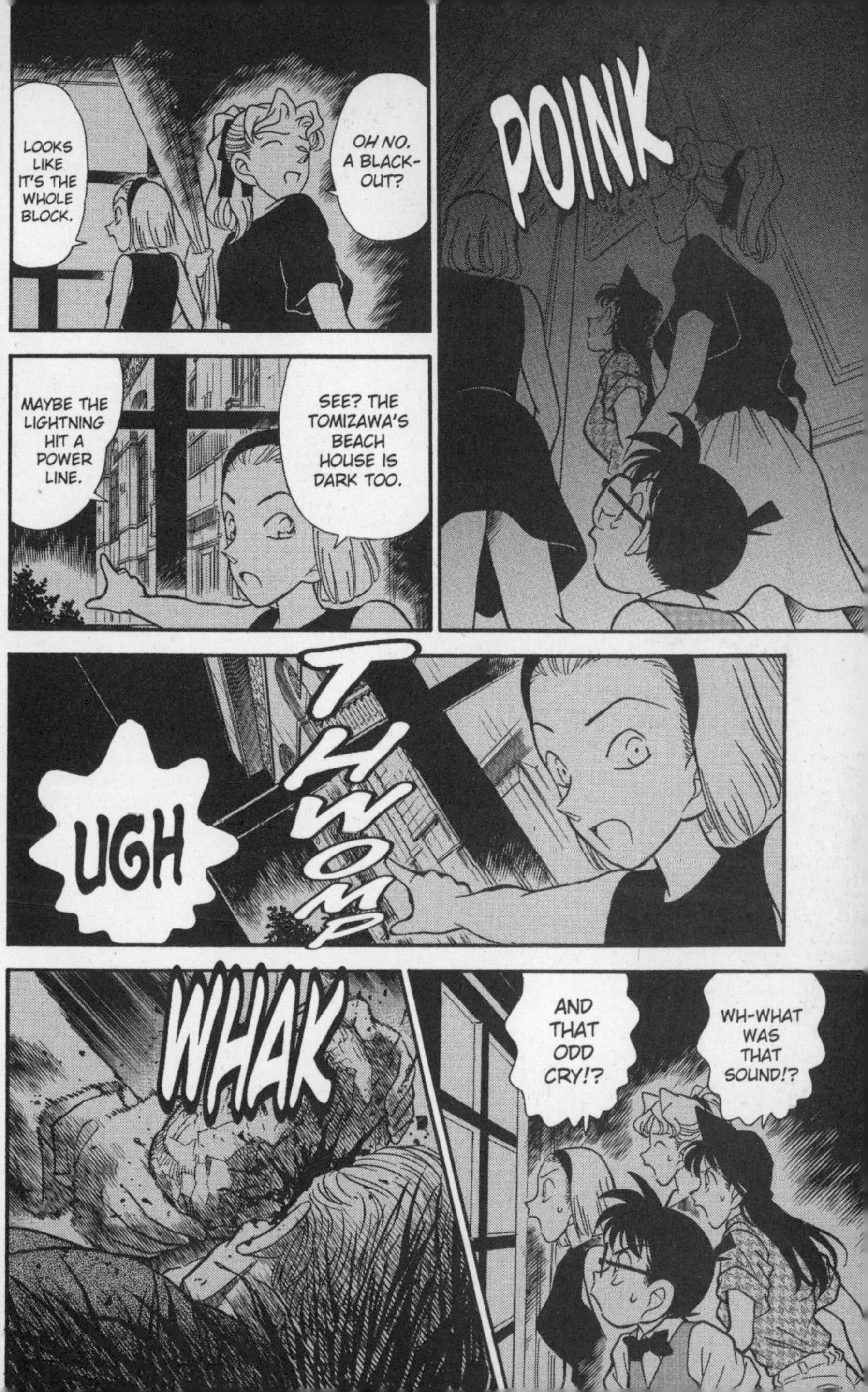
POINK
OH NO. A BLACK-OUT?
LOOKS LIKE IT'S THE WHOLE BLOCK.
SEE? THE TOMIZAWA'S BEACH HOUSE IS DARK TOO.
MAYBE THE LIGHTNING HIT A POWER LINE.
THWOMP
UGH
WH-WHAT WAS THAT SOUND!?
AND THAT ODD CRY!?
WHAK

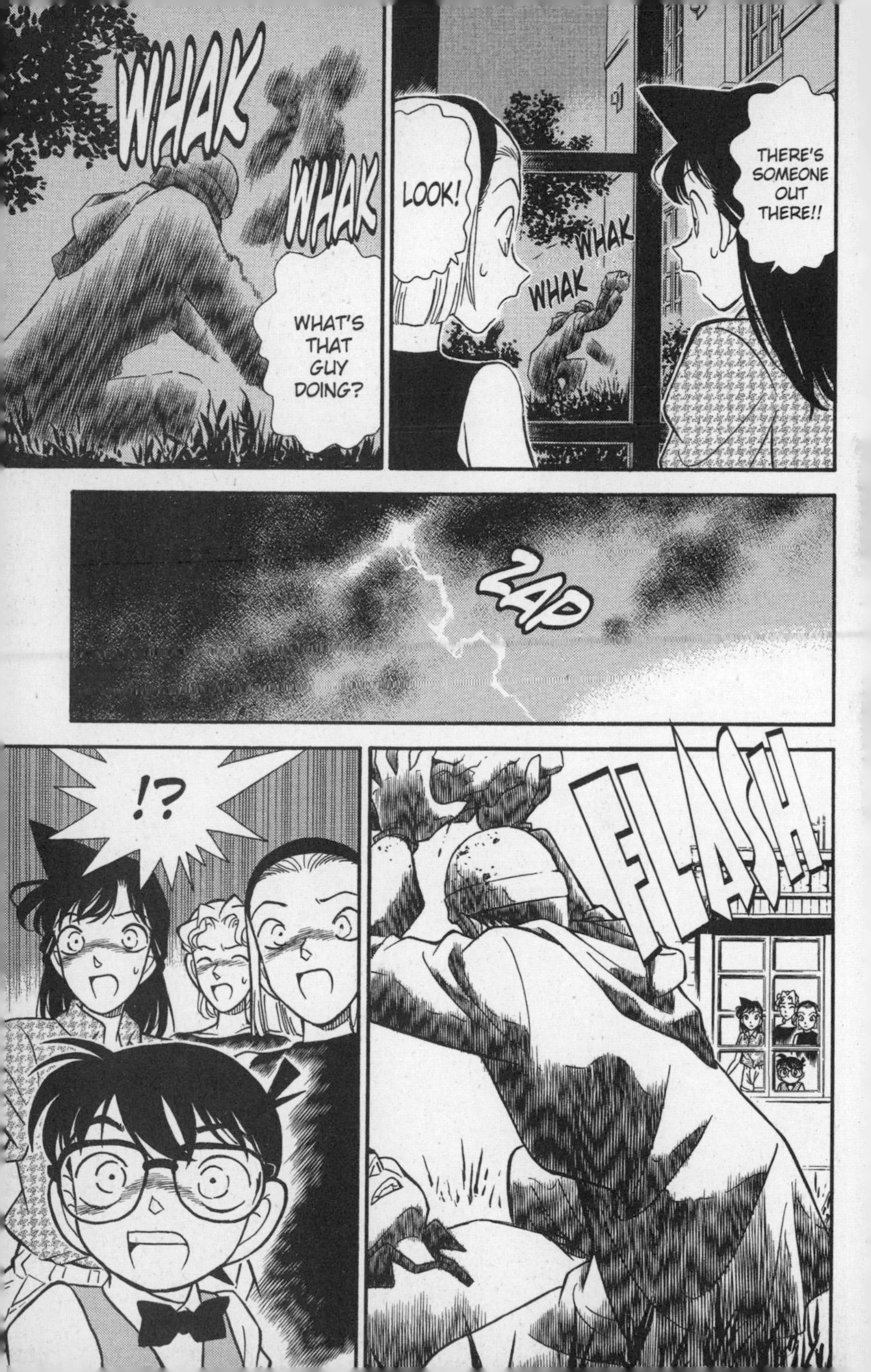
THERE'S SOMEONE OUT THERE!!
LOOK!
WHAK
WHAK
WHAK
WHAK
WHAT'S THAT GUY DOING?
ZAP
FLASH
!?

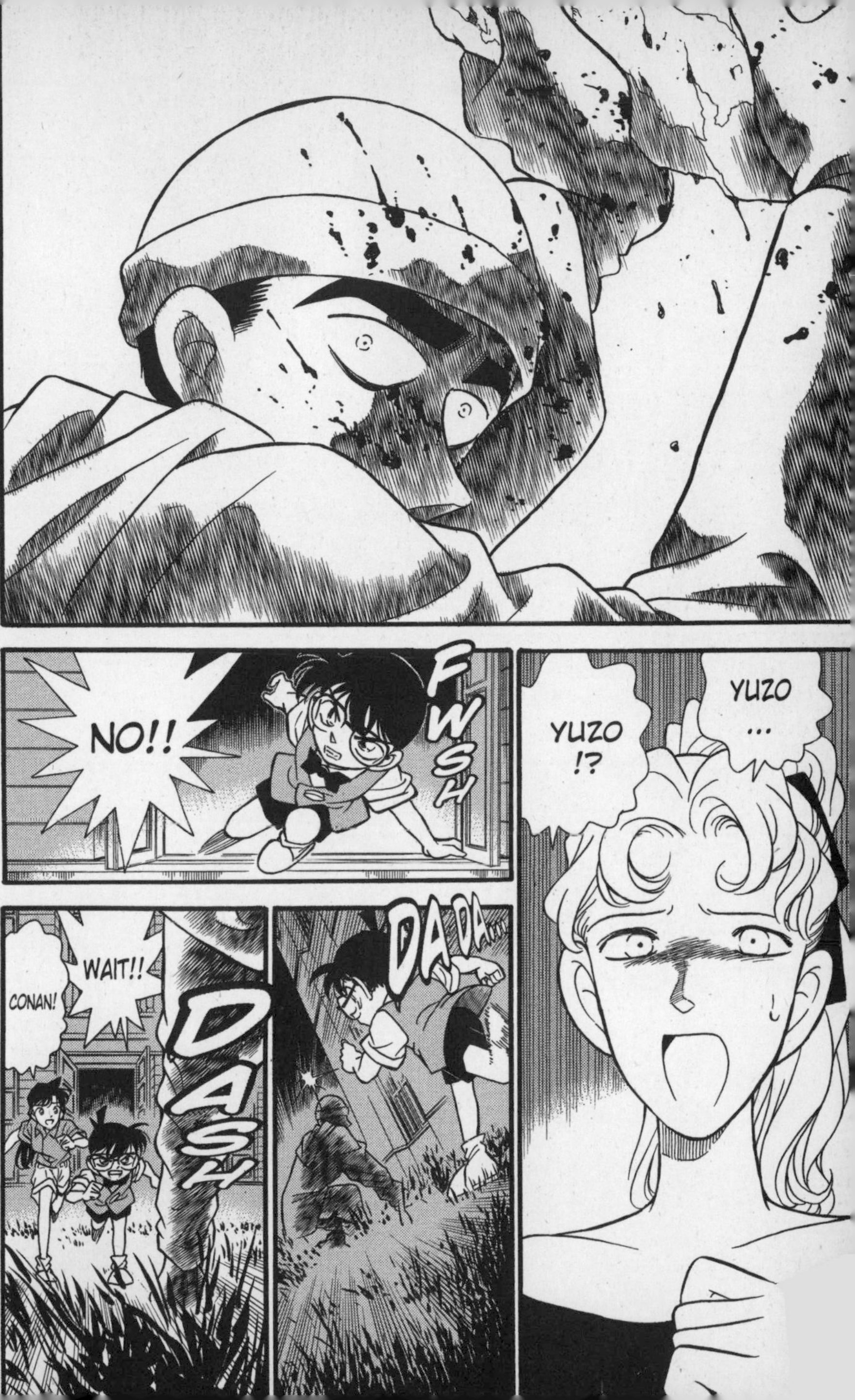
YUZO ...
YUZO !?
NO!!
FWSH
DA DA...
DASH
WAIT!!
CONAN!

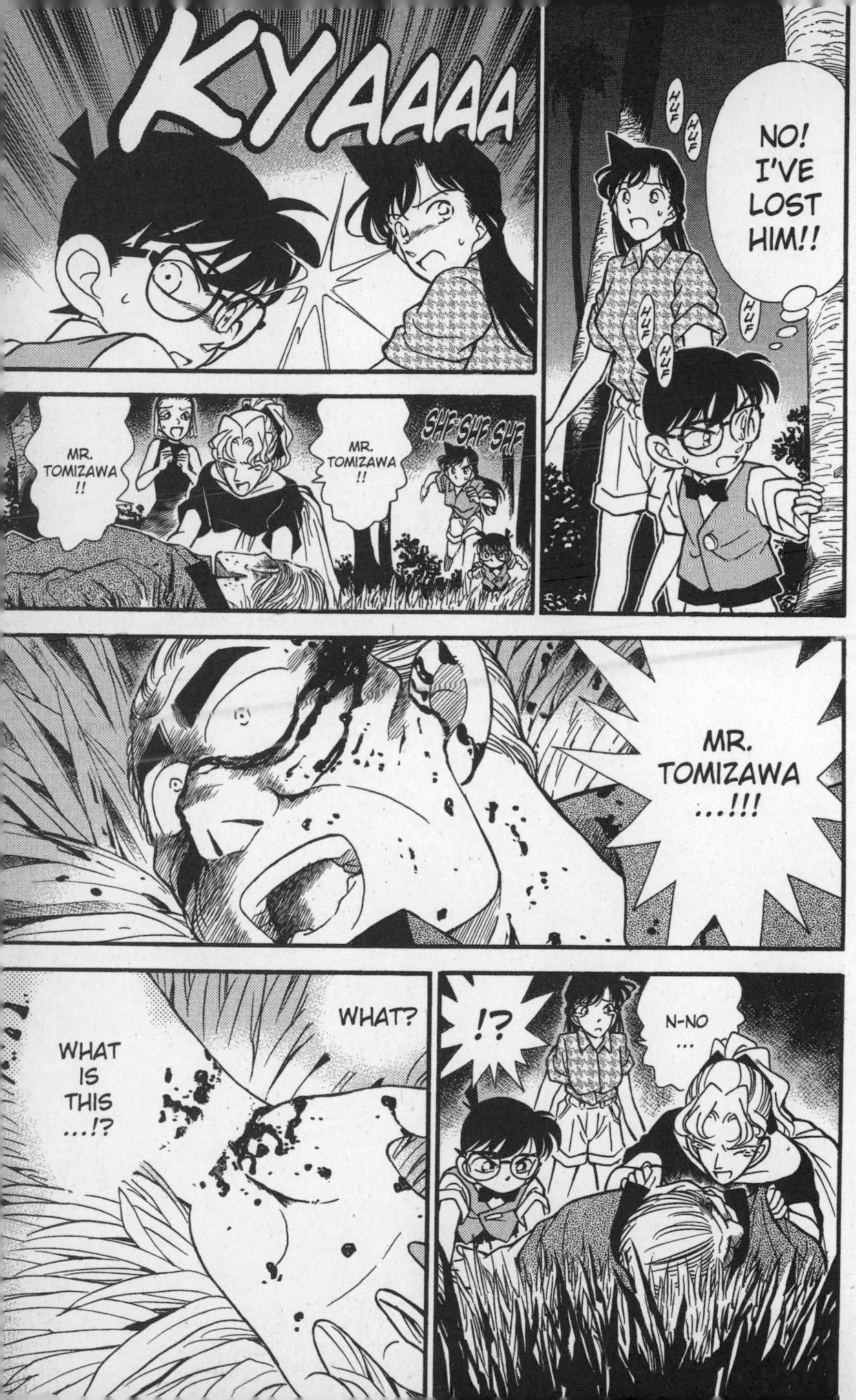
HUF
HUF
NO! I'VE LOST HIM!!
HUF
HUF
HUF
KYAAAA
SHF SHF SHF
MR. TOMIZAWA !!
MR. TOMIZAWA !!
MR. TOMIZAWA ...!!!
N-NO ...
!?
WHAT?
WHAT IS THIS ...!?

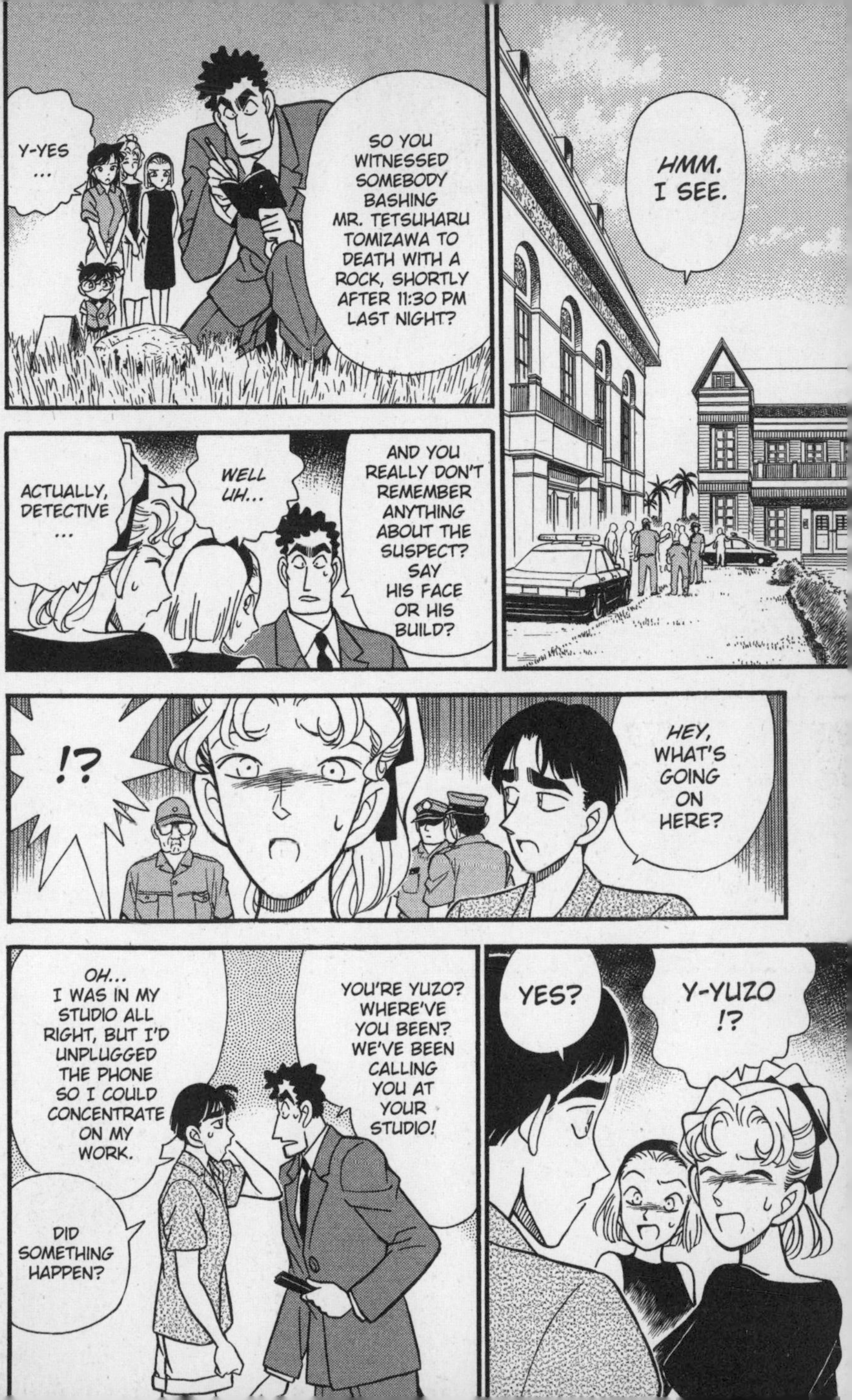
HMM. I SEE.
SO YOU WITNESSED SOMEBODY BASHING MR. TETSUHARU TOMIZAWA TO DEATH WITH A ROCK, SHORTLY AFTER 11:30 PM LAST NIGHT?
Y-YES ...
AND YOU REALLY DON'T REMEMBER ANYTHING ABOUT THE SUSPECT? SAY HIS FACE OR HIS BUILD?
WELL UH...
ACTUALLY, DETECTIVE ...
HEY, WHAT'S GOING ON HERE?
!?
Y-YUZO !?
YES?
YOU'RE YUZO? WHERE'VE YOU BEEN? WE'VE BEEN CALLING YOU AT YOUR STUDIO!
OH... I WAS IN MY STUDIO ALL RIGHT, BUT I'D UNPLUGGED THE PHONE SO I COULD CONCENTRATE ON MY WORK.
DID SOMETHING HAPPEN?

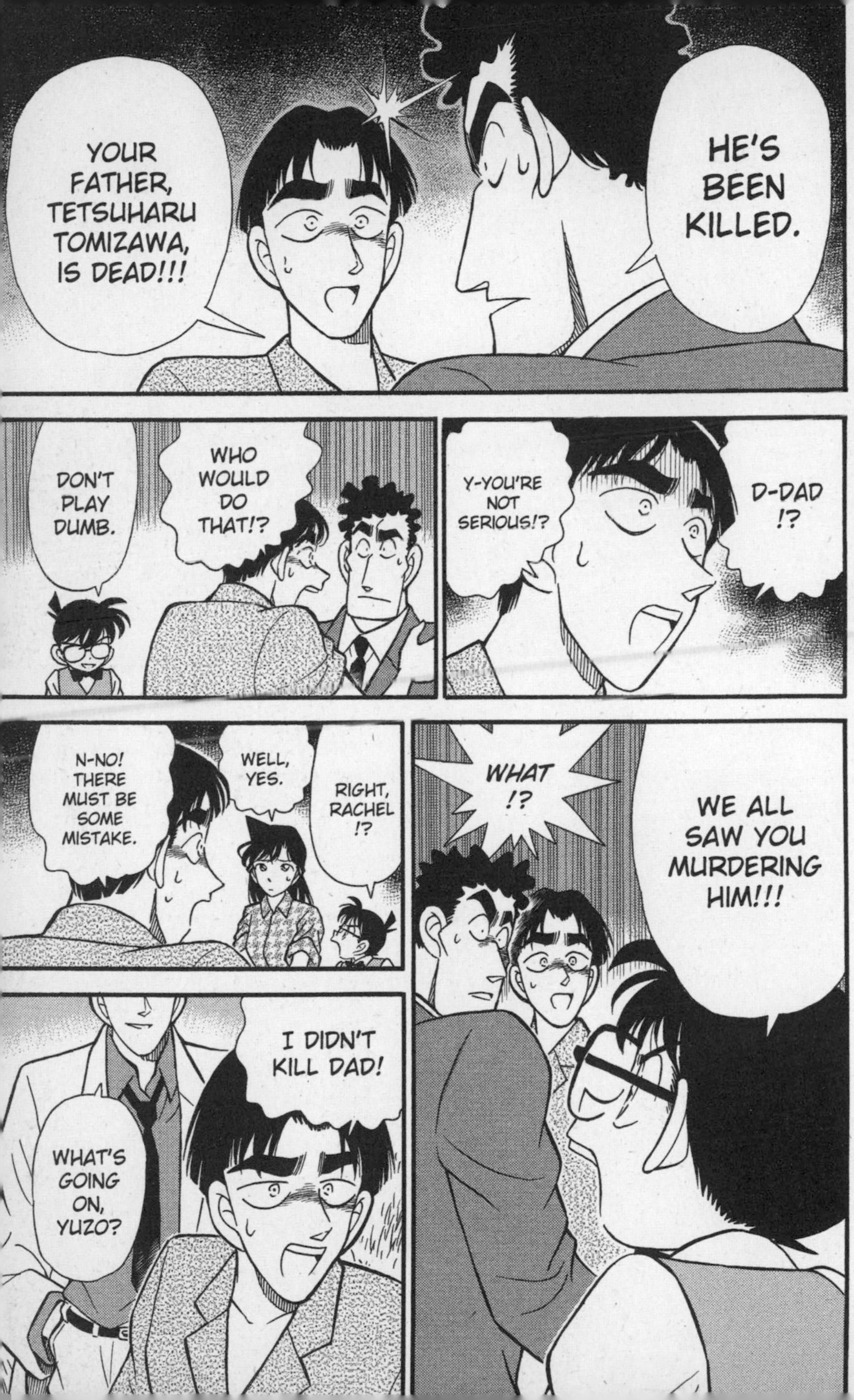
HE'S BEEN KILLED.
YOUR FATHER, TETSUHARU TOMIZAWA, IS DEAD!!!
D-DAD !?
Y-YOU'RE NOT SERIOUS!?
WHO WOULD DO THAT!?
DON'T PLAY DUMB.
WE ALL SAW YOU MURDERING HIM!!!
WHAT !?
RIGHT, RACHEL !?
WELL, YES.
N-NO! THERE MUST BE SOME MISTAKE.
I DIDN'T KILL DAD!
WHAT'S GOING ON, YUZO?

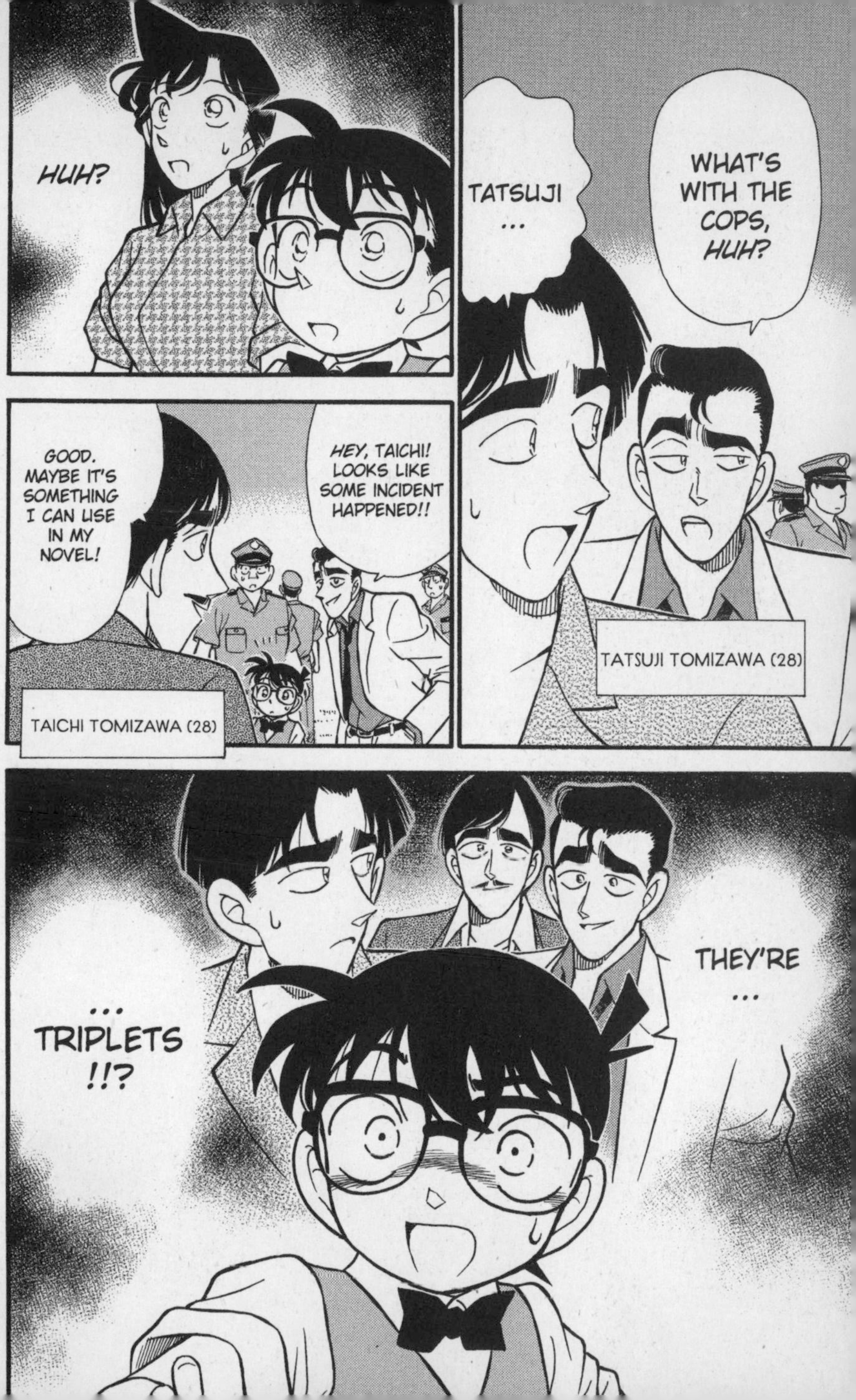
WHAT'S WITH THE COPS, HUH?
TATSUJI ...
TATSUJI TOMIZAWA (28)
HUH?
HEY, TAICHI! LOOKS LIKE SOME INCIDENT HAPPENED!!
GOOD. MAYBE IT'S SOMETHING I CAN USE IN MY NOVEL!
TAICHI TOMIZAWA (28)
THEY'RE ...
... TRIPLETS !!?

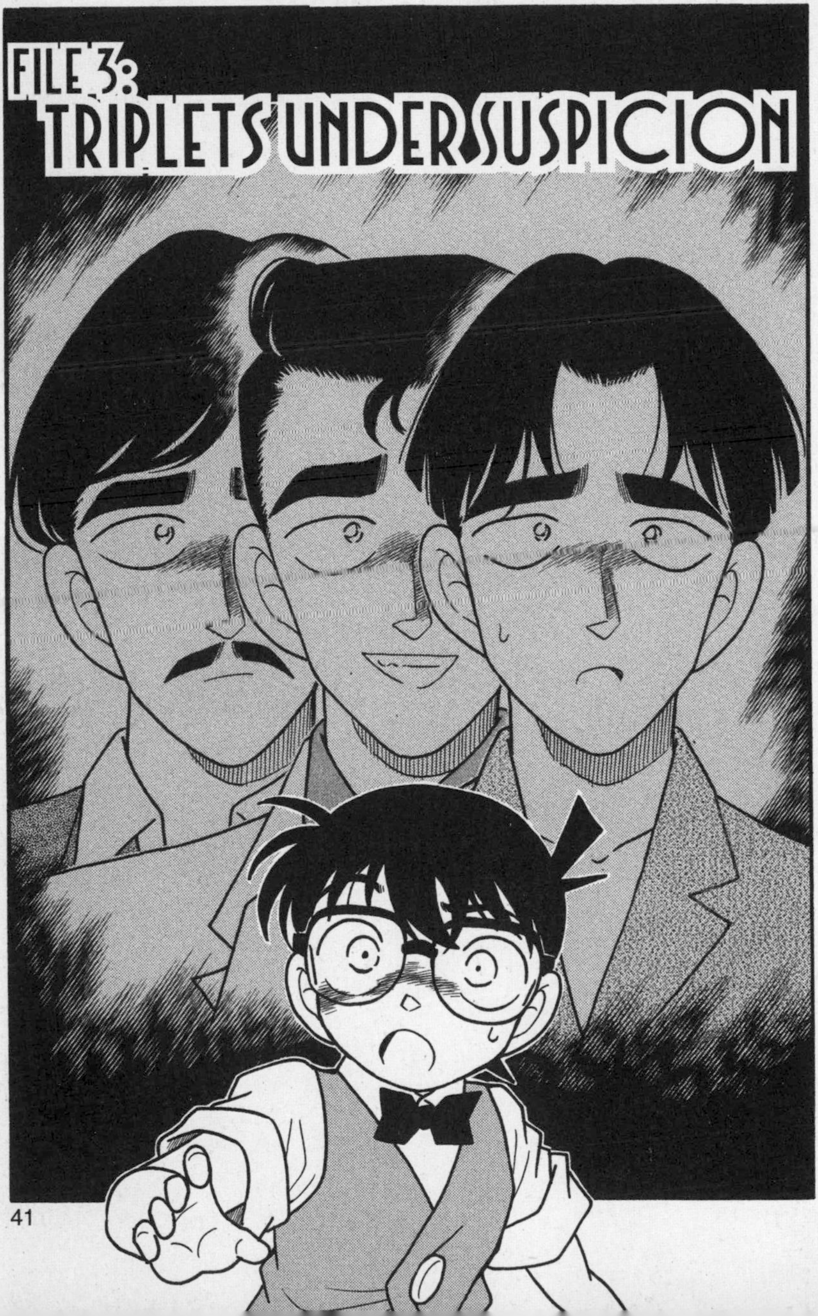
FILE 3:
TRIPLETS UNDER SUSPICION

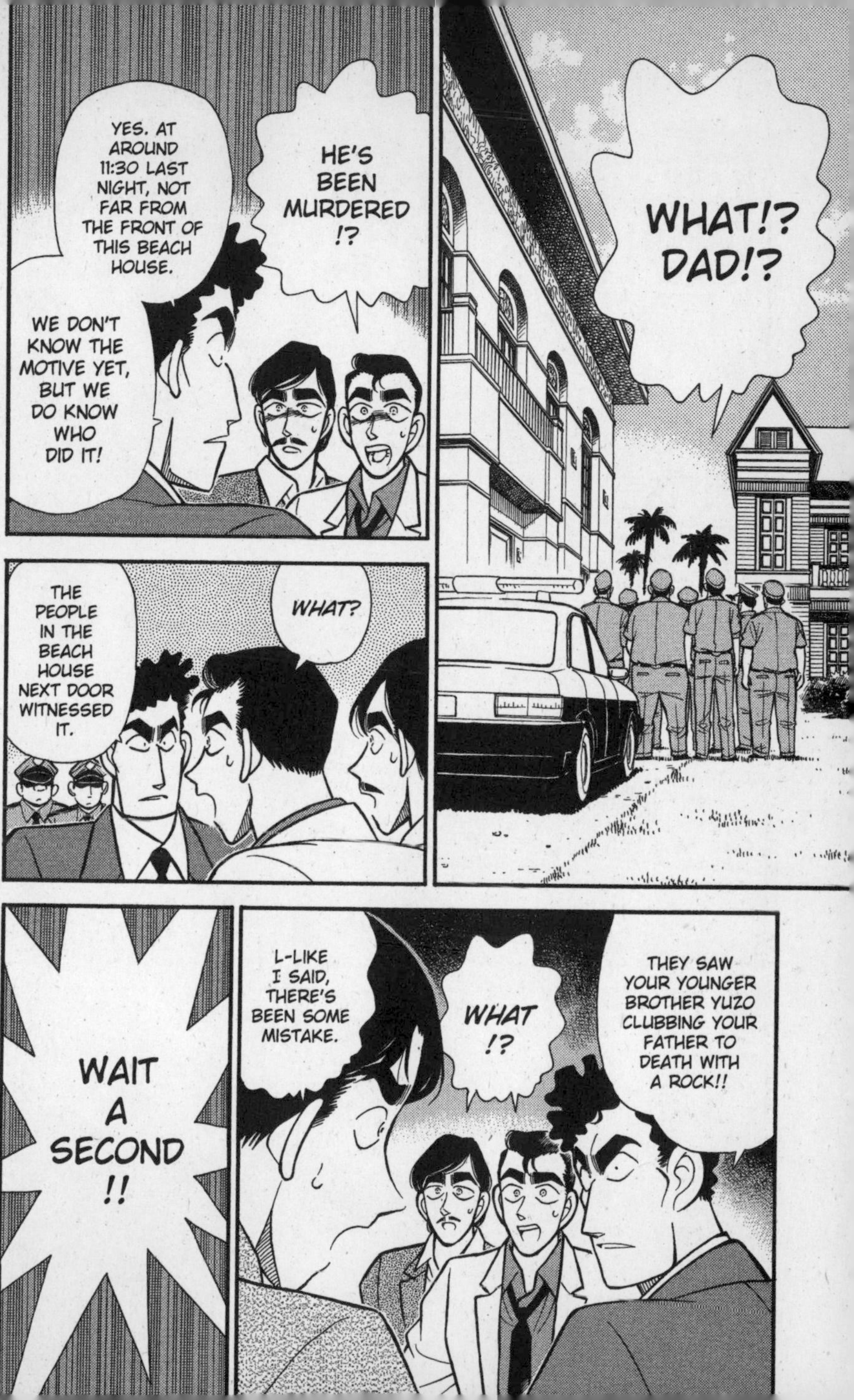
WHAT!? DAD!?
HE'S BEEN MURDERED !?
YES. AT AROUND 11:30 LAST NIGHT, NOT FAR FROM THE FRONT OF THIS BEACH HOUSE.
WE DON'T KNOW THE MOTIVE YET, BUT WE DO KNOW WHO DID IT!
WHAT?
THE PEOPLE IN THE BEACH HOUSE NEXT DOOR WITNESSED IT.
THEY SAW YOUR YOUNGER BROTHER YUZO CLUBBING YOUR FATHER TO DEATH WITH A ROCK!!
WHAT !?
L-LIKE I SAID, THERE'S BEEN SOME MISTAKE.
WAIT A SECOND !!

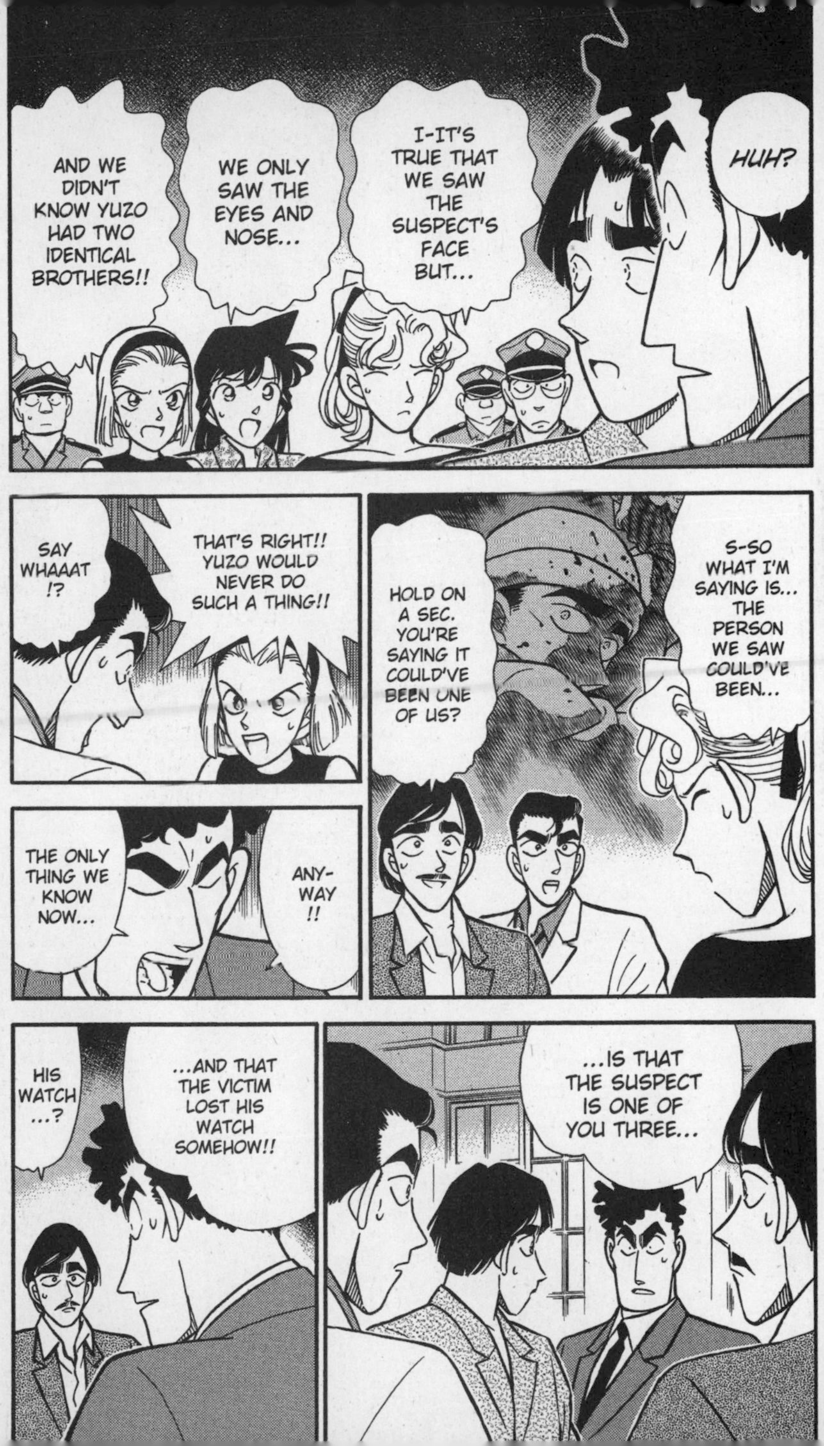
HUH?
I-IT'S TRUE THAT WE SAW THE SUSPECT'S FACE BUT...
WE ONLY SAW THE EYES AND NOSE...
AND WE DIDN'T KNOW YUZO HAD TWO IDENTICAL BROTHERS!!
S-SO WHAT I'M SAYING IS... THE PERSON WE SAW COULD'VE BEEN...
HOLD ON A SEC. YOU'RE SAYING IT COULD'VE BEEN ONE OF US?
THAT'S RIGHT!! YUZO WOULD NEVER DO SUCH A THING!!
SAY WHAAAT!?
ANY-WAY!!
THE ONLY THING WE KNOW NOW...
...IS THAT THE SUSPECT IS ONE OF YOU THREE...
...AND THAT THE VICTIM LOST HIS WATCH SOMEHOW!!
HIS WATCH...?

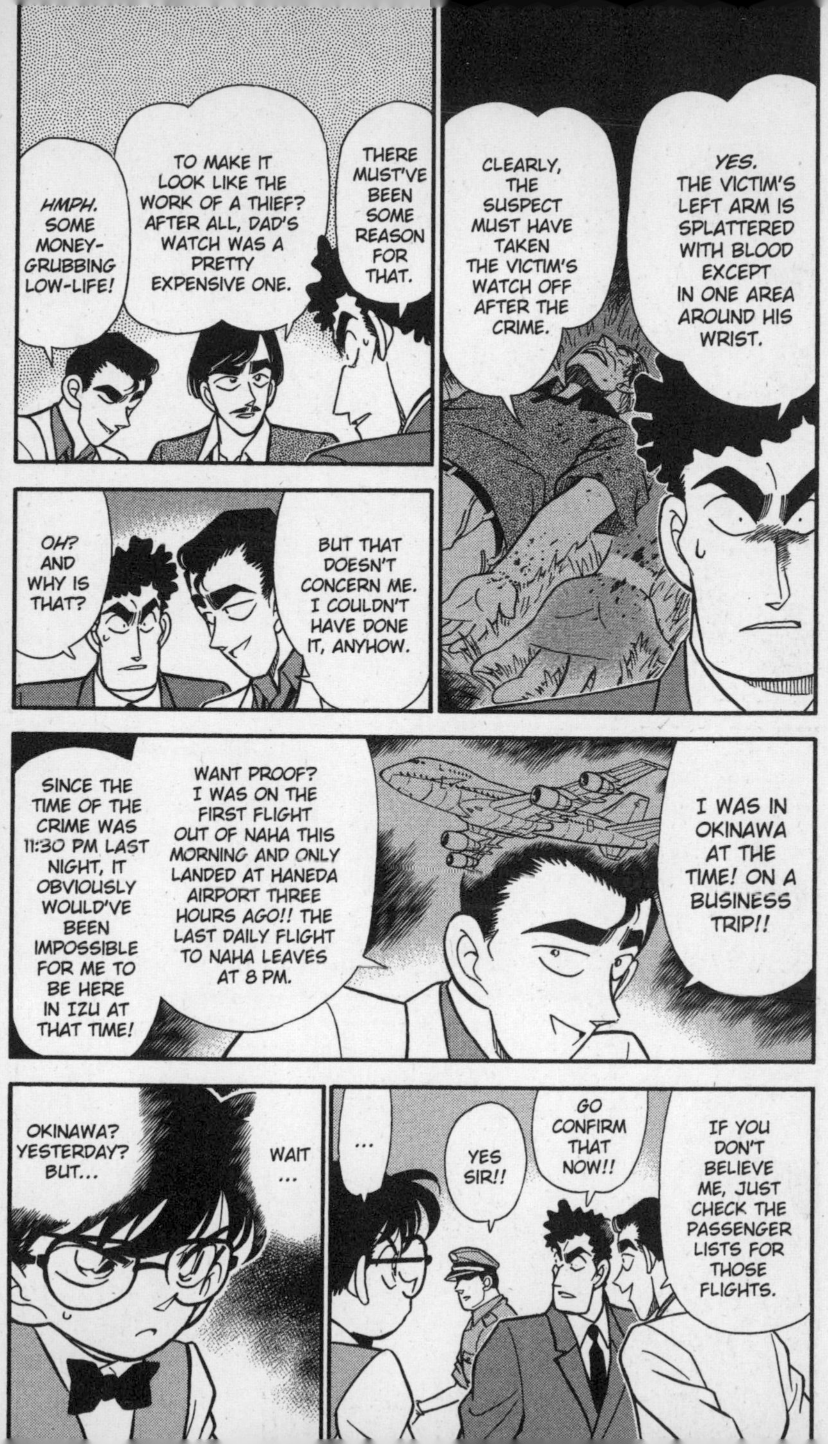
YES. THE VICTIM'S LEFT ARM IS SPLATTERED WITH BLOOD EXCEPT IN ONE AREA AROUND HIS WRIST.
CLEARLY, THE SUSPECT MUST HAVE TAKEN THE VICTIM'S WATCH OFF AFTER THE CRIME.
THERE MUST'VE BEEN SOME REASON FOR THAT.
TO MAKE IT LOOK LIKE THE WORK OF A THIEF? AFTER ALL, DAD'S WATCH WAS A PRETTY EXPENSIVE ONE.
HMPH. SOME MONEY-GRUBBING LOW-LIFE!
BUT THAT DOESN'T CONCERN ME. I COULDN'T HAVE DONE IT, ANYHOW.
OH? AND WHY IS THAT?
I WAS IN OKINAWA AT THE TIME! ON A BUSINESS TRIP!!
WANT PROOF? I WAS ON THE FIRST FLIGHT OUT OF NAHA THIS MORNING AND ONLY LANDED AT HANEDA AIRPORT THREE HOURS AGO!! THE LAST DAILY FLIGHT TO NAHA LEAVES AT 8 PM.
SINCE THE TIME OF THE CRIME WAS 11:30 PM LAST NIGHT, IT OBVIOUSLY WOULD'VE BEEN IMPOSSIBLE FOR ME TO BE HERE IN IZU AT THAT TIME!
IF YOU DON'T BELIEVE ME, JUST CHECK THE PASSENGER LISTS FOR THOSE FLIGHTS.
GO CONFIRM THAT NOW!!
YES SIR!!
...
WAIT ...
OKINAWA? YESTERDAY? BUT...

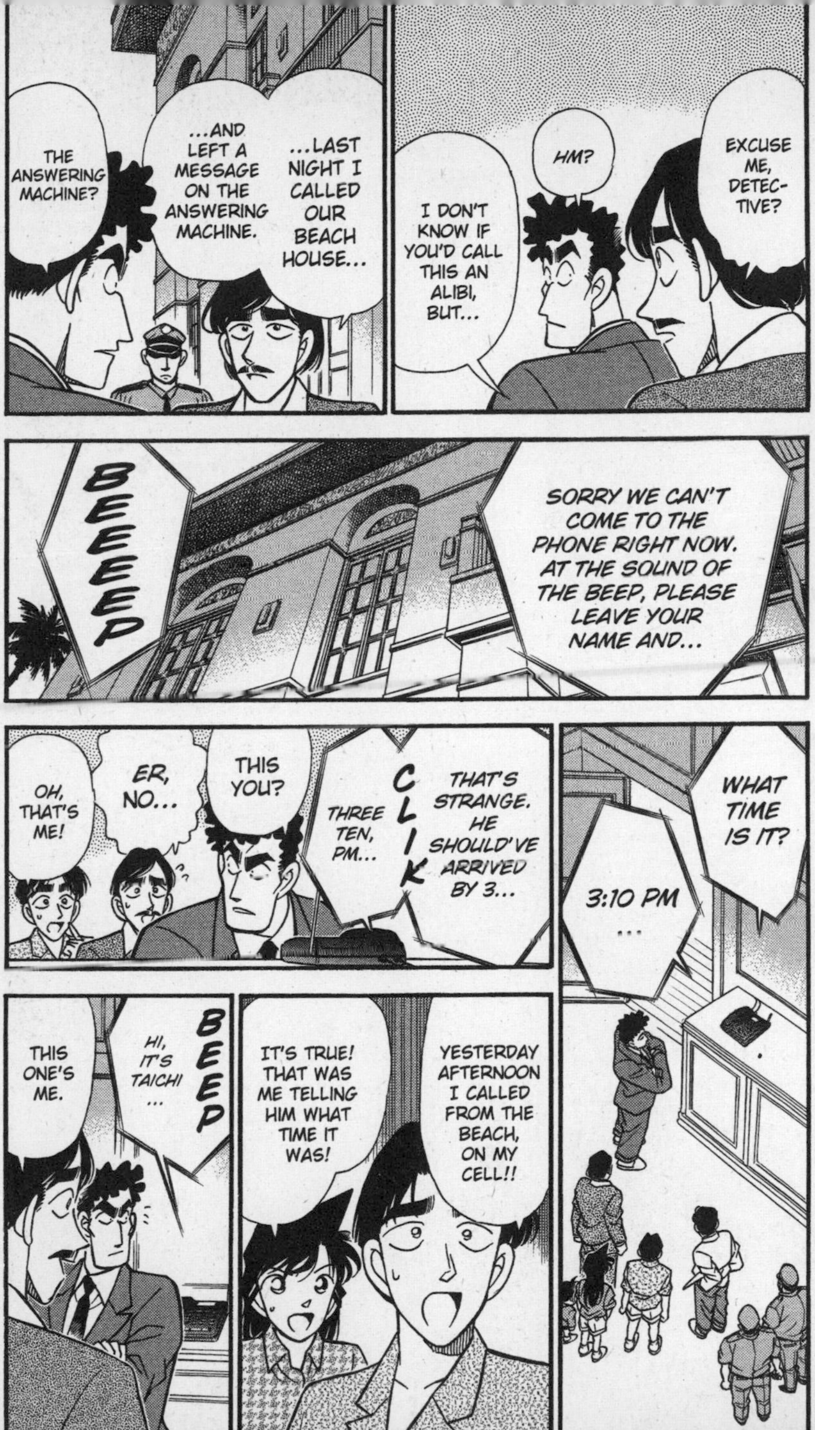
EXCUSE ME, DETECTIVE?
HM?
I DON'T KNOW IF YOU'D CALL THIS AN ALIBI, BUT...
...LAST NIGHT I CALLED OUR BEACH HOUSE...
...AND LEFT A MESSAGE ON THE ANSWERING MACHINE.
THE ANSWERING MACHINE?
SORRY WE CAN'T COME TO THE PHONE RIGHT NOW. AT THE SOUND OF THE BEEP, PLEASE LEAVE YOUR NAME AND...
BEEEEP
WHAT TIME IS IT?
3:10 PM ...
THAT'S STRANGE. HE SHOULD'VE ARRIVED BY 3...
CLIK
THREE TEN, PM...
THIS YOU?
ER, NO...
OH, THAT'S ME!
YESTERDAY AFTERNOON I CALLED FROM THE BEACH, ON MY CELL!!
IT'S TRUE! THAT WAS ME TELLING HIM WHAT TIME IT WAS!
BEEP
HI, IT'S TAICHI ...
THIS ONE'S ME.

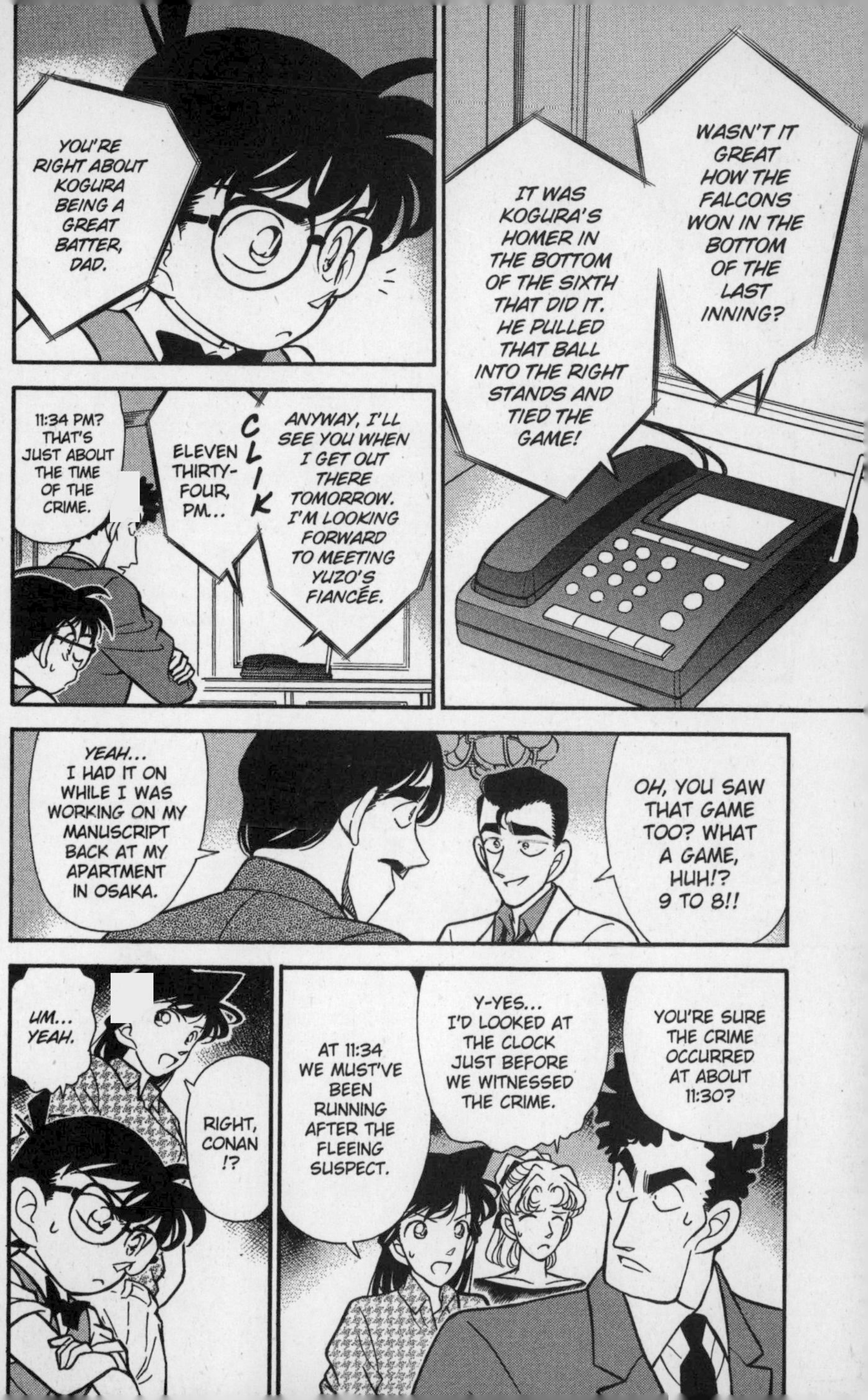
WASN'T IT GREAT HOW THE FALCONS WON IN THE BOTTOM OF THE LAST INNING?
IT WAS KOGURA'S HOMER IN THE BOTTOM OF THE SIXTH THAT DID IT. HE PULLED THAT BALL INTO THE RIGHT STANDS AND TIED THE GAME!
YOU'RE RIGHT ABOUT KOGURA BEING A GREAT BATTER, DAD.
ANYWAY, I'LL SEE YOU WHEN I GET OUT THERE TOMORROW. I'M LOOKING FORWARD TO MEETING YUZO'S FIANCÉE.
CLIK
ELEVEN THIRTY-FOUR, PM...
11:34 PM? THAT'S JUST ABOUT THE TIME OF THE CRIME.
OH, YOU SAW THAT GAME TOO? WHAT A GAME, HUH!? 9 TO 8!!
YEAH... I HAD IT ON WHILE I WAS WORKING ON MY MANUSCRIPT BACK AT MY APARTMENT IN OSAKA.
YOU'RE SURE THE CRIME OCCURRED AT ABOUT 11:30?
Y-YES... I'D LOOKED AT THE CLOCK JUST BEFORE WE WITNESSED THE CRIME.
AT 11:34 WE MUST'VE BEEN RUNNING AFTER THE FLEEING SUSPECT.
RIGHT, CONAN!?
UM... YEAH.

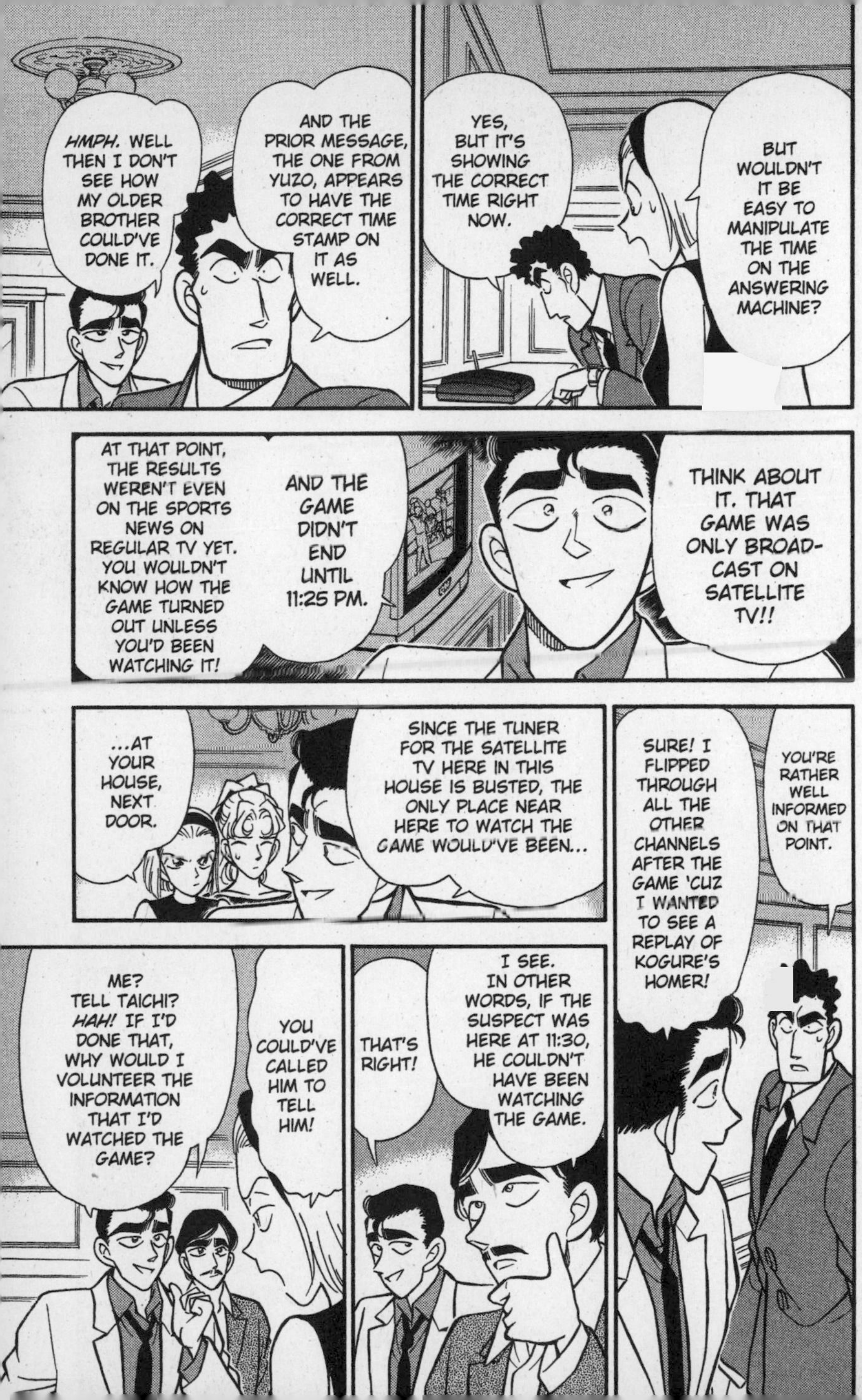
BUT WOULDN'T IT BE EASY TO MANIPULATE THE TIME ON THE ANSWERING MACHINE?
YES, BUT IT'S SHOWING THE CORRECT TIME RIGHT NOW.
AND THE PRIOR MESSAGE, THE ONE FROM YUZO, APPEARS TO HAVE THE CORRECT TIME STAMP ON IT AS WELL.
HMPH. WELL THEN I DON'T SEE HOW MY OLDER BROTHER COULD'VE DONE IT.
THINK ABOUT IT. THAT GAME WAS ONLY BROAD-CAST ON SATELLITE TV!!
AND THE GAME DIDN'T END UNTIL 11:25 PM.
AT THAT POINT, THE RESULTS WEREN'T EVEN ON THE SPORTS NEWS ON REGULAR TV YET. YOU WOULDN'T KNOW HOW THE GAME TURNED OUT UNLESS YOU'D BEEN WATCHING IT!
YOU'RE RATHER WELL INFORMED ON THAT POINT.
SURE! I FLIPPED THROUGH ALL THE OTHER CHANNELS AFTER THE GAME 'CUZ I WANTED TO SEE A REPLAY OF KOGURE'S HOMER!
SINCE THE TUNER FOR THE SATELLITE TV HERE IN THIS HOUSE IS BUSTED, THE ONLY PLACE NEAR HERE TO WATCH THE GAME WOULD'VE BEEN...
...AT YOUR HOUSE, NEXT DOOR.
I SEE. IN OTHER WORDS, IF THE SUSPECT WAS HERE AT 11:30, HE COULDN'T HAVE BEEN WATCHING THE GAME.
THAT'S RIGHT!
YOU COULD'VE CALLED HIM TO TELL HIM!
ME? TELL TAICHI? *HAH!* IF I'D DONE THAT, WHY WOULD I VOLUNTEER THE INFORMATION THAT I'D WATCHED THE GAME?

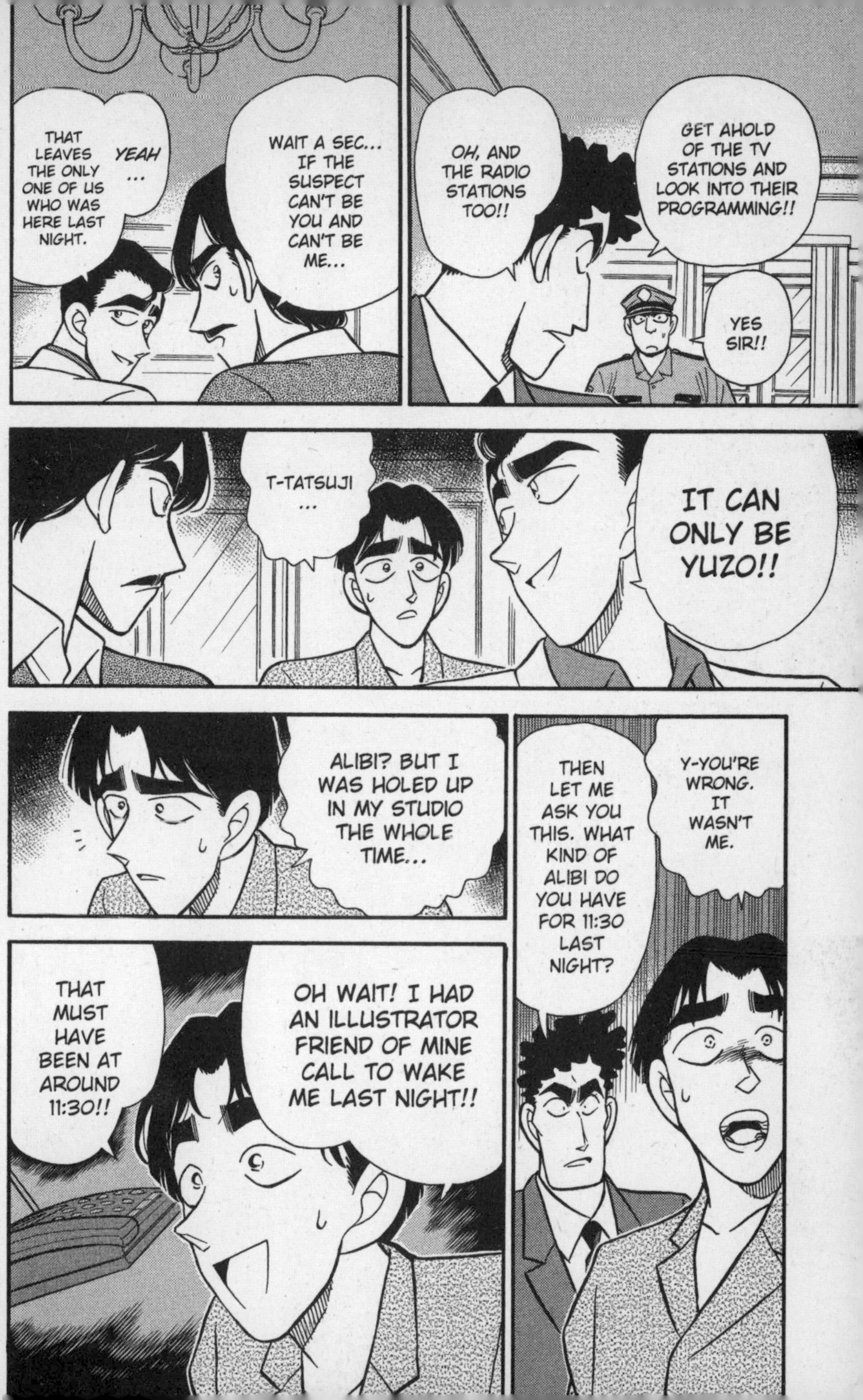
GET AHOLD OF THE TV STATIONS AND LOOK INTO THEIR PROGRAMMING!!
OH, AND THE RADIO STATIONS TOO!!
YES SIR!!
WAIT A SEC... IF THE SUSPECT CAN'T BE YOU AND CAN'T BE ME...
THAT LEAVES THE ONLY ONE OF US WHO WAS HERE LAST NIGHT.
YEAH ...
IT CAN ONLY BE YUZO!!
T-TATSUJI ...
Y-YOU'RE WRONG. IT WASN'T ME.
THEN LET ME ASK YOU THIS. WHAT KIND OF ALIBI DO YOU HAVE FOR 11:30 LAST NIGHT?
ALIBI? BUT I WAS HOLED UP IN MY STUDIO THE WHOLE TIME...
OH WAIT! I HAD AN ILLUSTRATOR FRIEND OF MINE CALL TO WAKE ME LAST NIGHT!!
THAT MUST HAVE BEEN AT AROUND 11:30!!

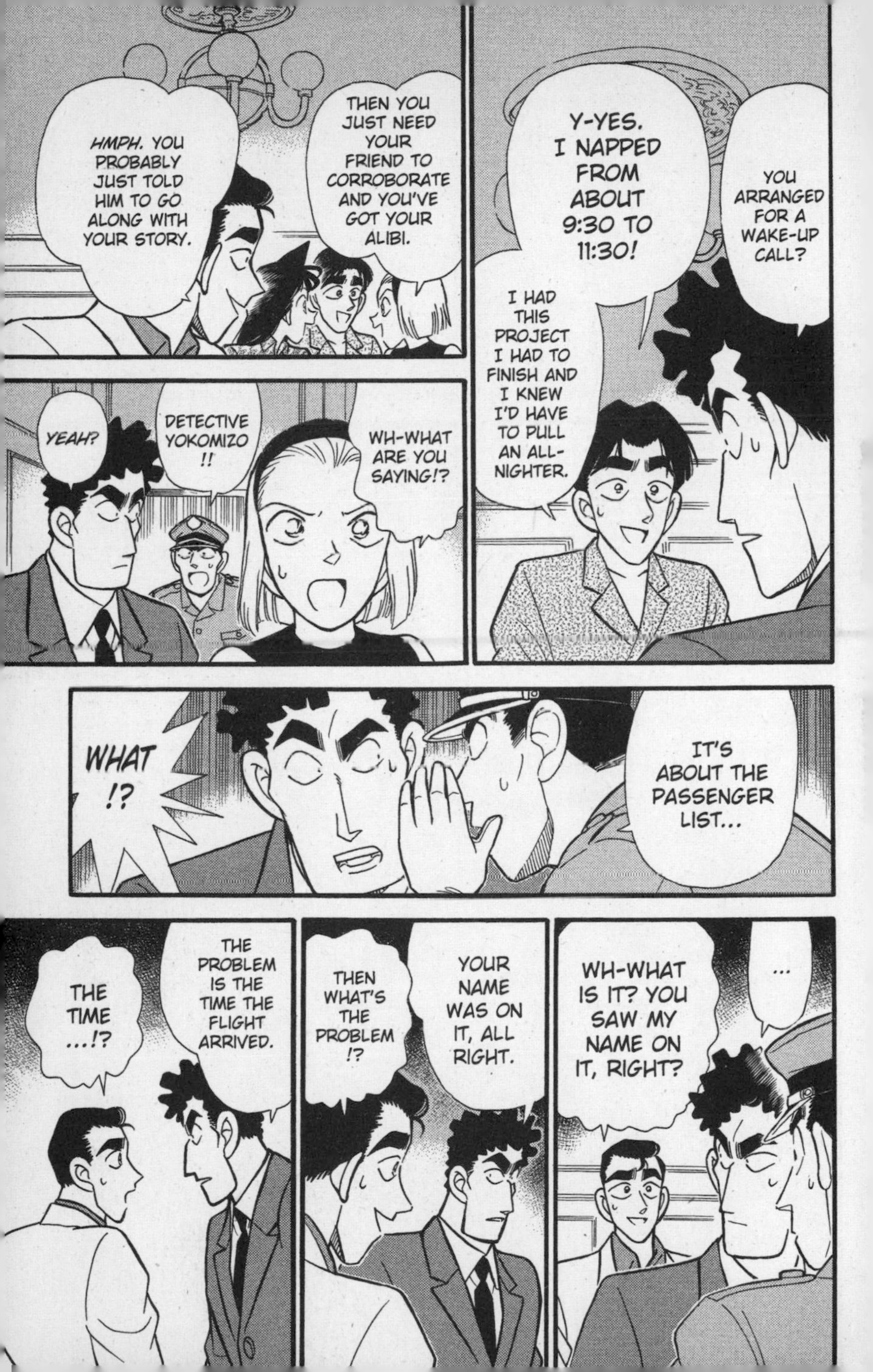
YOU ARRANGED FOR A WAKE-UP CALL?
Y-YES. I NAPPED FROM ABOUT 9:30 TO 11:30!
I HAD THIS PROJECT I HAD TO FINISH AND I KNEW I'D HAVE TO PULL AN ALL-NIGHTER.
THEN YOU JUST NEED YOUR FRIEND TO CORROBORATE AND YOU'VE GOT YOUR ALIBI.
HMPH. YOU PROBABLY JUST TOLD HIM TO GO ALONG WITH YOUR STORY.
WH-WHAT ARE YOU SAYING!?
DETECTIVE YOKOMIZO !!
YEAH?
IT'S ABOUT THE PASSENGER LIST...
WHAT !?
...
WH-WHAT IS IT? YOU SAW MY NAME ON IT, RIGHT?
YOUR NAME WAS ON IT, ALL RIGHT.
THEN WHAT'S THE PROBLEM !?
THE PROBLEM IS THE TIME THE FLIGHT ARRIVED.
THE TIME ...!?

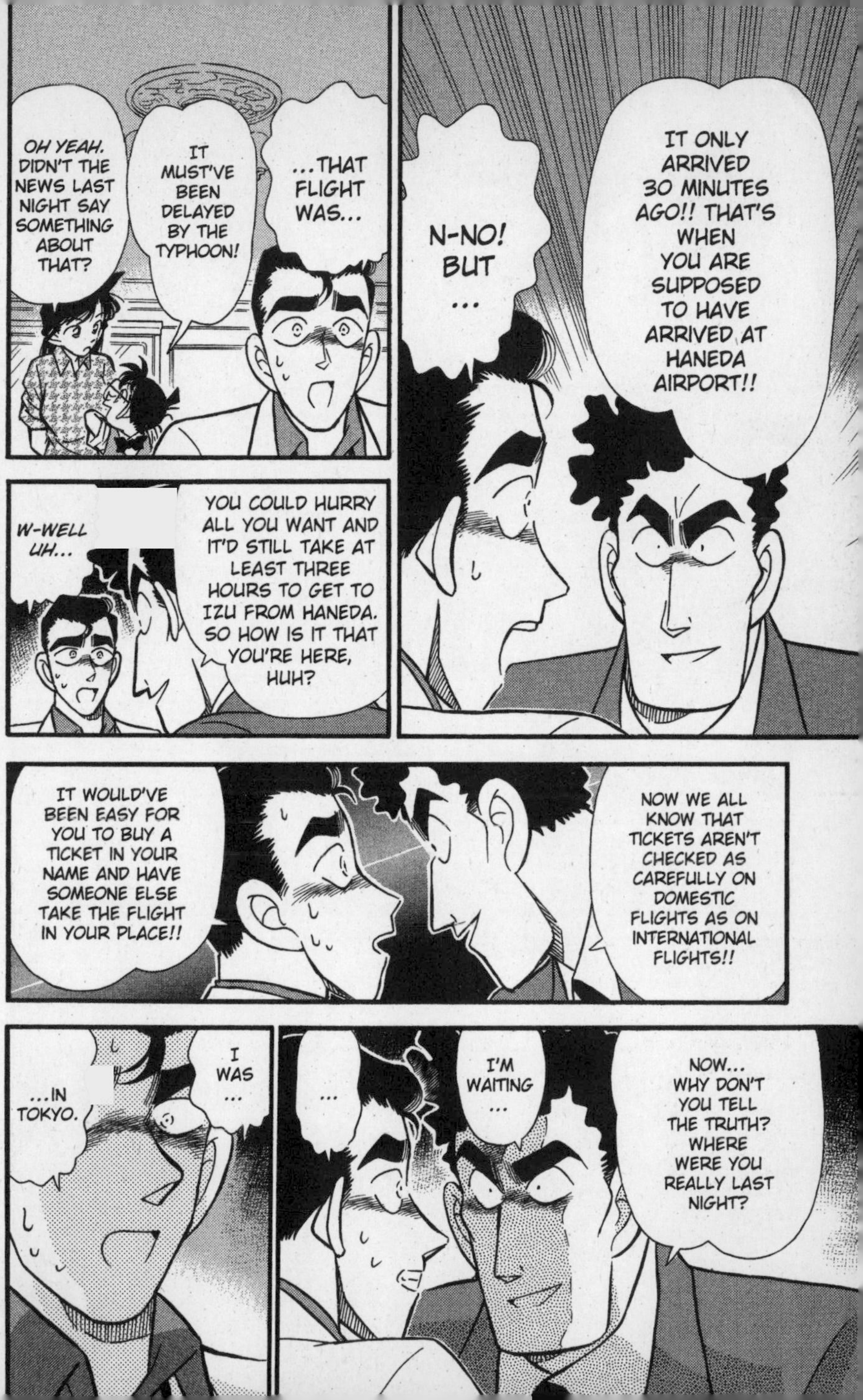
...THAT FLIGHT WAS...
IT MUST'VE BEEN DELAYED BY THE TYPHOON!
OH YEAH. DIDN'T THE NEWS LAST NIGHT SAY SOMETHING ABOUT THAT?
IT ONLY ARRIVED 30 MINUTES AGO!! THAT'S WHEN YOU ARE SUPPOSED TO HAVE ARRIVED AT HANEDA AIRPORT!!
N-NO! BUT ...
YOU COULD HURRY ALL YOU WANT AND IT'D STILL TAKE AT LEAST THREE HOURS TO GET TO IZU FROM HANEDA. SO HOW IS IT THAT YOU'RE HERE, HUH?
W-WELL UH...
NOW WE ALL KNOW THAT TICKETS AREN'T CHECKED AS CAREFULLY ON DOMESTIC FLIGHTS AS ON INTERNATIONAL FLIGHTS!!
IT WOULD'VE BEEN EASY FOR YOU TO BUY A TICKET IN YOUR NAME AND HAVE SOMEONE ELSE TAKE THE FLIGHT IN YOUR PLACE!!
NOW... WHY DON'T YOU TELL THE TRUTH? WHERE WERE YOU REALLY LAST NIGHT?
I'M WAITING ...
...
I WAS ...
...IN TOKYO.

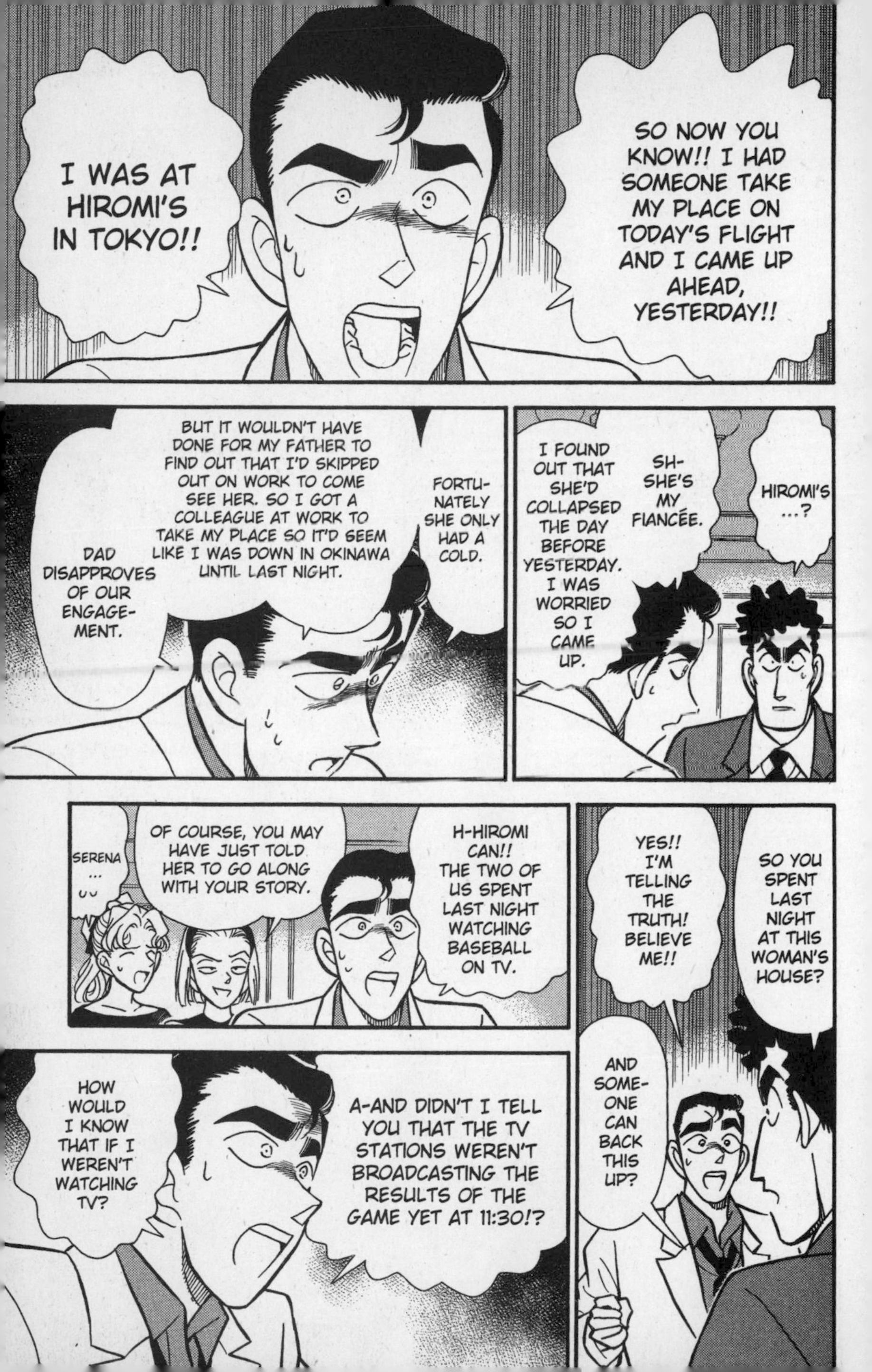
SO NOW YOU KNOW!! I HAD SOMEONE TAKE MY PLACE ON TODAY'S FLIGHT AND I CAME UP AHEAD, YESTERDAY!!
I WAS AT HIROMI'S IN TOKYO!!
HIROMI'S ...?
SH- SHE'S MY FIANCÉE.
I FOUND OUT THAT SHE'D COLLAPSED THE DAY BEFORE YESTERDAY. I WAS WORRIED SO I CAME UP.
FORTUNATELY SHE ONLY HAD A COLD.
BUT IT WOULDN'T HAVE DONE FOR MY FATHER TO FIND OUT THAT I'D SKIPPED OUT ON WORK TO COME SEE HER. SO I GOT A COLLEAGUE AT WORK TO TAKE MY PLACE SO IT'D SEEM LIKE I WAS DOWN IN OKINAWA UNTIL LAST NIGHT.
DAD DISAPPROVES OF OUR ENGAGEMENT.
SO YOU SPENT LAST NIGHT AT THIS WOMAN'S HOUSE?
YES!! I'M TELLING THE TRUTH! BELIEVE ME!!
AND SOMEONE CAN BACK THIS UP?
H-HIROMI CAN!! THE TWO OF US SPENT LAST NIGHT WATCHING BASEBALL ON TV.
OF COURSE, YOU MAY HAVE JUST TOLD HER TO GO ALONG WITH YOUR STORY.
SERENA ...
A-AND DIDN'T I TELL YOU THAT THE TV STATIONS WEREN'T BROADCASTING THE RESULTS OF THE GAME YET AT 11:30!?
HOW WOULD I KNOW THAT IF I WEREN'T WATCHING TV?

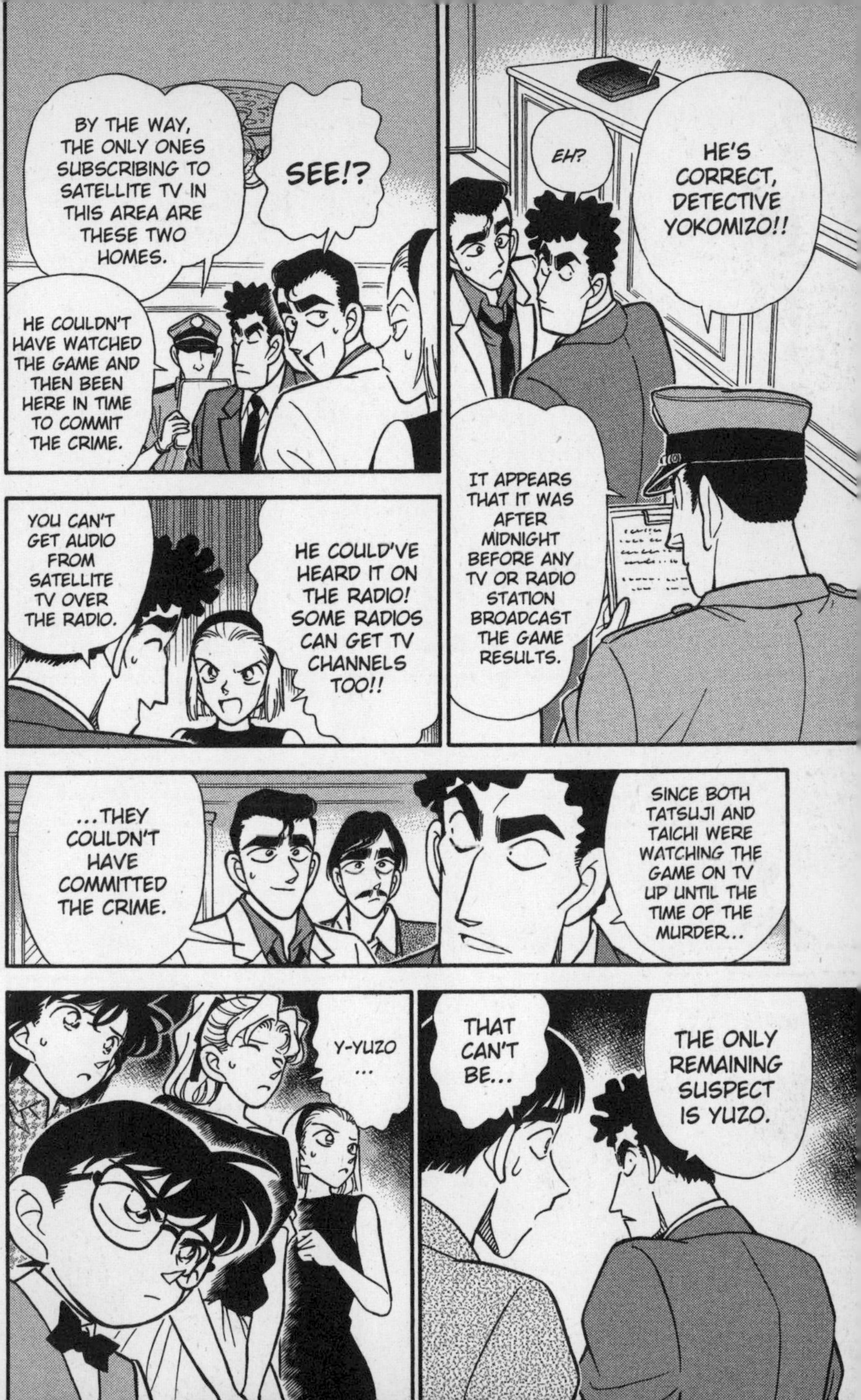
HE'S CORRECT, DETECTIVE YOKOMIZO!!
EH?
IT APPEARS THAT IT WAS AFTER MIDNIGHT BEFORE ANY TV OR RADIO STATION BROADCAST THE GAME RESULTS.
SEE!?
BY THE WAY, THE ONLY ONES SUBSCRIBING TO SATELLITE TV IN THIS AREA ARE THESE TWO HOMES.
HE COULDN'T HAVE WATCHED THE GAME AND THEN BEEN HERE IN TIME TO COMMIT THE CRIME.
HE COULD'VE HEARD IT ON THE RADIO! SOME RADIOS CAN GET TV CHANNELS TOO!!
YOU CAN'T GET AUDIO FROM SATELLITE TV OVER THE RADIO.
SINCE BOTH TATSUJI AND TAICHI WERE WATCHING THE GAME ON TV UP UNTIL THE TIME OF THE MURDER...
...THEY COULDN'T HAVE COMMITTED THE CRIME.
THE ONLY REMAINING SUSPECT IS YUZO.
THAT CAN'T BE...
Y-YUZO ...

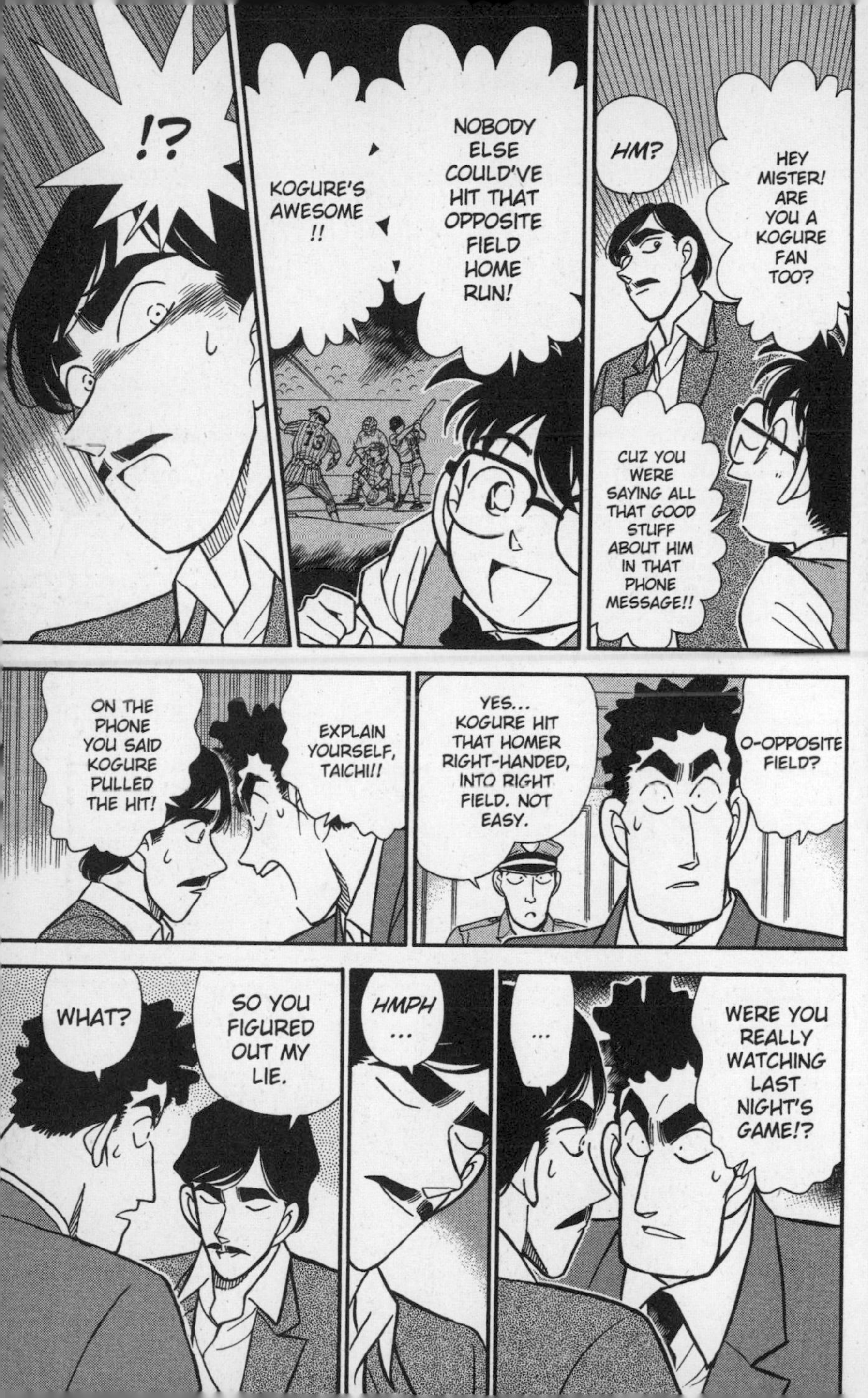
HEY MISTER! ARE YOU A KOGURE FAN TOO?
HM?
CUZ YOU WERE SAYING ALL THAT GOOD STUFF ABOUT HIM IN THAT PHONE MESSAGE!!
NOBODY ELSE COULD'VE HIT THAT OPPOSITE FIELD HOME RUN!
KOGURE'S AWESOME !!
!?
O-OPPOSITE FIELD?
YES... KOGURE HIT THAT HOMER RIGHT-HANDED, INTO RIGHT FIELD. NOT EASY.
EXPLAIN YOURSELF, TAICHI!!
ON THE PHONE YOU SAID KOGURE PULLED THE HIT!
WERE YOU REALLY WATCHING LAST NIGHT'S GAME!?
...
HMPH ...
SO YOU FIGURED OUT MY LIE.
WHAT?

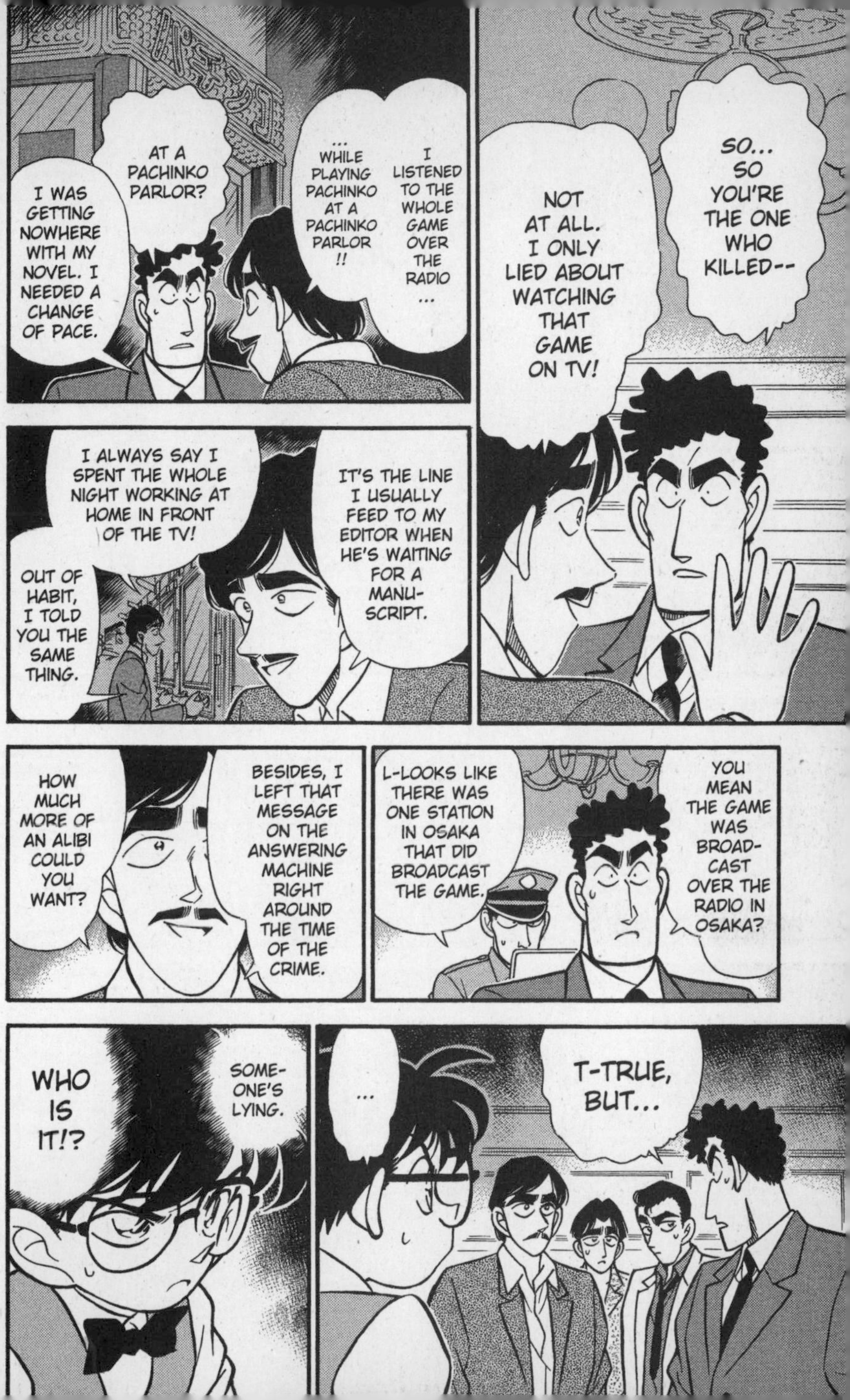
SO... SO YOU'RE THE ONE WHO KILLED--
NOT AT ALL. I ONLY LIED ABOUT WATCHING THAT GAME ON TV!
I LISTENED TO THE WHOLE GAME OVER THE RADIO ...
... WHILE PLAYING PACHINKO AT A PACHINKO PARLOR !!
AT A PACHINKO PARLOR?
I WAS GETTING NOWHERE WITH MY NOVEL. I NEEDED A CHANGE OF PACE.
IT'S THE LINE I USUALLY FEED TO MY EDITOR WHEN HE'S WAITING FOR A MANU-SCRIPT.
I ALWAYS SAY I SPENT THE WHOLE NIGHT WORKING AT HOME IN FRONT OF THE TV!
OUT OF HABIT, I TOLD YOU THE SAME THING.
YOU MEAN THE GAME WAS BROAD-CAST OVER THE RADIO IN OSAKA?
L-LOOKS LIKE THERE WAS ONE STATION IN OSAKA THAT DID BROADCAST THE GAME.
BESIDES, I LEFT THAT MESSAGE ON THE ANSWERING MACHINE RIGHT AROUND THE TIME OF THE CRIME.
HOW MUCH MORE OF AN ALIBI COULD YOU WANT?
T-TRUE, BUT...
...
SOME-ONE'S LYING.
WHO IS IT!?

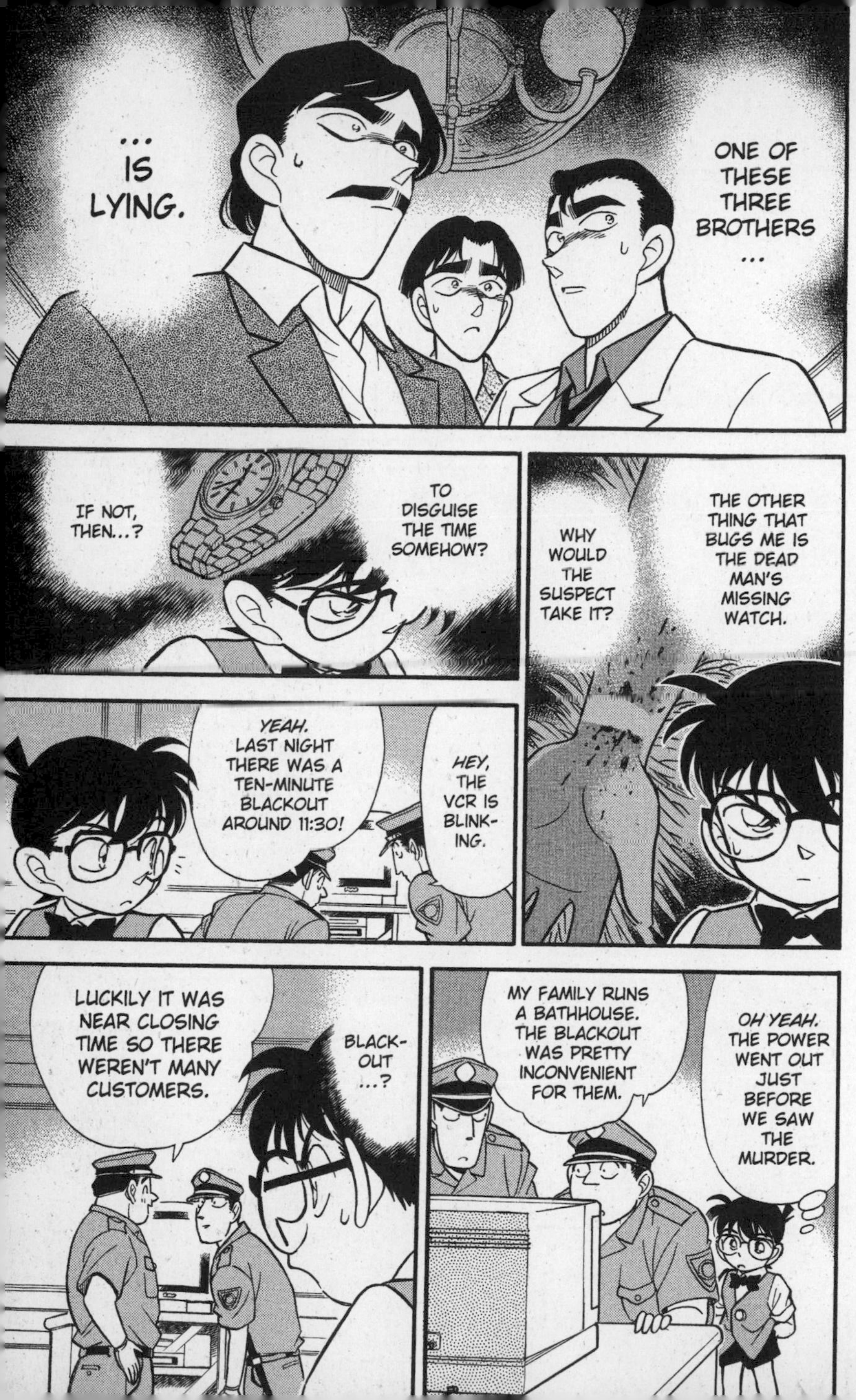

ONE OF THESE THREE BROTHERS ...
... IS LYING.
THE OTHER THING THAT BUGS ME IS THE DEAD MAN'S MISSING WATCH.
WHY WOULD THE SUSPECT TAKE IT?
TO DISGUISE THE TIME SOMEHOW?
IF NOT, THEN...?
HEY, THE VCR IS BLINK-ING.
YEAH. LAST NIGHT THERE WAS A TEN-MINUTE BLACKOUT AROUND 11:30!
OH YEAH. THE POWER WENT OUT JUST BEFORE WE SAW THE MURDER.
MY FAMILY RUNS A BATHHOUSE. THE BLACKOUT WAS PRETTY INCONVENIENT FOR THEM.
BLACK-OUT ...?
LUCKILY IT WAS NEAR CLOSING TIME SO THERE WEREN'T MANY CUSTOMERS.

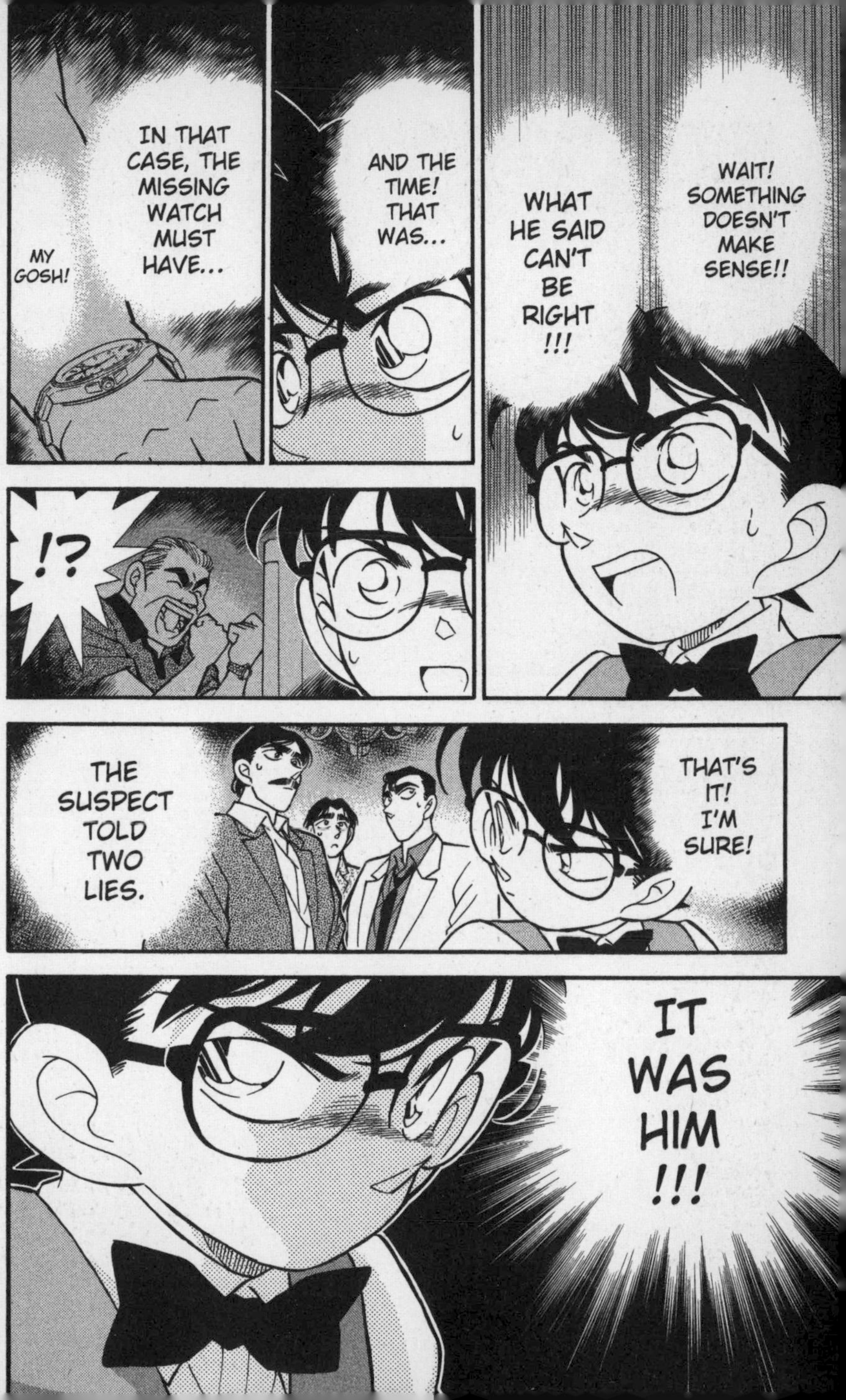
WAIT! SOMETHING DOESN'T MAKE SENSE!!
WHAT HE SAID CAN'T BE RIGHT !!!
AND THE TIME! THAT WAS...
IN THAT CASE, THE MISSING WATCH MUST HAVE...
MY GOSH!
!?
THAT'S IT! I'M SURE!
THE SUSPECT TOLD TWO LIES.
IT WAS HIM !!!

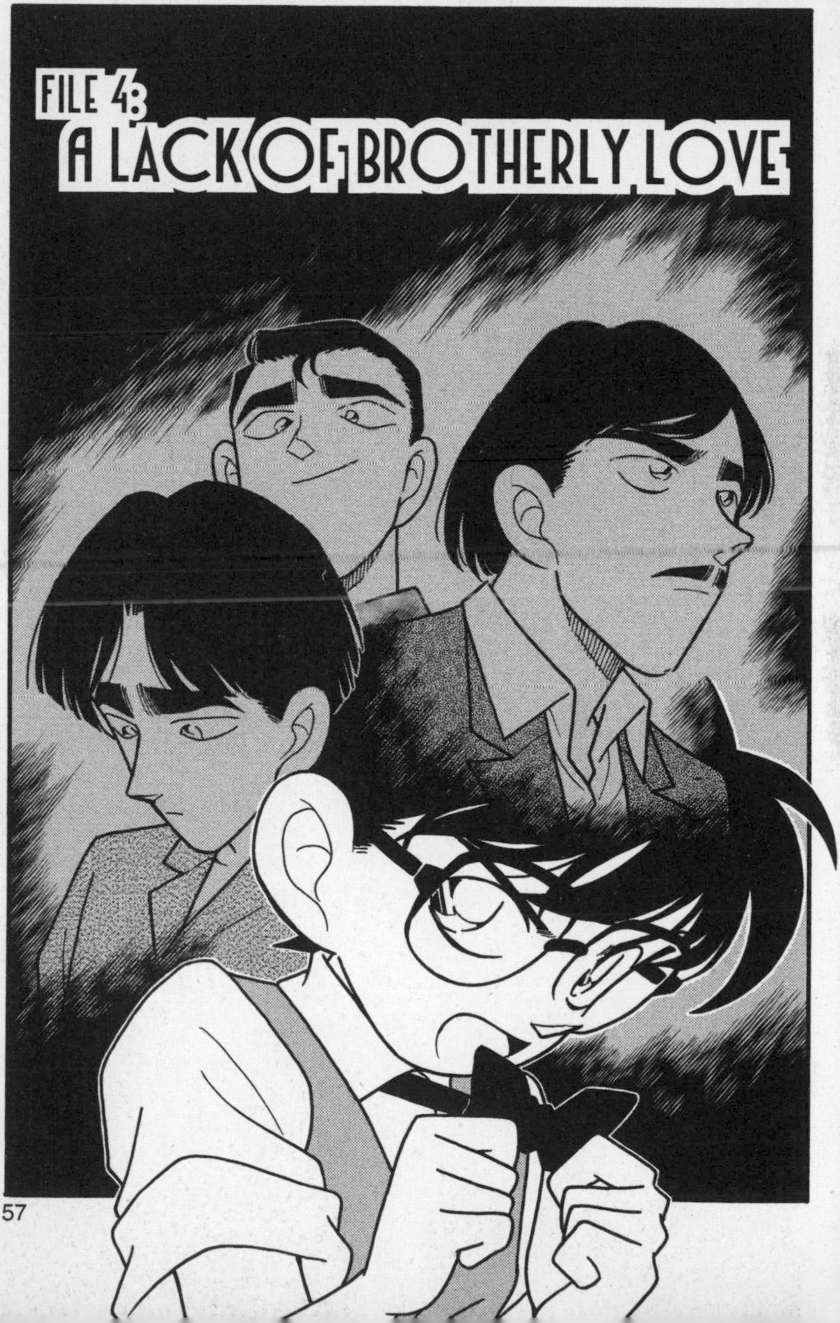
FILE 4:
A LACK OF BROTHERLY LOVE

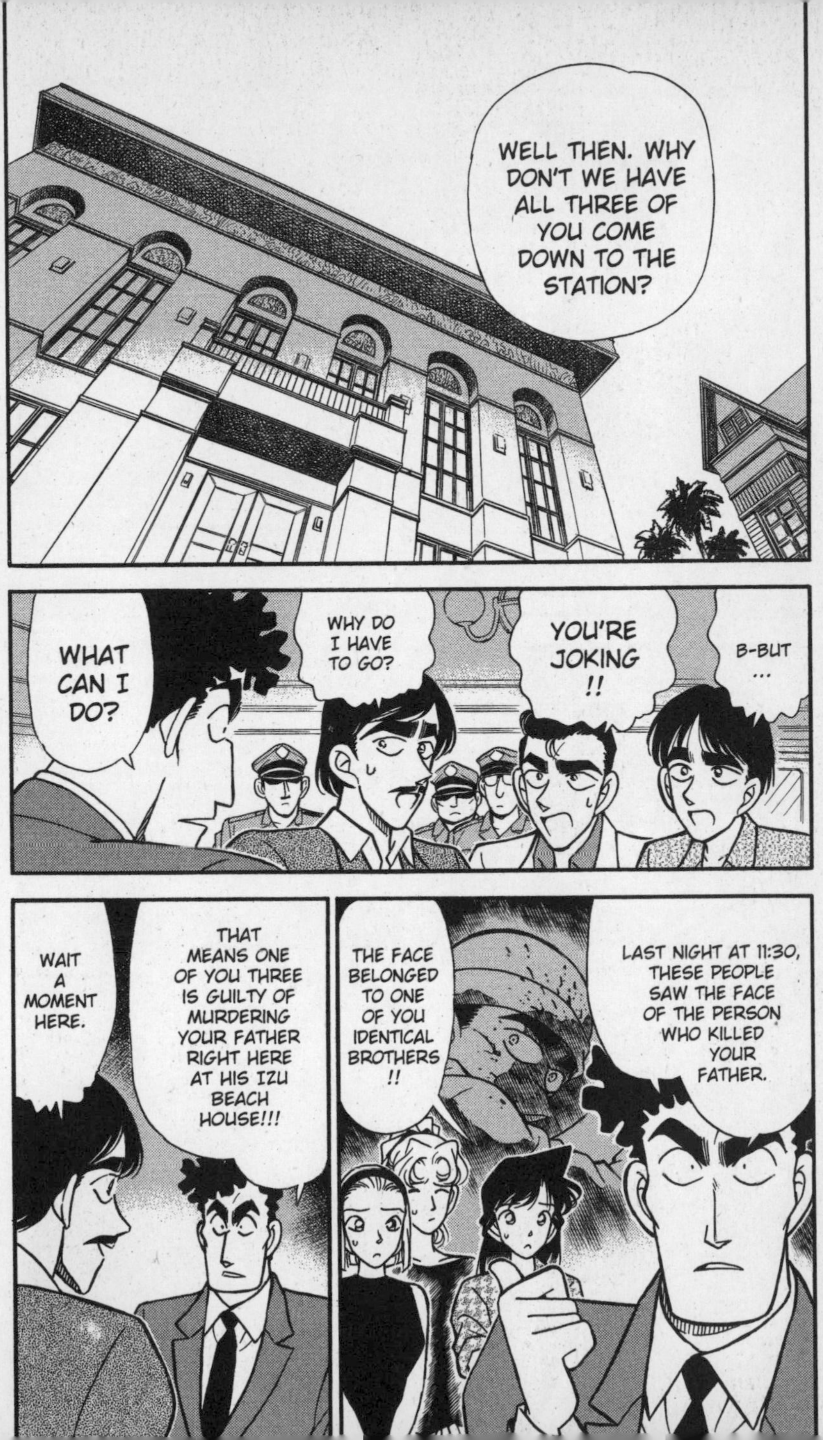
WELL THEN. WHY DON'T WE HAVE ALL THREE OF YOU COME DOWN TO THE STATION?
B-BUT ...
YOU'RE JOKING !!
WHY DO I HAVE TO GO?
WHAT CAN I DO?
LAST NIGHT AT 11:30, THESE PEOPLE SAW THE FACE OF THE PERSON WHO KILLED YOUR FATHER.
THE FACE BELONGED TO ONE OF YOU IDENTICAL BROTHERS !!
THAT MEANS ONE OF YOU THREE IS GUILTY OF MURDERING YOUR FATHER RIGHT HERE AT HIS IZU BEACH HOUSE!!!
WAIT A MOMENT HERE.

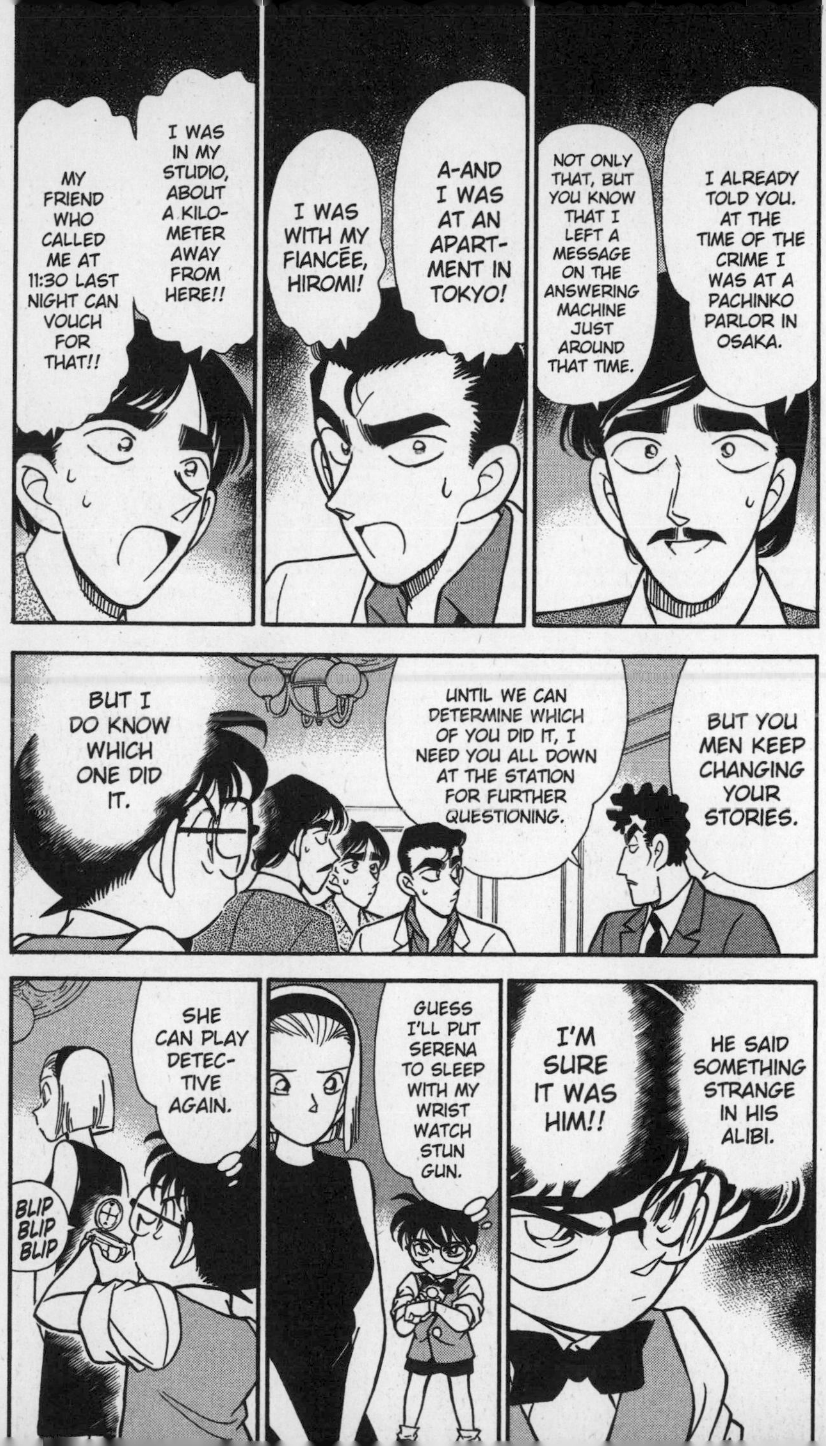
I ALREADY TOLD YOU. AT THE TIME OF THE CRIME I WAS AT A PACHINKO PARLOR IN OSAKA.
NOT ONLY THAT, BUT YOU KNOW THAT I LEFT A MESSAGE ON THE ANSWERING MACHINE JUST AROUND THAT TIME.
A-AND I WAS AT AN APARTMENT IN TOKYO!
I WAS WITH MY FIANCÉE, HIROMI!
I WAS IN MY STUDIO, ABOUT A KILOMETER AWAY FROM HERE!!
MY FRIEND WHO CALLED ME AT 11:30 LAST NIGHT CAN VOUCH FOR THAT!!
BUT YOU MEN KEEP CHANGING YOUR STORIES.
UNTIL WE CAN DETERMINE WHICH OF YOU DID IT, I NEED YOU ALL DOWN AT THE STATION FOR FURTHER QUESTIONING.
BUT I DO KNOW WHICH ONE DID IT.
HE SAID SOMETHING STRANGE IN HIS ALIBI.
I'M SURE IT WAS HIM!!
GUESS I'LL PUT SERENA TO SLEEP WITH MY WRIST WATCH STUN GUN.
SHE CAN PLAY DETECTIVE AGAIN.
BLIP BLIP BLIP

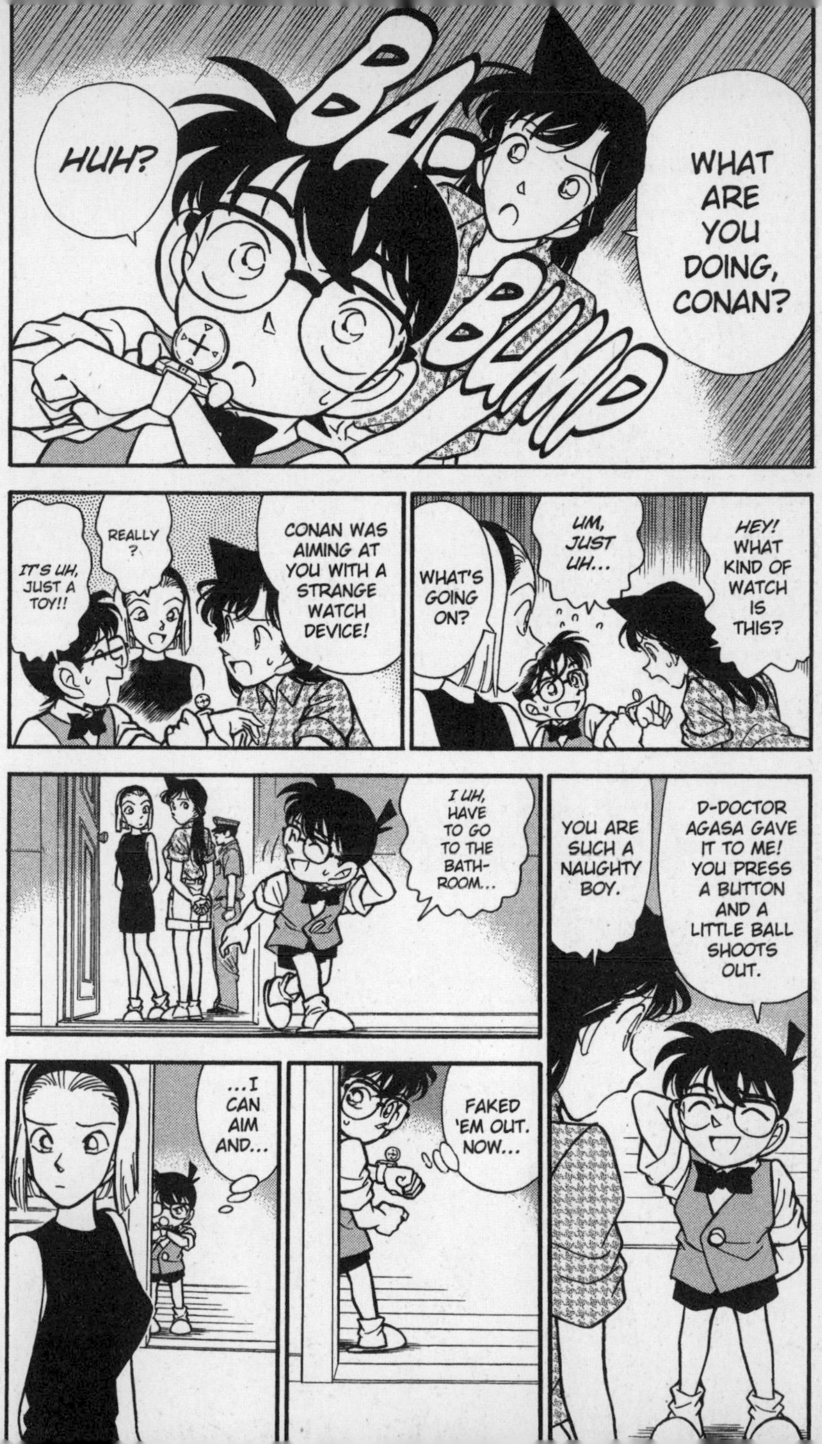
WHAT ARE YOU DOING, CONAN?
BA-BUMP
HUH?
HEY! WHAT KIND OF WATCH IS THIS?
UM, JUST UH...
WHAT'S GOING ON?
CONAN WAS AIMING AT YOU WITH A STRANGE WATCH DEVICE!
REALLY?
IT'S UH, JUST A TOY!!
D-DOCTOR AGASA GAVE IT TO ME! YOU PRESS A BUTTON AND A LITTLE BALL SHOOTS OUT.
YOU ARE SUCH A NAUGHTY BOY.
I UH, HAVE TO GO TO THE BATH-ROOM...
FAKED 'EM OUT. NOW...
...I CAN AIM AND...

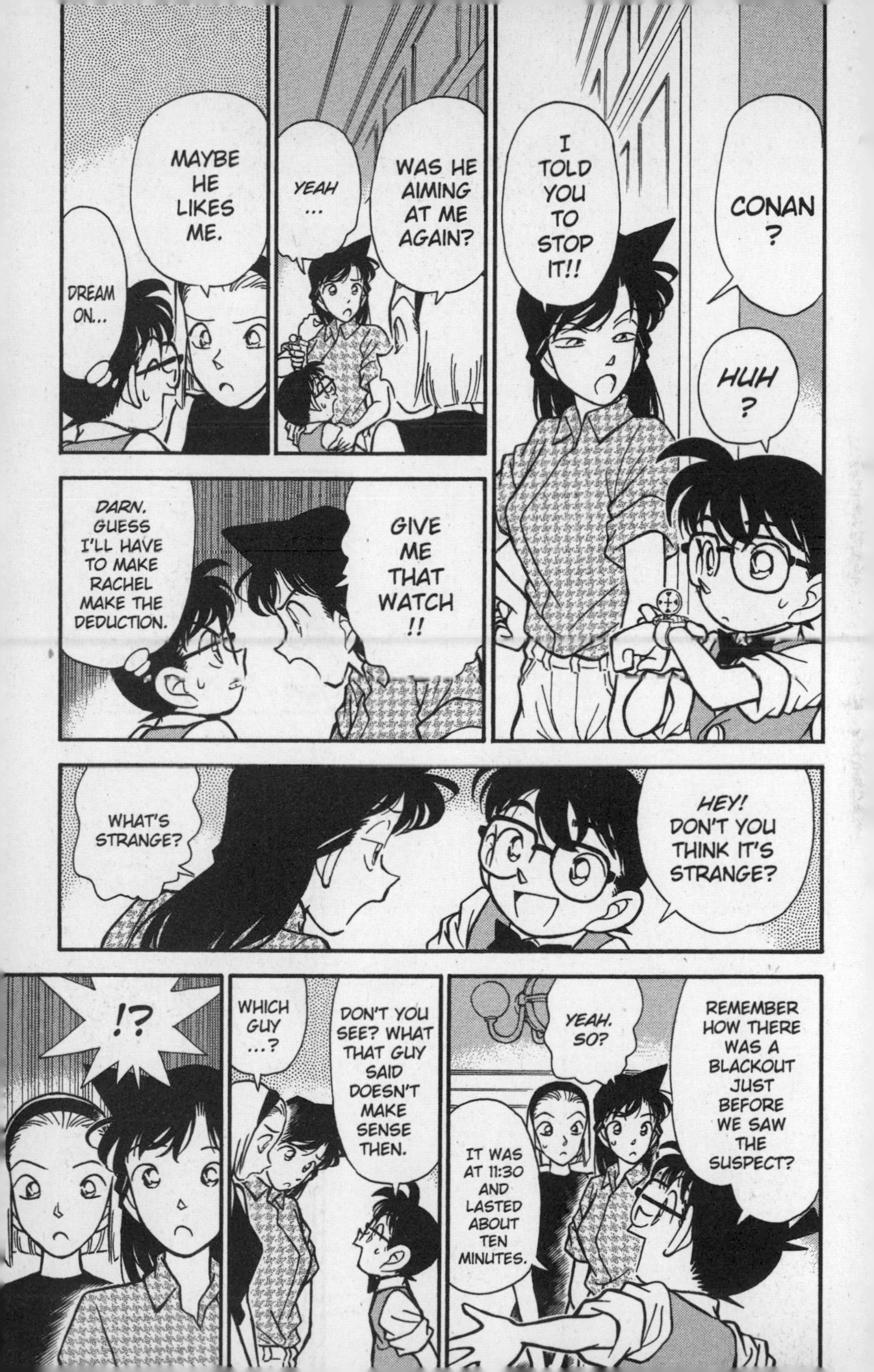
CONAN?
I TOLD YOU TO STOP IT!!
HUH?
WAS HE AIMING AT ME AGAIN?
YEAH...
MAYBE HE LIKES ME.
DREAM ON...
GIVE ME THAT WATCH!!
DARN. GUESS I'LL HAVE TO MAKE RACHEL MAKE THE DEDUCTION.
HEY! DON'T YOU THINK IT'S STRANGE?
WHAT'S STRANGE?
REMEMBER HOW THERE WAS A BLACKOUT JUST BEFORE WE SAW THE SUSPECT?
YEAH. SO?
IT WAS AT 11:30 AND LASTED ABOUT TEN MINUTES.
DON'T YOU SEE? WHAT THAT GUY SAID DOESN'T MAKE SENSE THEN.
WHICH GUY...?
!?

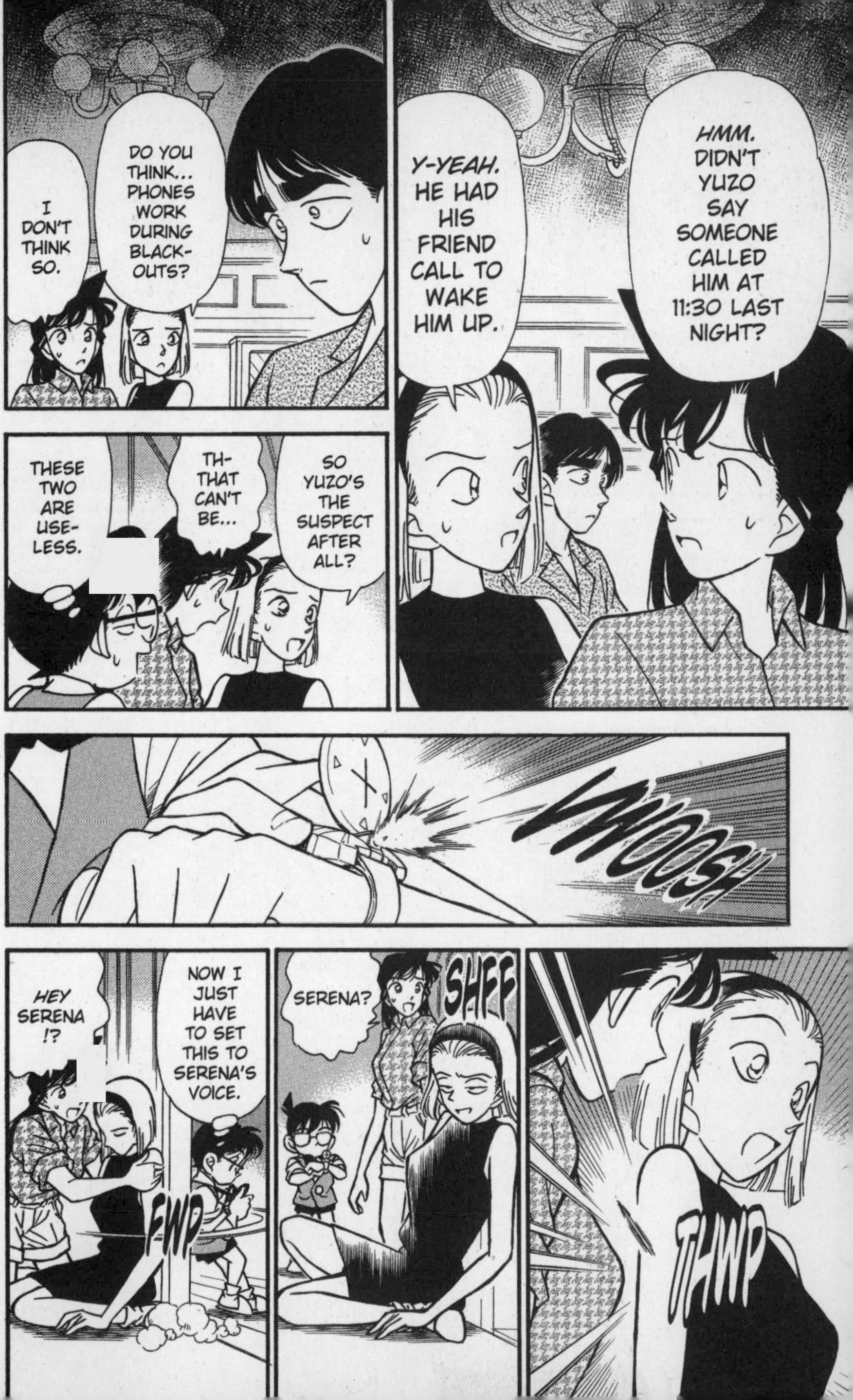
HMM. DIDN'T YUZO SAY SOMEONE CALLED HIM AT 11:30 LAST NIGHT?
Y-YEAH. HE HAD HIS FRIEND CALL TO WAKE HIM UP.
DO YOU THINK... PHONES WORK DURING BLACK-OUTS?
I DON'T THINK SO.
SO YUZO'S THE SUSPECT AFTER ALL?
TH-THAT CAN'T BE...
THESE TWO ARE USE-LESS.
WOOSH
THWP
SHFF
SERENA?
NOW I JUST HAVE TO SET THIS TO SERENA'S VOICE.
HEY SERENA!?
FWP

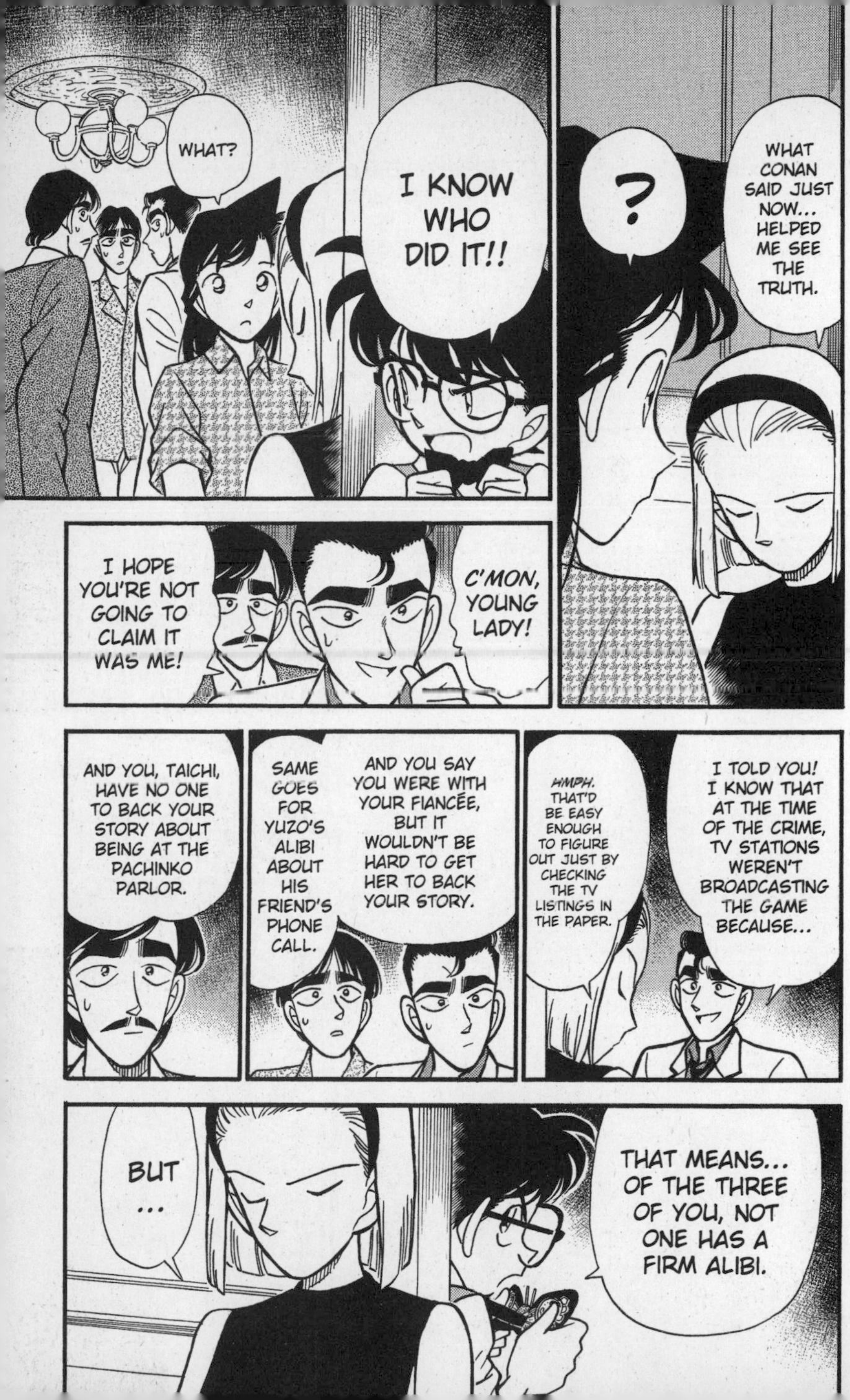

?
WHAT CONAN SAID JUST NOW... HELPED ME SEE THE TRUTH.
I KNOW WHO DID IT!!
WHAT?
C'MON, YOUNG LADY!
I HOPE YOU'RE NOT GOING TO CLAIM IT WAS ME!
I TOLD YOU! I KNOW THAT AT THE TIME OF THE CRIME, TV STATIONS WEREN'T BROADCASTING THE GAME BECAUSE...
HMPH. THAT'D BE EASY ENOUGH TO FIGURE OUT JUST BY CHECKING THE TV LISTINGS IN THE PAPER.
AND YOU SAY YOU WERE WITH YOUR FIANCÉE, BUT IT WOULDN'T BE HARD TO GET HER TO BACK YOUR STORY.
SAME GOES FOR YUZO'S ALIBI ABOUT HIS FRIEND'S PHONE CALL.
AND YOU, TAICHI, HAVE NO ONE TO BACK YOUR STORY ABOUT BEING AT THE PACHINKO PARLOR.
THAT MEANS... OF THE THREE OF YOU, NOT ONE HAS A FIRM ALIBI.
BUT ...

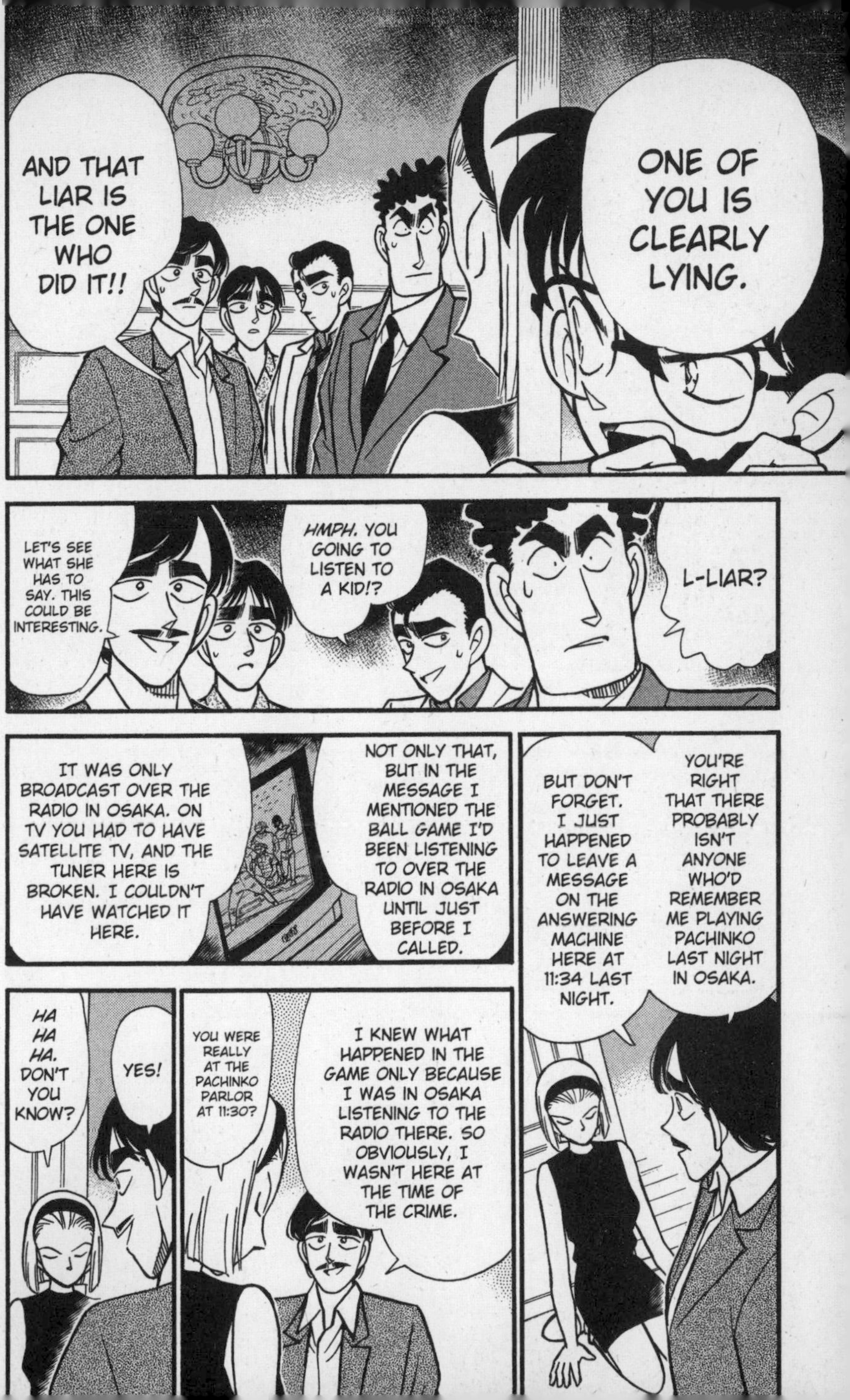
ONE OF YOU IS CLEARLY LYING.
AND THAT LIAR IS THE ONE WHO DID IT!!
L-LIAR?
HMPH. YOU GOING TO LISTEN TO A KID!?
LET'S SEE WHAT SHE HAS TO SAY. THIS COULD BE INTERESTING.
YOU'RE RIGHT THAT THERE PROBABLY ISN'T ANYONE WHO'D REMEMBER ME PLAYING PACHINKO LAST NIGHT IN OSAKA.
BUT DON'T FORGET. I JUST HAPPENED TO LEAVE A MESSAGE ON THE ANSWERING MACHINE HERE AT 11:34 LAST NIGHT.
NOT ONLY THAT, BUT IN THE MESSAGE I MENTIONED THE BALL GAME I'D BEEN LISTENING TO OVER THE RADIO IN OSAKA UNTIL JUST BEFORE I CALLED.
IT WAS ONLY BROADCAST OVER THE RADIO IN OSAKA. ON TV YOU HAD TO HAVE SATELLITE TV, AND THE TUNER HERE IS BROKEN. I COULDN'T HAVE WATCHED IT HERE.
I KNEW WHAT HAPPENED IN THE GAME ONLY BECAUSE I WAS IN OSAKA LISTENING TO THE RADIO THERE. SO OBVIOUSLY, I WASN'T HERE AT THE TIME OF THE CRIME.
YOU WERE REALLY AT THE PACHINKO PARLOR AT 11:30?
YES!
HA HA HA. DON'T YOU KNOW?

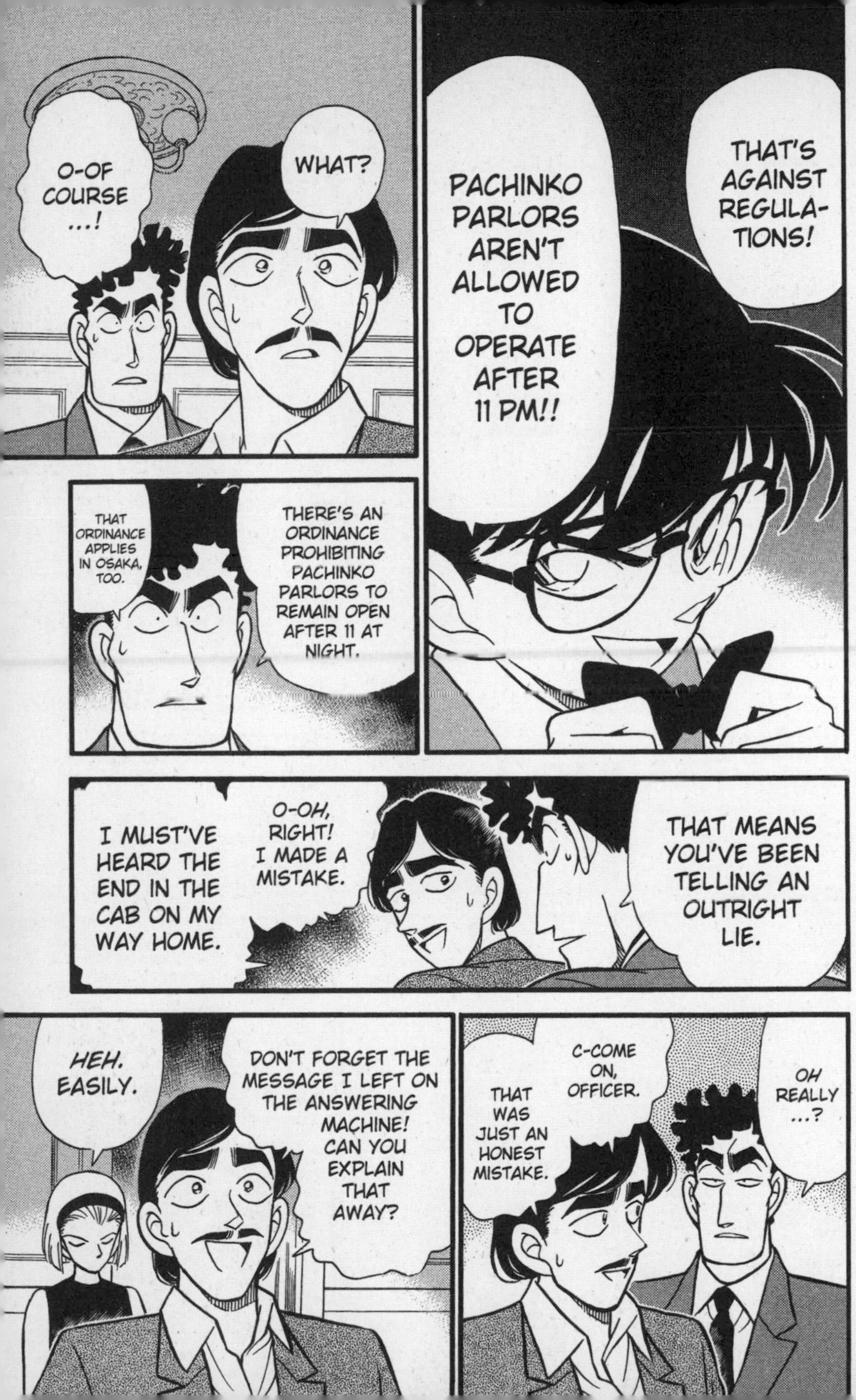
THAT'S AGAINST REGULA-TIONS!
PACHINKO PARLORS AREN'T ALLOWED TO OPERATE AFTER 11 PM!!
WHAT?
O-OF COURSE ...!
THERE'S AN ORDINANCE PROHIBITING PACHINKO PARLORS TO REMAIN OPEN AFTER 11 AT NIGHT.
THAT ORDINANCE APPLIES IN OSAKA, TOO.
THAT MEANS YOU'VE BEEN TELLING AN OUTRIGHT LIE.
O-OH, RIGHT! I MADE A MISTAKE.
I MUST'VE HEARD THE END IN THE CAB ON MY WAY HOME.
OH REALLY ...?
C-COME ON, OFFICER.
THAT WAS JUST AN HONEST MISTAKE.
DON'T FORGET THE MESSAGE I LEFT ON THE ANSWERING MACHINE! CAN YOU EXPLAIN THAT AWAY?
HEH. EASILY.

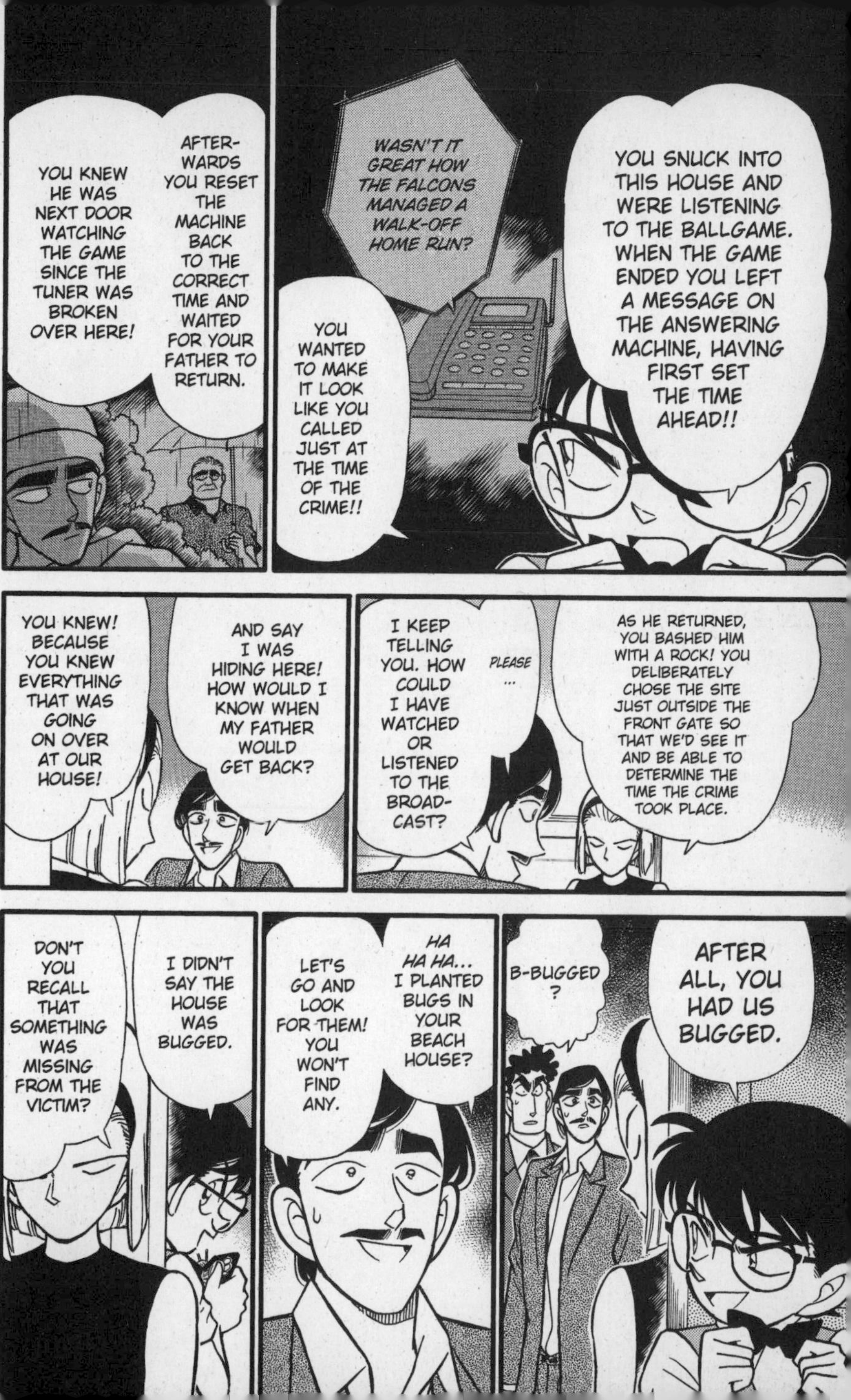
YOU SNUCK INTO THIS HOUSE AND WERE LISTENING TO THE BALLGAME. WHEN THE GAME ENDED YOU LEFT A MESSAGE ON THE ANSWERING MACHINE, HAVING FIRST SET THE TIME AHEAD!!
WASN'T IT GREAT HOW THE FALCONS MANAGED A WALK-OFF HOME RUN?
YOU WANTED TO MAKE IT LOOK LIKE YOU CALLED JUST AT THE TIME OF THE CRIME!!
AFTER-WARDS YOU RESET THE MACHINE BACK TO THE CORRECT TIME AND WAITED FOR YOUR FATHER TO RETURN.
YOU KNEW HE WAS NEXT DOOR WATCHING THE GAME SINCE THE TUNER WAS BROKEN OVER HERE!
AS HE RETURNED, YOU BASHED HIM WITH A ROCK! YOU DELIBERATELY CHOSE THE SITE JUST OUTSIDE THE FRONT GATE SO THAT WE'D SEE IT AND BE ABLE TO DETERMINE THE TIME THE CRIME TOOK PLACE.
PLEASE ...
I KEEP TELLING YOU. HOW COULD I HAVE WATCHED OR LISTENED TO THE BROAD-CAST?
AND SAY I WAS HIDING HERE! HOW WOULD I KNOW WHEN MY FATHER WOULD GET BACK?
YOU KNEW! BECAUSE YOU KNEW EVERYTHING THAT WAS GOING ON OVER AT OUR HOUSE!
AFTER ALL, YOU HAD US BUGGED.
B-BUGGED ?
HA HA HA... I PLANTED BUGS IN YOUR BEACH HOUSE?
LET'S GO AND LOOK FOR THEM! YOU WON'T FIND ANY.
I DIDN'T SAY THE HOUSE WAS BUGGED.
DON'T YOU RECALL THAT SOMETHING WAS MISSING FROM THE VICTIM?

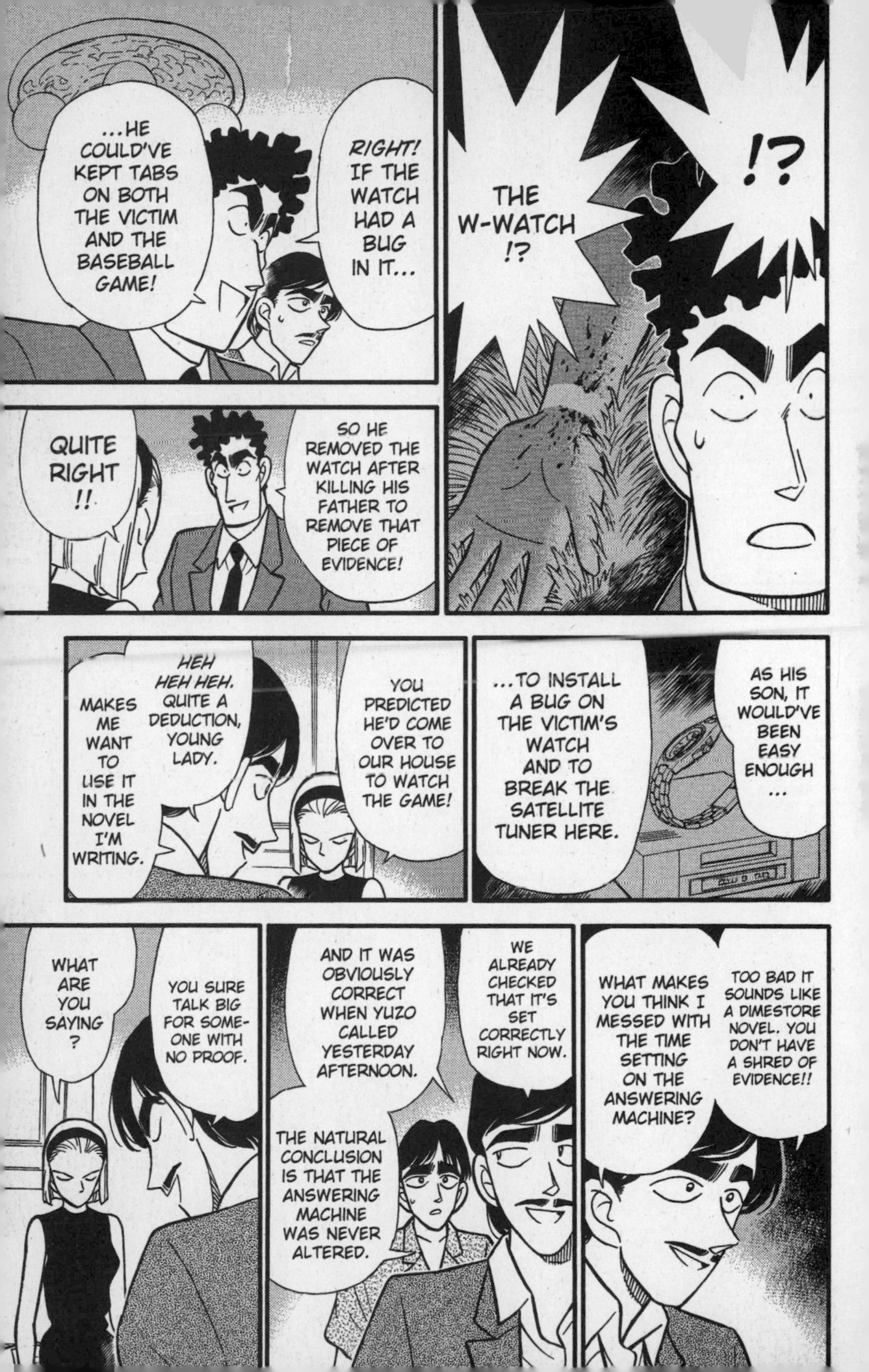
!?
THE W-WATCH !?
RIGHT! IF THE WATCH HAD A BUG IN IT...
...HE COULD'VE KEPT TABS ON BOTH THE VICTIM AND THE BASEBALL GAME!
SO HE REMOVED THE WATCH AFTER KILLING HIS FATHER TO REMOVE THAT PIECE OF EVIDENCE!
QUITE RIGHT !!
AS HIS SON, IT WOULD'VE BEEN EASY ENOUGH ...
...TO INSTALL A BUG ON THE VICTIM'S WATCH AND TO BREAK THE SATELLITE TUNER HERE.
YOU PREDICTED HE'D COME OVER TO OUR HOUSE TO WATCH THE GAME!
HEH HEH HEH. QUITE A DEDUCTION, YOUNG LADY.
MAKES ME WANT TO USE IT IN THE NOVEL I'M WRITING.
TOO BAD IT SOUNDS LIKE A DIMESTORE NOVEL. YOU DON'T HAVE A SHRED OF EVIDENCE!!
WHAT MAKES YOU THINK I MESSED WITH THE TIME SETTING ON THE ANSWERING MACHINE?
WE ALREADY CHECKED THAT IT'S SET CORRECTLY RIGHT NOW.
AND IT WAS OBVIOUSLY CORRECT WHEN YUZO CALLED YESTERDAY AFTERNOON.
THE NATURAL CONCLUSION IS THAT THE ANSWERING MACHINE WAS NEVER ALTERED.
YOU SURE TALK BIG FOR SOME-ONE WITH NO PROOF.
WHAT ARE YOU SAYING ?

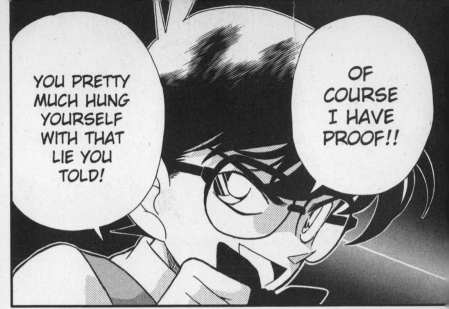

OF COURSE I HAVE PROOF!!
YOU PRETTY MUCH HUNG YOURSELF WITH THAT LIE YOU TOLD!
HUH !?
WHAT !?
YOU WERE HERE LAST NIGHT, SO YOU SHOULD REMEMBER! THERE WAS A TEN-MINUTE POWER OUTAGE STARTING AT 11:30 LAST NIGHT!!
P-POWER OUTAGE !?
YOU DO KNOW WHAT HAPPENS TO ANSWERING MACHINES AFTER A BLACKOUT?
!?

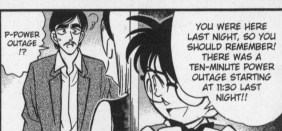

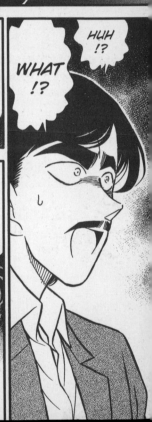

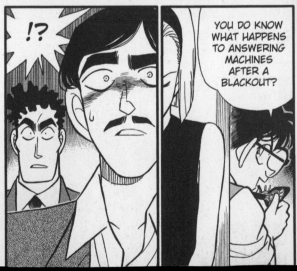

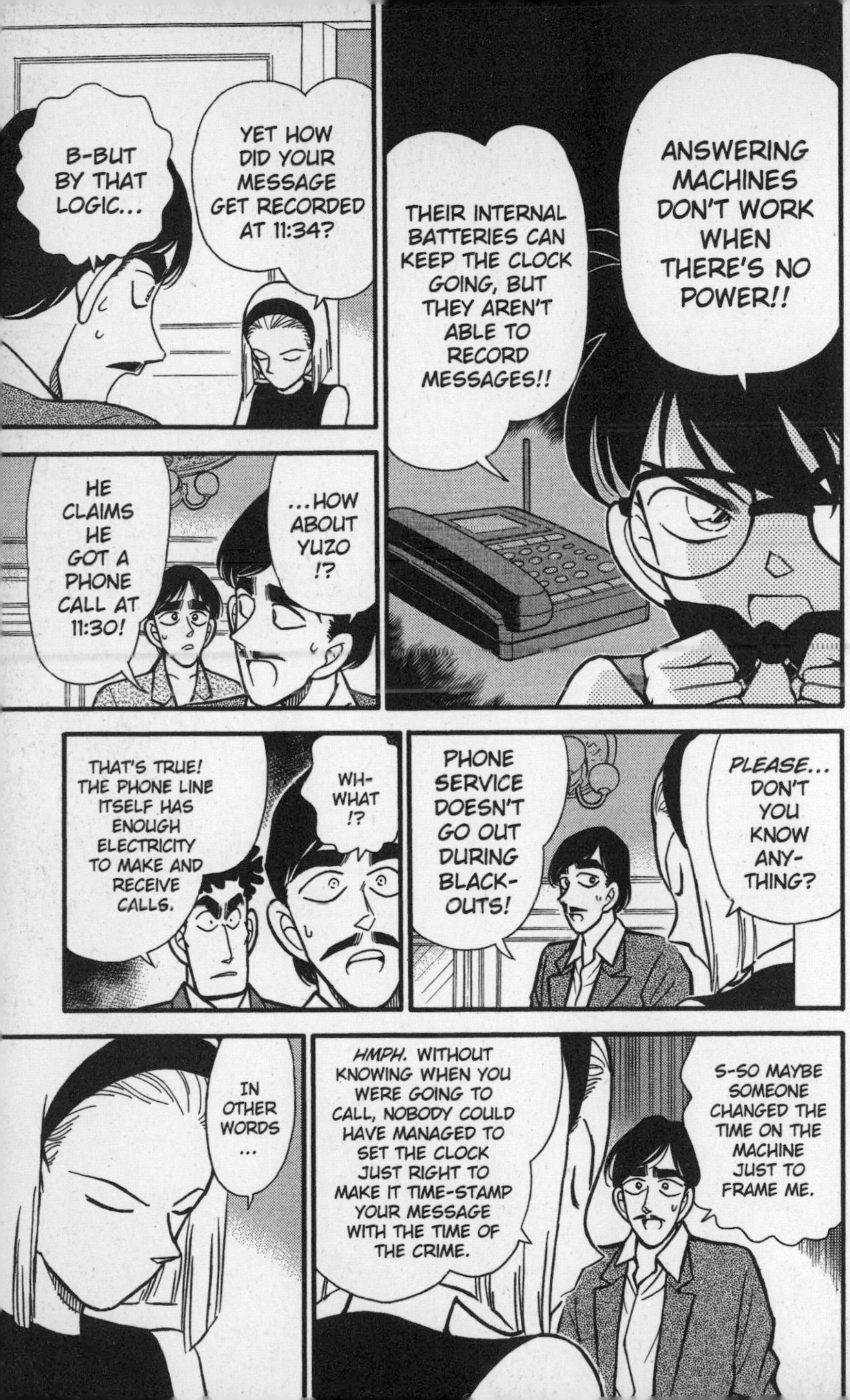
ANSWERING MACHINES DON'T WORK WHEN THERE'S NO POWER!!
THEIR INTERNAL BATTERIES CAN KEEP THE CLOCK GOING, BUT THEY AREN'T ABLE TO RECORD MESSAGES!!
YET HOW DID YOUR MESSAGE GET RECORDED AT 11:34?
B-BUT BY THAT LOGIC...
...HOW ABOUT YUZO!?
HE CLAIMS HE GOT A PHONE CALL AT 11:30!
PLEASE... DON'T YOU KNOW ANY-THING?
PHONE SERVICE DOESN'T GO OUT DURING BLACK-OUTS!
WH-WHAT!?
THAT'S TRUE! THE PHONE LINE ITSELF HAS ENOUGH ELECTRICITY TO MAKE AND RECEIVE CALLS.
S-SO MAYBE SOMEONE CHANGED THE TIME ON THE MACHINE JUST TO FRAME ME.
HMPH. WITHOUT KNOWING WHEN YOU WERE GOING TO CALL, NOBODY COULD HAVE MANAGED TO SET THE CLOCK JUST RIGHT TO MAKE IT TIME-STAMP YOUR MESSAGE WITH THE TIME OF THE CRIME.
IN OTHER WORDS...

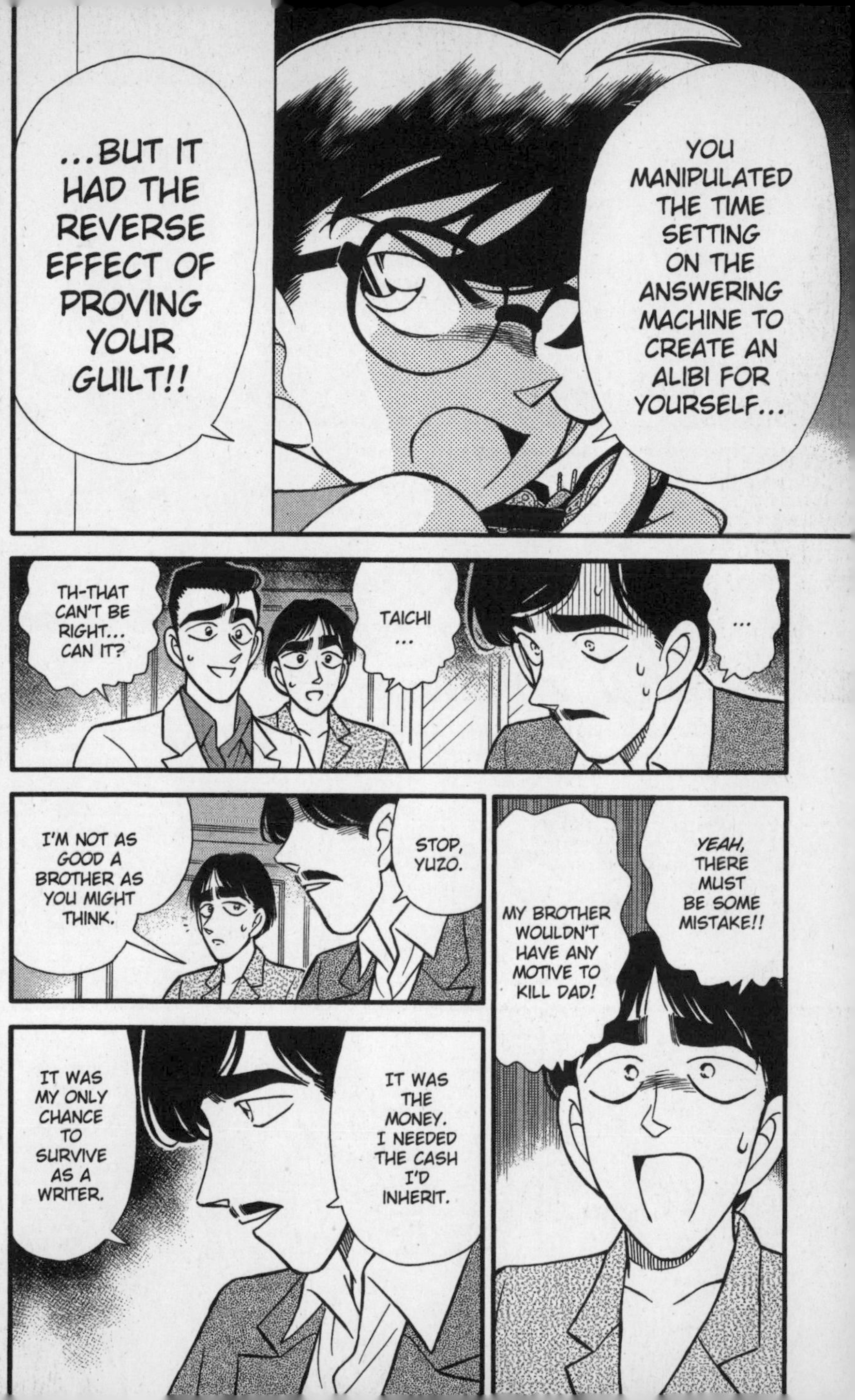
YOU MANIPULATED THE TIME SETTING ON THE ANSWERING MACHINE TO CREATE AN ALIBI FOR YOURSELF...
...BUT IT HAD THE REVERSE EFFECT OF PROVING YOUR GUILT!!
...
TAICHI ...
TH-THAT CAN'T BE RIGHT... CAN IT?
YEAH, THERE MUST BE SOME MISTAKE!!
MY BROTHER WOULDN'T HAVE ANY MOTIVE TO KILL DAD!
STOP, YUZO.
I'M NOT AS GOOD A BROTHER AS YOU MIGHT THINK.
IT WAS THE MONEY. I NEEDED THE CASH I'D INHERIT.
IT WAS MY ONLY CHANCE TO SURVIVE AS A WRITER.

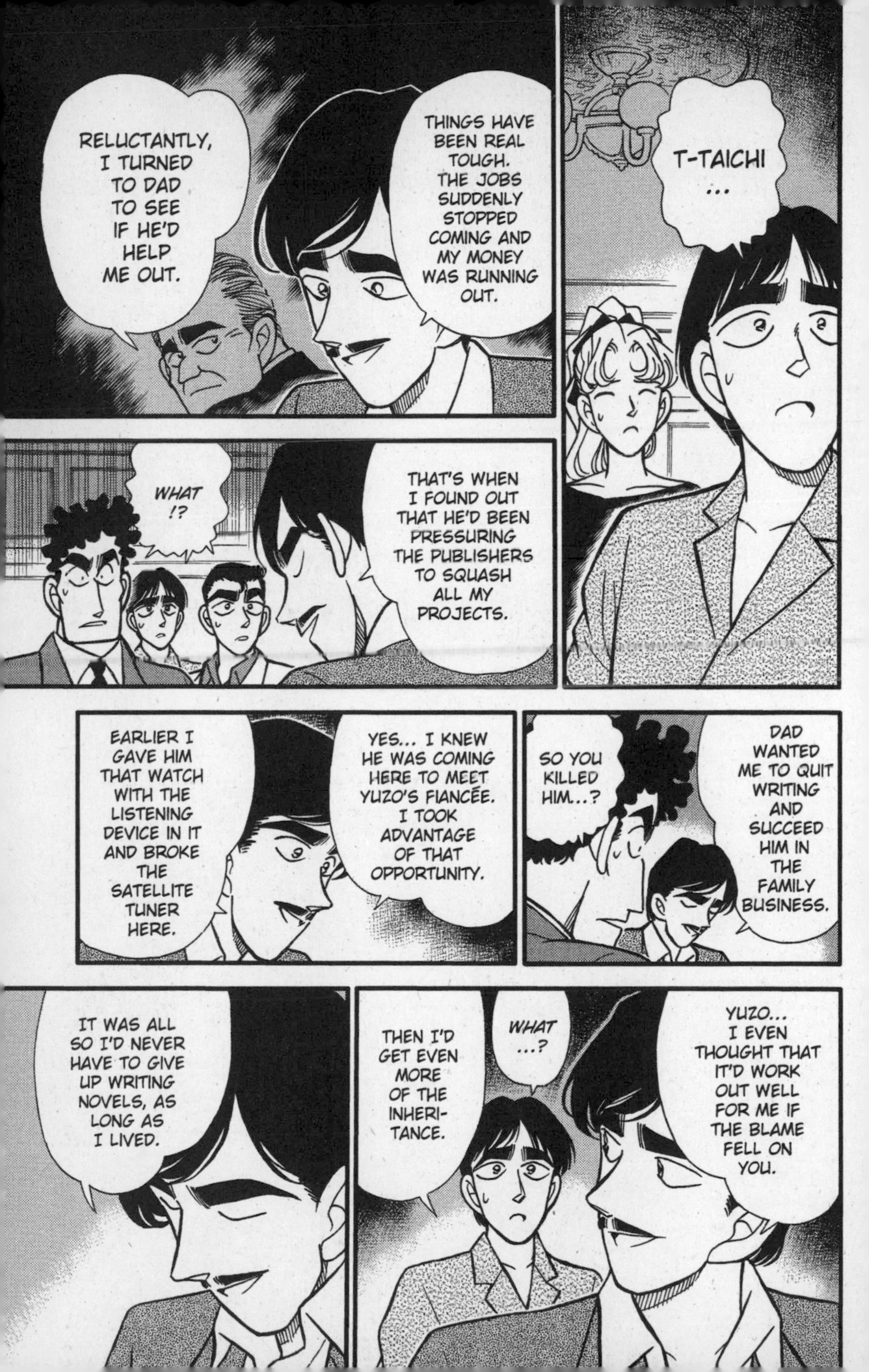
T-TAICHI ...
THINGS HAVE BEEN REAL TOUGH. THE JOBS SUDDENLY STOPPED COMING AND MY MONEY WAS RUNNING OUT.
RELUCTANTLY, I TURNED TO DAD TO SEE IF HE'D HELP ME OUT.
THAT'S WHEN I FOUND OUT THAT HE'D BEEN PRESSURING THE PUBLISHERS TO SQUASH ALL MY PROJECTS.
WHAT !?
DAD WANTED ME TO QUIT WRITING AND SUCCEED HIM IN THE FAMILY BUSINESS.
SO YOU KILLED HIM...?
YES... I KNEW HE WAS COMING HERE TO MEET YUZO'S FIANCÉE. I TOOK ADVANTAGE OF THAT OPPORTUNITY.
EARLIER I GAVE HIM THAT WATCH WITH THE LISTENING DEVICE IN IT AND BROKE THE SATELLITE TUNER HERE.
YUZO... I EVEN THOUGHT THAT IT'D WORK OUT WELL FOR ME IF THE BLAME FELL ON YOU.
THEN I'D GET EVEN MORE OF THE INHERI-TANCE.
WHAT ...?
IT WAS ALL SO I'D NEVER HAVE TO GIVE UP WRITING NOVELS, AS LONG AS I LIVED.

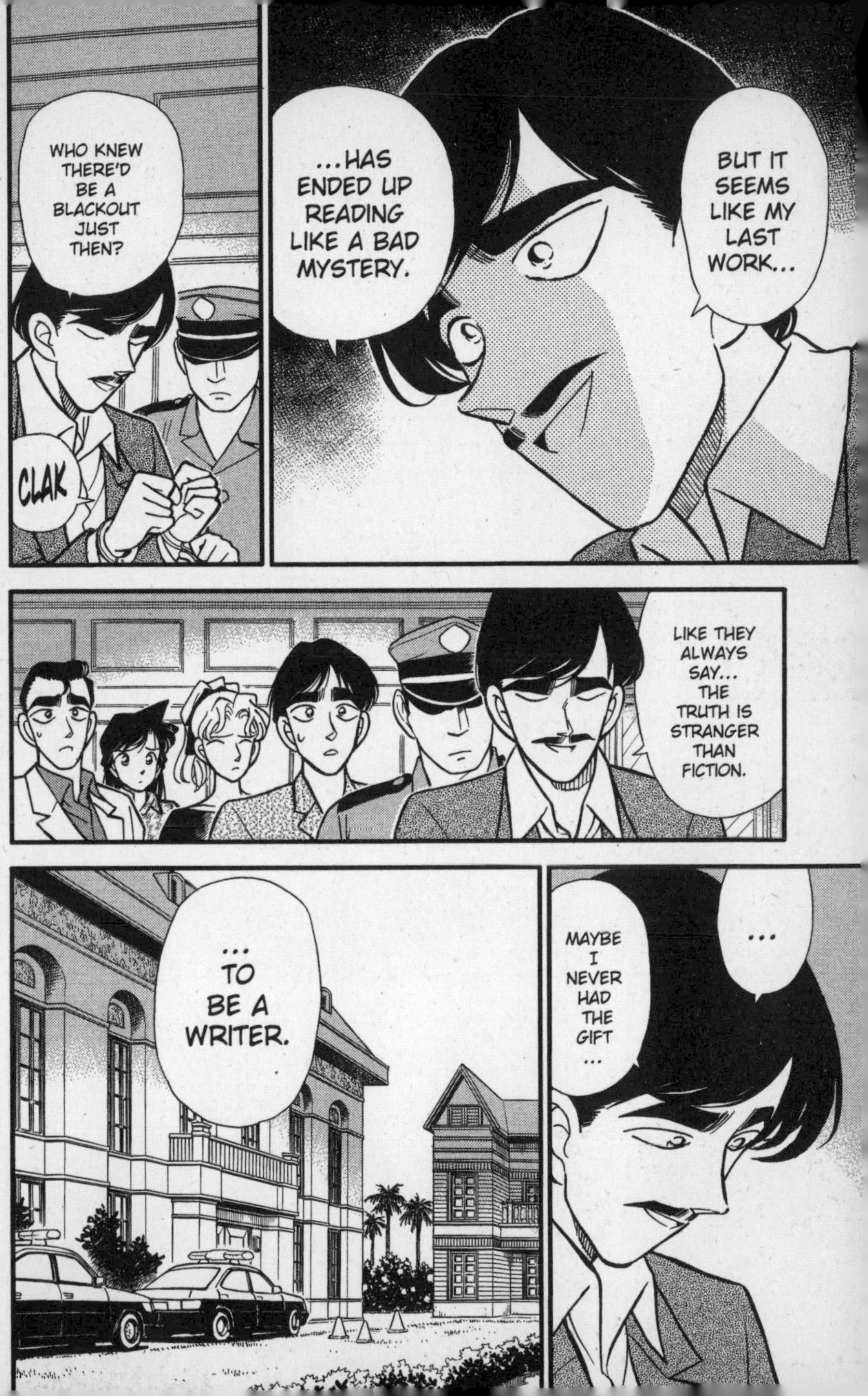
BUT IT SEEMS LIKE MY LAST WORK...
...HAS ENDED UP READING LIKE A BAD MYSTERY.
WHO KNEW THERE'D BE A BLACKOUT JUST THEN?
CLAK
LIKE THEY ALWAYS SAY... THE TRUTH IS STRANGER THAN FICTION.
...
MAYBE I NEVER HAD THE GIFT ...
... TO BE A WRITER.

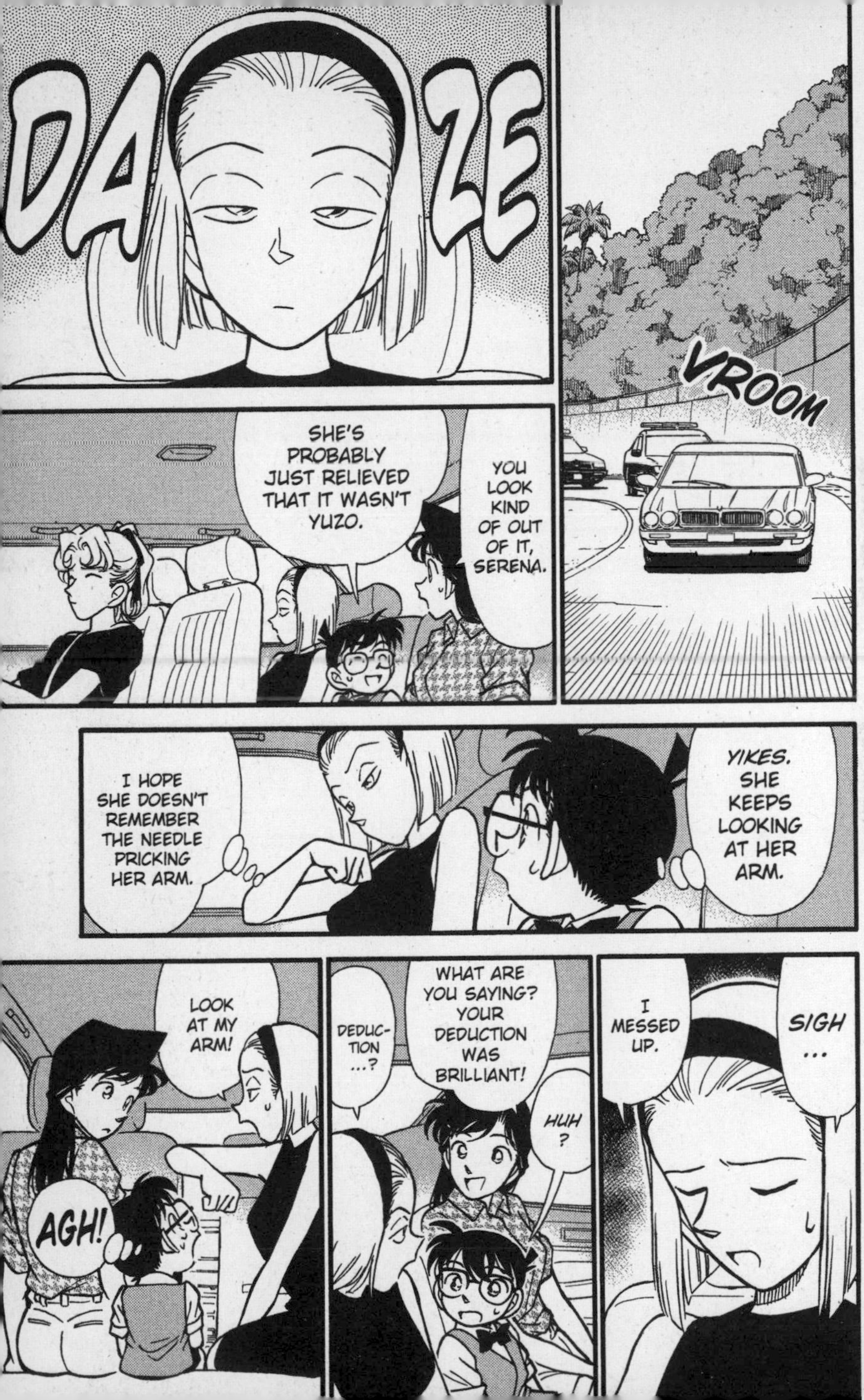
VROOM
DAZE
YOU LOOK KIND OF OUT OF IT, SERENA.
SHE'S PROBABLY JUST RELIEVED THAT IT WASN'T YUZO.
YIKES. SHE KEEPS LOOKING AT HER ARM.
I HOPE SHE DOESN'T REMEMBER THE NEEDLE PRICKING HER ARM.
SIGH...
I MESSED UP.
WHAT ARE YOU SAYING? YOUR DEDUCTION WAS BRILLIANT!
DEDUCTION...?
HUH?
LOOK AT MY ARM!
AGH!

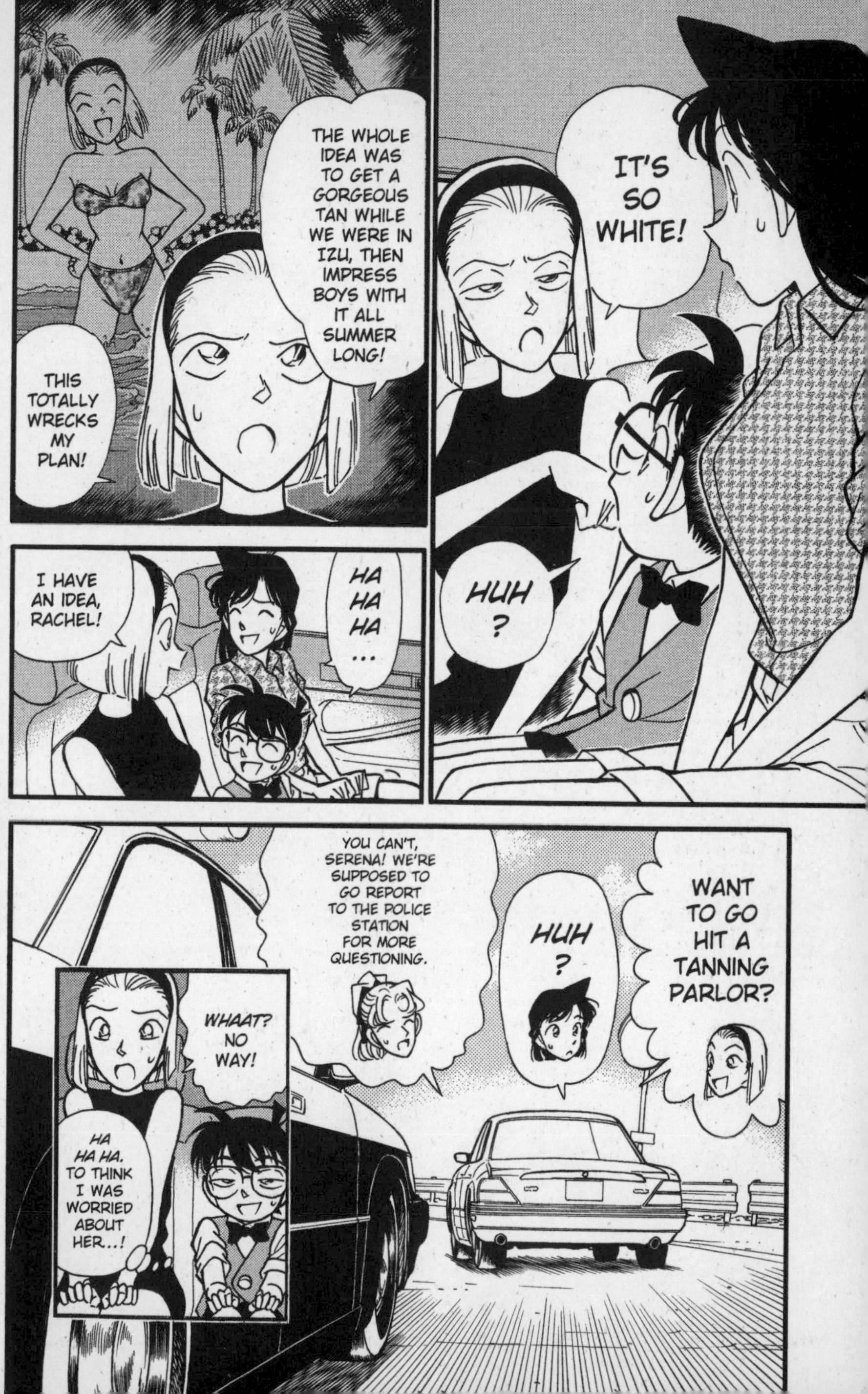
IT'S SO WHITE!
HUH?
THE WHOLE IDEA WAS TO GET A GORGEOUS TAN WHILE WE WERE IN IZU, THEN IMPRESS BOYS WITH IT ALL SUMMER LONG!
THIS TOTALLY WRECKS MY PLAN!
HA HA HA ...
I HAVE AN IDEA, RACHEL!
WANT TO GO HIT A TANNING PARLOR?
HUH?
YOU CAN'T, SERENA! WE'RE SUPPOSED TO GO REPORT TO THE POLICE STATION FOR MORE QUESTIONING.
WHAAT? NO WAY!
HA HA HA. TO THINK I WAS WORRIED ABOUT HER...!

FILE 5:
THE FALLING CORPSE

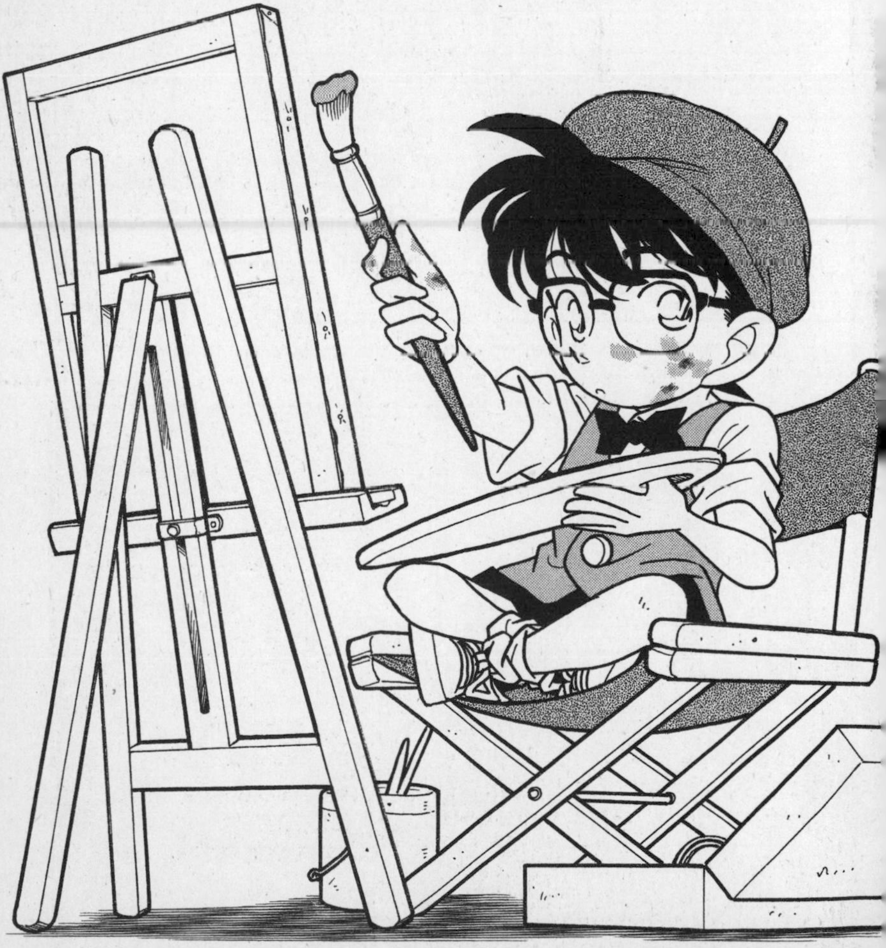

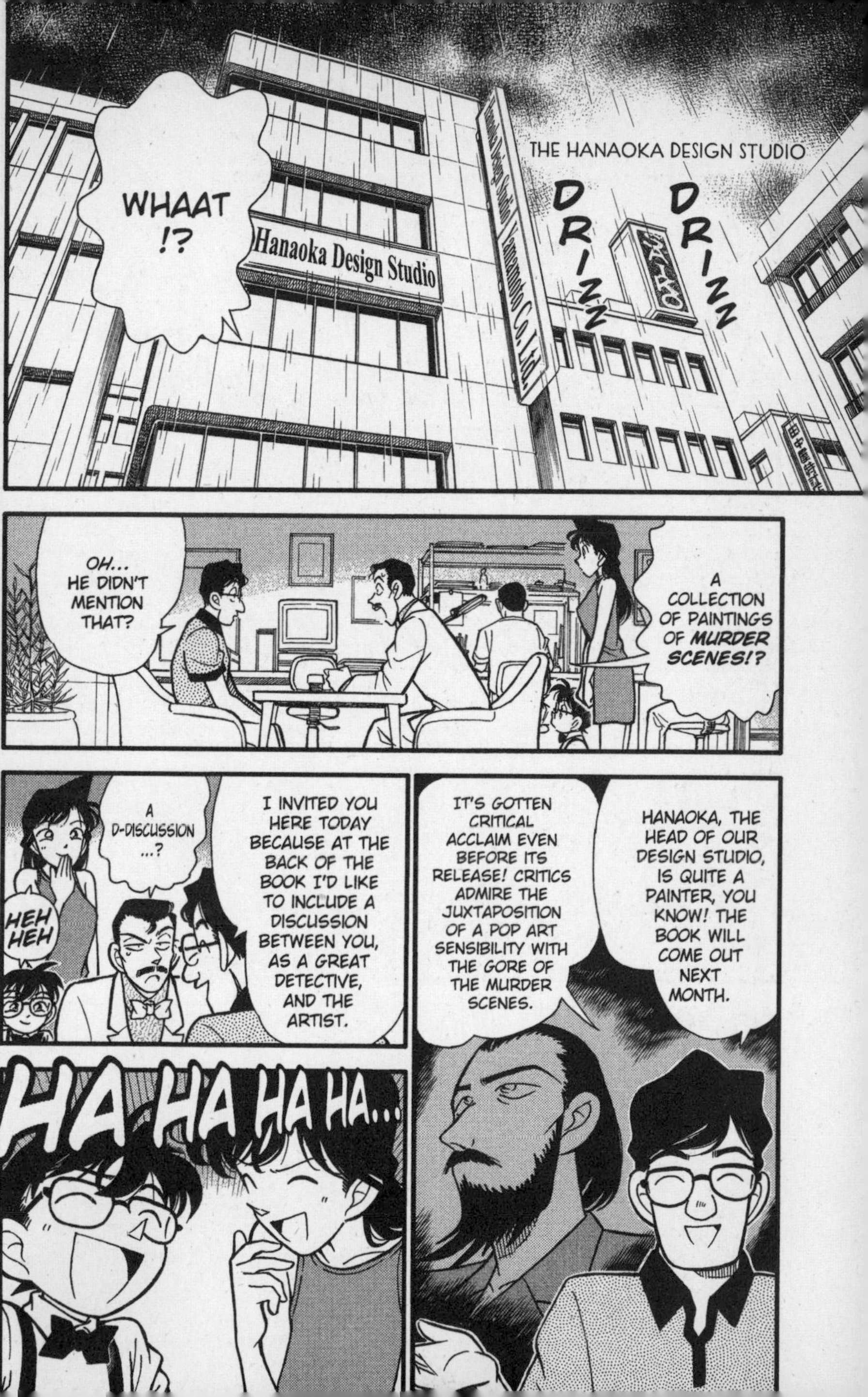
THE HANAOKA DESIGN STUDIO
DRIZZ DRIZZ
Hanaoka Design Studio
WHAAT !?
A COLLECTION OF PAINTINGS OF MURDER SCENES!?
OH... HE DIDN'T MENTION THAT?
HANAOKA, THE HEAD OF OUR DESIGN STUDIO, IS QUITE A PAINTER, YOU KNOW! THE BOOK WILL COME OUT NEXT MONTH.
IT'S GOTTEN CRITICAL ACCLAIM EVEN BEFORE ITS RELEASE! CRITICS ADMIRE THE JUXTAPOSITION OF A POP ART SENSIBILITY WITH THE GORE OF THE MURDER SCENES.
I INVITED YOU HERE TODAY BECAUSE AT THE BACK OF THE BOOK I'D LIKE TO INCLUDE A DISCUSSION BETWEEN YOU, AS A GREAT DETECTIVE, AND THE ARTIST.
A D-DISCUSSION ...?
HEH HEH
HA HA HA HA HA...

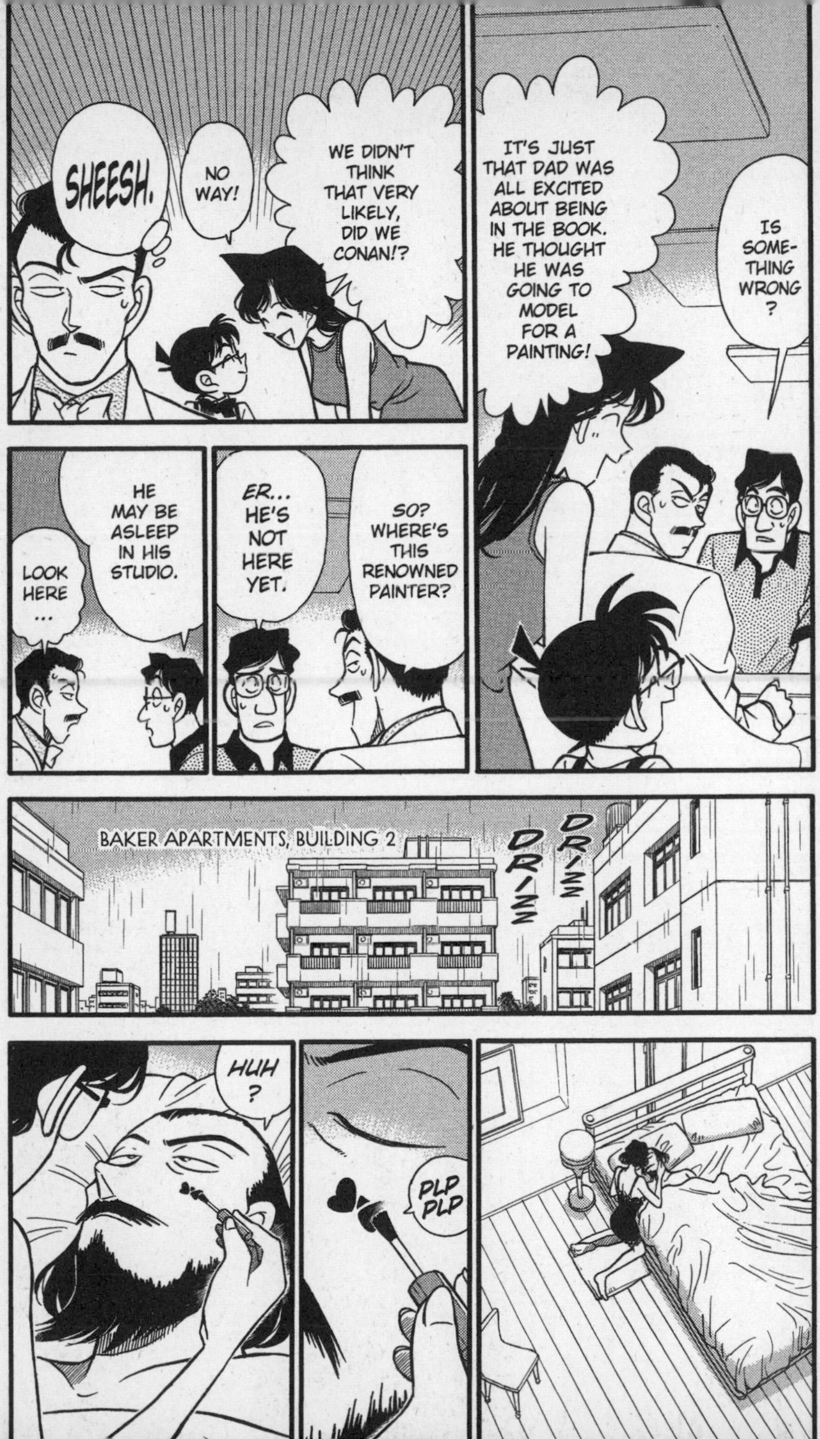
IS SOMETHING WRONG?
IT'S JUST THAT DAD WAS ALL EXCITED ABOUT BEING IN THE BOOK. HE THOUGHT HE WAS GOING TO MODEL FOR A PAINTING!
WE DIDN'T THINK THAT VERY LIKELY, DID WE CONAN!?
NO WAY!
SHEESH.
SO? WHERE'S THIS RENOWNED PAINTER?
ER... HE'S NOT HERE YET.
HE MAY BE ASLEEP IN HIS STUDIO.
LOOK HERE ...
DRIZZ
DRIZZ
BAKER APARTMENTS, BUILDING 2
PLP PLP
HUH?

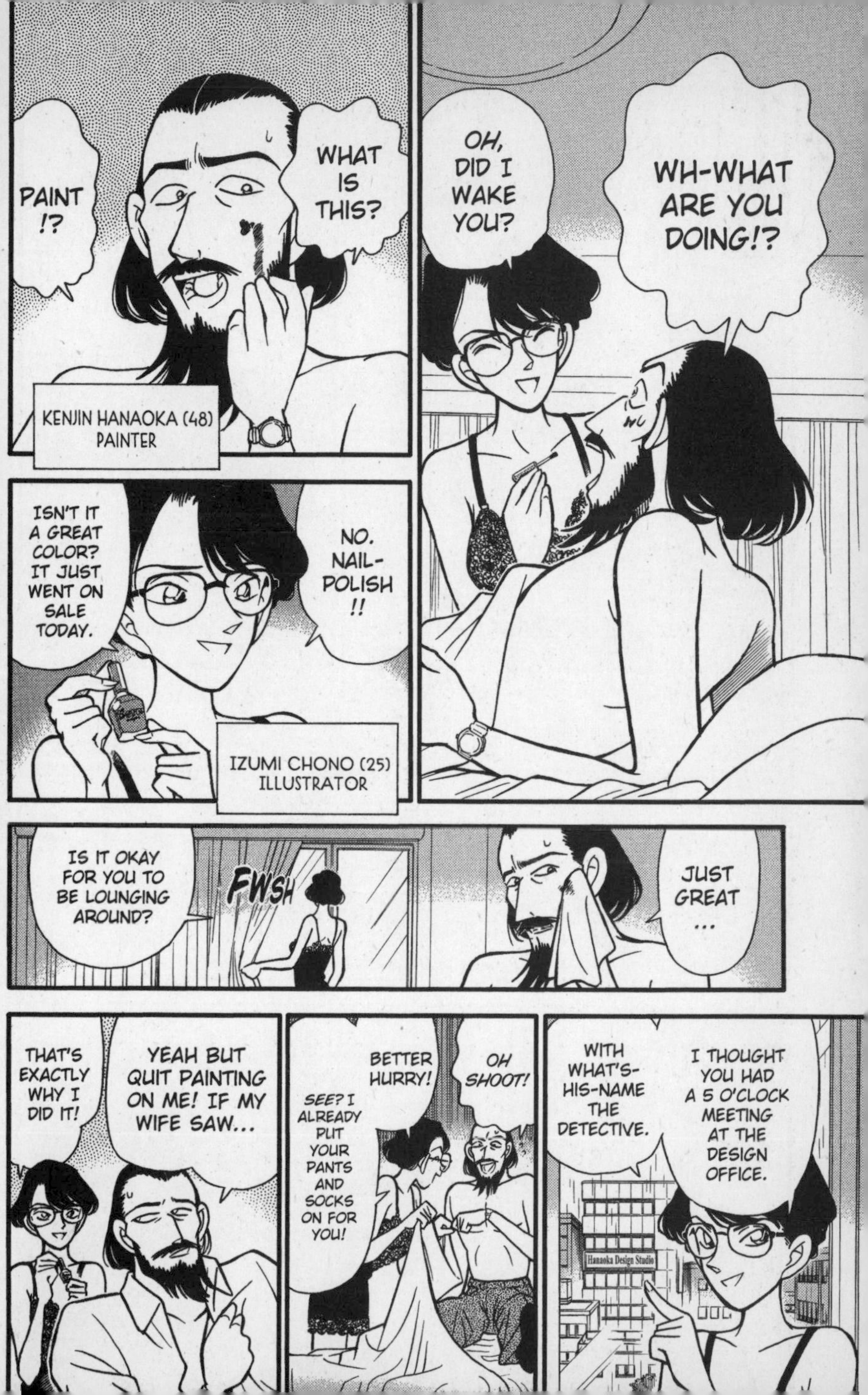
WH-WHAT ARE YOU DOING!?
OH, DID I WAKE YOU?
WHAT IS THIS?
PAINT!?
KENJIN HANAOKA (48) PAINTER
NO. NAIL-POLISH!!
ISN'T IT A GREAT COLOR? IT JUST WENT ON SALE TODAY.
IZUMI CHONO (25) ILLUSTRATOR
JUST GREAT...
FWSH
IS IT OKAY FOR YOU TO BE LOUNGING AROUND?
I THOUGHT YOU HAD A 5 O'CLOCK MEETING AT THE DESIGN OFFICE.
WITH WHAT'S-HIS-NAME THE DETECTIVE.
Hanaoka Design Studio
OH SHOOT!
BETTER HURRY!
SEE? I ALREADY PUT YOUR PANTS AND SOCKS ON FOR YOU!
YEAH BUT QUIT PAINTING ON ME! IF MY WIFE SAW...
THAT'S EXACTLY WHY I DID IT!

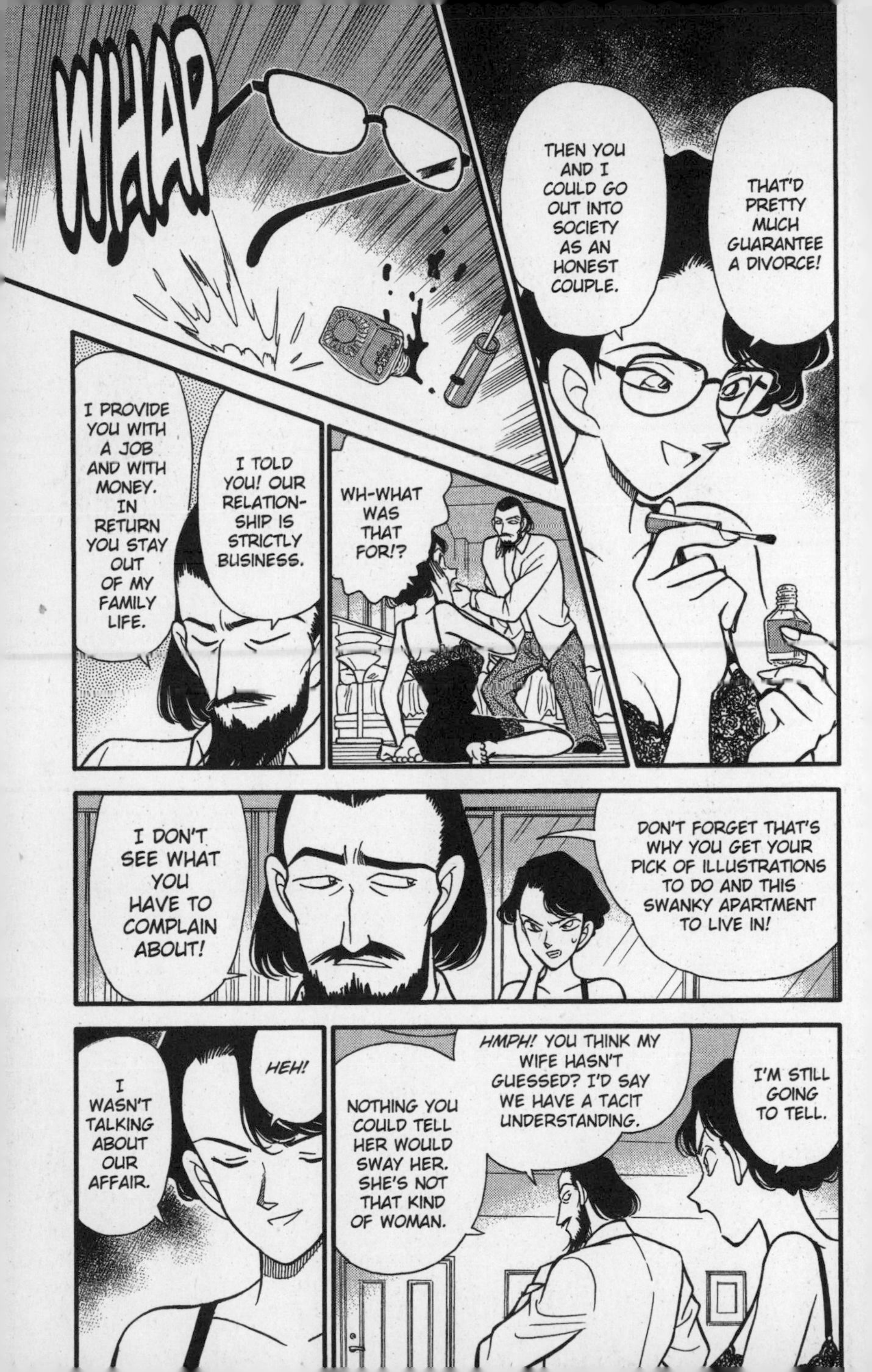
THAT'D PRETTY MUCH GUARANTEE A DIVORCE!
THEN YOU AND I COULD GO OUT INTO SOCIETY AS AN HONEST COUPLE.
WHAP
WH-WHAT WAS THAT FOR!?
I TOLD YOU! OUR RELATIONSHIP IS STRICTLY BUSINESS.
I PROVIDE YOU WITH A JOB AND WITH MONEY. IN RETURN YOU STAY OUT OF MY FAMILY LIFE.
DON'T FORGET THAT'S WHY YOU GET YOUR PICK OF ILLUSTRATIONS TO DO AND THIS SWANKY APARTMENT TO LIVE IN!
I DON'T SEE WHAT YOU HAVE TO COMPLAIN ABOUT!
I'M STILL GOING TO TELL.
HMPH! YOU THINK MY WIFE HASN'T GUESSED? I'D SAY WE HAVE A TACIT UNDERSTANDING.
NOTHING YOU COULD TELL HER WOULD SWAY HER. SHE'S NOT THAT KIND OF WOMAN.
HEH!
I WASN'T TALKING ABOUT OUR AFFAIR.

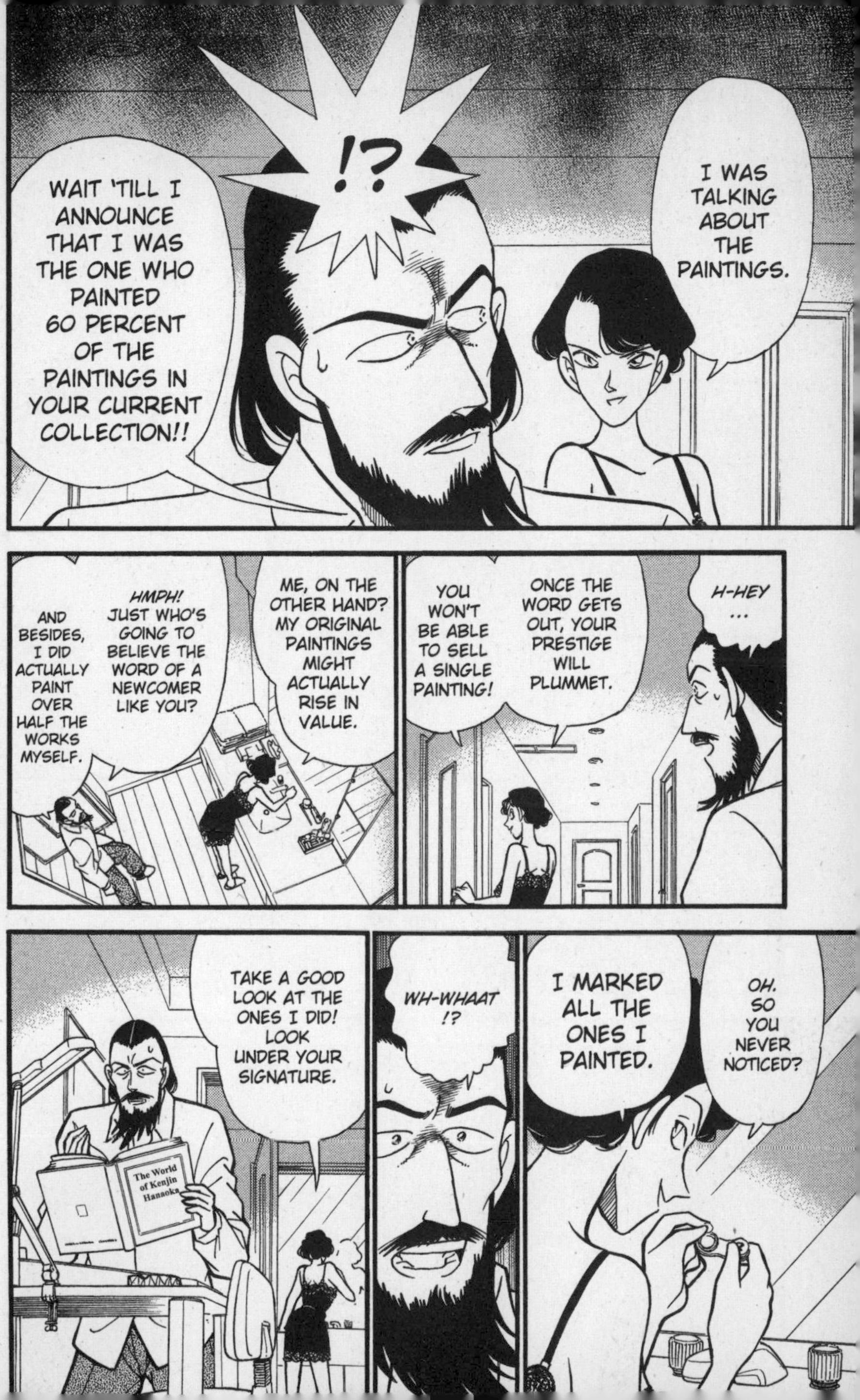
I WAS TALKING ABOUT THE PAINTINGS.
!?
WAIT 'TILL I ANNOUNCE THAT I WAS THE ONE WHO PAINTED 60 PERCENT OF THE PAINTINGS IN YOUR CURRENT COLLECTION!!
H-HEY ...
ONCE THE WORD GETS OUT, YOUR PRESTIGE WILL PLUMMET.
YOU WON'T BE ABLE TO SELL A SINGLE PAINTING!
ME, ON THE OTHER HAND? MY ORIGINAL PAINTINGS MIGHT ACTUALLY RISE IN VALUE.
HMPH! JUST WHO'S GOING TO BELIEVE THE WORD OF A NEWCOMER LIKE YOU?
AND BESIDES, I DID ACTUALLY PAINT OVER HALF THE WORKS MYSELF.
OH. SO YOU NEVER NOTICED?
I MARKED ALL THE ONES I PAINTED.
WH-WHAAT !?
TAKE A GOOD LOOK AT THE ONES I DID! LOOK UNDER YOUR SIGNATURE.
The World of Kenjin Hanaoka

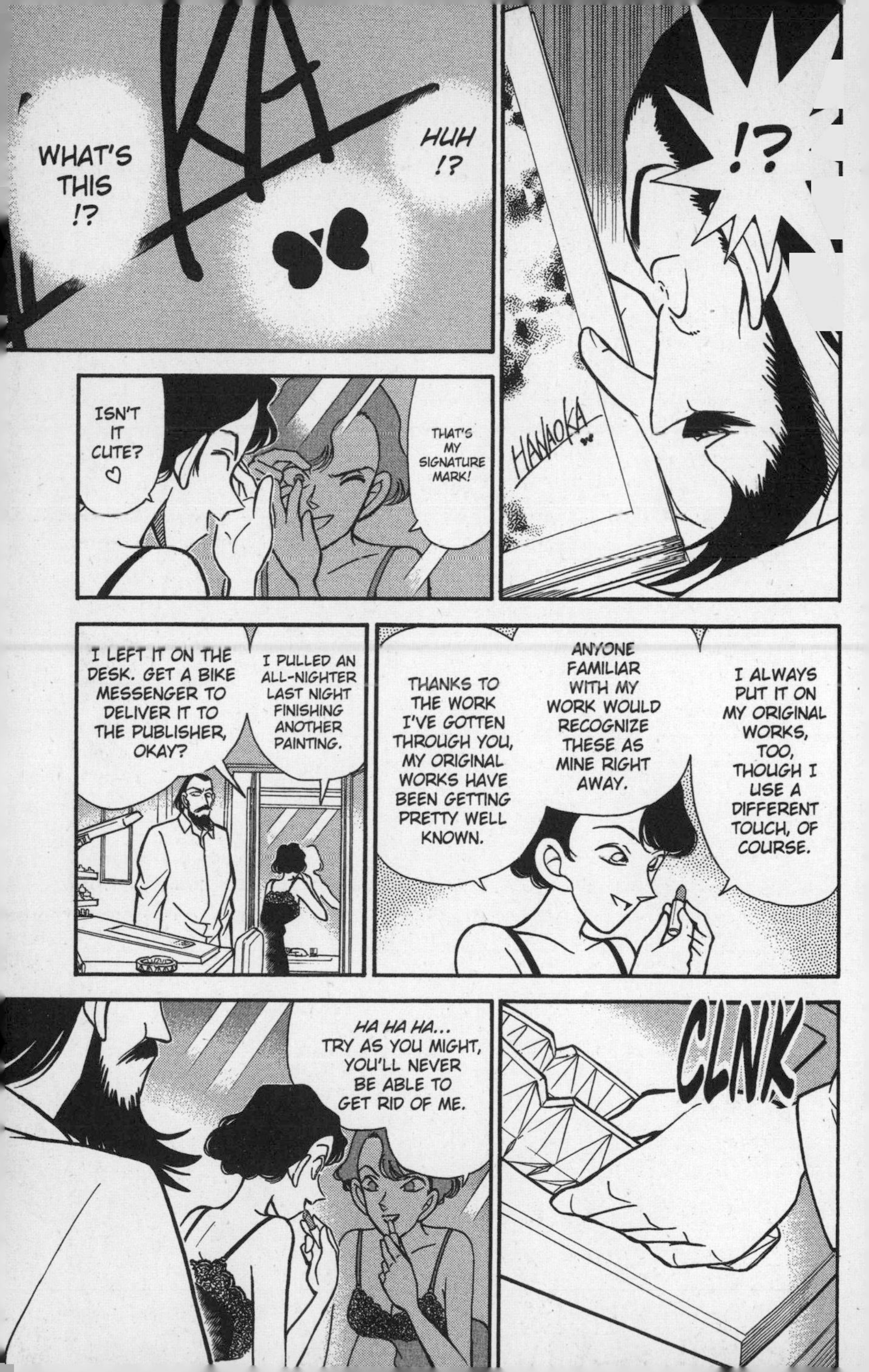
!?
HANAOKA
HUH !?
KA
WHAT'S THIS !?
THAT'S MY SIGNATURE MARK!
ISN'T IT CUTE? ♡
I ALWAYS PUT IT ON MY ORIGINAL WORKS, TOO, THOUGH I USE A DIFFERENT TOUCH, OF COURSE.
ANYONE FAMILIAR WITH MY WORK WOULD RECOGNIZE THESE AS MINE RIGHT AWAY.
THANKS TO THE WORK I'VE GOTTEN THROUGH YOU, MY ORIGINAL WORKS HAVE BEEN GETTING PRETTY WELL KNOWN.
I PULLED AN ALL-NIGHTER LAST NIGHT FINISHING ANOTHER PAINTING.
I LEFT IT ON THE DESK. GET A BIKE MESSENGER TO DELIVER IT TO THE PUBLISHER, OKAY?
CLNK
HA HA HA... TRY AS YOU MIGHT, YOU'LL NEVER BE ABLE TO GET RID OF ME.

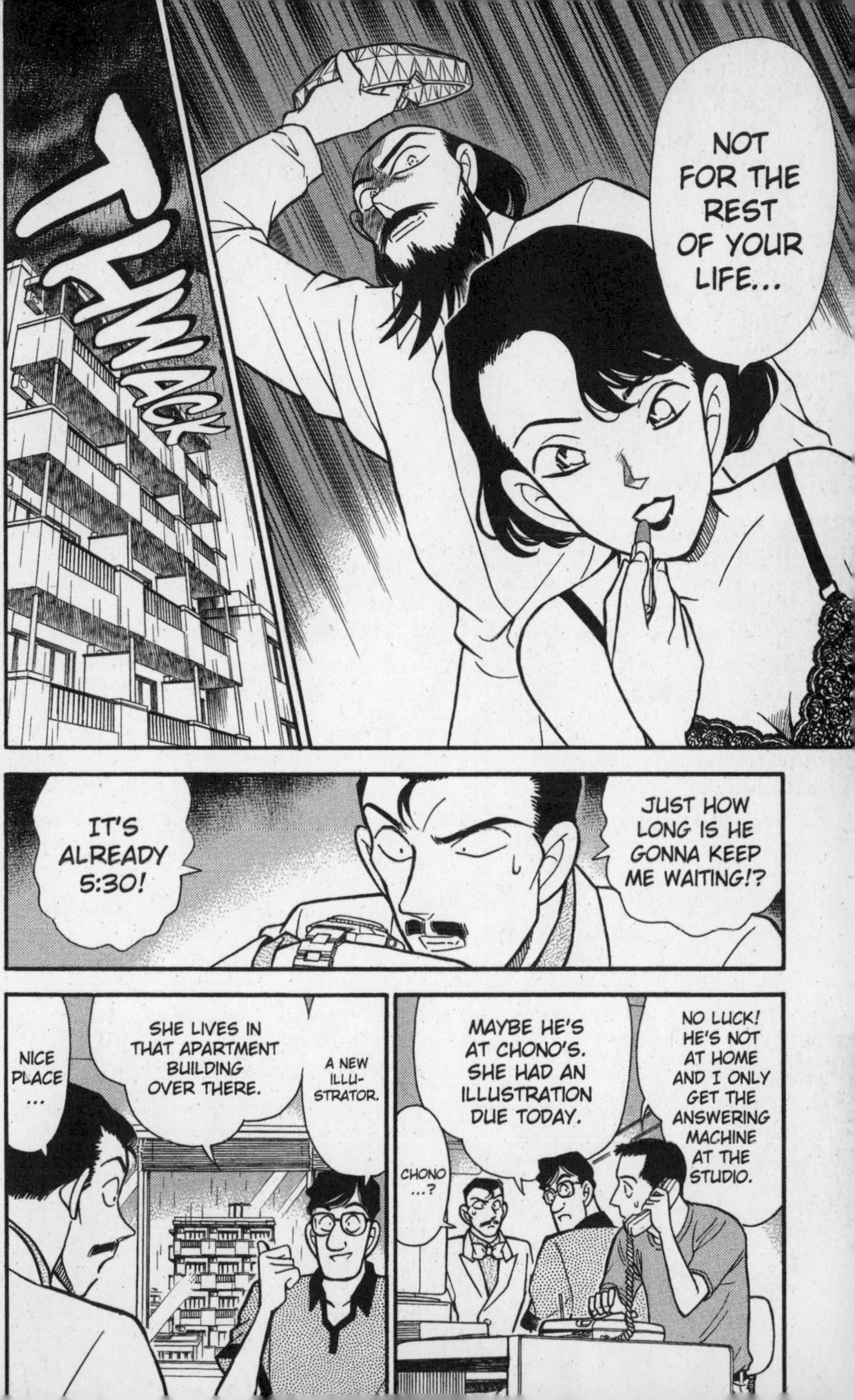
NOT FOR THE REST OF YOUR LIFE...
THWACK
JUST HOW LONG IS HE GONNA KEEP ME WAITING!?
IT'S ALREADY 5:30!
NO LUCK! HE'S NOT AT HOME AND I ONLY GET THE ANSWERING MACHINE AT THE STUDIO.
MAYBE HE'S AT CHONO'S. SHE HAD AN ILLUSTRATION DUE TODAY.
CHONO ...?
A NEW ILLU-STRATOR.
SHE LIVES IN THAT APARTMENT BUILDING OVER THERE.
NICE PLACE ...

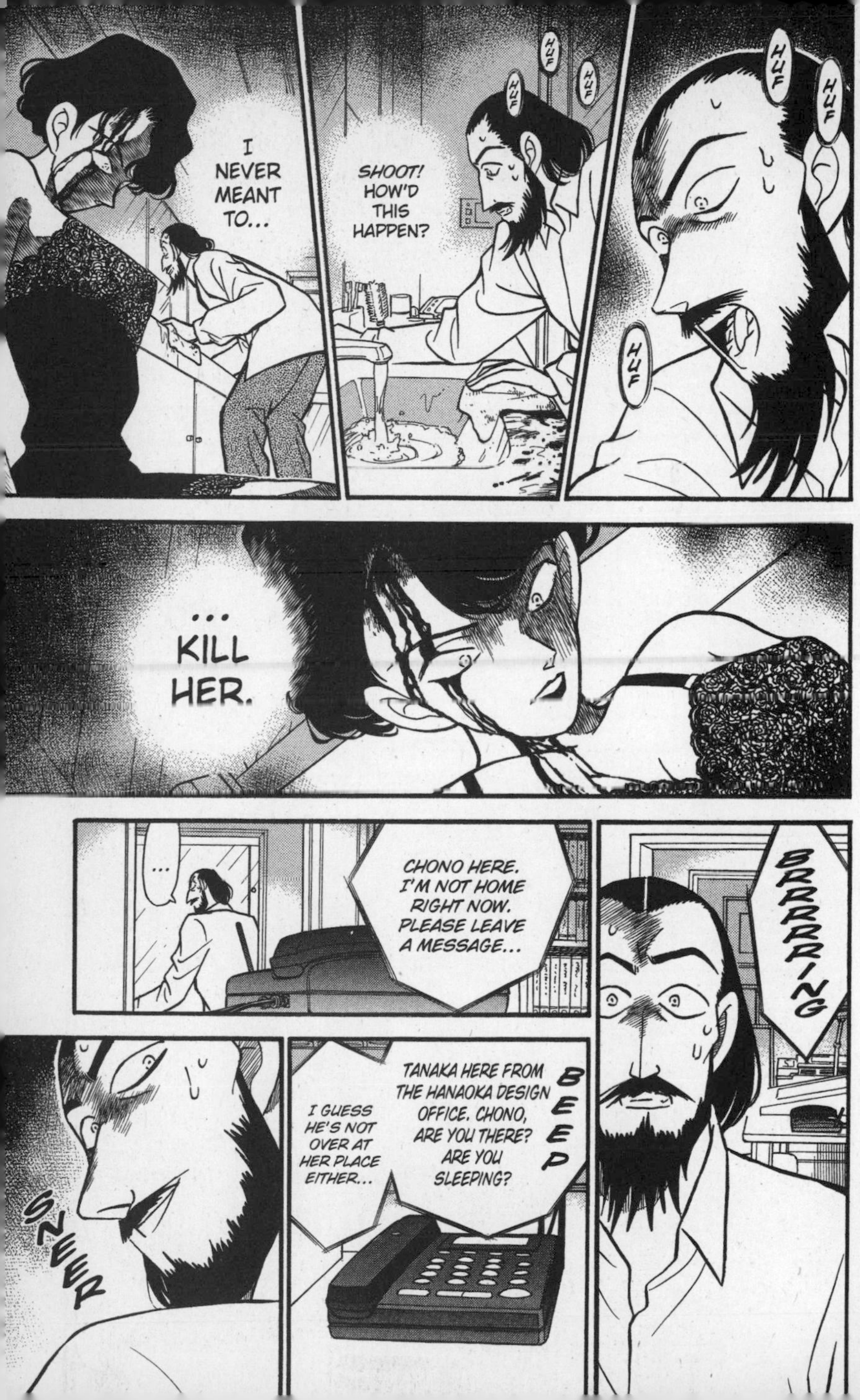
HUF
HUF
HUF
HUF
HUF
HUF
SHOOT! HOW'D THIS HAPPEN?
I NEVER MEANT TO...
... KILL HER.
BRRRRRING
CHONO HERE. I'M NOT HOME RIGHT NOW. PLEASE LEAVE A MESSAGE...
...
BEEP
TANAKA HERE FROM THE HANAOKA DESIGN OFFICE. CHONO, ARE YOU THERE? ARE YOU SLEEPING?
I GUESS HE'S NOT OVER AT HER PLACE EITHER...
SNEER

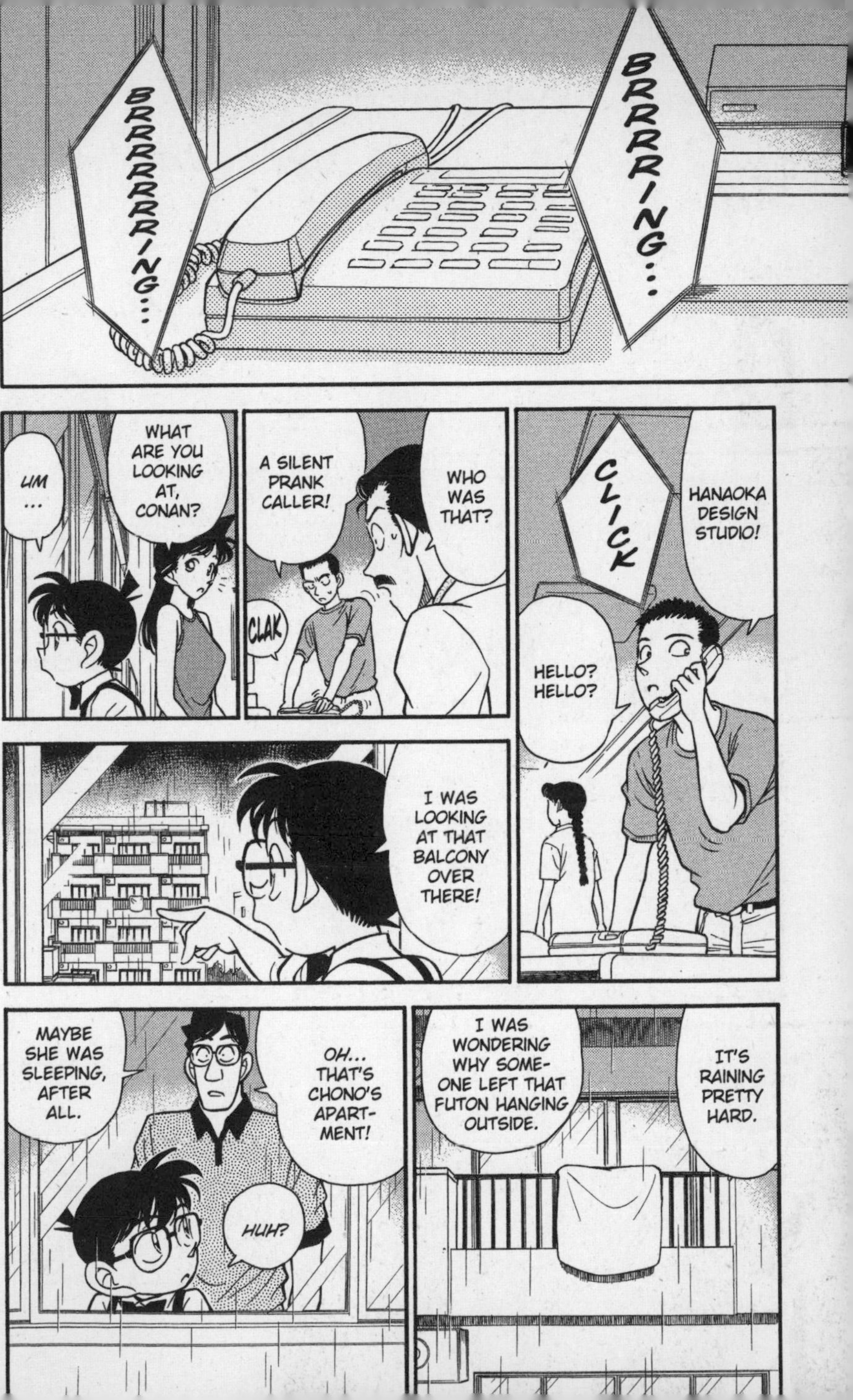
BRRRRING...
BRRRRRRING...
HANAOKA DESIGN STUDIO!
CLICK
HELLO? HELLO?
WHO WAS THAT?
A SILENT PRANK CALLER!
CLAK
WHAT ARE YOU LOOKING AT, CONAN?
UM ...
I WAS LOOKING AT THAT BALCONY OVER THERE!
IT'S RAINING PRETTY HARD.
I WAS WONDERING WHY SOME-ONE LEFT THAT FUTON HANGING OUTSIDE.
OH... THAT'S CHONO'S APART-MENT!
MAYBE SHE WAS SLEEPING, AFTER ALL.
HUH?

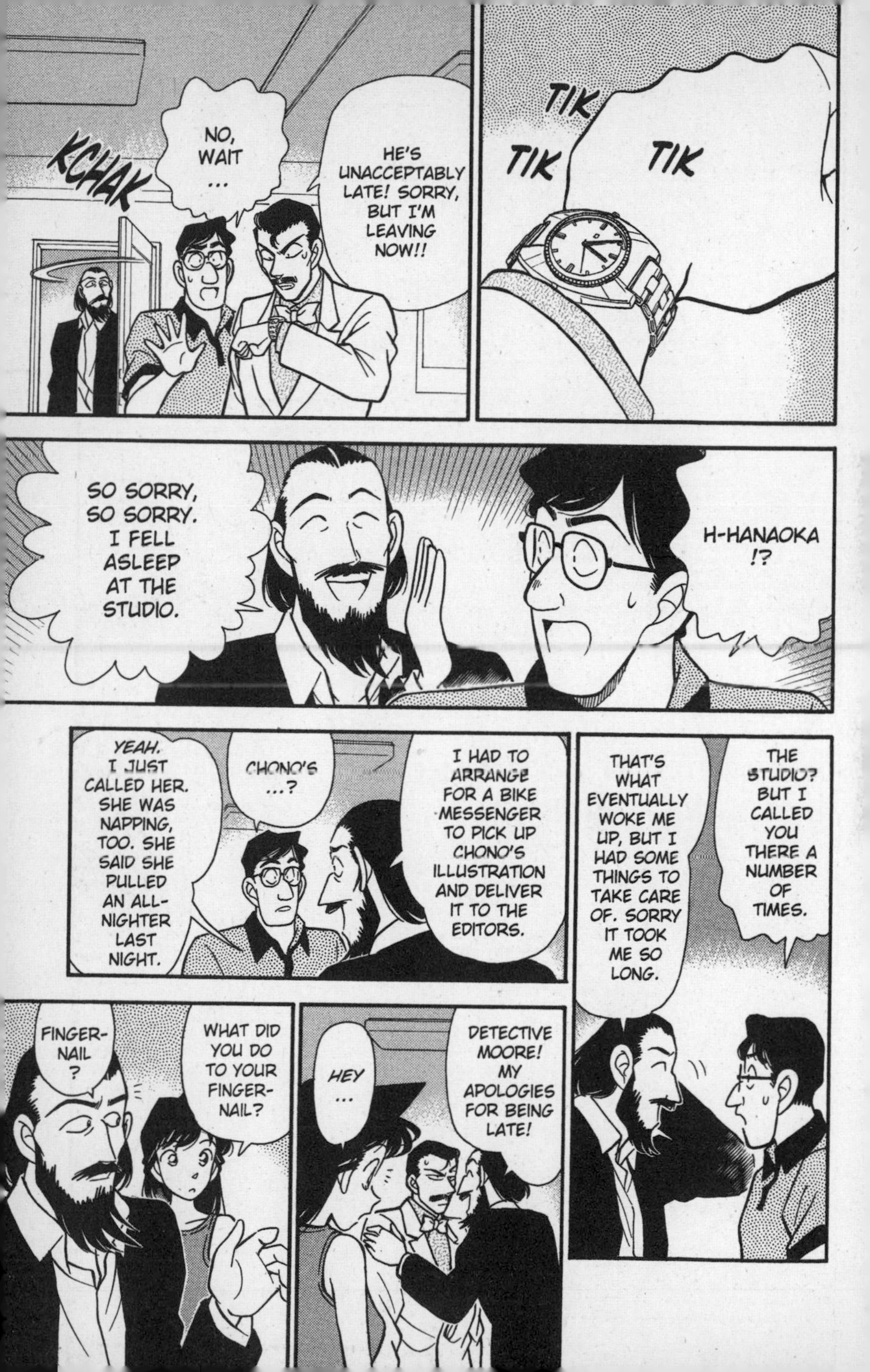
TIK
TIK
TIK
HE'S UNACCEPTABLY LATE! SORRY, BUT I'M LEAVING NOW!!
NO, WAIT ...
KCHAK
H-HANAOKA !?
SO SORRY, SO SORRY. I FELL ASLEEP AT THE STUDIO.
THE STUDIO? BUT I CALLED YOU THERE A NUMBER OF TIMES.
THAT'S WHAT EVENTUALLY WOKE ME UP, BUT I HAD SOME THINGS TO TAKE CARE OF. SORRY IT TOOK ME SO LONG.
I HAD TO ARRANGE FOR A BIKE MESSENGER TO PICK UP CHONO'S ILLUSTRATION AND DELIVER IT TO THE EDITORS.
CHONO'S ...?
YEAH. I JUST CALLED HER. SHE WAS NAPPING, TOO. SHE SAID SHE PULLED AN ALL-NIGHTER LAST NIGHT.
DETECTIVE MOORE! MY APOLOGIES FOR BEING LATE!
HEY ...
WHAT DID YOU DO TO YOUR FINGER-NAIL?
FINGER-NAIL ?

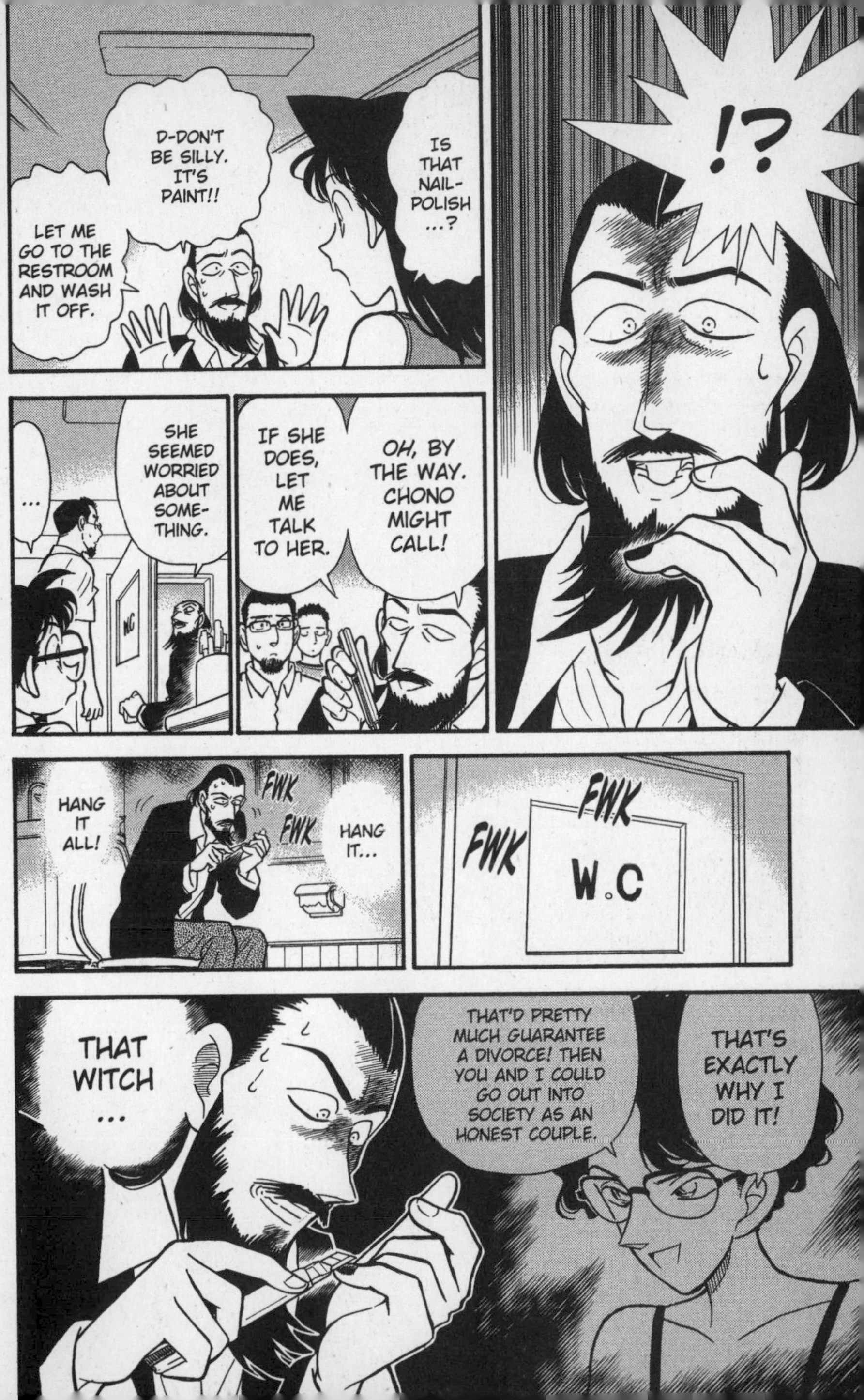
!?
IS THAT NAIL-POLISH ...?
D-DON'T BE SILLY. IT'S PAINT!!
LET ME GO TO THE RESTROOM AND WASH IT OFF.
OH, BY THE WAY. CHONO MIGHT CALL!
IF SHE DOES, LET ME TALK TO HER.
SHE SEEMED WORRIED ABOUT SOME-THING.
...
FWK
FWK
W.C
HANG IT...
FWK
FWK
HANG IT ALL!
THAT'S EXACTLY WHY I DID IT!
THAT'D PRETTY MUCH GUARANTEE A DIVORCE! THEN YOU AND I COULD GO OUT INTO SOCIETY AS AN HONEST COUPLE.
THAT WITCH ...

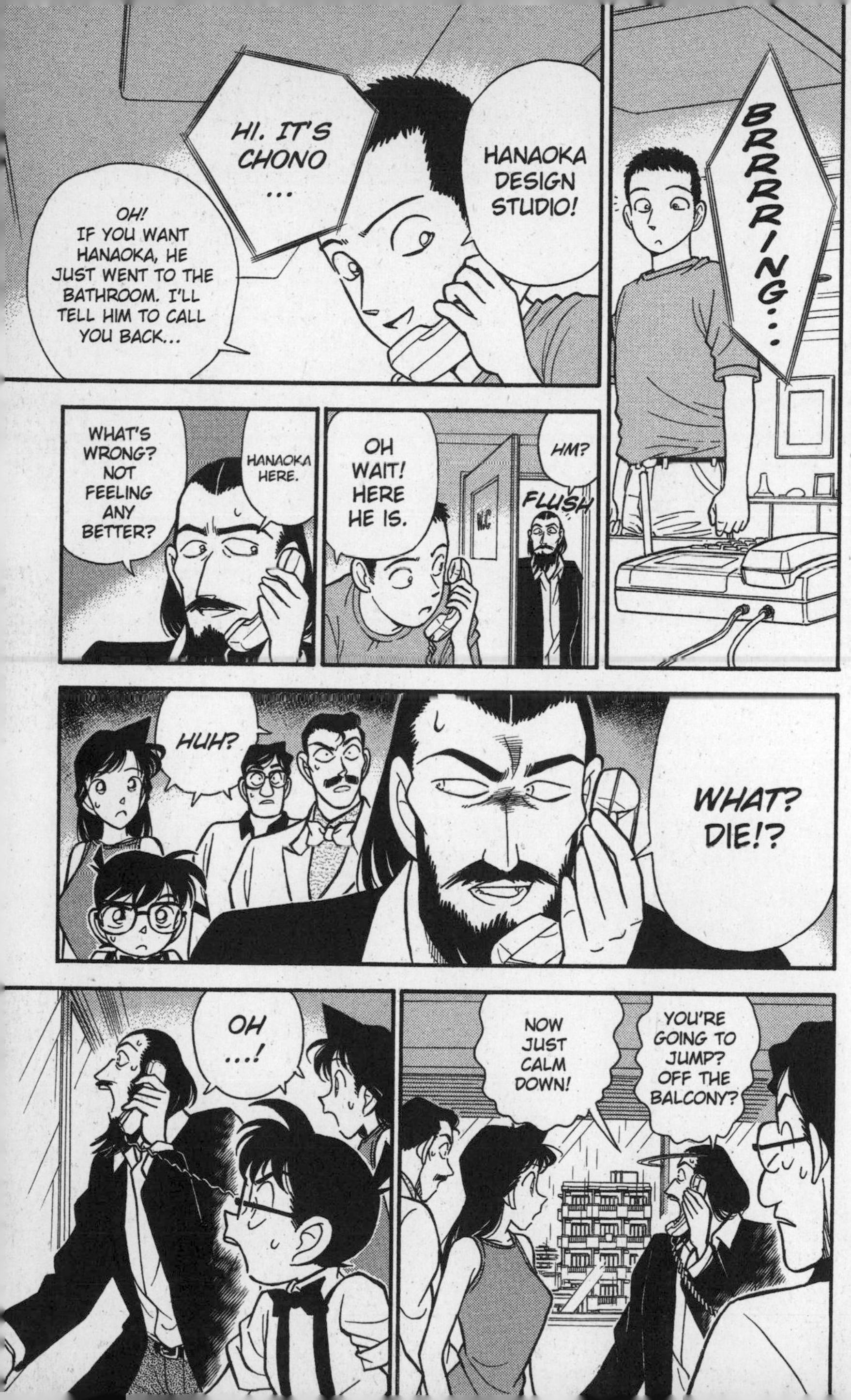
BRRRRING...
HANAOKA DESIGN STUDIO!
HI. IT'S CHONO ...
OH! IF YOU WANT HANAOKA, HE JUST WENT TO THE BATHROOM. I'LL TELL HIM TO CALL YOU BACK...
HM?
OH WAIT! HERE HE IS.
FLUSH
HANAOKA HERE.
WHAT'S WRONG? NOT FEELING ANY BETTER?
WHAT? DIE!?
HUH?
YOU'RE GOING TO JUMP? OFF THE BALCONY?
NOW JUST CALM DOWN!
OH ...!

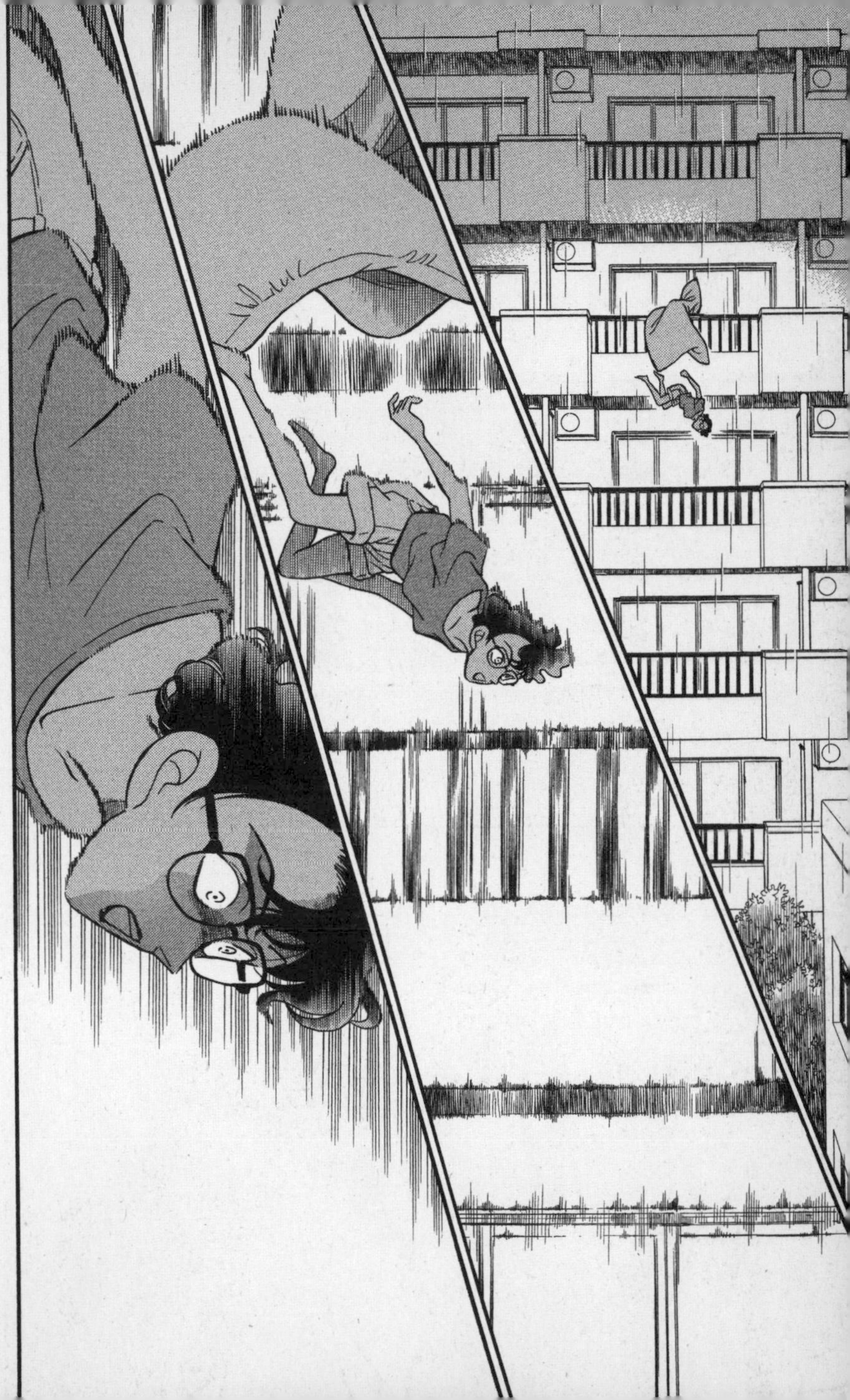

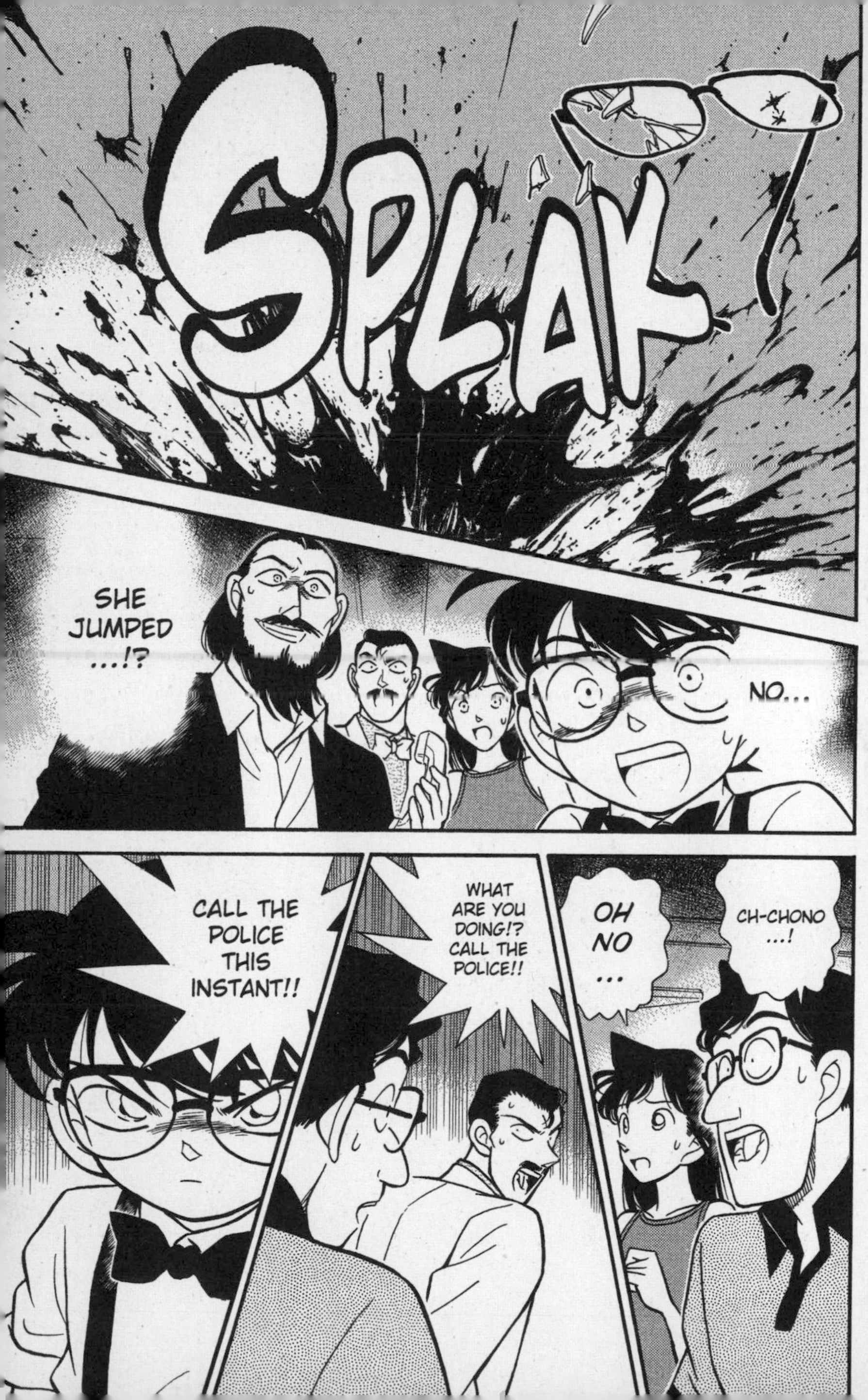
SPLAK
NO...
SHE JUMPED ...!?
CH-CHONO ...!
OH NO ...
WHAT ARE YOU DOING!? CALL THE POLICE!!
CALL THE POLICE THIS INSTANT!!

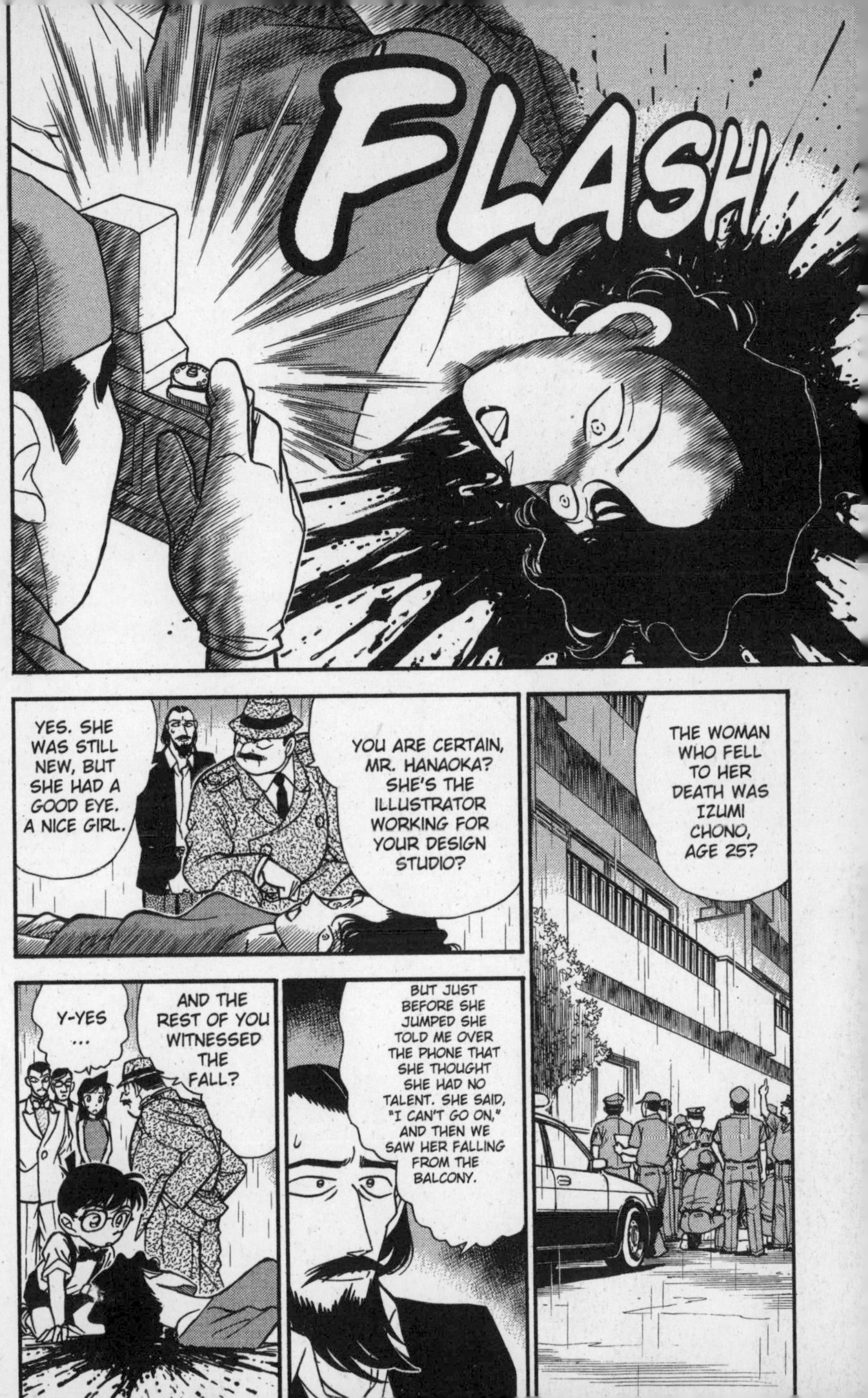
FLASH
THE WOMAN WHO FELL TO HER DEATH WAS IZUMI CHONO, AGE 25?
YOU ARE CERTAIN, MR. HANAOKA? SHE'S THE ILLUSTRATOR WORKING FOR YOUR DESIGN STUDIO?
YES. SHE WAS STILL NEW, BUT SHE HAD A GOOD EYE. A NICE GIRL.
BUT JUST BEFORE SHE JUMPED SHE TOLD ME OVER THE PHONE THAT SHE THOUGHT SHE HAD NO TALENT. SHE SAID, "I CAN'T GO ON," AND THEN WE SAW HER FALLING FROM THE BALCONY.
AND THE REST OF YOU WITNESSED THE FALL?
Y-YES ...

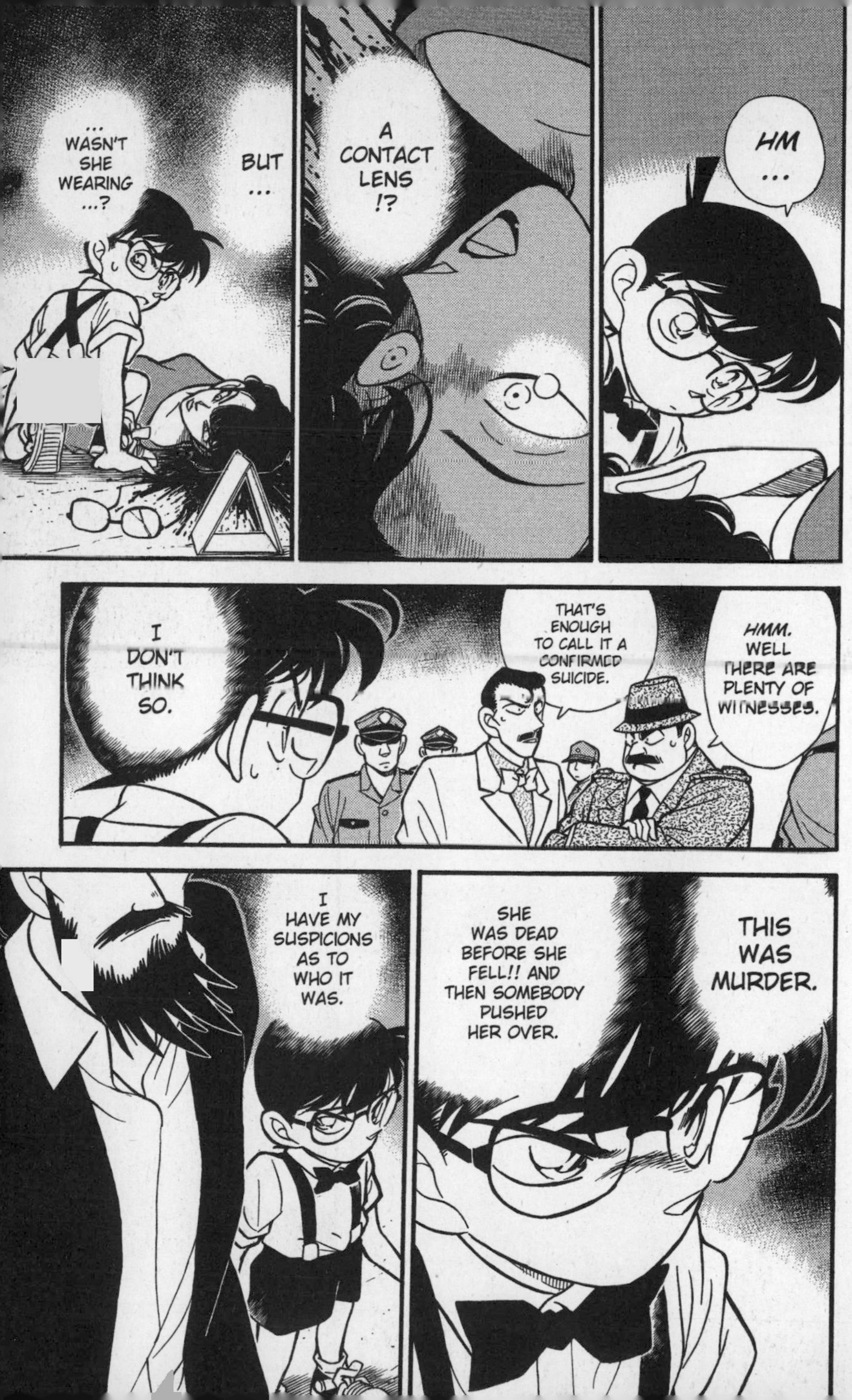
HM ...
A CONTACT LENS !?
BUT ...
... WASN'T SHE WEARING ...?
HMM. WELL THERE ARE PLENTY OF WITNESSES.
THAT'S ENOUGH TO CALL IT A CONFIRMED SUICIDE.
I DON'T THINK SO.
THIS WAS MURDER.
SHE WAS DEAD BEFORE SHE FELL!! AND THEN SOMEBODY PUSHED HER OVER.
I HAVE MY SUSPICIONS AS TO WHO IT WAS.

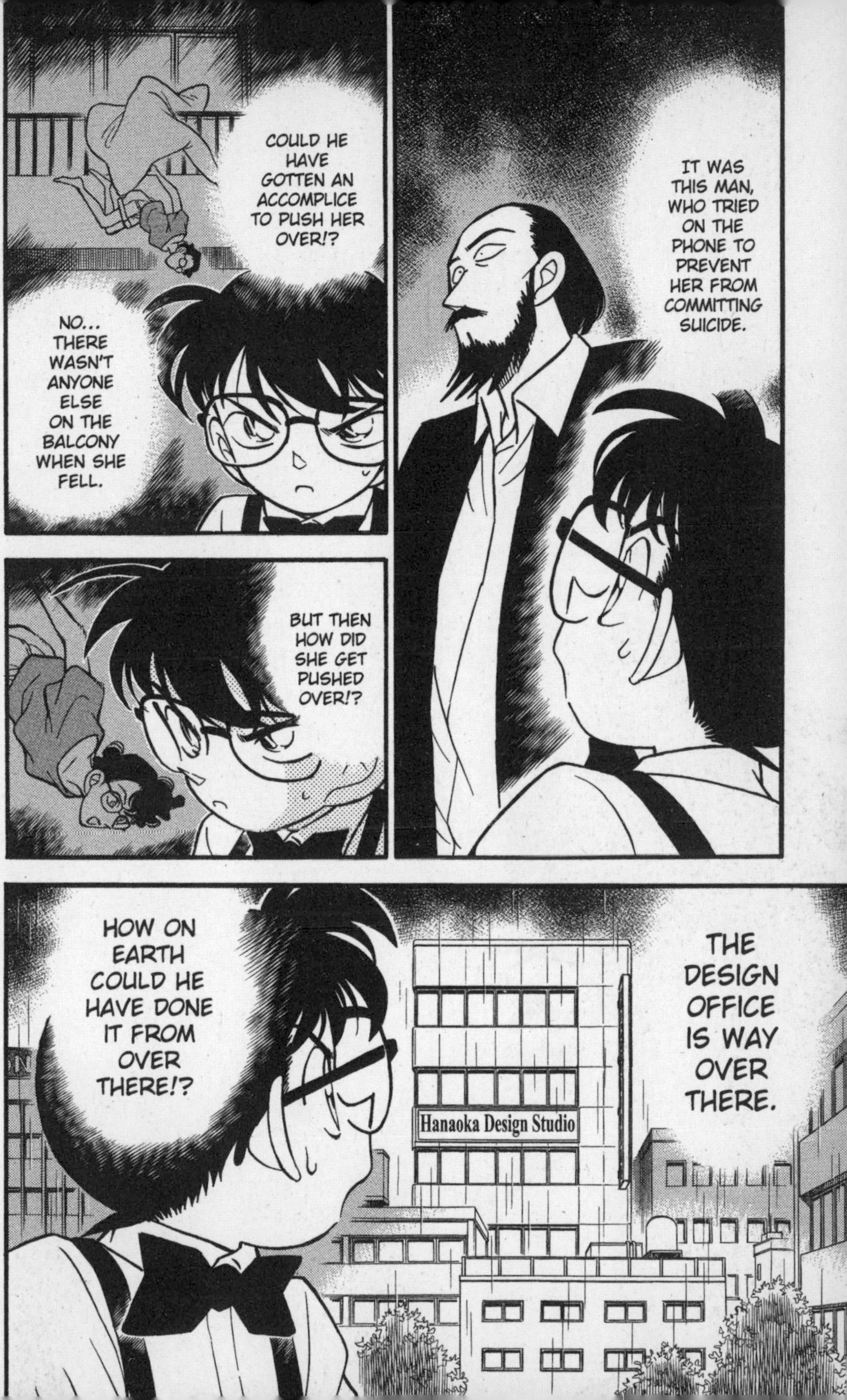
IT WAS THIS MAN, WHO TRIED ON THE PHONE TO PREVENT HER FROM COMMITTING SUICIDE.
COULD HE HAVE GOTTEN AN ACCOMPLICE TO PUSH HER OVER!?
NO... THERE WASN'T ANYONE ELSE ON THE BALCONY WHEN SHE FELL.
BUT THEN HOW DID SHE GET PUSHED OVER!?
THE DESIGN OFFICE IS WAY OVER THERE.
Hanaoka Design Studio
HOW ON EARTH COULD HE HAVE DONE IT FROM OVER THERE!?

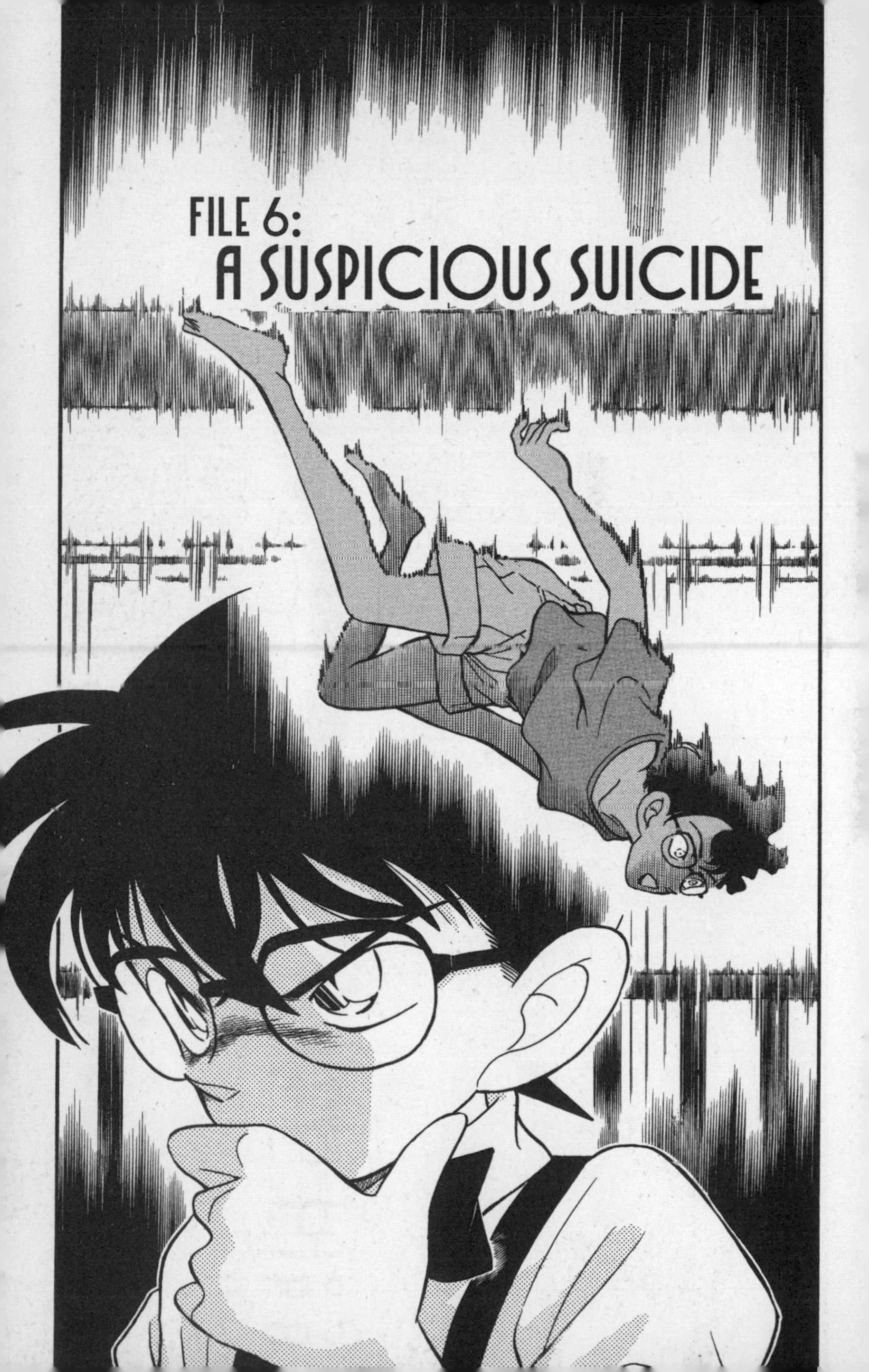
FILE 6:
A SUSPICIOUS SUICIDE

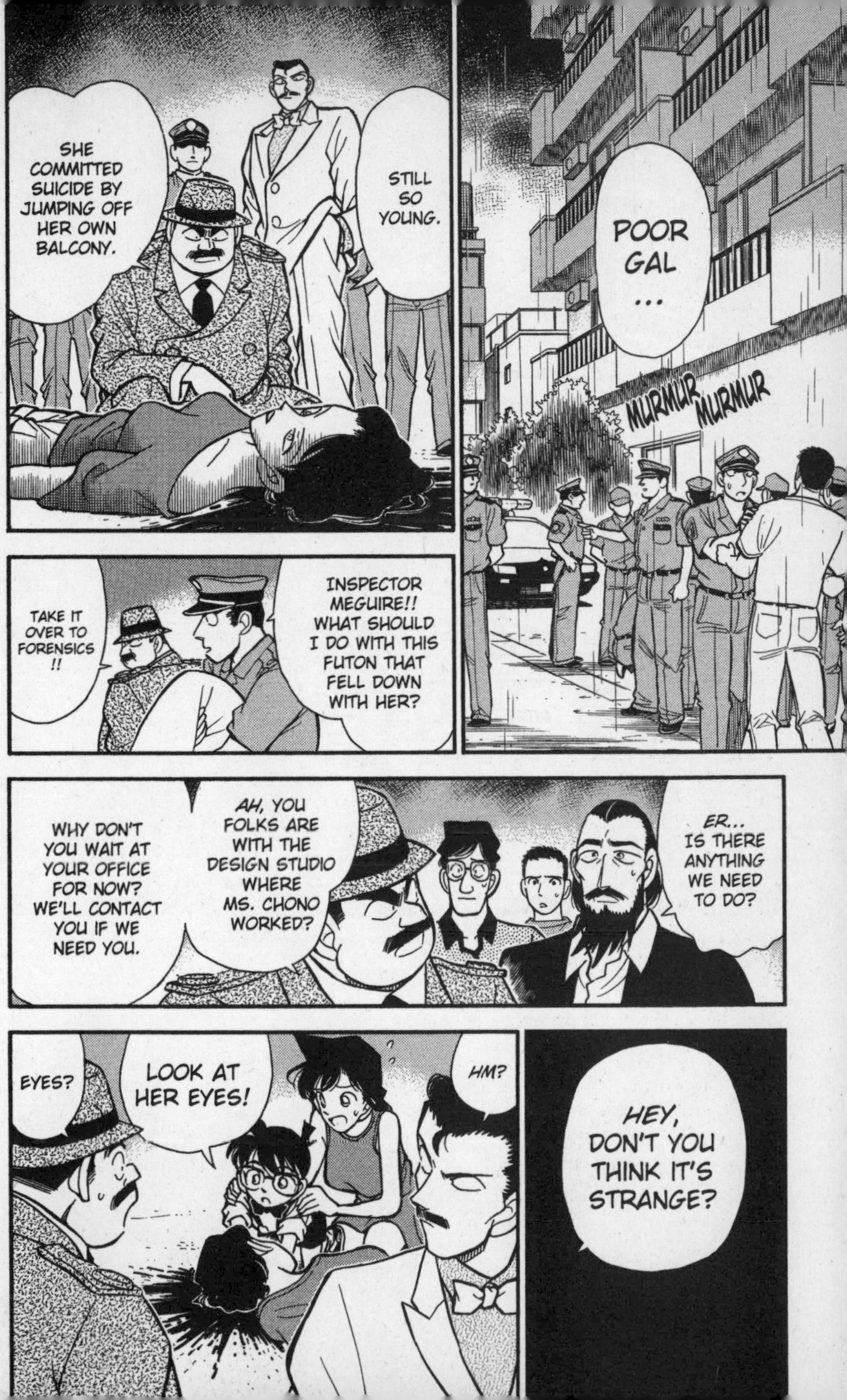
POOR GAL ...
MURMUR MURMUR
STILL SO YOUNG.
SHE COMMITTED SUICIDE BY JUMPING OFF HER OWN BALCONY.
INSPECTOR MEGUIRE!! WHAT SHOULD I DO WITH THIS FUTON THAT FELL DOWN WITH HER?
TAKE IT OVER TO FORENSICS !!
ER... IS THERE ANYTHING WE NEED TO DO?
AH, YOU FOLKS ARE WITH THE DESIGN STUDIO WHERE MS. CHONO WORKED?
WHY DON'T YOU WAIT AT YOUR OFFICE FOR NOW? WE'LL CONTACT YOU IF WE NEED YOU.
HEY, DON'T YOU THINK IT'S STRANGE?
HM?
LOOK AT HER EYES!
EYES?

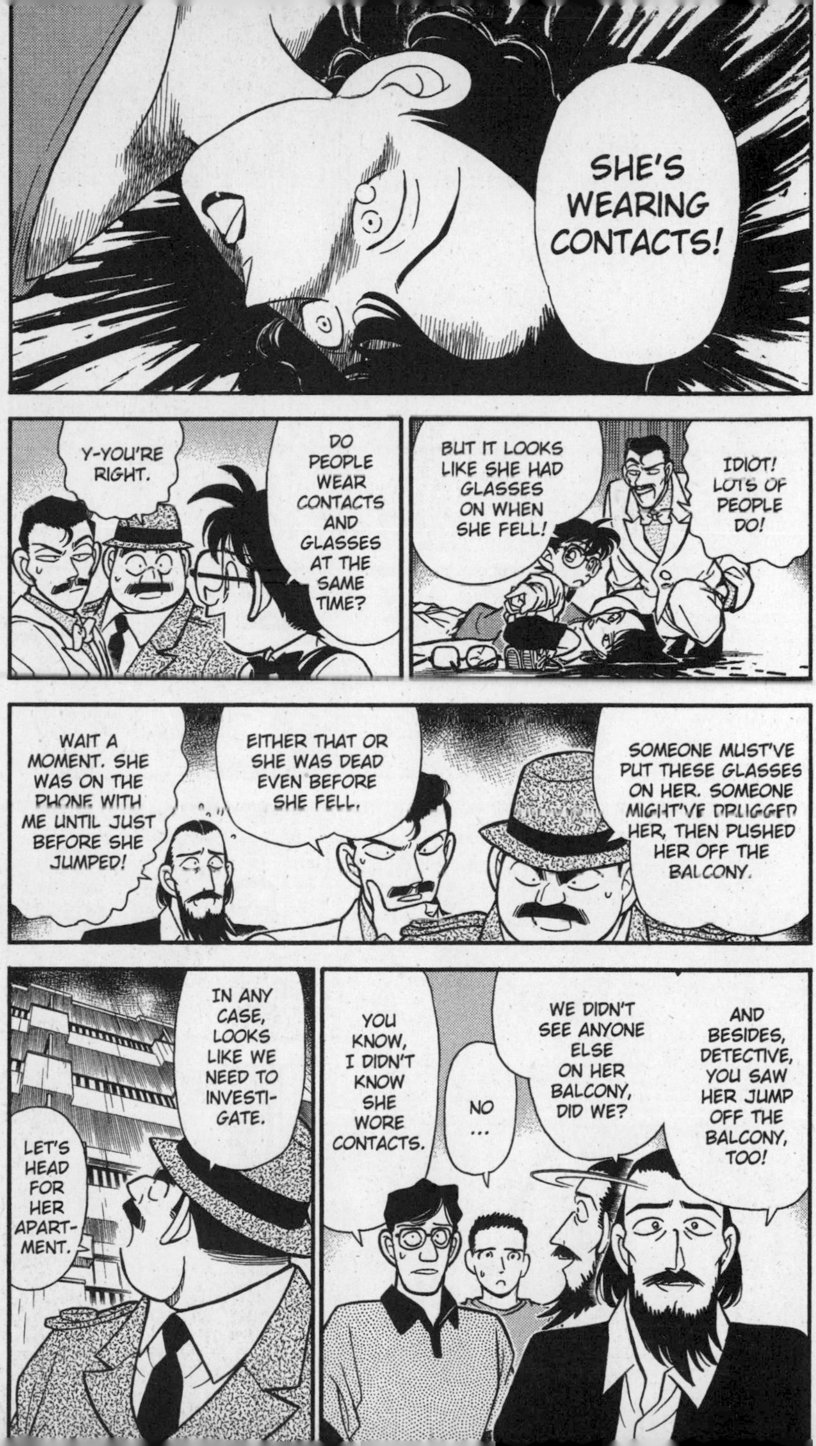
SHE'S WEARING CONTACTS!
IDIOT! LOTS OF PEOPLE DO!
BUT IT LOOKS LIKE SHE HAD GLASSES ON WHEN SHE FELL!
DO PEOPLE WEAR CONTACTS AND GLASSES AT THE SAME TIME?
Y-YOU'RE RIGHT.
SOMEONE MUST'VE PUT THESE GLASSES ON HER. SOMEONE MIGHT'VE DRUGGED HER, THEN PUSHED HER OFF THE BALCONY.
EITHER THAT OR SHE WAS DEAD EVEN BEFORE SHE FELL.
WAIT A MOMENT. SHE WAS ON THE PHONE WITH ME UNTIL JUST BEFORE SHE JUMPED!
AND BESIDES, DETECTIVE, YOU SAW HER JUMP OFF THE BALCONY, TOO!
WE DIDN'T SEE ANYONE ELSE ON HER BALCONY, DID WE?
NO ...
YOU KNOW, I DIDN'T KNOW SHE WORE CONTACTS.
IN ANY CASE, LOOKS LIKE WE NEED TO INVESTI-GATE.
LET'S HEAD FOR HER APART-MENT.

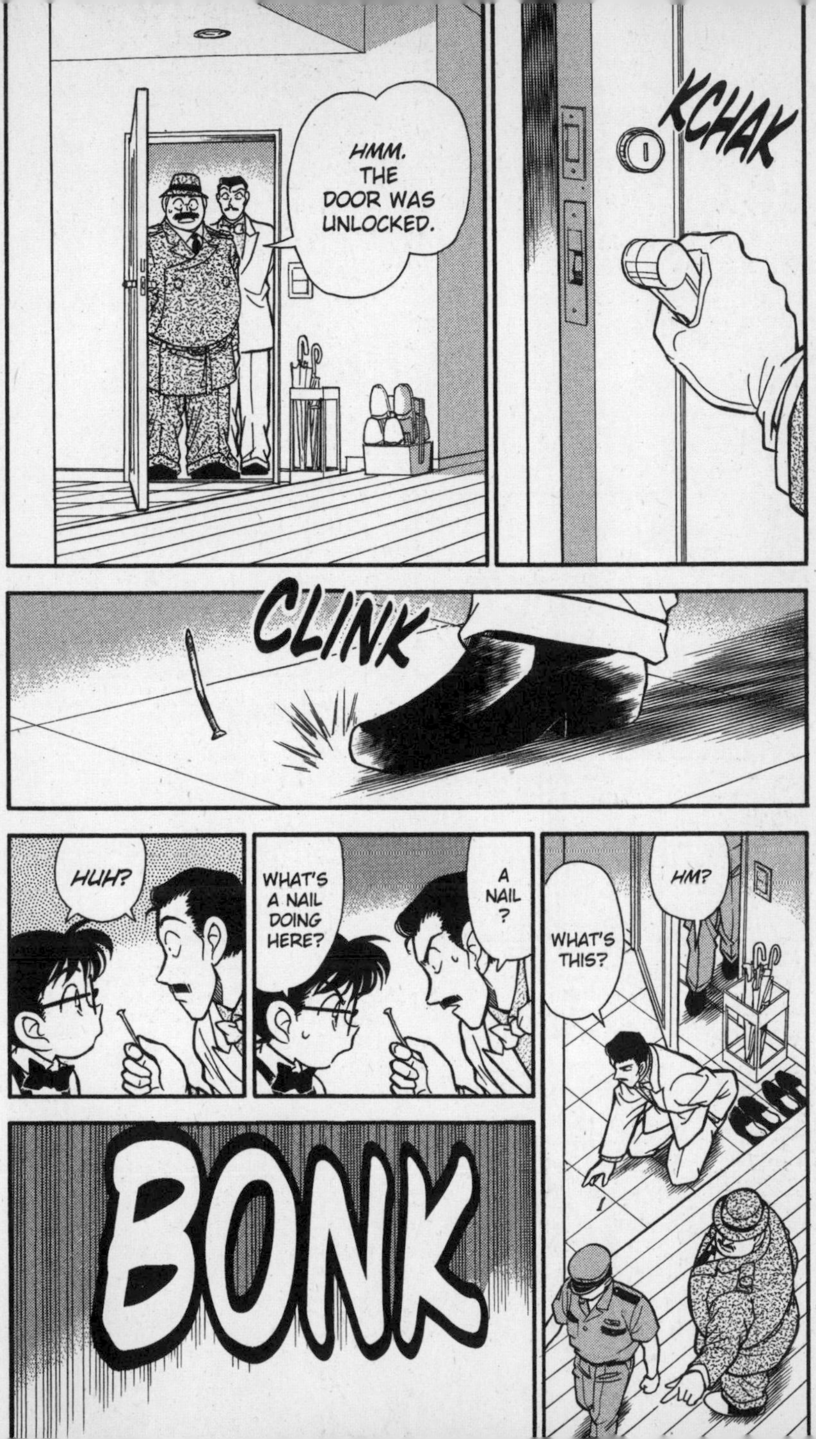
KCHAK
HMM. THE DOOR WAS UNLOCKED.
CLINK
HM?
WHAT'S THIS?
A NAIL?
WHAT'S A NAIL DOING HERE?
HUH?
BONK

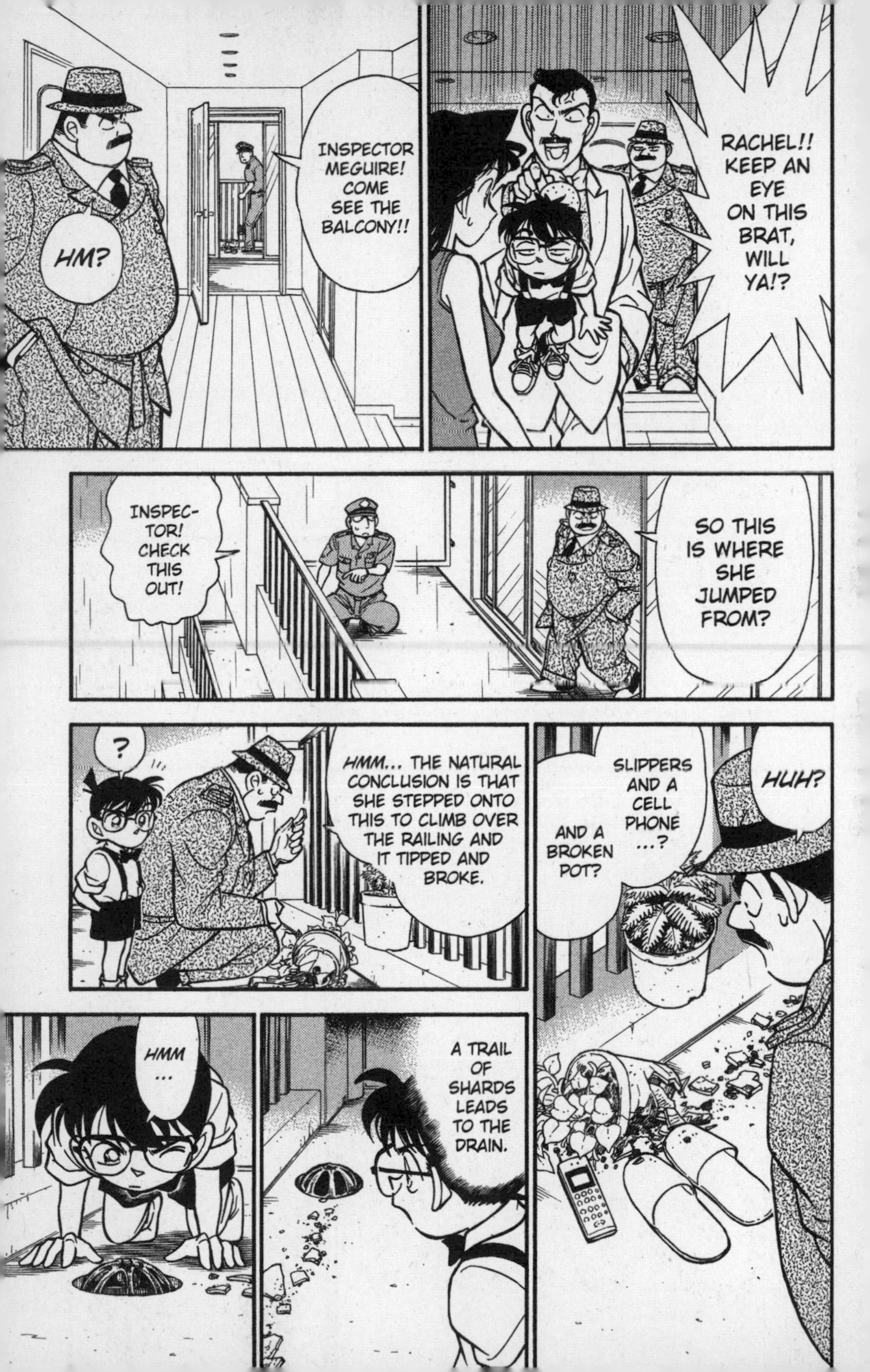
RACHEL!! KEEP AN EYE ON THIS BRAT, WILL YA!?
INSPECTOR MEGUIRE! COME SEE THE BALCONY!!
HM?
SO THIS IS WHERE SHE JUMPED FROM?
INSPECTOR! CHECK THIS OUT!
HUH?
SLIPPERS AND A CELL PHONE ...?
AND A BROKEN POT?
HMM... THE NATURAL CONCLUSION IS THAT SHE STEPPED ONTO THIS TO CLIMB OVER THE RAILING AND IT TIPPED AND BROKE.
?
A TRAIL OF SHARDS LEADS TO THE DRAIN.
HMM ...

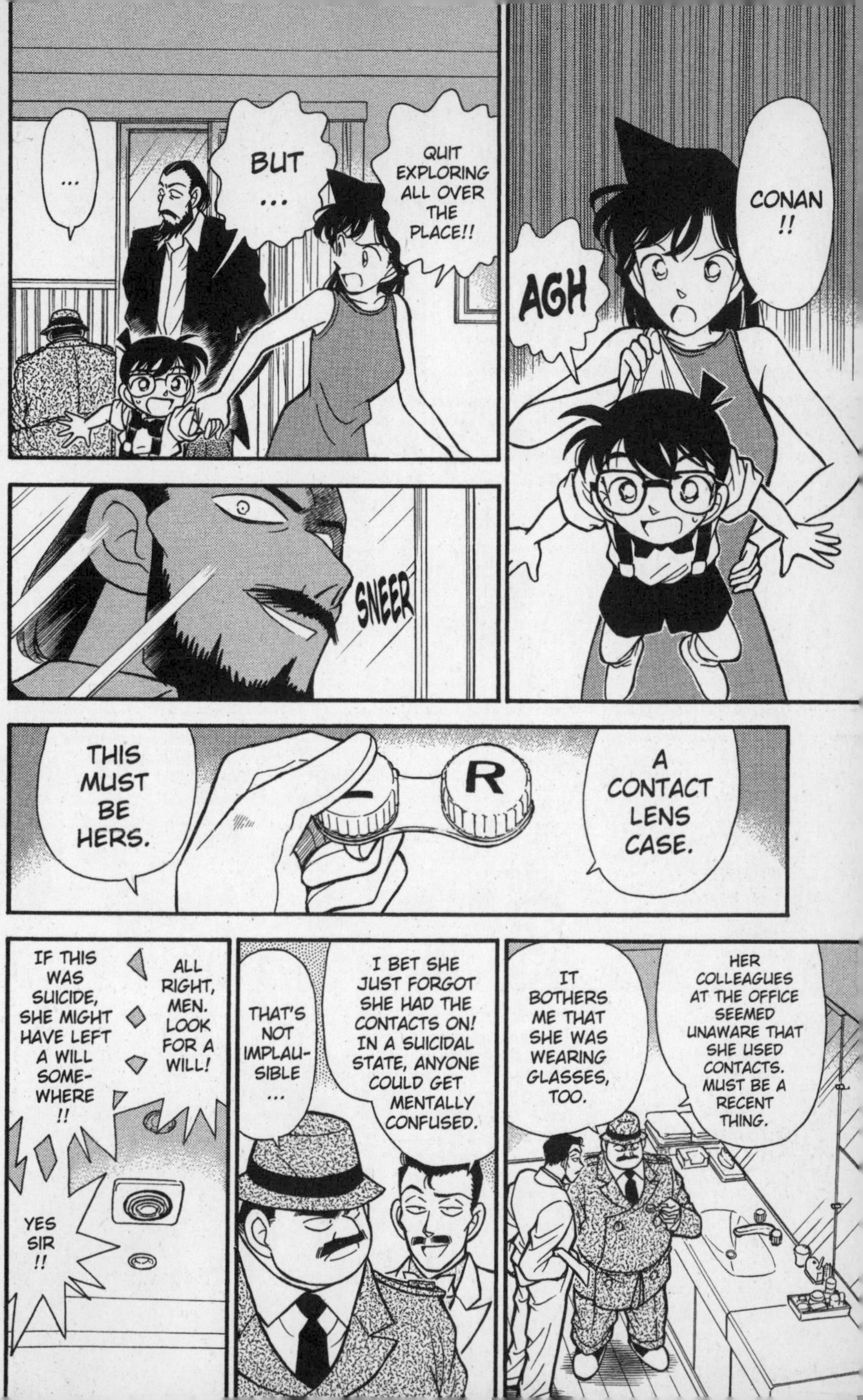
CONAN !!
AGH
QUIT EXPLORING ALL OVER THE PLACE!!
BUT ...
...
SNEER
A CONTACT LENS CASE.
THIS MUST BE HERS.
HER COLLEAGUES AT THE OFFICE SEEMED UNAWARE THAT SHE USED CONTACTS. MUST BE A RECENT THING.
IT BOTHERS ME THAT SHE WAS WEARING GLASSES, TOO.
I BET SHE JUST FORGOT SHE HAD THE CONTACTS ON! IN A SUICIDAL STATE, ANYONE COULD GET MENTALLY CONFUSED.
THAT'S NOT IMPLAU-SIBLE ...
ALL RIGHT, MEN. LOOK FOR A WILL!
IF THIS WAS SUICIDE, SHE MIGHT HAVE LEFT A WILL SOME-WHERE !!
YES SIR !!

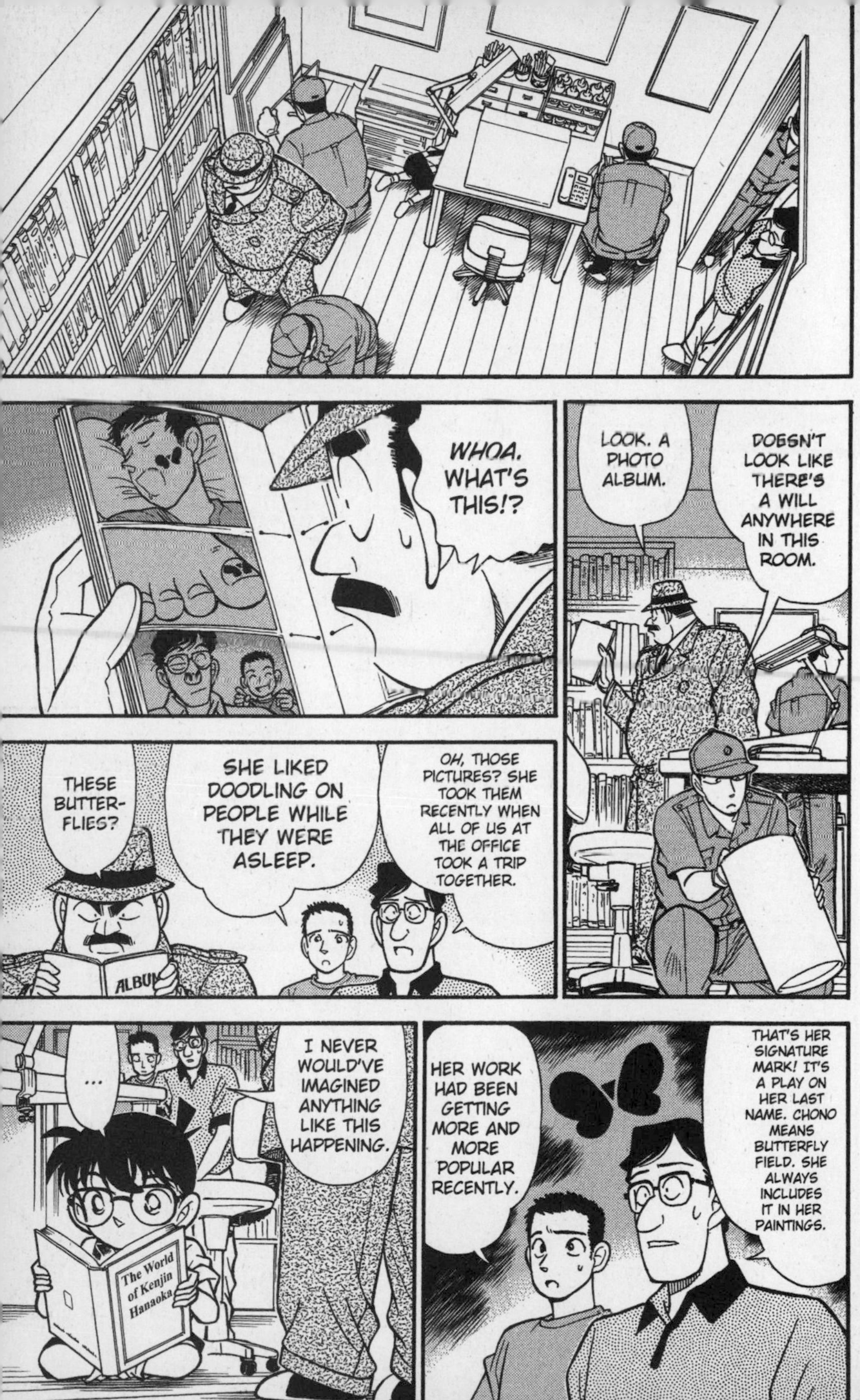
DOESN'T LOOK LIKE THERE'S A WILL ANYWHERE IN THIS ROOM.
LOOK. A PHOTO ALBUM.
WHOA. WHAT'S THIS!?
OH, THOSE PICTURES? SHE TOOK THEM RECENTLY WHEN ALL OF US AT THE OFFICE TOOK A TRIP TOGETHER.
SHE LIKED DOODLING ON PEOPLE WHILE THEY WERE ASLEEP.
THESE BUTTERFLIES?
ALBUM
THAT'S HER SIGNATURE MARK! IT'S A PLAY ON HER LAST NAME. CHONO MEANS BUTTERFLY FIELD. SHE ALWAYS INCLUDES IT IN HER PAINTINGS.
HER WORK HAD BEEN GETTING MORE AND MORE POPULAR RECENTLY.
I NEVER WOULD'VE IMAGINED ANYTHING LIKE THIS HAPPENING.
...
The World of Kenjin Hanaoka

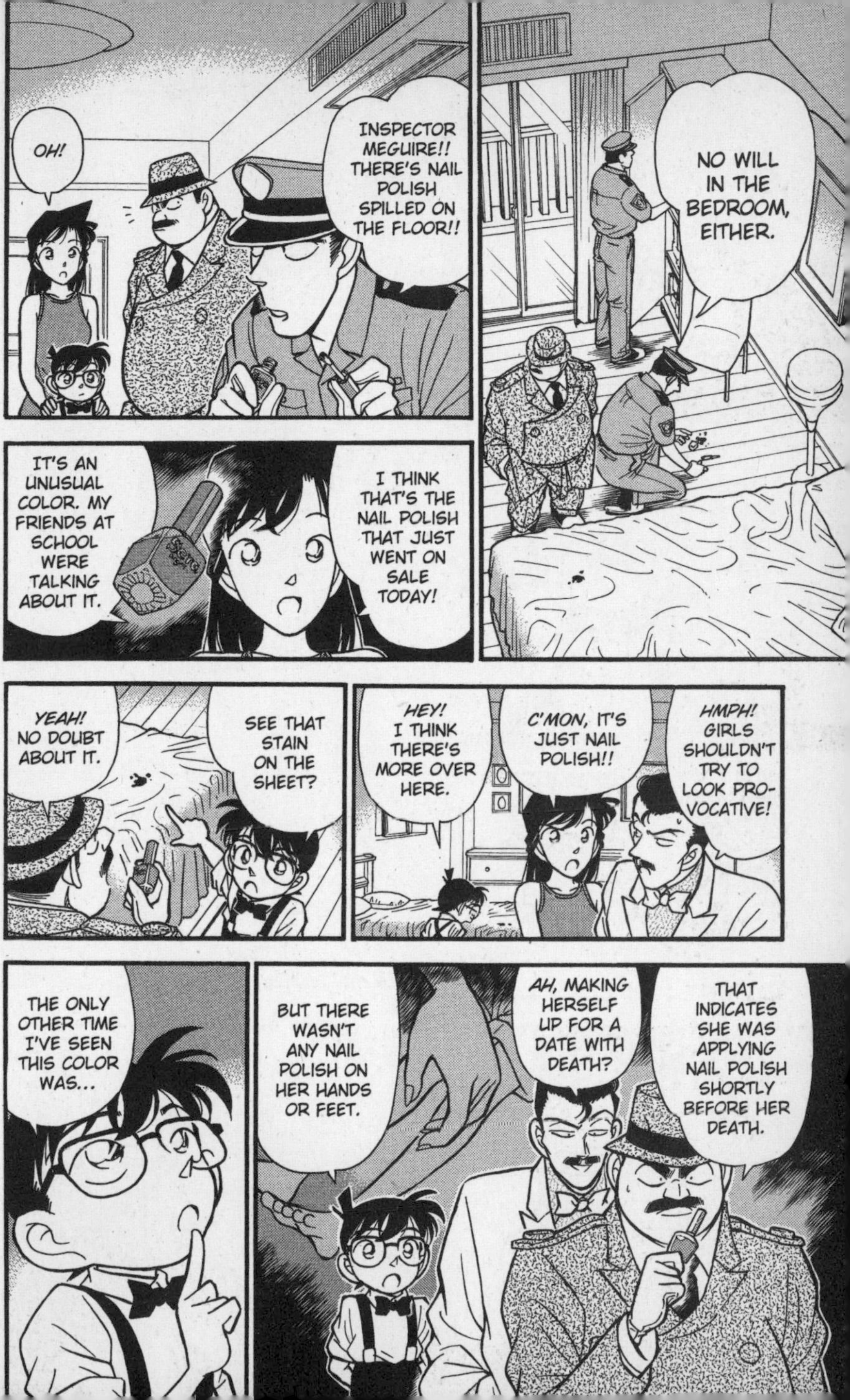
NO WILL IN THE BEDROOM, EITHER.
INSPECTOR MEGUIRE!! THERE'S NAIL POLISH SPILLED ON THE FLOOR!!
OH!
I THINK THAT'S THE NAIL POLISH THAT JUST WENT ON SALE TODAY!
IT'S AN UNUSUAL COLOR. MY FRIENDS AT SCHOOL WERE TALKING ABOUT IT.
HMPH! GIRLS SHOULDN'T TRY TO LOOK PRO-VOCATIVE!
C'MON, IT'S JUST NAIL POLISH!!
HEY! I THINK THERE'S MORE OVER HERE.
SEE THAT STAIN ON THE SHEET?
YEAH! NO DOUBT ABOUT IT.
THAT INDICATES SHE WAS APPLYING NAIL POLISH SHORTLY BEFORE HER DEATH.
AH, MAKING HERSELF UP FOR A DATE WITH DEATH?
BUT THERE WASN'T ANY NAIL POLISH ON HER HANDS OR FEET.
THE ONLY OTHER TIME I'VE SEEN THIS COLOR WAS...

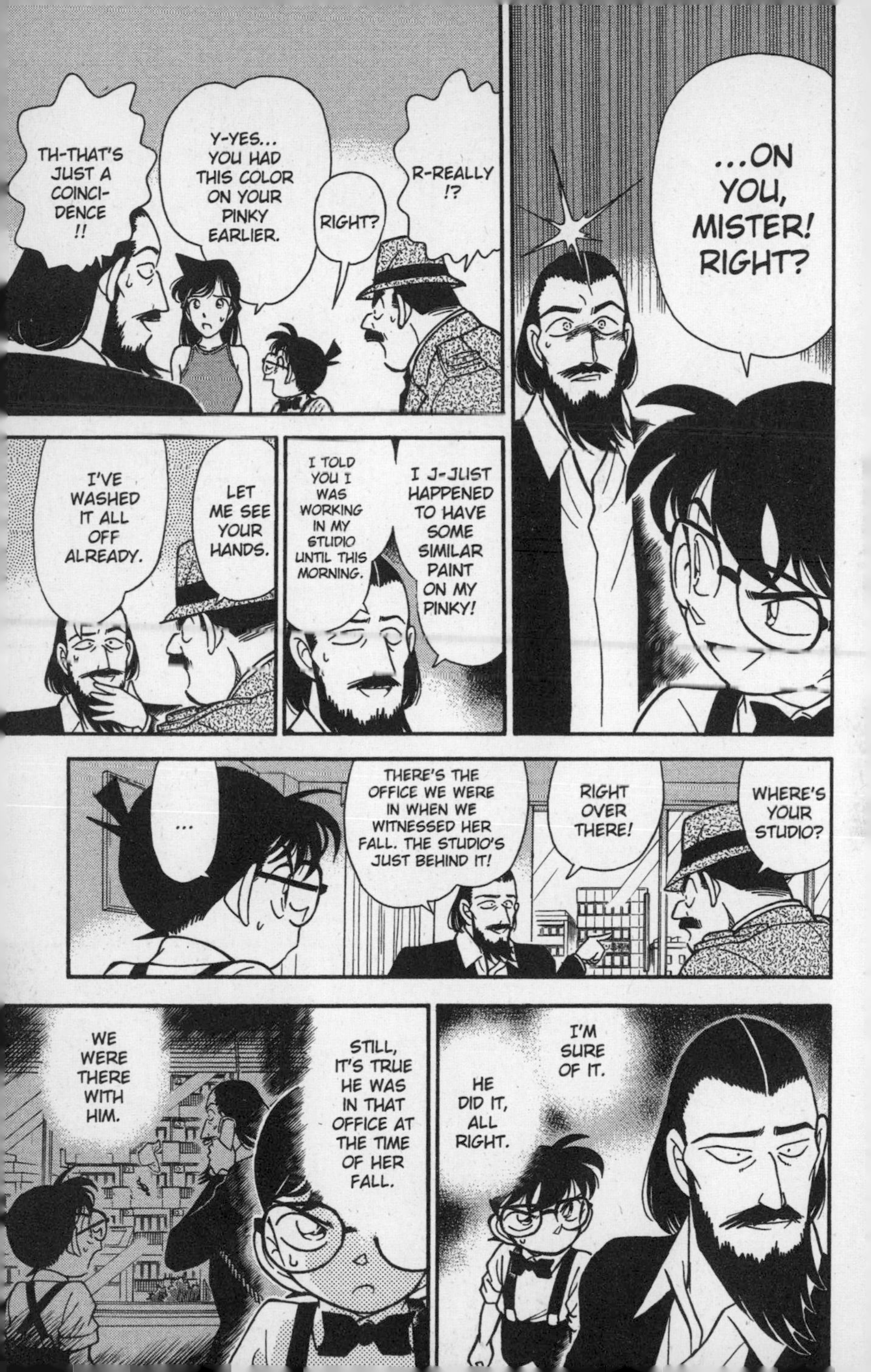
...ON YOU, MISTER! RIGHT?
R-REALLY !?
RIGHT?
Y-YES... YOU HAD THIS COLOR ON YOUR PINKY EARLIER.
TH-THAT'S JUST A COINCIDENCE !!
I J-JUST HAPPENED TO HAVE SOME SIMILAR PAINT ON MY PINKY!
I TOLD YOU I WAS WORKING IN MY STUDIO UNTIL THIS MORNING.
LET ME SEE YOUR HANDS.
I'VE WASHED IT ALL OFF ALREADY.
WHERE'S YOUR STUDIO?
RIGHT OVER THERE!
THERE'S THE OFFICE WE WERE IN WHEN WE WITNESSED HER FALL. THE STUDIO'S JUST BEHIND IT!
...
I'M SURE OF IT.
HE DID IT, ALL RIGHT.
STILL, IT'S TRUE HE WAS IN THAT OFFICE AT THE TIME OF HER FALL.
WE WERE THERE WITH HIM.

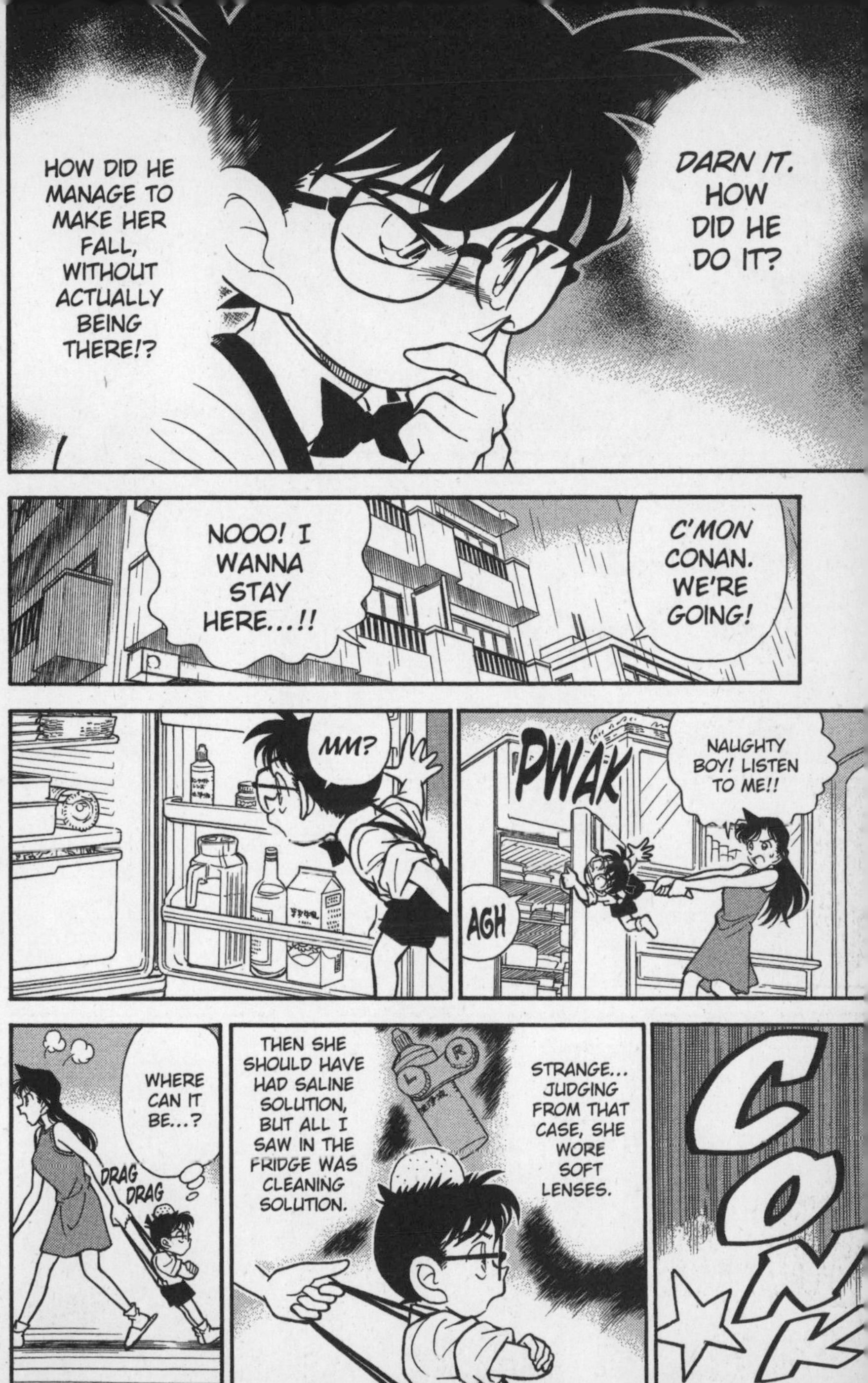
DARN IT. HOW DID HE DO IT?
HOW DID HE MANAGE TO MAKE HER FALL, WITHOUT ACTUALLY BEING THERE!?
C'MON CONAN. WE'RE GOING!
NOOO! I WANNA STAY HERE...!!
NAUGHTY BOY! LISTEN TO ME!!
PWAK
AGH
MM?
CONK
STRANGE... JUDGING FROM THAT CASE, SHE WORE SOFT LENSES.
THEN SHE SHOULD HAVE HAD SALINE SOLUTION, BUT ALL I SAW IN THE FRIDGE WAS CLEANING SOLUTION.
WHERE CAN IT BE...?
DRAG
DRAG

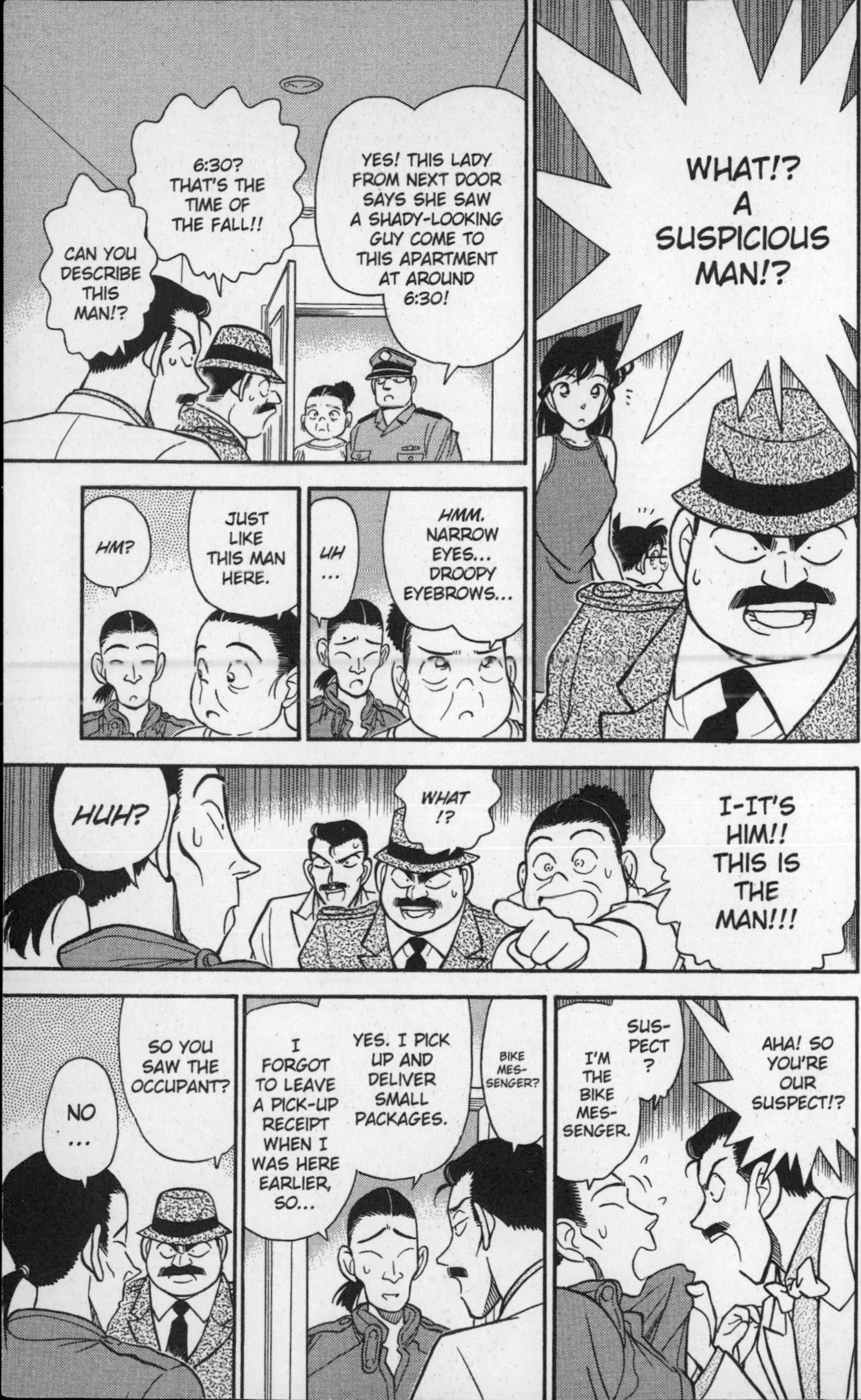
WHAT!? A SUSPICIOUS MAN!?
YES! THIS LADY FROM NEXT DOOR SAYS SHE SAW A SHADY-LOOKING GUY COME TO THIS APARTMENT AT AROUND 6:30!
6:30? THAT'S THE TIME OF THE FALL!!
CAN YOU DESCRIBE THIS MAN!?
HMM. NARROW EYES... DROOPY EYEBROWS...
UH ...
JUST LIKE THIS MAN HERE.
HM?
I-IT'S HIM!! THIS IS THE MAN!!!
WHAT !?
HUH?
AHA! SO YOU'RE OUR SUSPECT!?
SUS-PECT ?
I'M THE BIKE MES-SENGER.
BIKE MES-SENGER?
YES. I PICK UP AND DELIVER SMALL PACKAGES.
I FORGOT TO LEAVE A PICK-UP RECEIPT WHEN I WAS HERE EARLIER, SO...
SO YOU SAW THE OCCUPANT?
NO ...

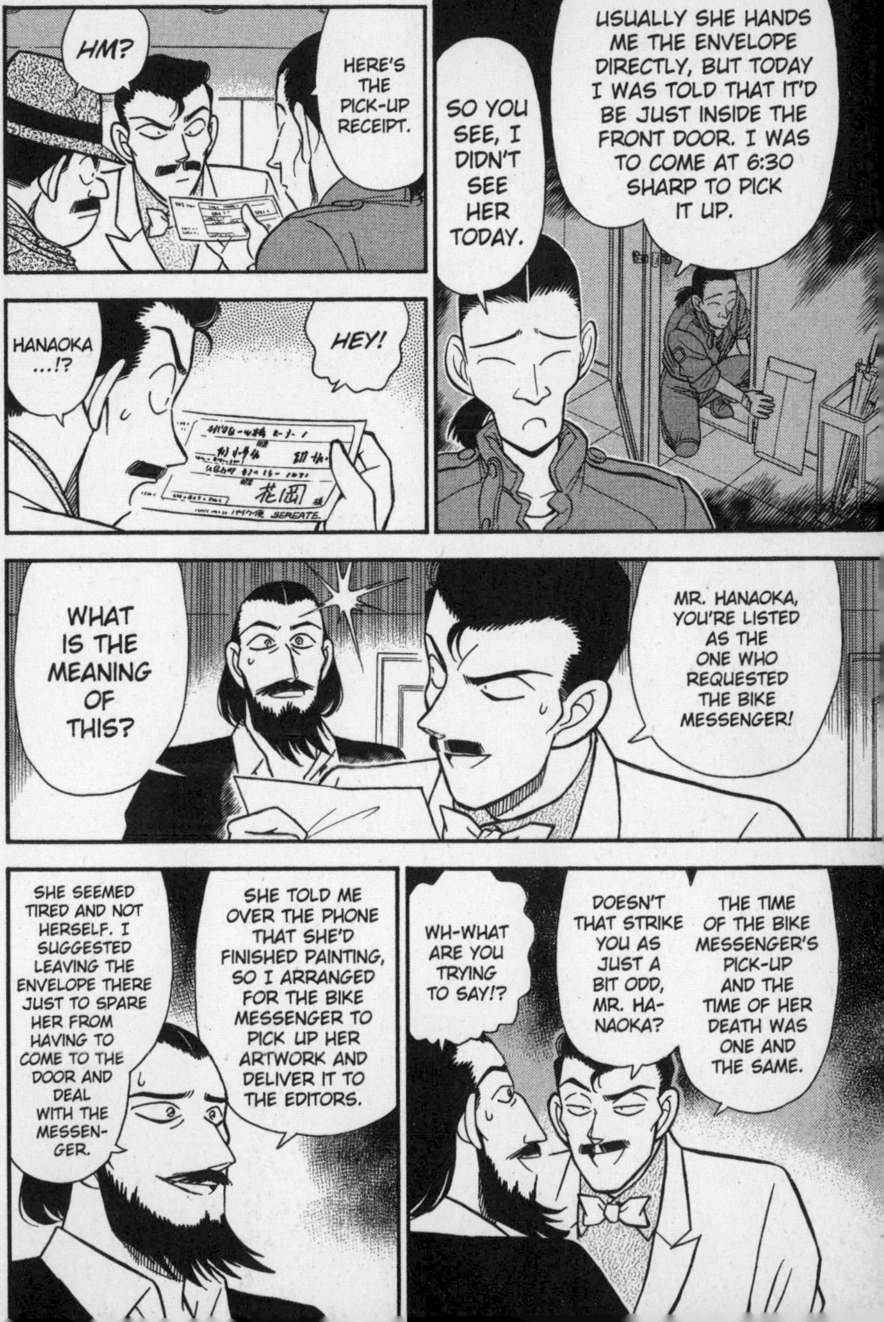
USUALLY SHE HANDS ME THE ENVELOPE DIRECTLY, BUT TODAY I WAS TOLD THAT IT'D BE JUST INSIDE THE FRONT DOOR. I WAS TO COME AT 6:30 SHARP TO PICK IT UP.
SO YOU SEE, I DIDN'T SEE HER TODAY.
HERE'S THE PICK-UP RECEIPT.
HM?
HEY!
HANAOKA ...!?
MR. HANAOKA, YOU'RE LISTED AS THE ONE WHO REQUESTED THE BIKE MESSENGER!
WHAT IS THE MEANING OF THIS?
THE TIME OF THE BIKE MESSENGER'S PICK-UP AND THE TIME OF HER DEATH WAS ONE AND THE SAME.
DOESN'T THAT STRIKE YOU AS JUST A BIT ODD, MR. HA-NAOKA?
WH-WHAT ARE YOU TRYING TO SAY!?
SHE TOLD ME OVER THE PHONE THAT SHE'D FINISHED PAINTING, SO I ARRANGED FOR THE BIKE MESSENGER TO PICK UP HER ARTWORK AND DELIVER IT TO THE EDITORS.
SHE SEEMED TIRED AND NOT HERSELF. I SUGGESTED LEAVING THE ENVELOPE THERE JUST TO SPARE HER FROM HAVING TO COME TO THE DOOR AND DEAL WITH THE MESSEN-GER.

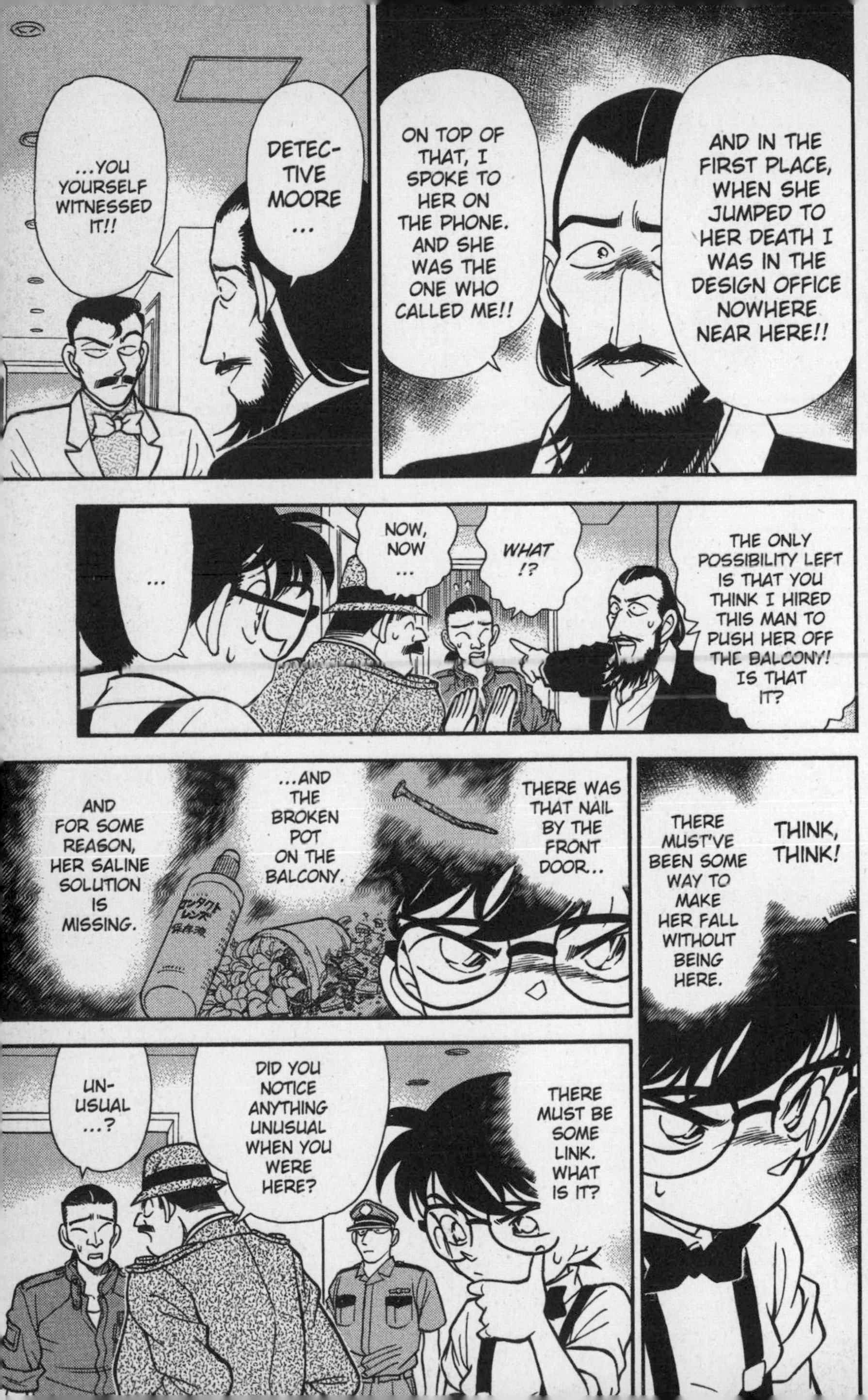
AND IN THE FIRST PLACE, WHEN SHE JUMPED TO HER DEATH I WAS IN THE DESIGN OFFICE NOWHERE NEAR HERE!!
ON TOP OF THAT, I SPOKE TO HER ON THE PHONE. AND SHE WAS THE ONE WHO CALLED ME!!
DETEC-TIVE MOORE ...
...YOU YOURSELF WITNESSED IT!!
THE ONLY POSSIBILITY LEFT IS THAT YOU THINK I HIRED THIS MAN TO PUSH HER OFF THE BALCONY! IS THAT IT?
WHAT !?
NOW, NOW ...
...
THINK, THINK!
THERE MUST'VE BEEN SOME WAY TO MAKE HER FALL WITHOUT BEING HERE.
THERE WAS THAT NAIL BY THE FRONT DOOR...
...AND THE BROKEN POT ON THE BALCONY.
AND FOR SOME REASON, HER SALINE SOLUTION IS MISSING.
THERE MUST BE SOME LINK. WHAT IS IT?
DID YOU NOTICE ANYTHING UNUSUAL WHEN YOU WERE HERE?
UN-USUAL ...?

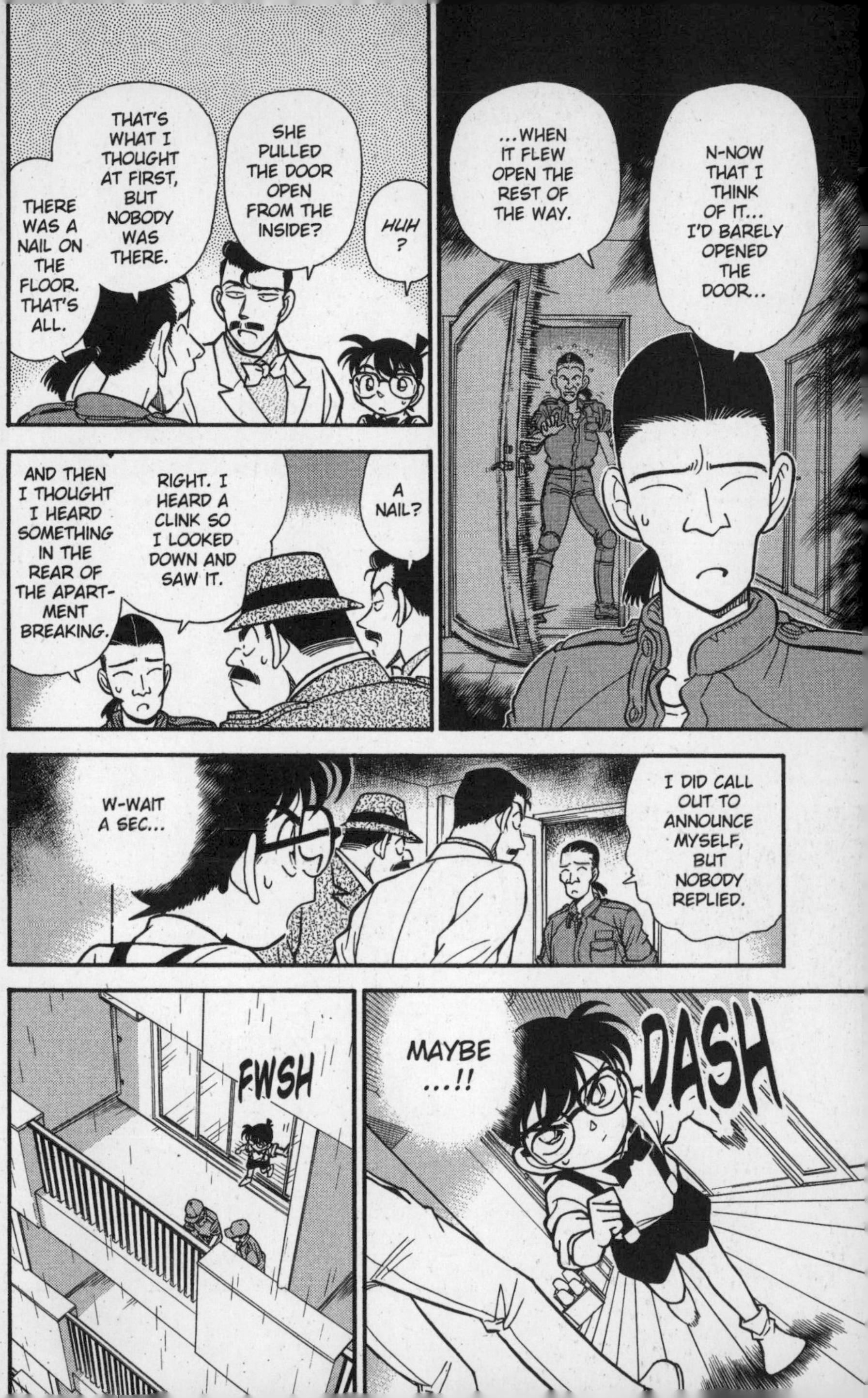
N-NOW THAT I THINK OF IT... I'D BARELY OPENED THE DOOR...
...WHEN IT FLEW OPEN THE REST OF THE WAY.
HUH?
SHE PULLED THE DOOR OPEN FROM THE INSIDE?
THAT'S WHAT I THOUGHT AT FIRST, BUT NOBODY WAS THERE.
THERE WAS A NAIL ON THE FLOOR. THAT'S ALL.
A NAIL?
RIGHT. I HEARD A CLINK SO I LOOKED DOWN AND SAW IT.
AND THEN I THOUGHT I HEARD SOMETHING IN THE REAR OF THE APARTMENT BREAKING.
I DID CALL OUT TO ANNOUNCE MYSELF, BUT NOBODY REPLIED.
W-WAIT A SEC...
DASH
MAYBE ...!!
FWSH

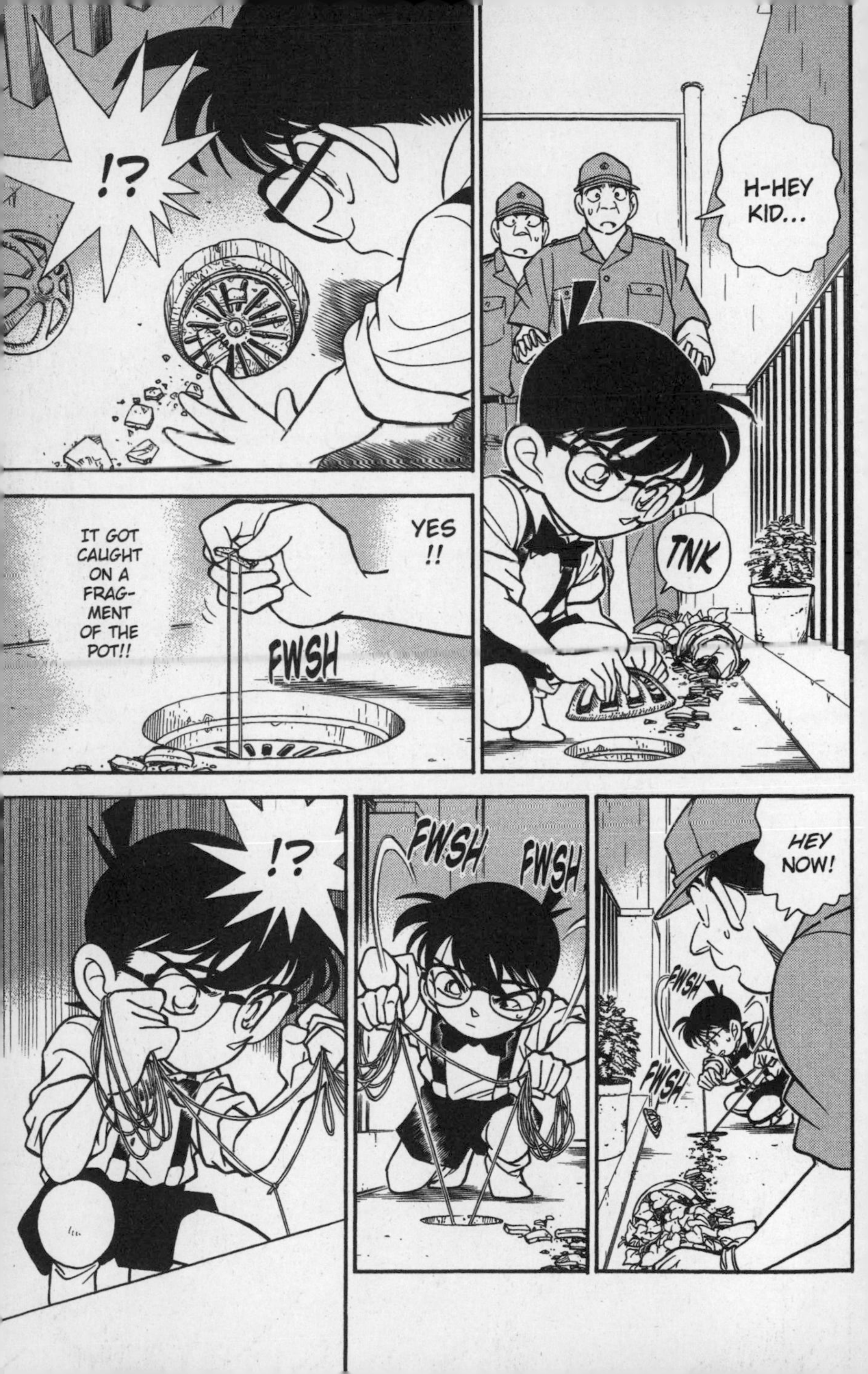
H-HEY KID...
TNK
!?
YES!!
IT GOT CAUGHT ON A FRAG-MENT OF THE POT!!
FWSH
HEY NOW!
FWSH
FWSH
FWSH
FWSH
!?

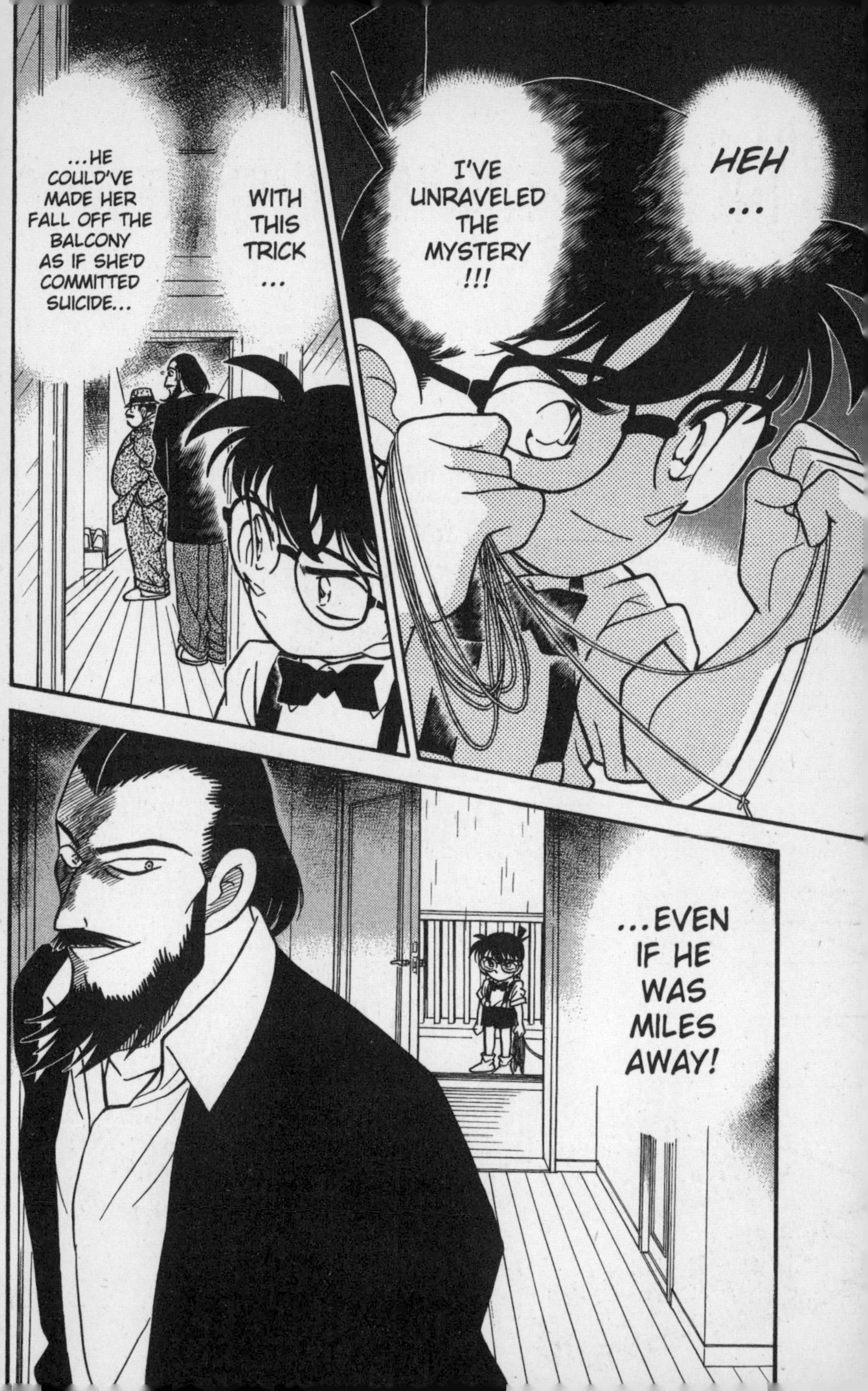
HEH ...
I'VE UNRAVELED THE MYSTERY !!!
WITH THIS TRICK ...
...HE COULD'VE MADE HER FALL OFF THE BALCONY AS IF SHE'D COMMITTED SUICIDE...
...EVEN IF HE WAS MILES AWAY!

FILE 7:
THE FLOWER AND THE BUTTERFLY

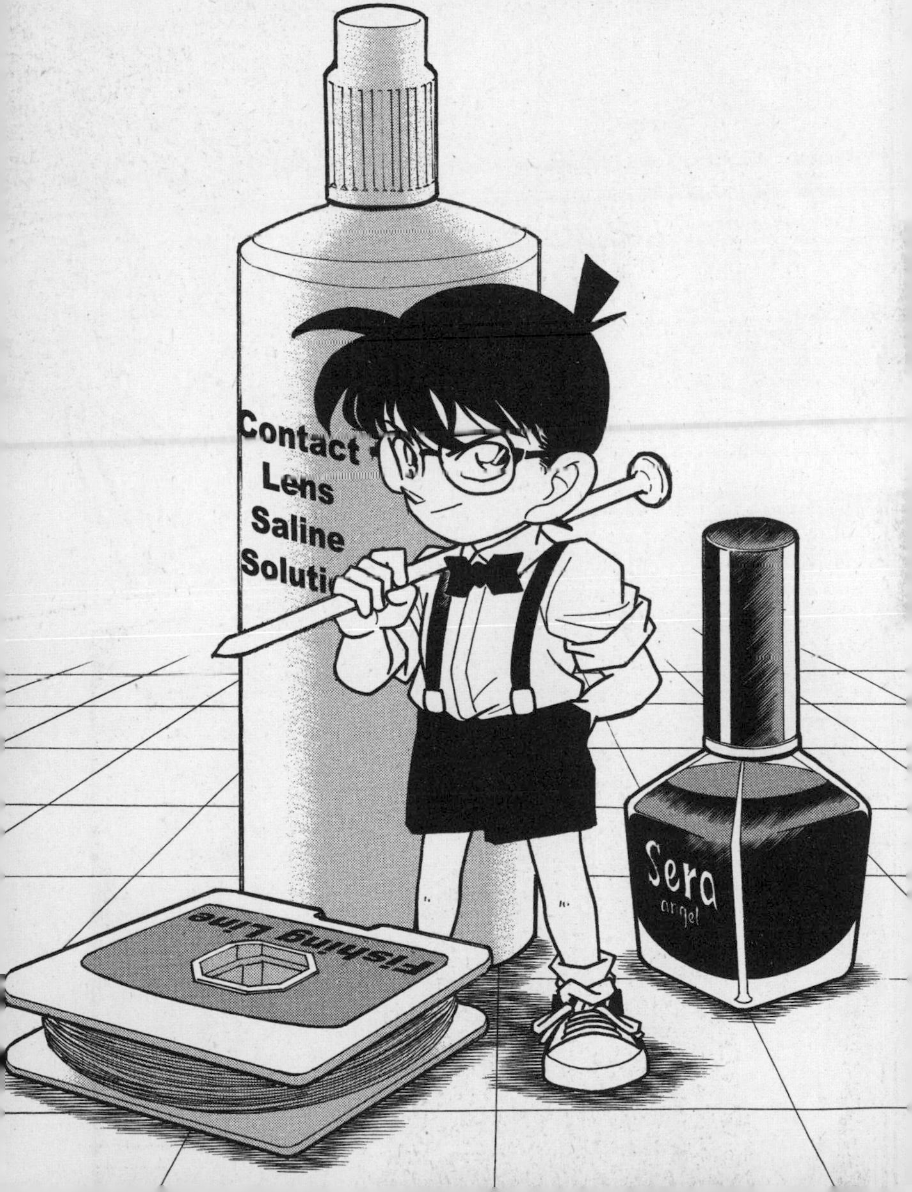
Contact
Lens
Saline
Soluti
Fishing Line
Sera
angel

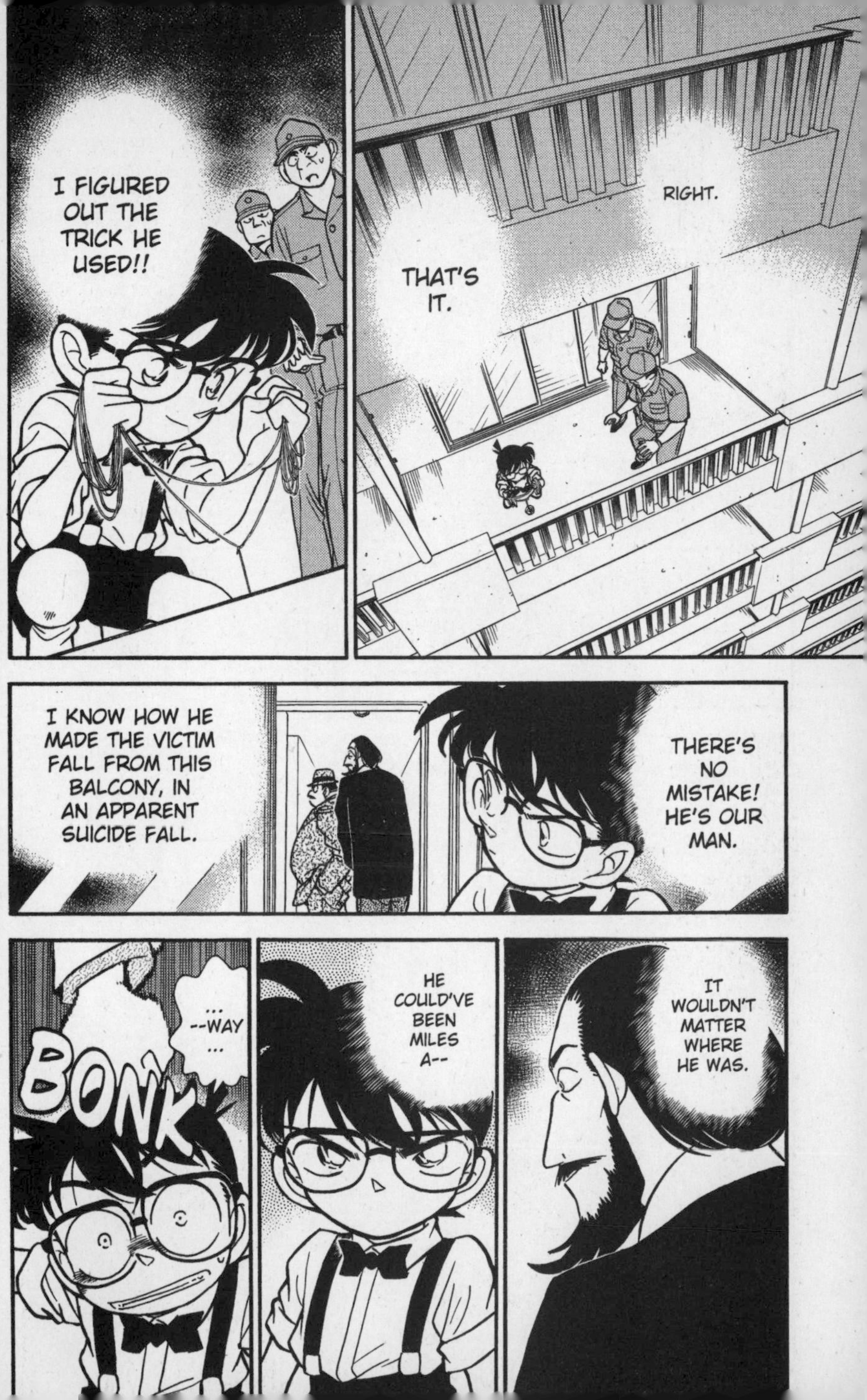
RIGHT.
THAT'S IT.
I FIGURED OUT THE TRICK HE USED!!
THERE'S NO MISTAKE! HE'S OUR MAN.
I KNOW HOW HE MADE THE VICTIM FALL FROM THIS BALCONY, IN AN APPARENT SUICIDE FALL.
IT WOULDN'T MATTER WHERE HE WAS.
HE COULD'VE BEEN MILES A--
... --WAY ...
BONK

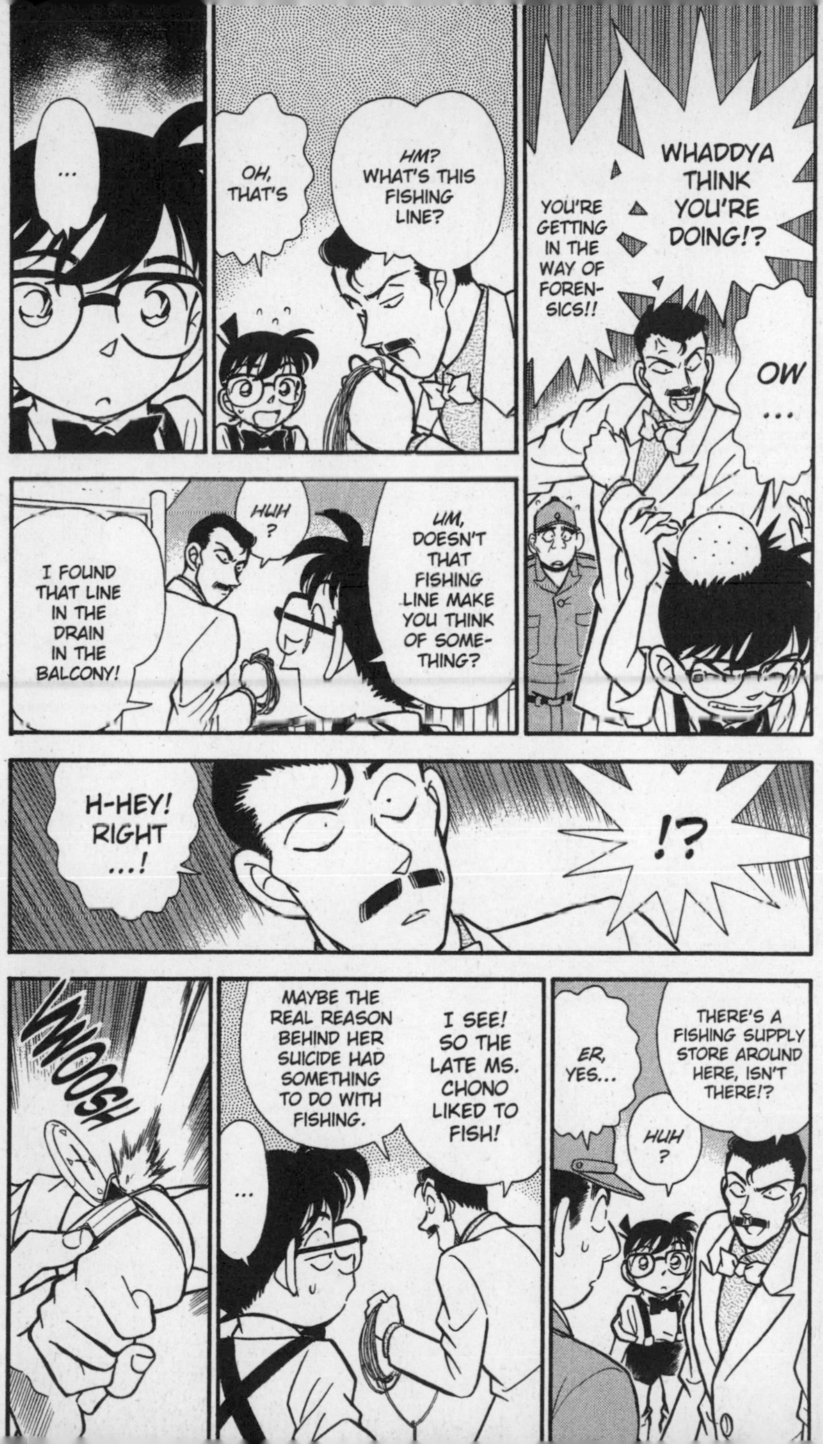
WHADDYA THINK YOU'RE DOING!?
YOU'RE GETTING IN THE WAY OF FOREN-SICS!!
OW ...
HM? WHAT'S THIS FISHING LINE?
OH, THAT'S
...
UM, DOESN'T THAT FISHING LINE MAKE YOU THINK OF SOME-THING?
HUH ?
I FOUND THAT LINE IN THE DRAIN IN THE BALCONY!
!?
H-HEY! RIGHT ...!
THERE'S A FISHING SUPPLY STORE AROUND HERE, ISN'T THERE!?
HUH ?
ER, YES...
I SEE! SO THE LATE MS. CHONO LIKED TO FISH!
MAYBE THE REAL REASON BEHIND HER SUICIDE HAD SOMETHING TO DO WITH FISHING.
...
WOOSH

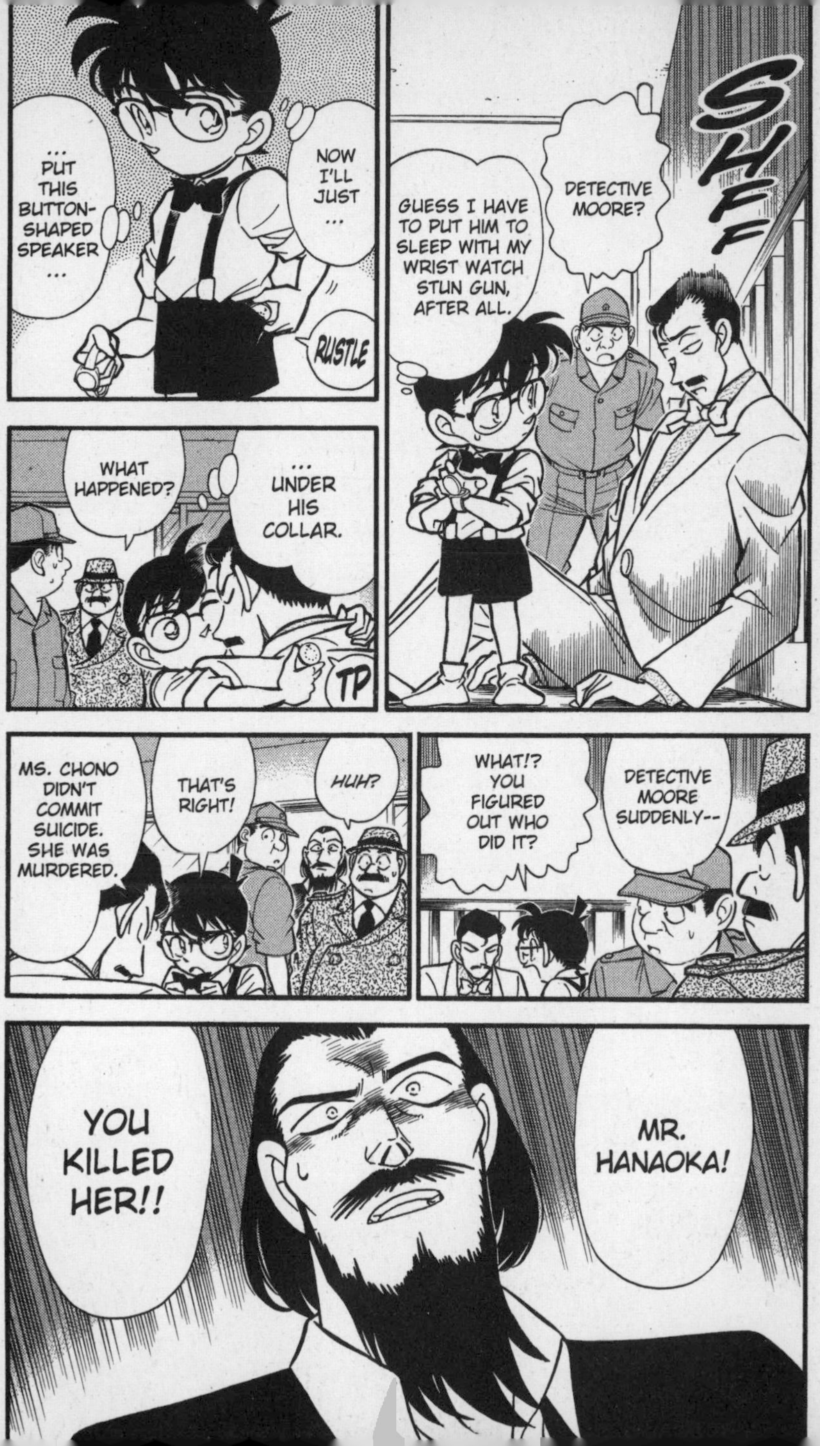
SHFF
DETECTIVE MOORE?
GUESS I HAVE TO PUT HIM TO SLEEP WITH MY WRIST WATCH STUN GUN, AFTER ALL.
NOW I'LL JUST ...
... PUT THIS BUTTON-SHAPED SPEAKER ...
RUSTLE
... UNDER HIS COLLAR.
WHAT HAPPENED?
TP
DETECTIVE MOORE SUDDENLY--
WHAT!? YOU FIGURED OUT WHO DID IT?
HUH?
THAT'S RIGHT!
MS. CHONO DIDN'T COMMIT SUICIDE. SHE WAS MURDERED.
MR. HANAOKA!
YOU KILLED HER!!

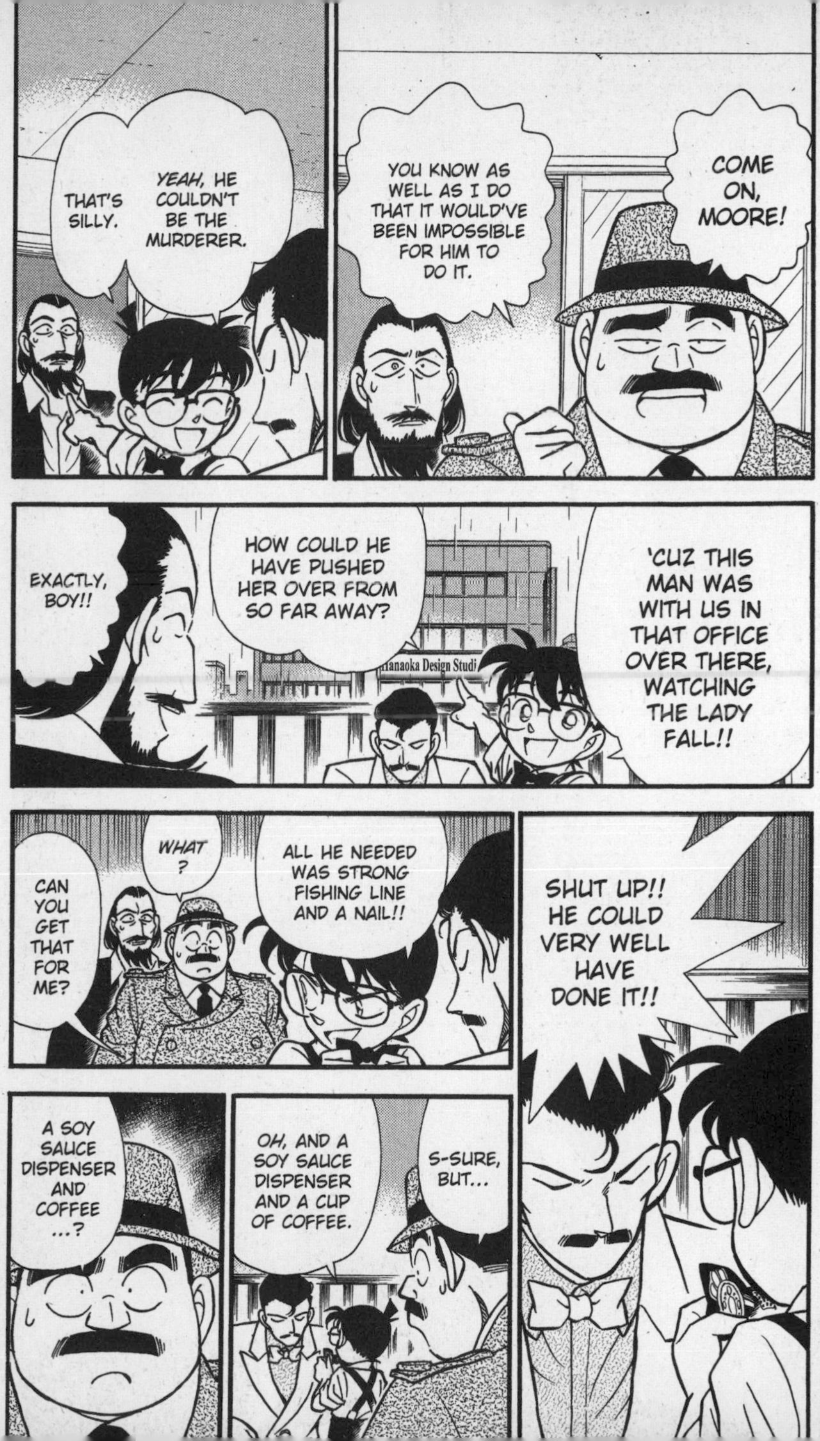
COME ON, MOORE!
YOU KNOW AS WELL AS I DO THAT IT WOULD'VE BEEN IMPOSSIBLE FOR HIM TO DO IT.
YEAH, HE COULDN'T BE THE MURDERER.
THAT'S SILLY.
'CUZ THIS MAN WAS WITH US IN THAT OFFICE OVER THERE, WATCHING THE LADY FALL!!
Hanaoka Design Studi
HOW COULD HE HAVE PUSHED HER OVER FROM SO FAR AWAY?
EXACTLY, BOY!!
SHUT UP!! HE COULD VERY WELL HAVE DONE IT!!
ALL HE NEEDED WAS STRONG FISHING LINE AND A NAIL!!
WHAT?
CAN YOU GET THAT FOR ME?
S-SURE, BUT...
OH, AND A SOY SAUCE DISPENSER AND A CUP OF COFFEE.
A SOY SAUCE DISPENSER AND COFFEE ...?

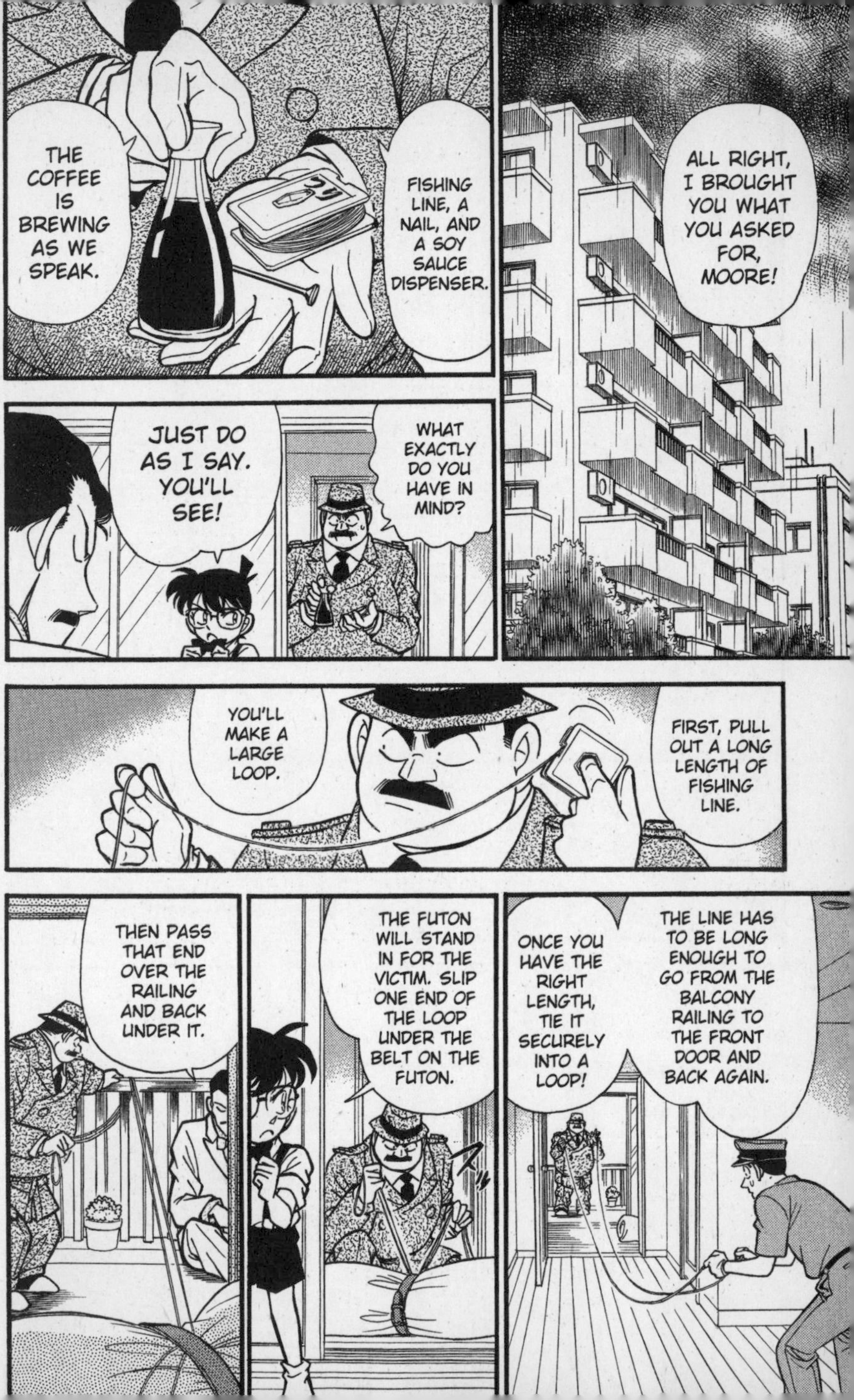
ALL RIGHT, I BROUGHT YOU WHAT YOU ASKED FOR, MOORE!
FISHING LINE, A NAIL, AND A SOY SAUCE DISPENSER.
THE COFFEE IS BREWING AS WE SPEAK.
WHAT EXACTLY DO YOU HAVE IN MIND?
JUST DO AS I SAY. YOU'LL SEE!
FIRST, PULL OUT A LONG LENGTH OF FISHING LINE.
YOU'LL MAKE A LARGE LOOP.
THE LINE HAS TO BE LONG ENOUGH TO GO FROM THE BALCONY RAILING TO THE FRONT DOOR AND BACK AGAIN.
ONCE YOU HAVE THE RIGHT LENGTH, TIE IT SECURELY INTO A LOOP!
THE FUTON WILL STAND IN FOR THE VICTIM. SLIP ONE END OF THE LOOP UNDER THE BELT ON THE FUTON.
THEN PASS THAT END OVER THE RAILING AND BACK UNDER IT.

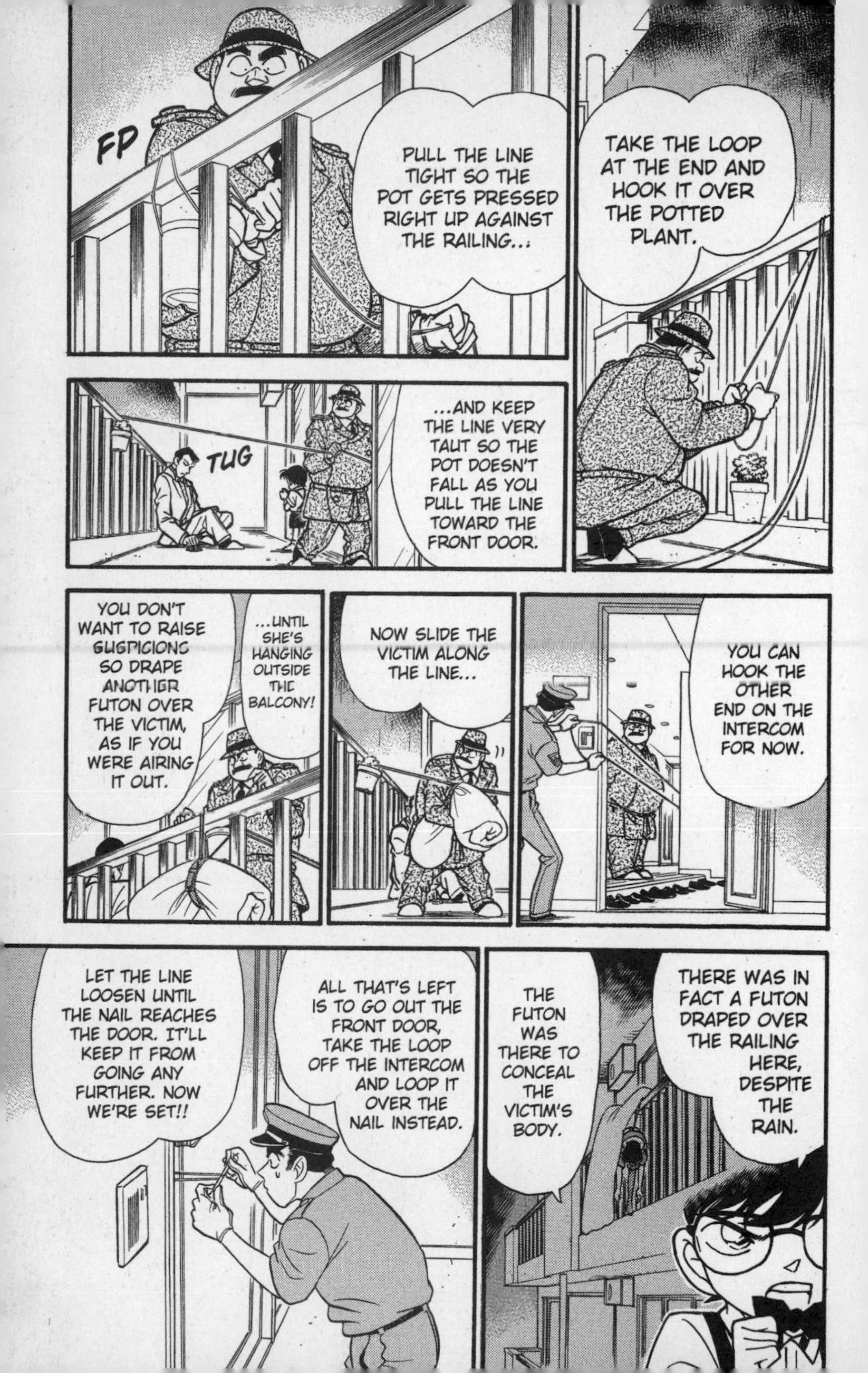
TAKE THE LOOP AT THE END AND HOOK IT OVER THE POTTED PLANT.
PULL THE LINE TIGHT SO THE POT GETS PRESSED RIGHT UP AGAINST THE RAILING...
FP
...AND KEEP THE LINE VERY TAUT SO THE POT DOESN'T FALL AS YOU PULL THE LINE TOWARD THE FRONT DOOR.
TUG
YOU CAN HOOK THE OTHER END ON THE INTERCOM FOR NOW.
NOW SLIDE THE VICTIM ALONG THE LINE...
...UNTIL SHE'S HANGING OUTSIDE THE BALCONY!
YOU DON'T WANT TO RAISE SUSPICIONS SO DRAPE ANOTHER FUTON OVER THE VICTIM, AS IF YOU WERE AIRING IT OUT.
THERE WAS IN FACT A FUTON DRAPED OVER THE RAILING HERE, DESPITE THE RAIN.
THE FUTON WAS THERE TO CONCEAL THE VICTIM'S BODY.
ALL THAT'S LEFT IS TO GO OUT THE FRONT DOOR, TAKE THE LOOP OFF THE INTERCOM AND LOOP IT OVER THE NAIL INSTEAD.
LET THE LINE LOOSEN UNTIL THE NAIL REACHES THE DOOR. IT'LL KEEP IT FROM GOING ANY FURTHER. NOW WE'RE SET!!

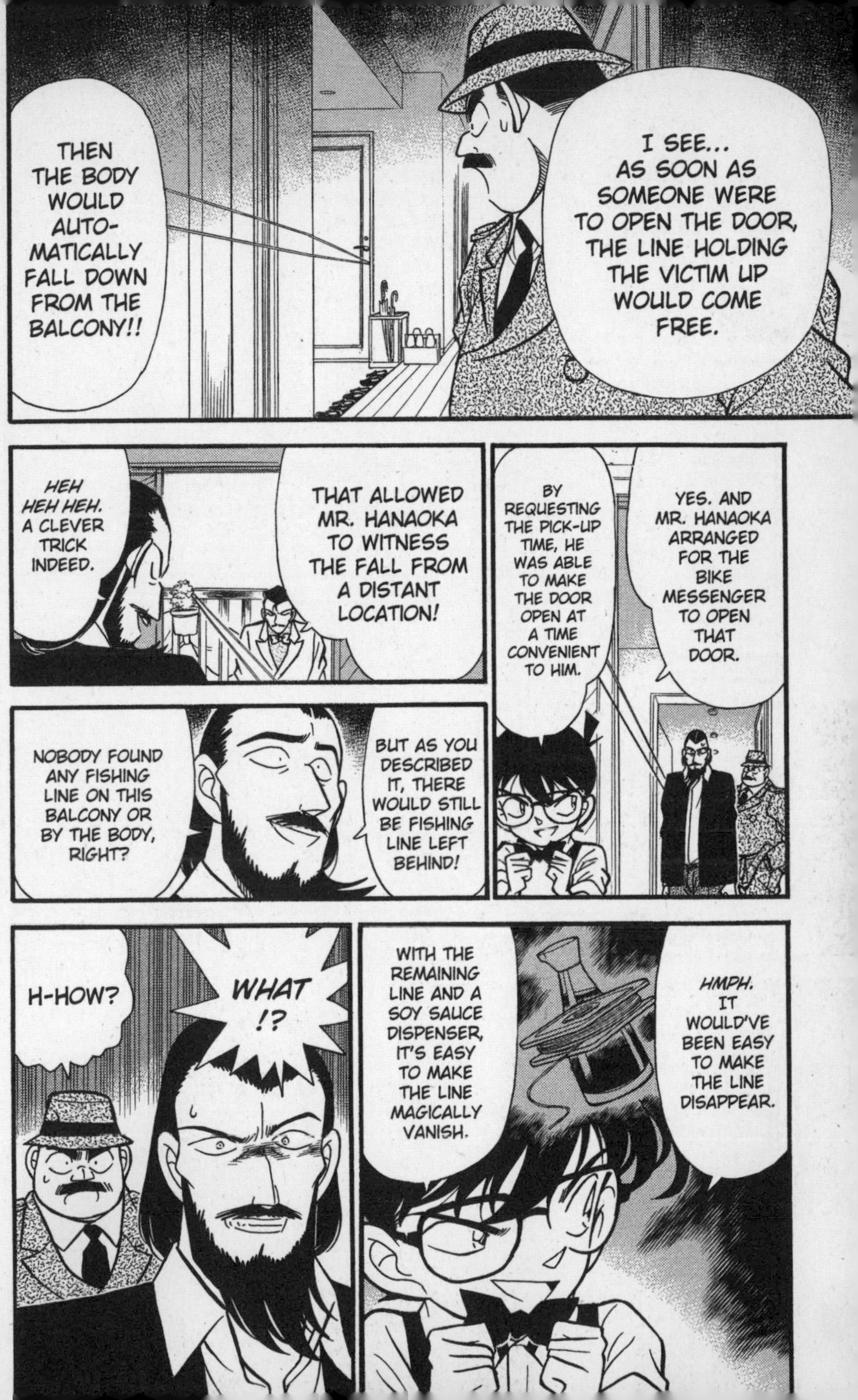
I SEE... AS SOON AS SOMEONE WERE TO OPEN THE DOOR, THE LINE HOLDING THE VICTIM UP WOULD COME FREE.
THEN THE BODY WOULD AUTO-MATICALLY FALL DOWN FROM THE BALCONY!!
YES. AND MR. HANAOKA ARRANGED FOR THE BIKE MESSENGER TO OPEN THAT DOOR.
BY REQUESTING THE PICK-UP TIME, HE WAS ABLE TO MAKE THE DOOR OPEN AT A TIME CONVENIENT TO HIM.
THAT ALLOWED MR. HANAOKA TO WITNESS THE FALL FROM A DISTANT LOCATION!
HEH HEH HEH. A CLEVER TRICK INDEED.
BUT AS YOU DESCRIBED IT, THERE WOULD STILL BE FISHING LINE LEFT BEHIND!
NOBODY FOUND ANY FISHING LINE ON THIS BALCONY OR BY THE BODY, RIGHT?
HMPH. IT WOULD'VE BEEN EASY TO MAKE THE LINE DISAPPEAR.
WITH THE REMAINING LINE AND A SOY SAUCE DISPENSER, IT'S EASY TO MAKE THE LINE MAGICALLY VANISH.
WHAT !?
H-HOW?

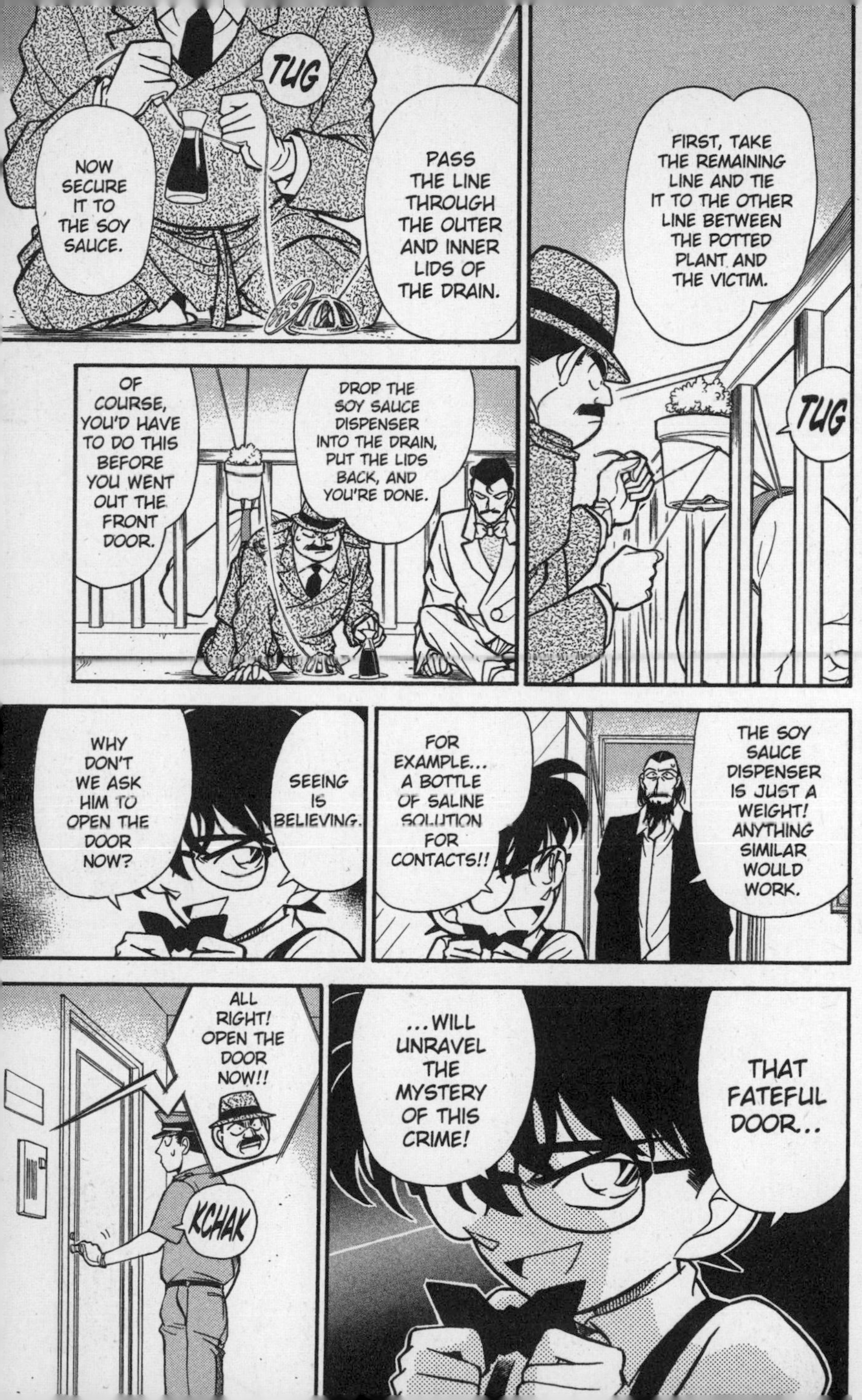
FIRST, TAKE THE REMAINING LINE AND TIE IT TO THE OTHER LINE BETWEEN THE POTTED PLANT AND THE VICTIM.
TUG
PASS THE LINE THROUGH THE OUTER AND INNER LIDS OF THE DRAIN.
TUG
NOW SECURE IT TO THE SOY SAUCE.
DROP THE SOY SAUCE DISPENSER INTO THE DRAIN, PUT THE LIDS BACK, AND YOU'RE DONE.
OF COURSE, YOU'D HAVE TO DO THIS BEFORE YOU WENT OUT THE FRONT DOOR.
THE SOY SAUCE DISPENSER IS JUST A WEIGHT! ANYTHING SIMILAR WOULD WORK.
FOR EXAMPLE... A BOTTLE OF SALINE SOLUTION FOR CONTACTS!!
SEEING IS BELIEVING.
WHY DON'T WE ASK HIM TO OPEN THE DOOR NOW?
THAT FATEFUL DOOR...
...WILL UNRAVEL THE MYSTERY OF THIS CRIME!
ALL RIGHT! OPEN THE DOOR NOW!!
KCHAK

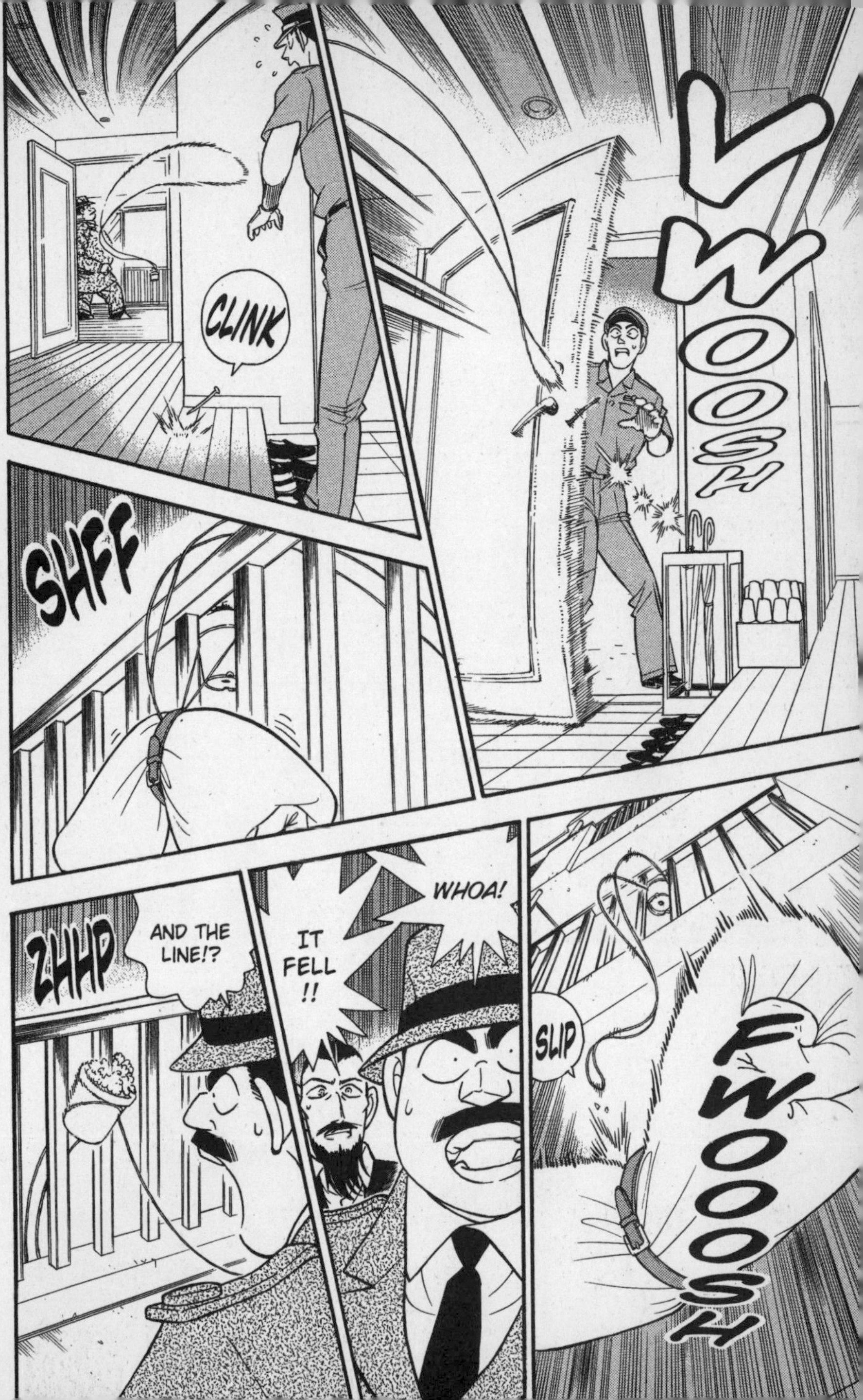
VWOOSH
CLINK
SHFF
SLIP
FWOOOSH
WHOA!
IT FELL!!
ZHHP
AND THE LINE!?

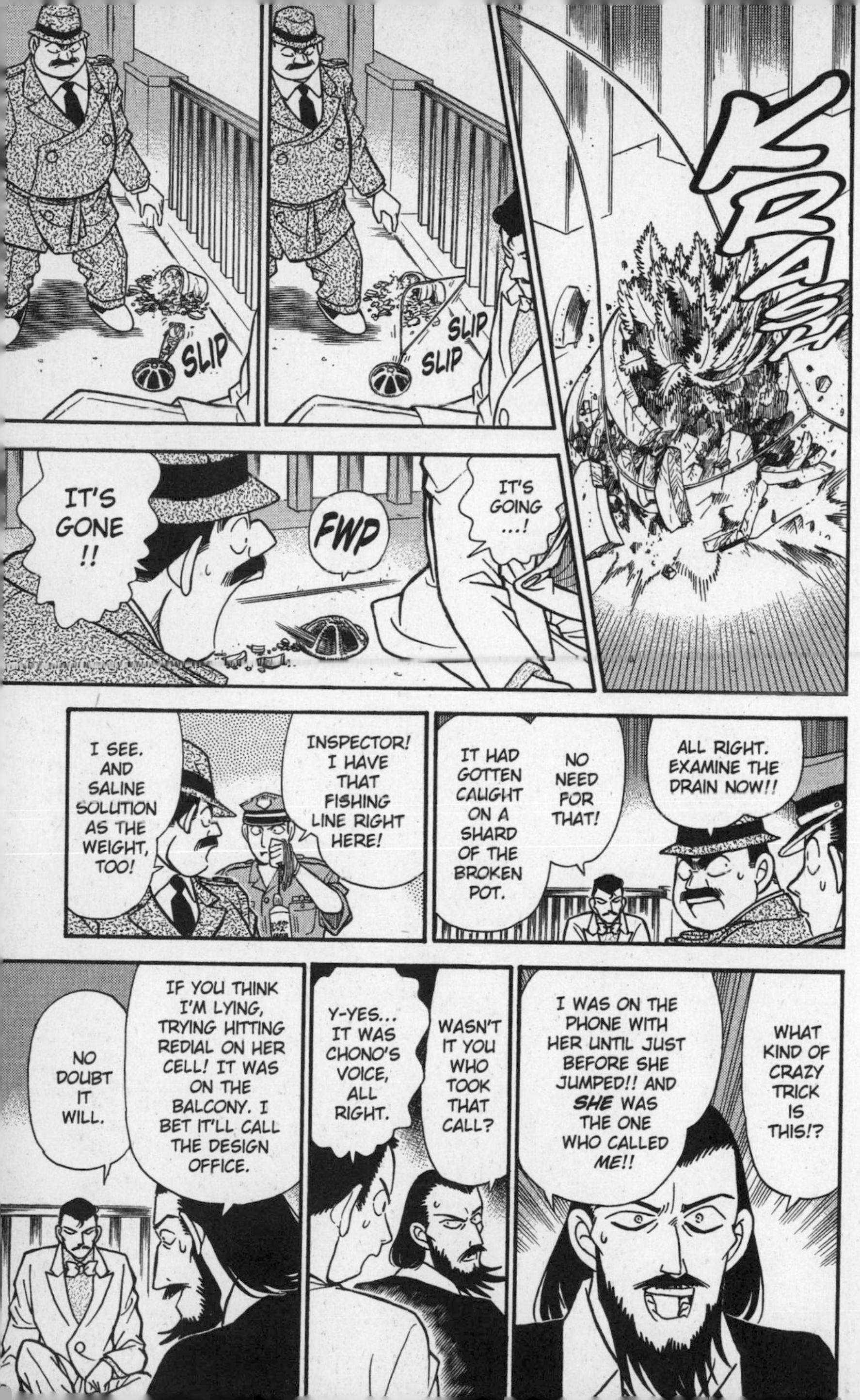
KRASH
SLIP
SLIP
SLIP
IT'S GOING ...!
FWP
IT'S GONE !!
ALL RIGHT. EXAMINE THE DRAIN NOW!!
NO NEED FOR THAT!
IT HAD GOTTEN CAUGHT ON A SHARD OF THE BROKEN POT.
INSPECTOR! I HAVE THAT FISHING LINE RIGHT HERE!
I SEE. AND SALINE SOLUTION AS THE WEIGHT, TOO!
WHAT KIND OF CRAZY TRICK IS THIS!?
I WAS ON THE PHONE WITH HER UNTIL JUST BEFORE SHE JUMPED!! AND *SHE* WAS THE ONE WHO CALLED *ME*!!
WASN'T IT YOU WHO TOOK THAT CALL?
Y-YES... IT WAS CHONO'S VOICE, ALL RIGHT.
IF YOU THINK I'M LYING, TRYING HITTING REDIAL ON HER CELL! IT WAS ON THE BALCONY. I BET IT'LL CALL THE DESIGN OFFICE.
NO DOUBT IT WILL.

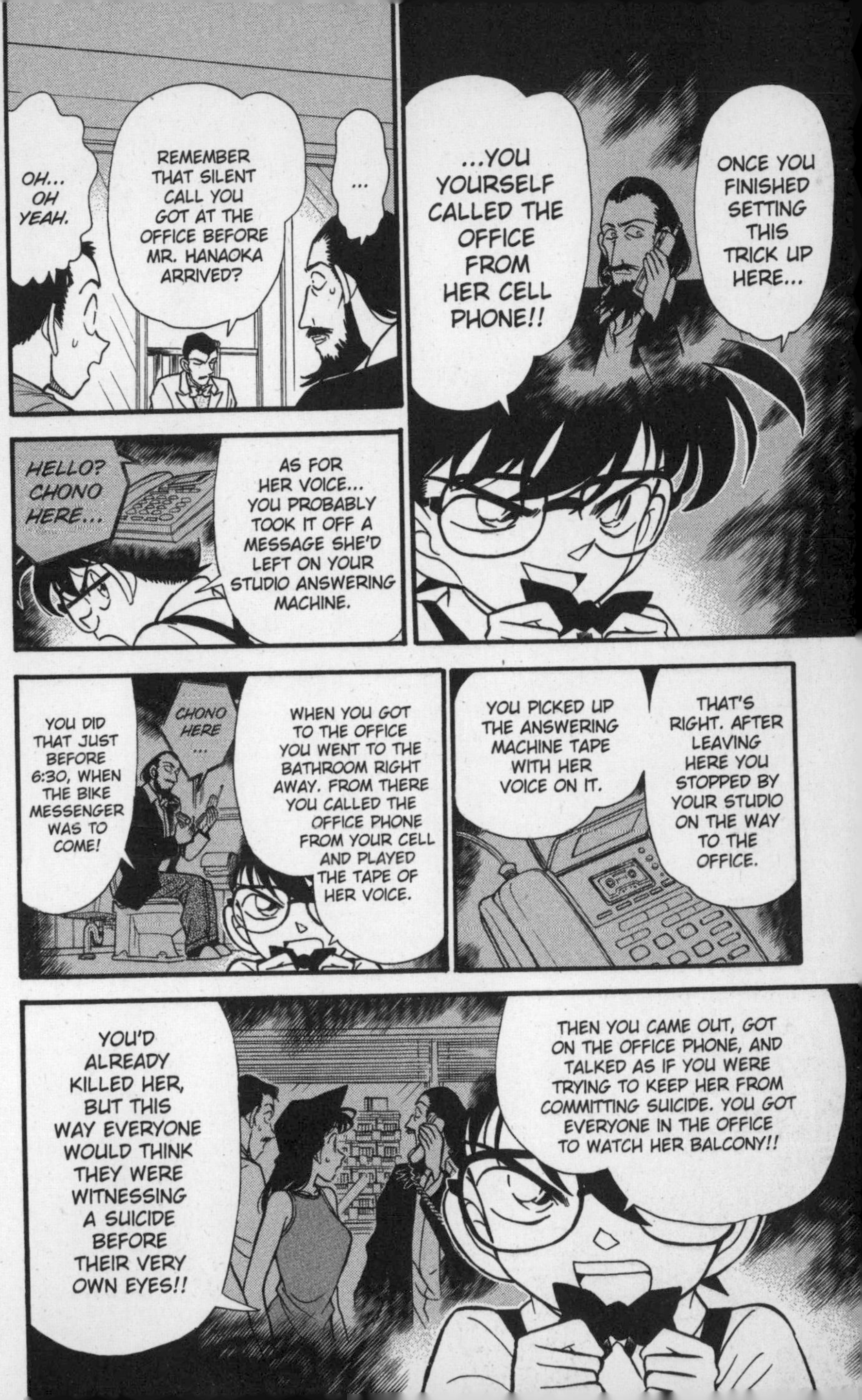
ONCE YOU FINISHED SETTING THIS TRICK UP HERE...
...YOU YOURSELF CALLED THE OFFICE FROM HER CELL PHONE!!
...
REMEMBER THAT SILENT CALL YOU GOT AT THE OFFICE BEFORE MR. HANAOKA ARRIVED?
OH... OH YEAH.
AS FOR HER VOICE... YOU PROBABLY TOOK IT OFF A MESSAGE SHE'D LEFT ON YOUR STUDIO ANSWERING MACHINE.
HELLO? CHONO HERE...
THAT'S RIGHT. AFTER LEAVING HERE YOU STOPPED BY YOUR STUDIO ON THE WAY TO THE OFFICE.
YOU PICKED UP THE ANSWERING MACHINE TAPE WITH HER VOICE ON IT.
WHEN YOU GOT TO THE OFFICE YOU WENT TO THE BATHROOM RIGHT AWAY. FROM THERE YOU CALLED THE OFFICE PHONE FROM YOUR CELL AND PLAYED THE TAPE OF HER VOICE.
CHONO HERE ...
YOU DID THAT JUST BEFORE 6:30, WHEN THE BIKE MESSENGER WAS TO COME!
THEN YOU CAME OUT, GOT ON THE OFFICE PHONE, AND TALKED AS IF YOU WERE TRYING TO KEEP HER FROM COMMITTING SUICIDE. YOU GOT EVERYONE IN THE OFFICE TO WATCH HER BALCONY!!
YOU'D ALREADY KILLED HER, BUT THIS WAY EVERYONE WOULD THINK THEY WERE WITNESSING A SUICIDE BEFORE THEIR VERY OWN EYES!!

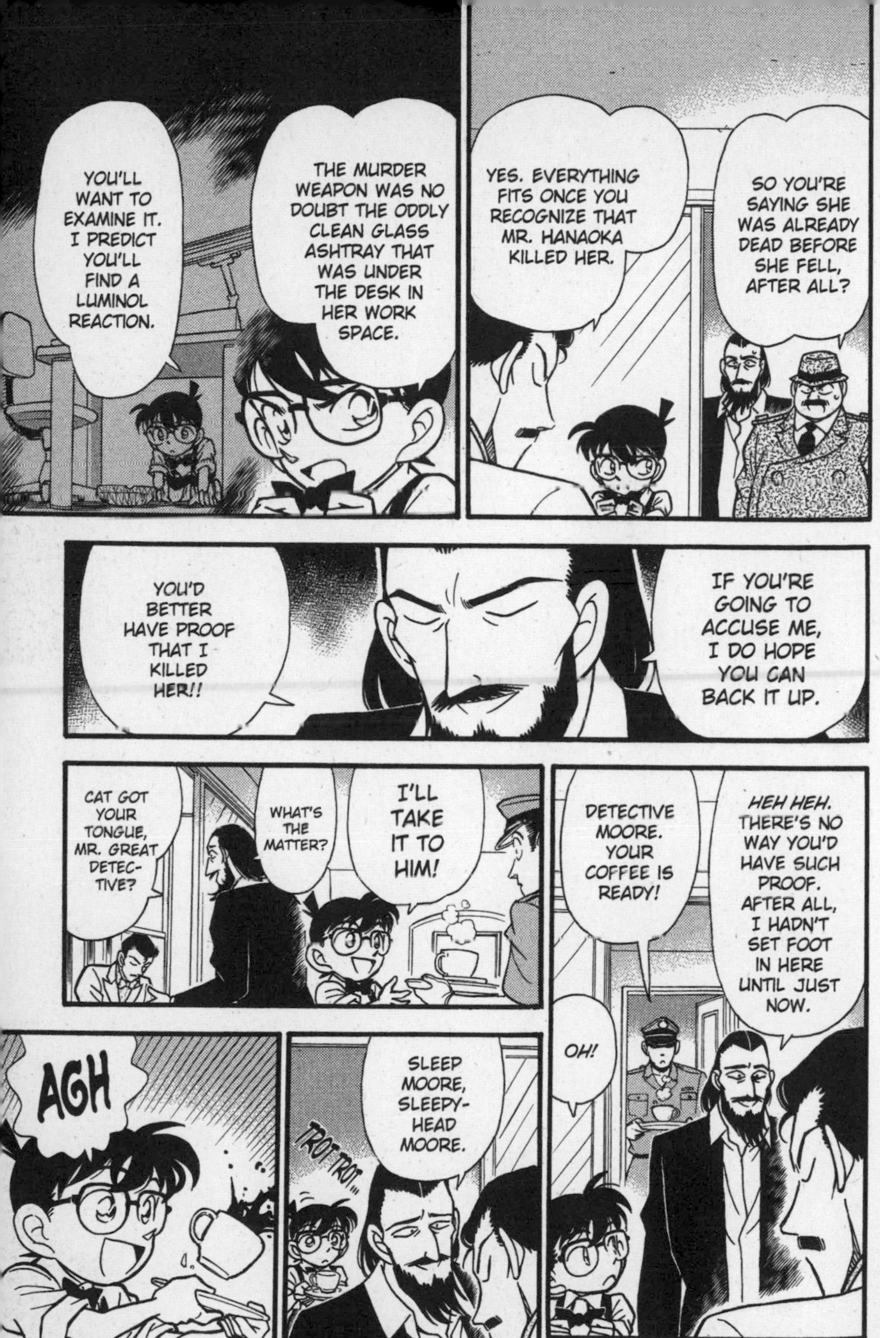
SO YOU'RE SAYING SHE WAS ALREADY DEAD BEFORE SHE FELL, AFTER ALL?
YES. EVERYTHING FITS ONCE YOU RECOGNIZE THAT MR. HANAOKA KILLED HER.
THE MURDER WEAPON WAS NO DOUBT THE ODDLY CLEAN GLASS ASHTRAY THAT WAS UNDER THE DESK IN HER WORK SPACE.
YOU'LL WANT TO EXAMINE IT. I PREDICT YOU'LL FIND A LUMINOL REACTION.
IF YOU'RE GOING TO ACCUSE ME, I DO HOPE YOU CAN BACK IT UP.
YOU'D BETTER HAVE PROOF THAT I KILLED HER!!
HEH HEH. THERE'S NO WAY YOU'D HAVE SUCH PROOF. AFTER ALL, I HADN'T SET FOOT IN HERE UNTIL JUST NOW.
DETECTIVE MOORE. YOUR COFFEE IS READY!
OH!
I'LL TAKE IT TO HIM!
WHAT'S THE MATTER?
CAT GOT YOUR TONGUE, MR. GREAT DETECTIVE?
SLEEP MOORE, SLEEPY-HEAD MOORE.
TROT TROT
AGH

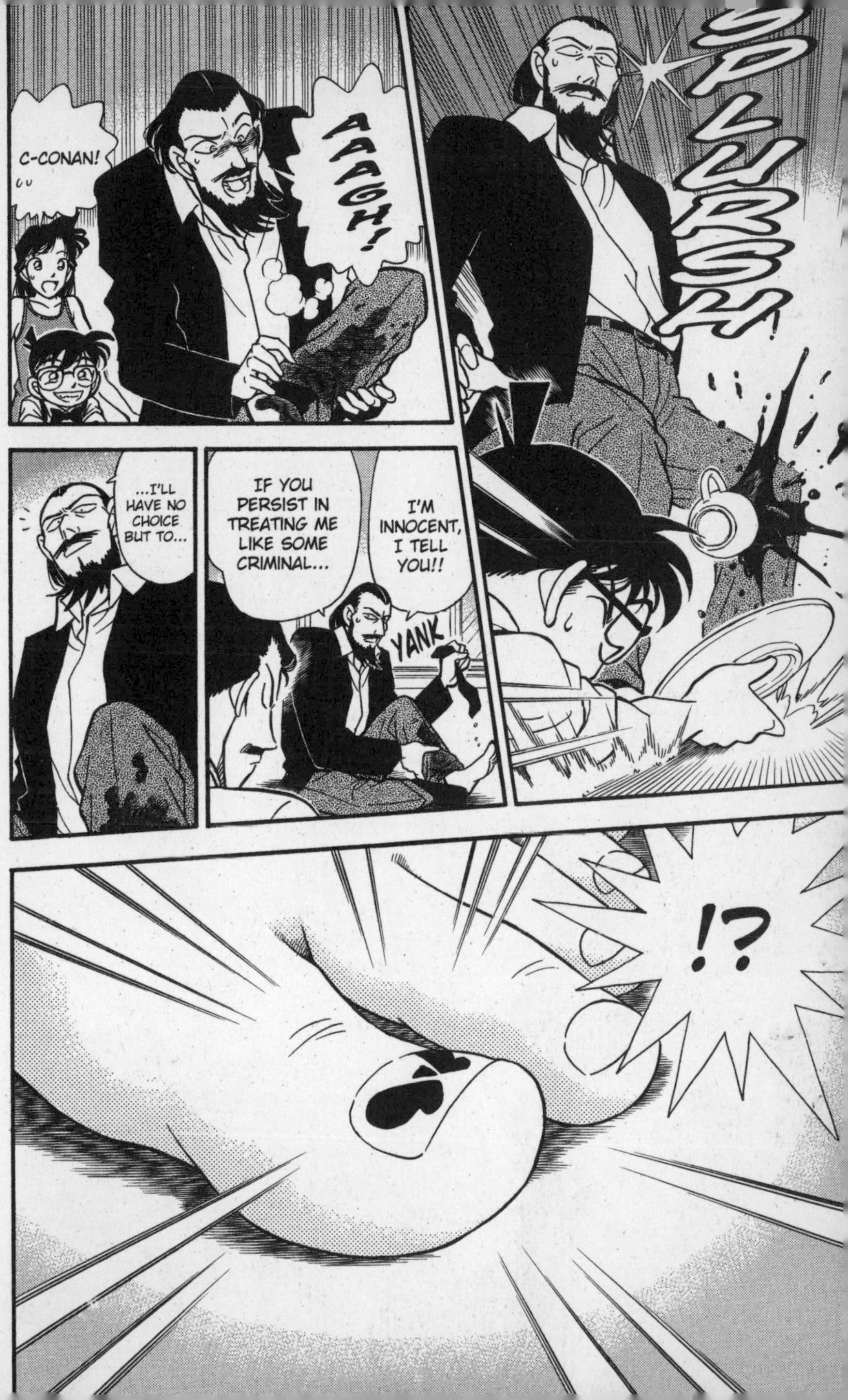
SPLURSH!
AAAGH!
C-CONAN!
I'M INNOCENT, I TELL YOU!!
IF YOU PERSIST IN TREATING ME LIKE SOME CRIMINAL...
YANK
...I'LL HAVE NO CHOICE BUT TO...
!?

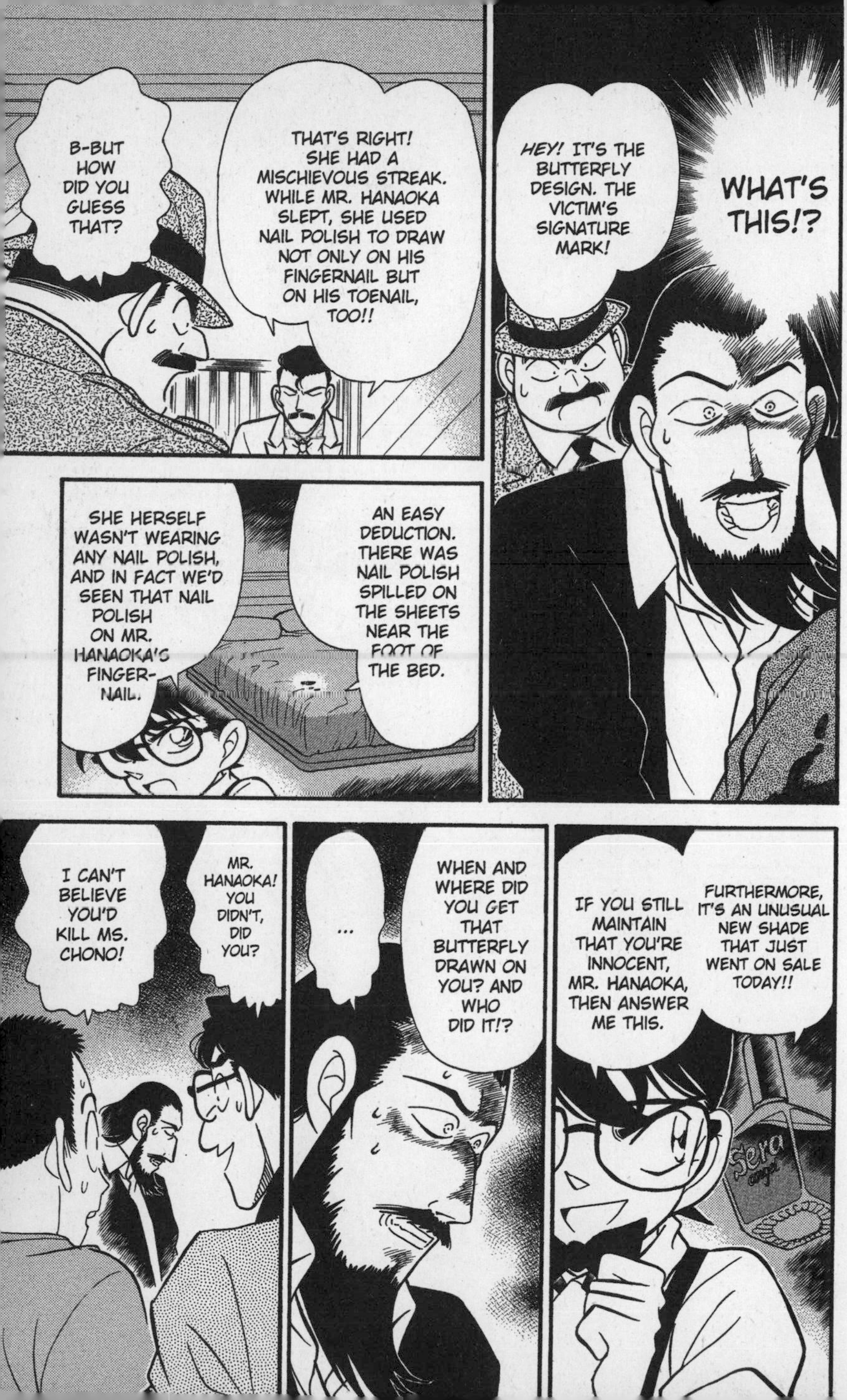
WHAT'S THIS!?
HEY! IT'S THE BUTTERFLY DESIGN. THE VICTIM'S SIGNATURE MARK!
THAT'S RIGHT! SHE HAD A MISCHIEVOUS STREAK. WHILE MR. HANAOKA SLEPT, SHE USED NAIL POLISH TO DRAW NOT ONLY ON HIS FINGERNAIL BUT ON HIS TOENAIL, TOO!!
B-BUT HOW DID YOU GUESS THAT?
AN EASY DEDUCTION. THERE WAS NAIL POLISH SPILLED ON THE SHEETS NEAR THE FOOT OF THE BED.
SHE HERSELF WASN'T WEARING ANY NAIL POLISH, AND IN FACT WE'D SEEN THAT NAIL POLISH ON MR. HANAOKA'S FINGER-NAIL.
FURTHERMORE, IT'S AN UNUSUAL NEW SHADE THAT JUST WENT ON SALE TODAY!!
IF YOU STILL MAINTAIN THAT YOU'RE INNOCENT, MR. HANAOKA, THEN ANSWER ME THIS.
sera angel
WHEN AND WHERE DID YOU GET THAT BUTTERFLY DRAWN ON YOU? AND WHO DID IT!?
...
MR. HANAOKA! YOU DIDN'T, DID YOU?
I CAN'T BELIEVE YOU'D KILL MS. CHONO!

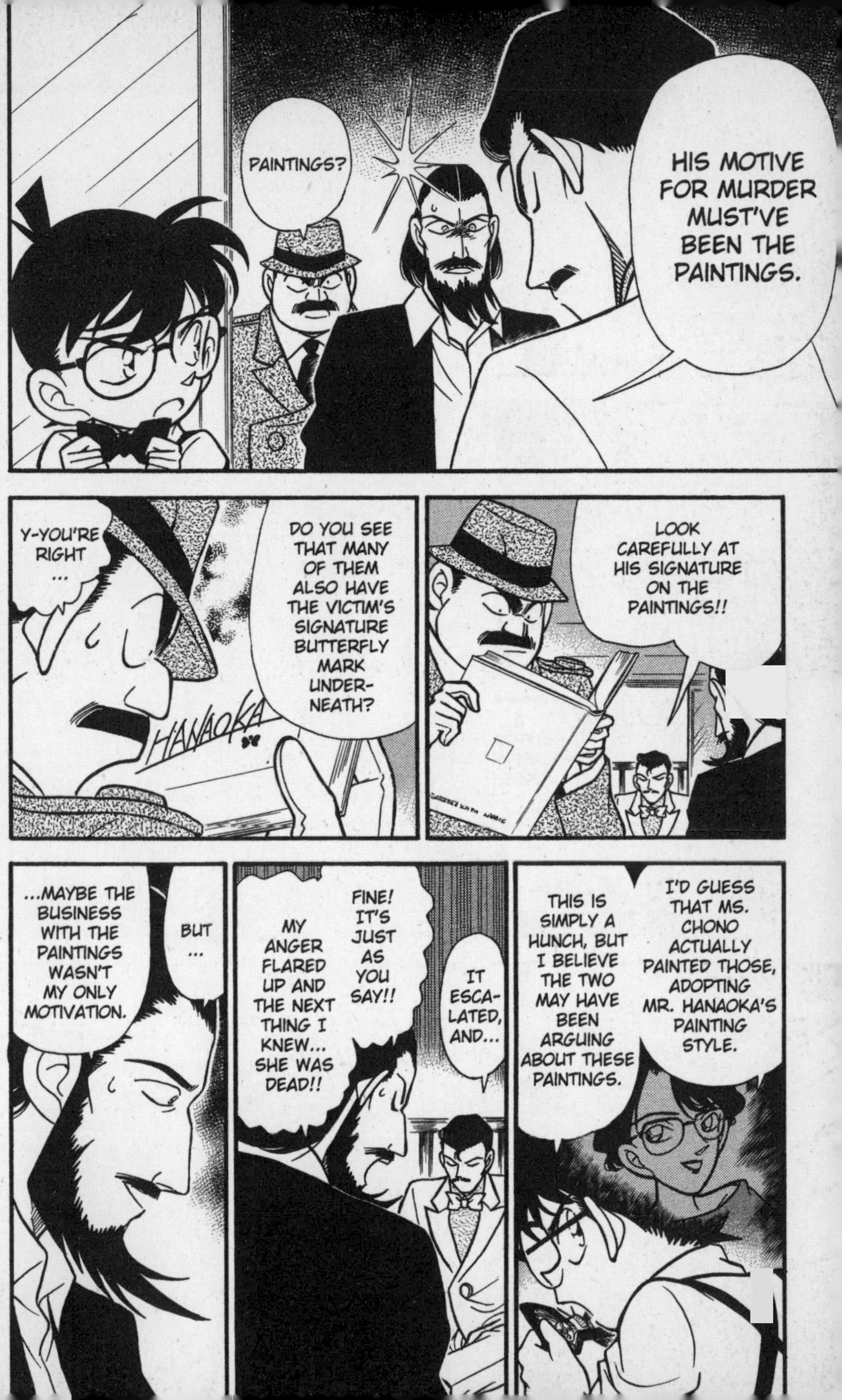
HIS MOTIVE FOR MURDER MUST'VE BEEN THE PAINTINGS.
PAINTINGS?
LOOK CAREFULLY AT HIS SIGNATURE ON THE PAINTINGS!!
DO YOU SEE THAT MANY OF THEM ALSO HAVE THE VICTIM'S SIGNATURE BUTTERFLY MARK UNDERNEATH?
HANAOKA
Y-YOU'RE RIGHT ...
I'D GUESS THAT MS. CHONO ACTUALLY PAINTED THOSE, ADOPTING MR. HANAOKA'S PAINTING STYLE.
THIS IS SIMPLY A HUNCH, BUT I BELIEVE THE TWO MAY HAVE BEEN ARGUING ABOUT THESE PAINTINGS.
IT ESCALATED, AND...
FINE! IT'S JUST AS YOU SAY!!
MY ANGER FLARED UP AND THE NEXT THING I KNEW... SHE WAS DEAD!!
BUT ...
...MAYBE THE BUSINESS WITH THE PAINTINGS WASN'T MY ONLY MOTIVATION.

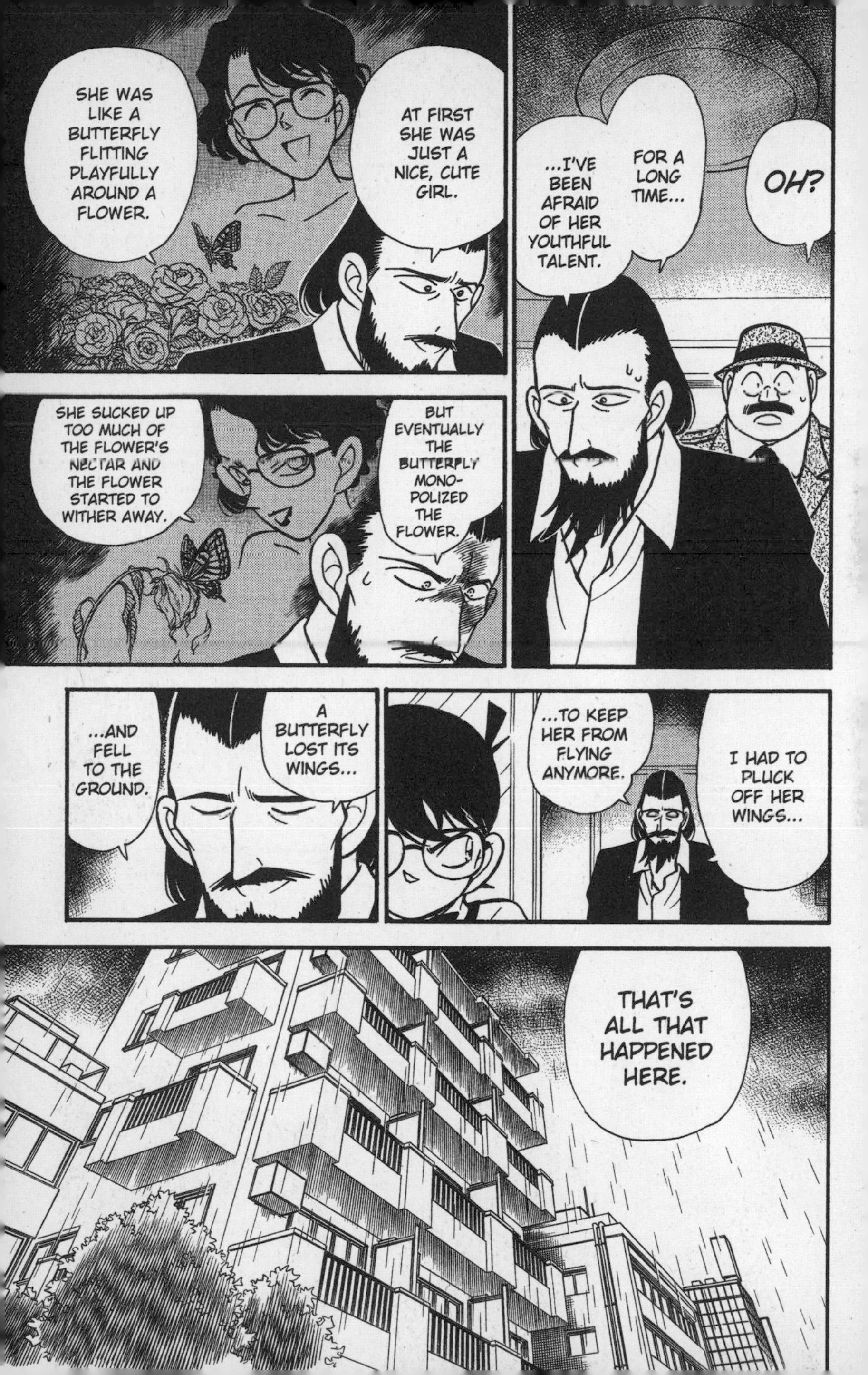
OH?
FOR A LONG TIME...
...I'VE BEEN AFRAID OF HER YOUTHFUL TALENT.
AT FIRST SHE WAS JUST A NICE, CUTE GIRL.
SHE WAS LIKE A BUTTERFLY FLITTING PLAYFULLY AROUND A FLOWER.
BUT EVENTUALLY THE BUTTERFLY MONO-POLIZED THE FLOWER.
SHE SUCKED UP TOO MUCH OF THE FLOWER'S NECTAR AND THE FLOWER STARTED TO WITHER AWAY.
I HAD TO PLUCK OFF HER WINGS...
...TO KEEP HER FROM FLYING ANYMORE.
A BUTTERFLY LOST ITS WINGS...
...AND FELL TO THE GROUND.
THAT'S ALL THAT HAPPENED HERE.

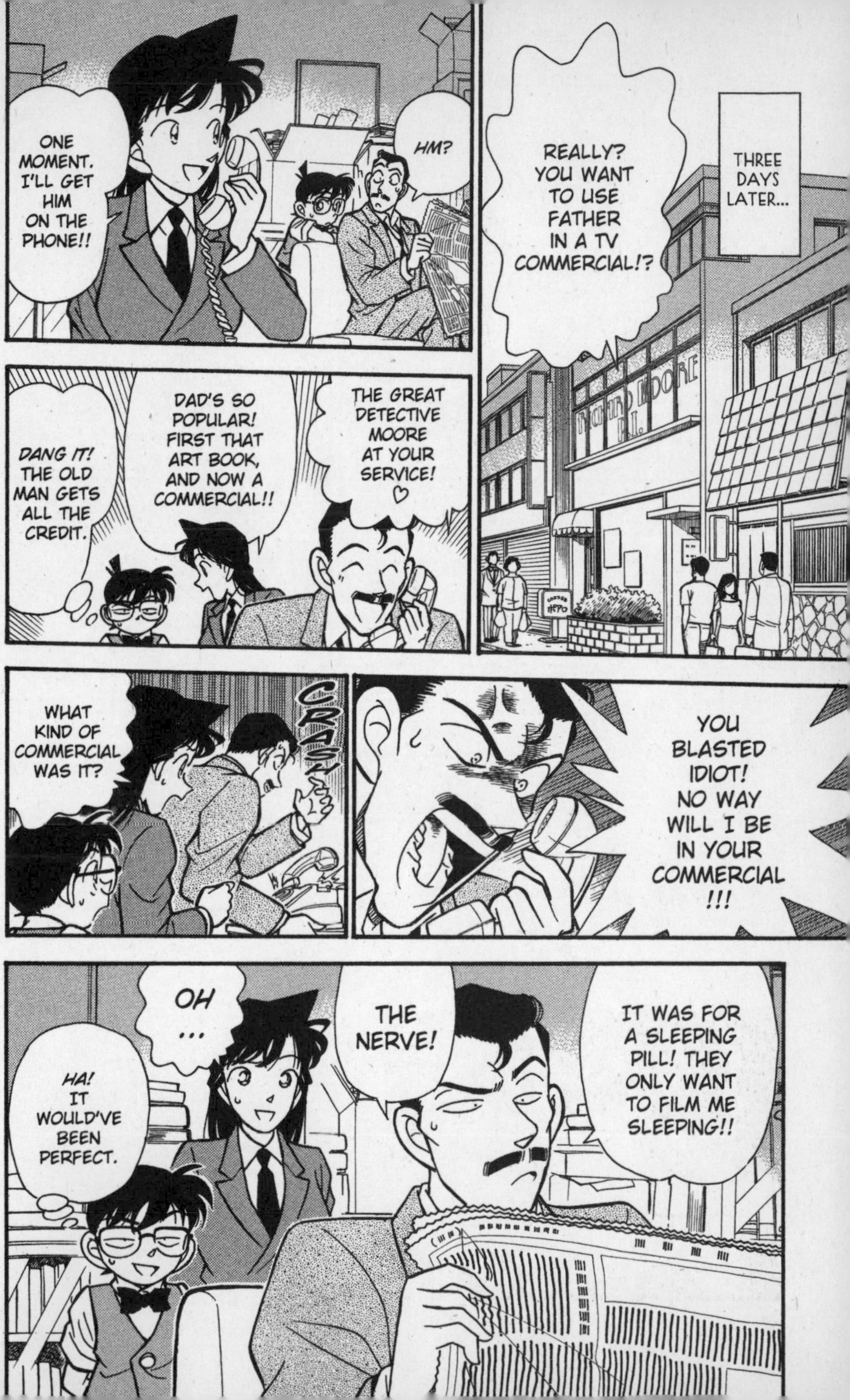
THREE DAYS LATER...
REALLY? YOU WANT TO USE FATHER IN A TV COMMERCIAL!?
RICHARD MOORE P.I.
HM?
ONE MOMENT. I'LL GET HIM ON THE PHONE!!
THE GREAT DETECTIVE MOORE AT YOUR SERVICE! ♡
DAD'S SO POPULAR! FIRST THAT ART BOOK, AND NOW A COMMERCIAL!!
DANG IT! THE OLD MAN GETS ALL THE CREDIT.
YOU BLASTED IDIOT! NO WAY WILL I BE IN YOUR COMMERCIAL !!!
CRASH
WHAT KIND OF COMMERCIAL WAS IT?
IT WAS FOR A SLEEPING PILL! THEY ONLY WANT TO FILM ME SLEEPING!!
THE NERVE!
OH ...
HA! IT WOULD'VE BEEN PERFECT.

FILE 8: THE VANISHING CRIMINAL

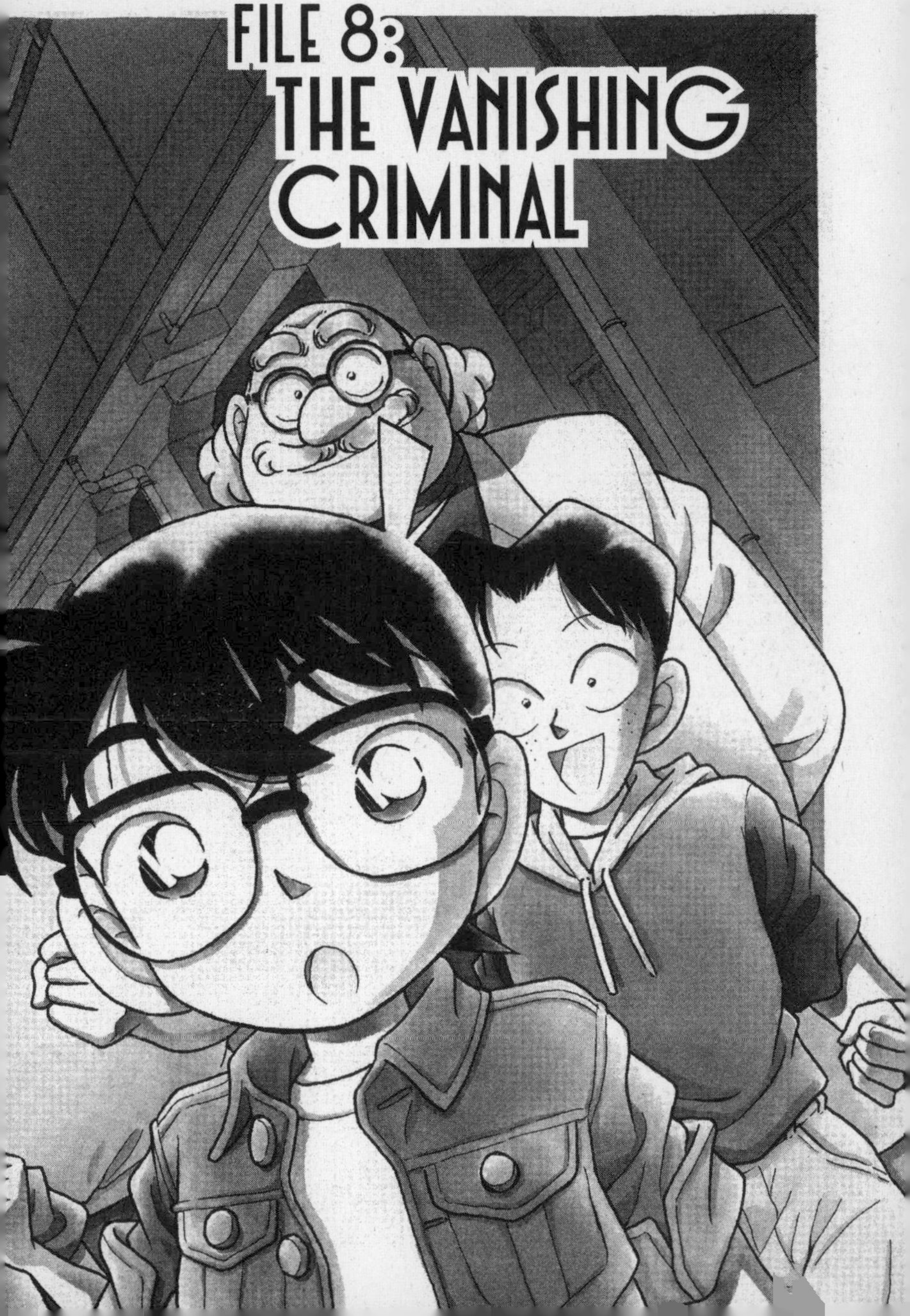

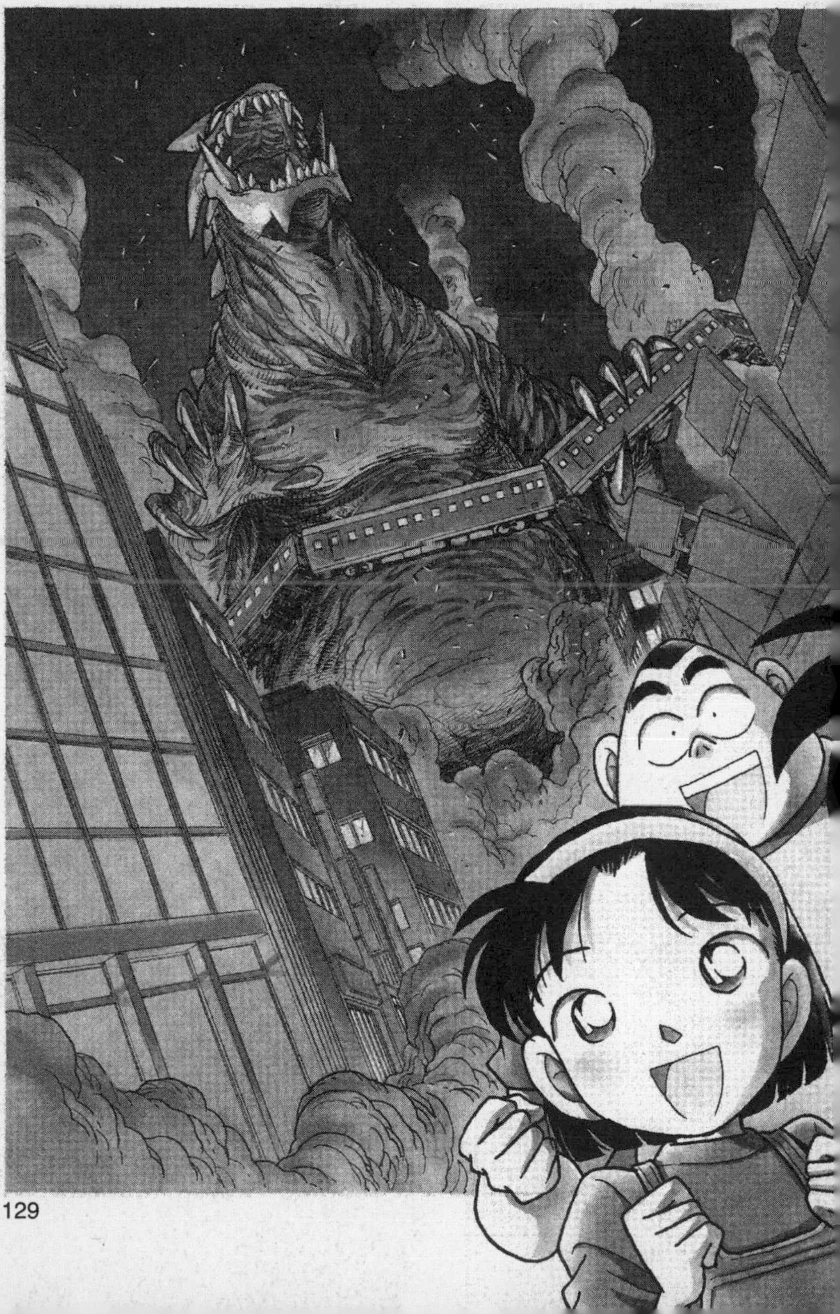

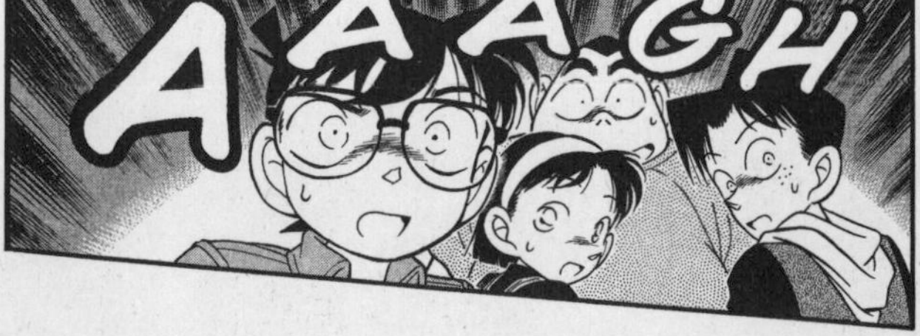
AAAGH

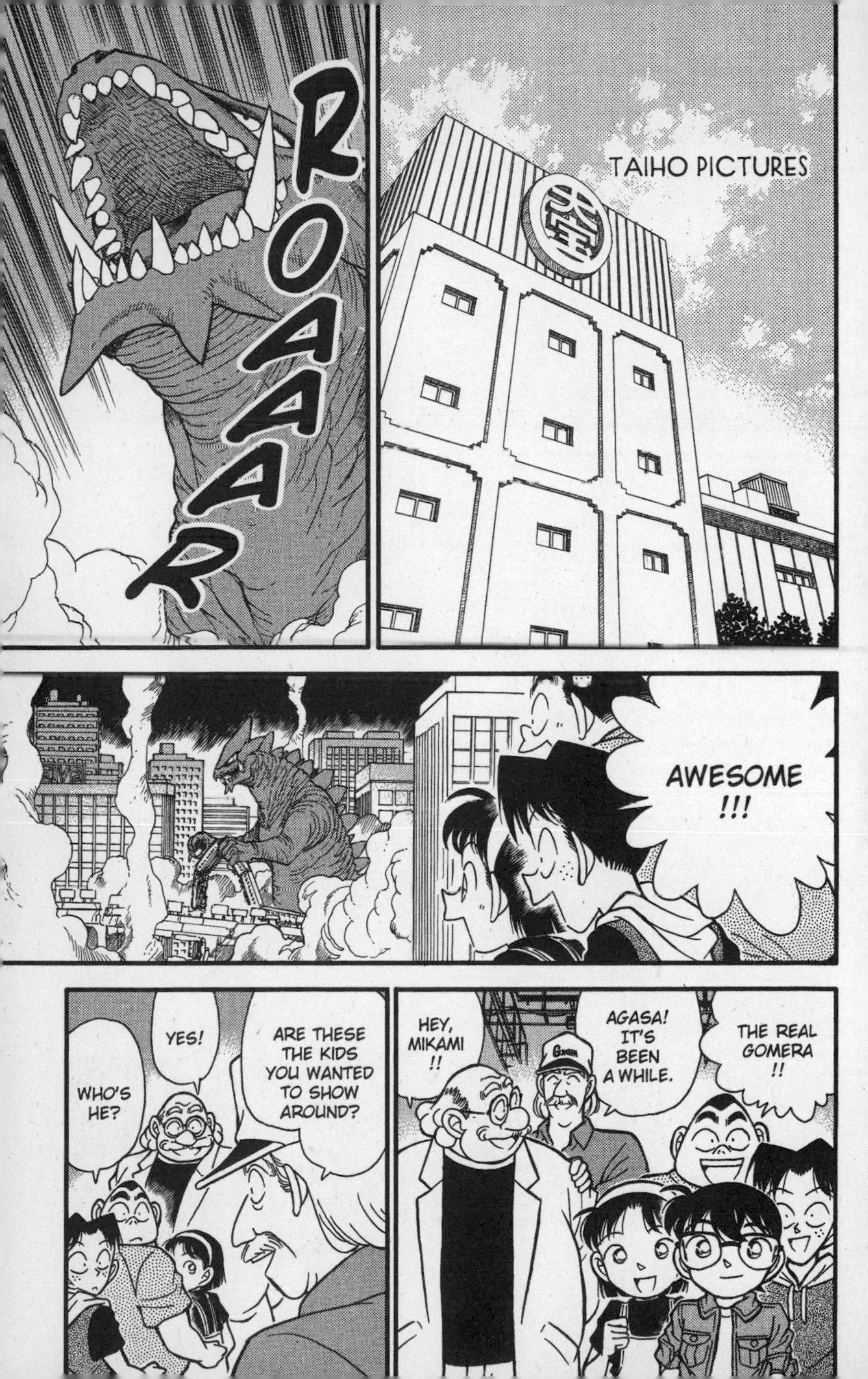
TAIHO PICTURES
ROAAAR
AWESOME !!!
THE REAL GOMERA !!
AGASA! IT'S BEEN A WHILE.
HEY, MIKAMI !!
ARE THESE THE KIDS YOU WANTED TO SHOW AROUND?
YES!
WHO'S HE?

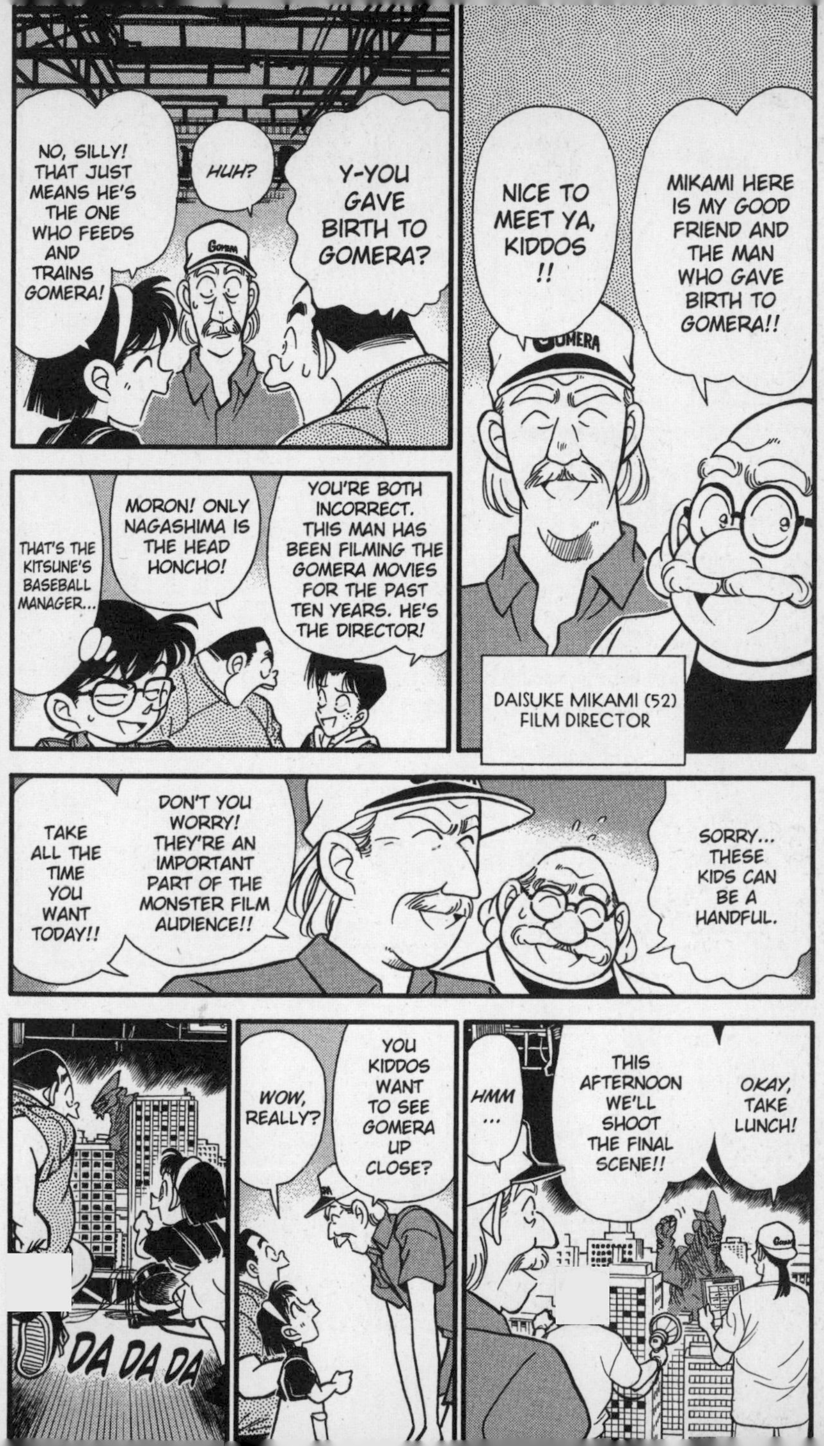
MIKAMI HERE IS MY GOOD FRIEND AND THE MAN WHO GAVE BIRTH TO GOMERA!!
NICE TO MEET YA, KIDDOS !!
DAISUKE MIKAMI (52) FILM DIRECTOR
Y-YOU GAVE BIRTH TO GOMERA?
HUH?
NO, SILLY! THAT JUST MEANS HE'S THE ONE WHO FEEDS AND TRAINS GOMERA!
YOU'RE BOTH INCORRECT. THIS MAN HAS BEEN FILMING THE GOMERA MOVIES FOR THE PAST TEN YEARS. HE'S THE DIRECTOR!
MORON! ONLY NAGASHIMA IS THE HEAD HONCHO!
THAT'S THE KITSUNE'S BASEBALL MANAGER...
SORRY... THESE KIDS CAN BE A HANDFUL.
DON'T YOU WORRY! THEY'RE AN IMPORTANT PART OF THE MONSTER FILM AUDIENCE!!
TAKE ALL THE TIME YOU WANT TODAY!!
OKAY, TAKE LUNCH!
THIS AFTERNOON WE'LL SHOOT THE FINAL SCENE!!
HMM ...
YOU KIDDOS WANT TO SEE GOMERA UP CLOSE?
WOW, REALLY?
DA DA DA

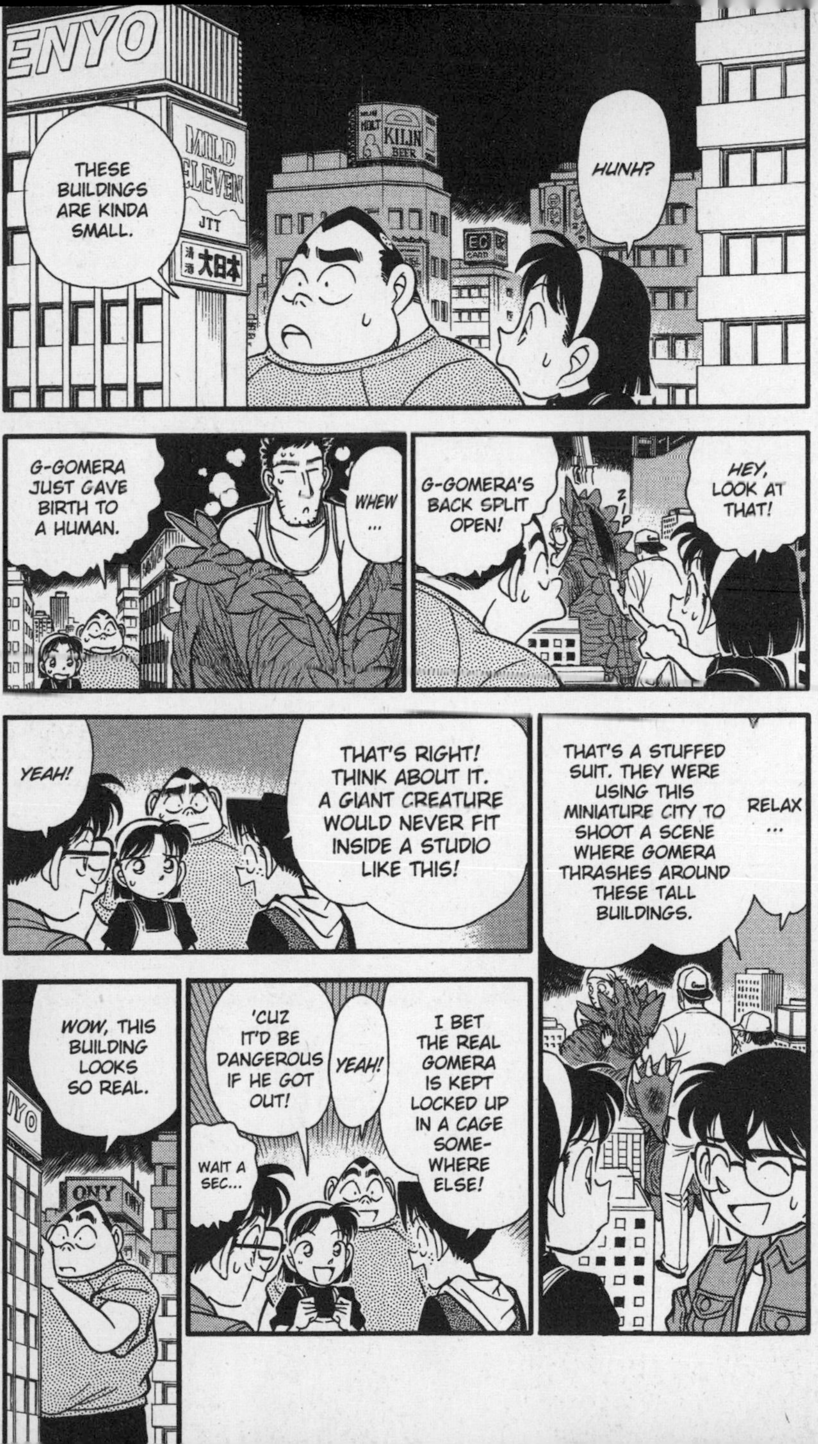
HUNH?
ENYO
MILD ELEVEN
JTT
大日本
KILIN BEER
THESE BUILDINGS ARE KINDA SMALL.
HEY, LOOK AT THAT!
ZIP
G-GOMERA'S BACK SPLIT OPEN!
WHEW ...
G-GOMERA JUST GAVE BIRTH TO A HUMAN.
RELAX ...
THAT'S A STUFFED SUIT. THEY WERE USING THIS MINIATURE CITY TO SHOOT A SCENE WHERE GOMERA THRASHES AROUND THESE TALL BUILDINGS.
THAT'S RIGHT! THINK ABOUT IT. A GIANT CREATURE WOULD NEVER FIT INSIDE A STUDIO LIKE THIS!
YEAH!
I BET THE REAL GOMERA IS KEPT LOCKED UP IN A CAGE SOME-WHERE ELSE!
YEAH!
'CUZ IT'D BE DANGEROUS IF HE GOT OUT!
WAIT A SEC...
WOW, THIS BUILDING LOOKS SO REAL.

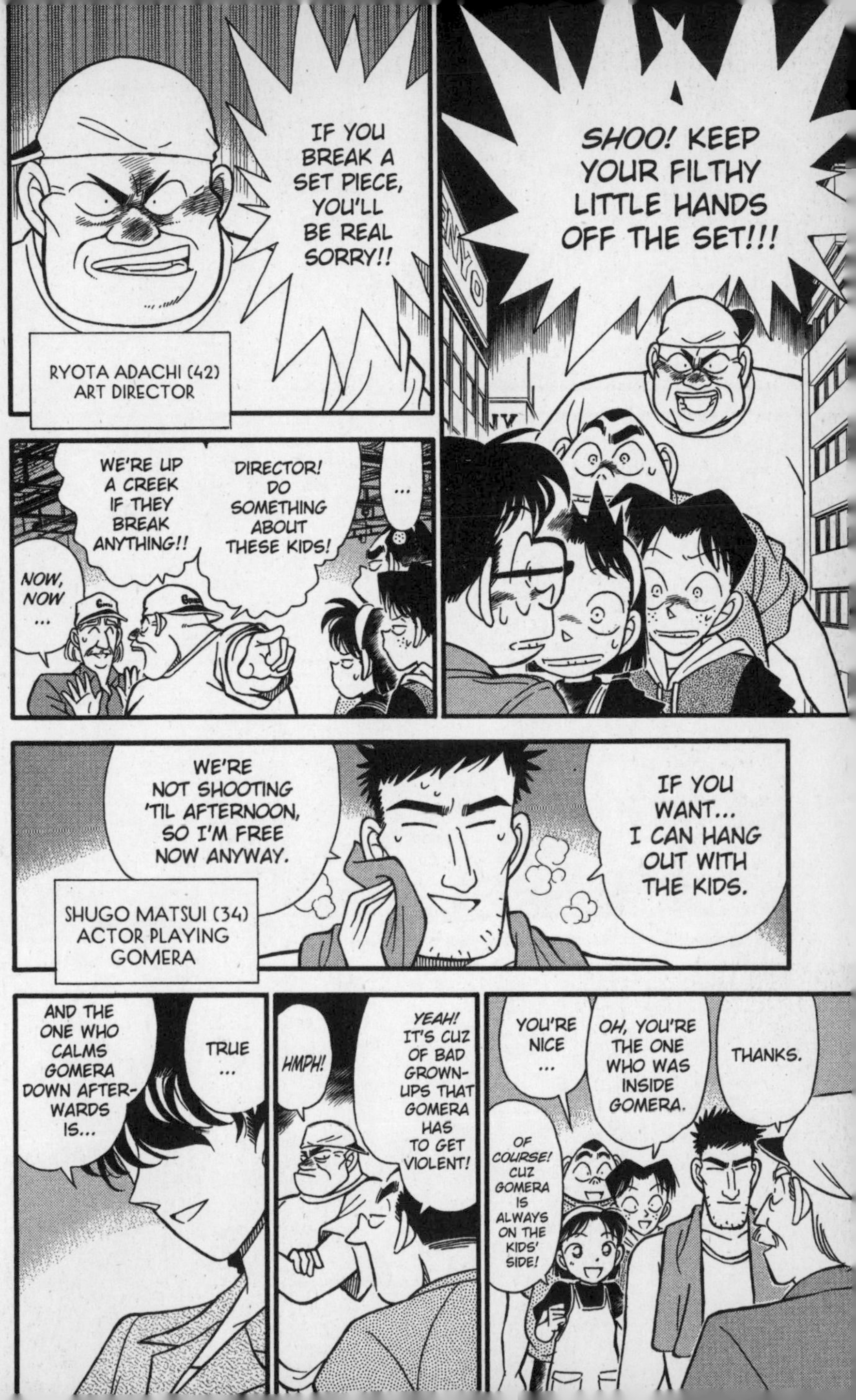
SHOO! KEEP YOUR FILTHY LITTLE HANDS OFF THE SET!!!
IF YOU BREAK A SET PIECE, YOU'LL BE REAL SORRY!!
RYOTA ADACHI (42) ART DIRECTOR
...
DIRECTOR! DO SOMETHING ABOUT THESE KIDS!
WE'RE UP A CREEK IF THEY BREAK ANYTHING!!
NOW, NOW ...
IF YOU WANT... I CAN HANG OUT WITH THE KIDS.
WE'RE NOT SHOOTING 'TIL AFTERNOON, SO I'M FREE NOW ANYWAY.
SHUGO MATSUI (34) ACTOR PLAYING GOMERA
THANKS.
OH, YOU'RE THE ONE WHO WAS INSIDE GOMERA.
YOU'RE NICE ...
OF COURSE! CUZ GOMERA IS ALWAYS ON THE KIDS' SIDE!
YEAH! IT'S CUZ OF BAD GROWN-UPS THAT GOMERA HAS TO GET VIOLENT!
HMPH!
TRUE ...
AND THE ONE WHO CALMS GOMERA DOWN AFTER-WARDS IS...

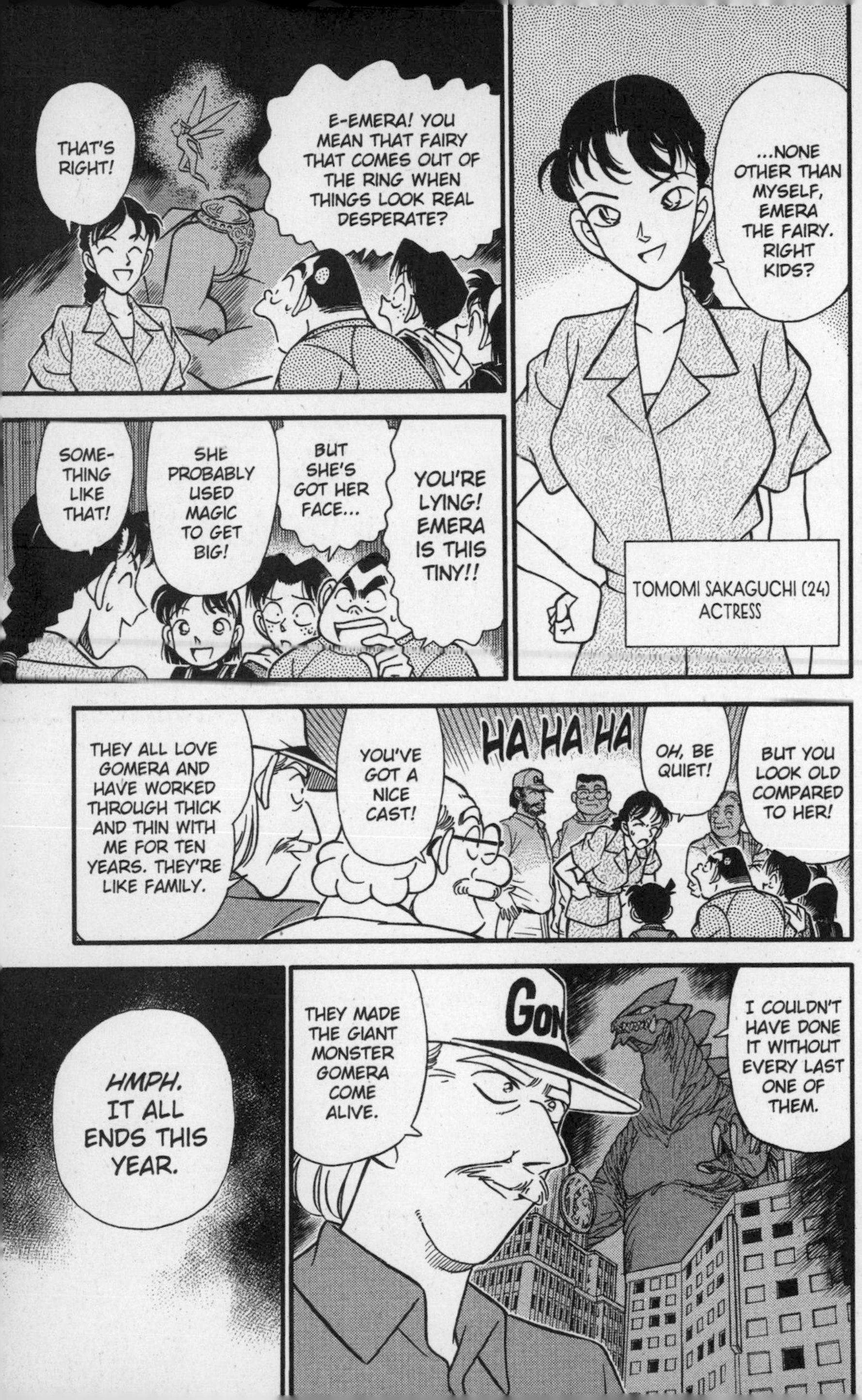
...NONE OTHER THAN MYSELF, EMERA THE FAIRY. RIGHT KIDS?
TOMOMI SAKAGUCHI (24) ACTRESS
E-EMERA! YOU MEAN THAT FAIRY THAT COMES OUT OF THE RING WHEN THINGS LOOK REAL DESPERATE?
THAT'S RIGHT!
YOU'RE LYING! EMERA IS THIS TINY!!
BUT SHE'S GOT HER FACE...
SHE PROBABLY USED MAGIC TO GET BIG!
SOME-THING LIKE THAT!
BUT YOU LOOK OLD COMPARED TO HER!
OH, BE QUIET!
HA HA HA
YOU'VE GOT A NICE CAST!
THEY ALL LOVE GOMERA AND HAVE WORKED THROUGH THICK AND THIN WITH ME FOR TEN YEARS. THEY'RE LIKE FAMILY.
I COULDN'T HAVE DONE IT WITHOUT EVERY LAST ONE OF THEM.
GON
THEY MADE THE GIANT MONSTER GOMERA COME ALIVE.
HMPH. IT ALL ENDS THIS YEAR.

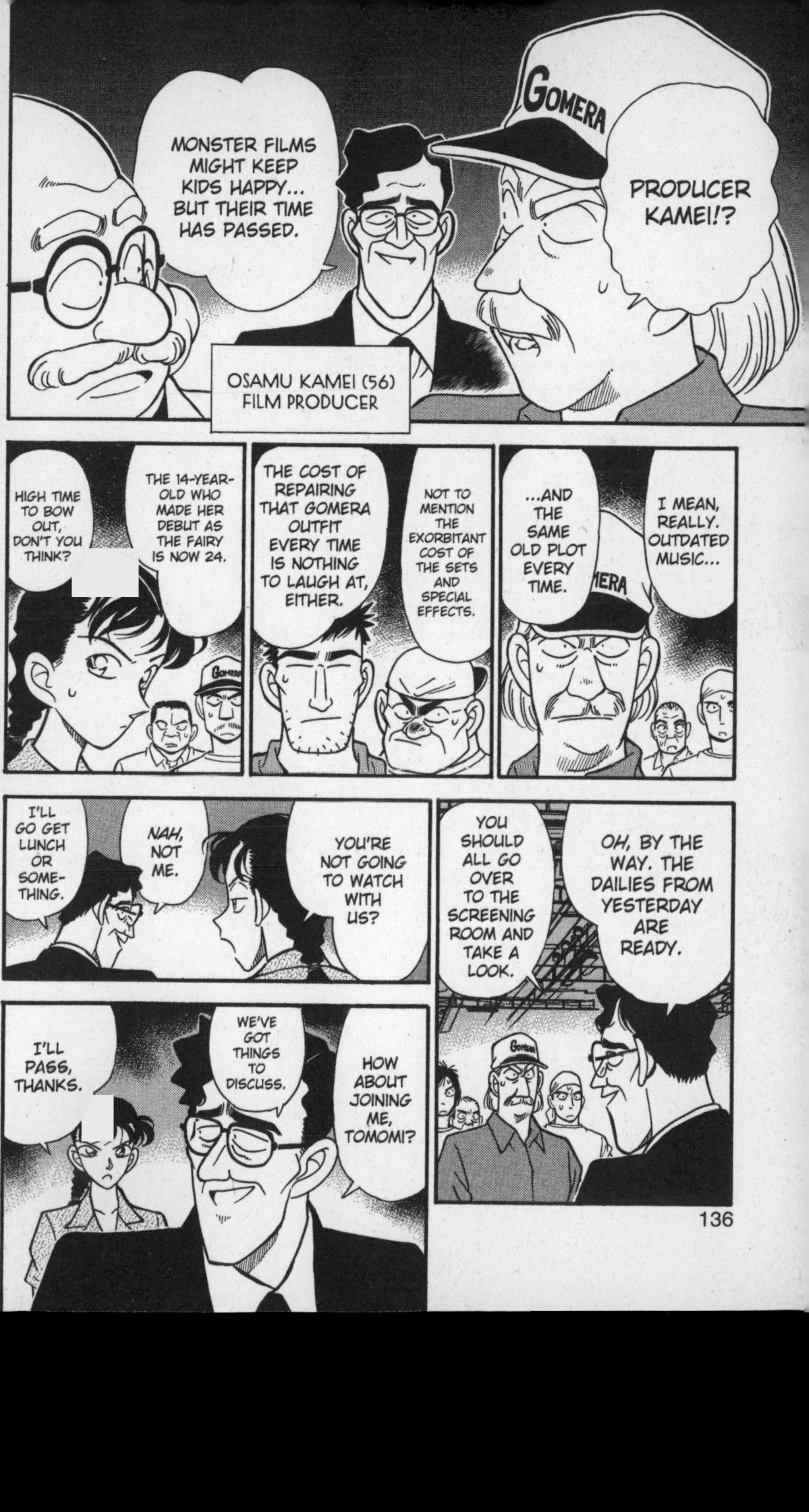
PRODUCER KAMEI!?
MONSTER FILMS MIGHT KEEP KIDS HAPPY... BUT THEIR TIME HAS PASSED.
OSAMU KAMEI (56) FILM PRODUCER
I MEAN, REALLY. OUTDATED MUSIC...
...AND THE SAME OLD PLOT EVERY TIME.
THE COST OF REPAIRING THAT GOMERA OUTFIT EVERY TIME IS NOTHING TO LAUGH AT, EITHER.
NOT TO MENTION THE EXORBITANT COST OF THE SETS AND SPECIAL EFFECTS.
THE 14-YEAR-OLD WHO MADE HER DEBUT AS THE FAIRY IS NOW 24.
HIGH TIME TO BOW OUT, DON'T YOU THINK?
OH, BY THE WAY. THE DAILIES FROM YESTERDAY ARE READY.
YOU SHOULD ALL GO OVER TO THE SCREENING ROOM AND TAKE A LOOK.
YOU'RE NOT GOING TO WATCH WITH US?
NAH, NOT ME.
I'LL GO GET LUNCH OR SOME-THING.
HOW ABOUT JOINING ME, TOMOMI?
WE'VE GOT THINGS TO DISCUSS.
I'LL PASS, THANKS.

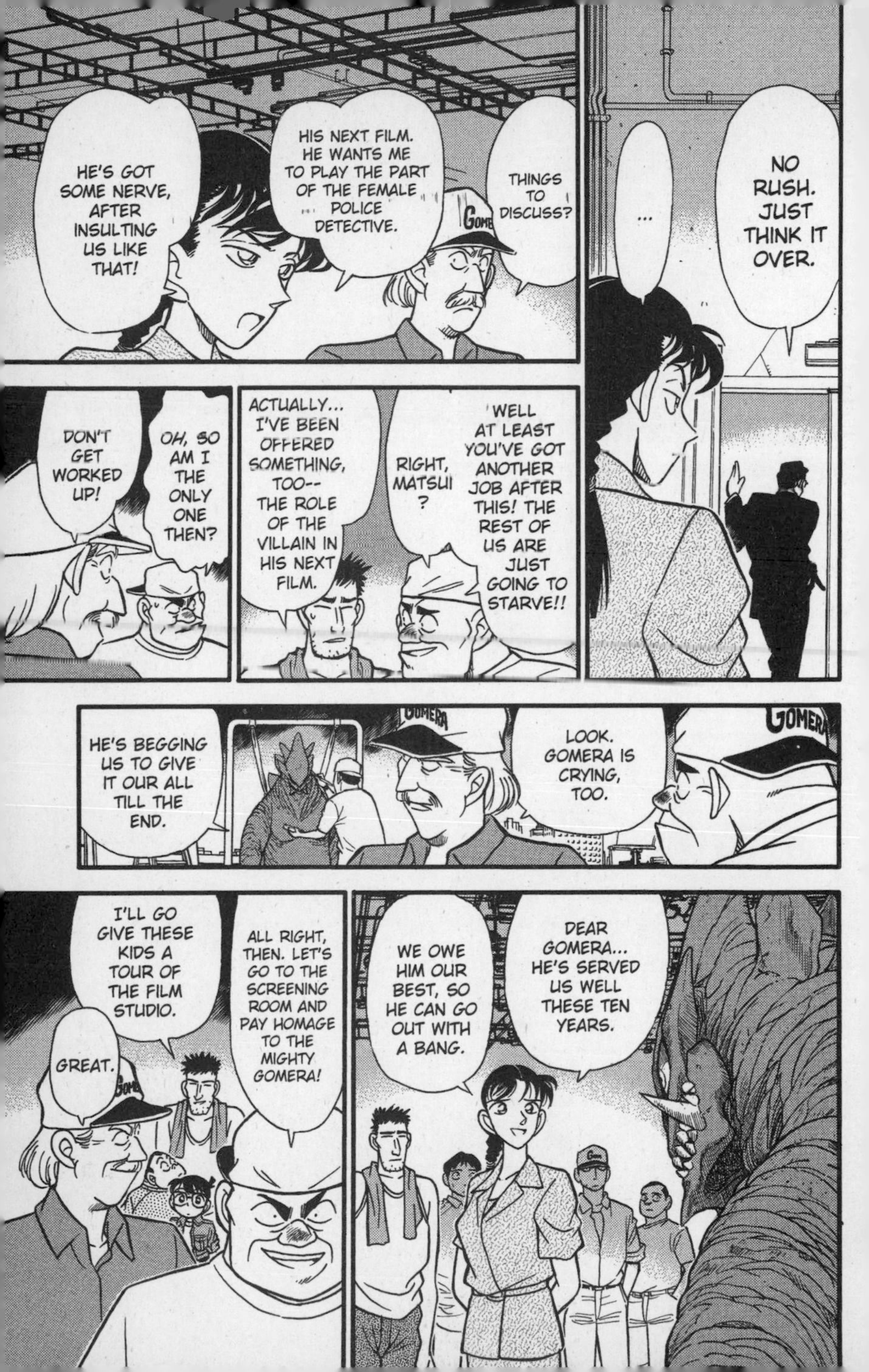
NO RUSH. JUST THINK IT OVER.
...
THINGS TO DISCUSS?
HIS NEXT FILM. HE WANTS ME TO PLAY THE PART OF THE FEMALE POLICE DETECTIVE.
HE'S GOT SOME NERVE, AFTER INSULTING US LIKE THAT!
WELL AT LEAST YOU'VE GOT ANOTHER JOB AFTER THIS! THE REST OF US ARE JUST GOING TO STARVE!!
RIGHT, MATSUI?
ACTUALLY... I'VE BEEN OFFERED SOMETHING, TOO-- THE ROLE OF THE VILLAIN IN HIS NEXT FILM.
OH, SO AM I THE ONLY ONE THEN?
DON'T GET WORKED UP!
LOOK. GOMERA IS CRYING, TOO.
HE'S BEGGING US TO GIVE IT OUR ALL TILL THE END.
DEAR GOMERA... HE'S SERVED US WELL THESE TEN YEARS.
WE OWE HIM OUR BEST, SO HE CAN GO OUT WITH A BANG.
ALL RIGHT, THEN. LET'S GO TO THE SCREENING ROOM AND PAY HOMAGE TO THE MIGHTY GOMERA!
I'LL GO GIVE THESE KIDS A TOUR OF THE FILM STUDIO.
GREAT.

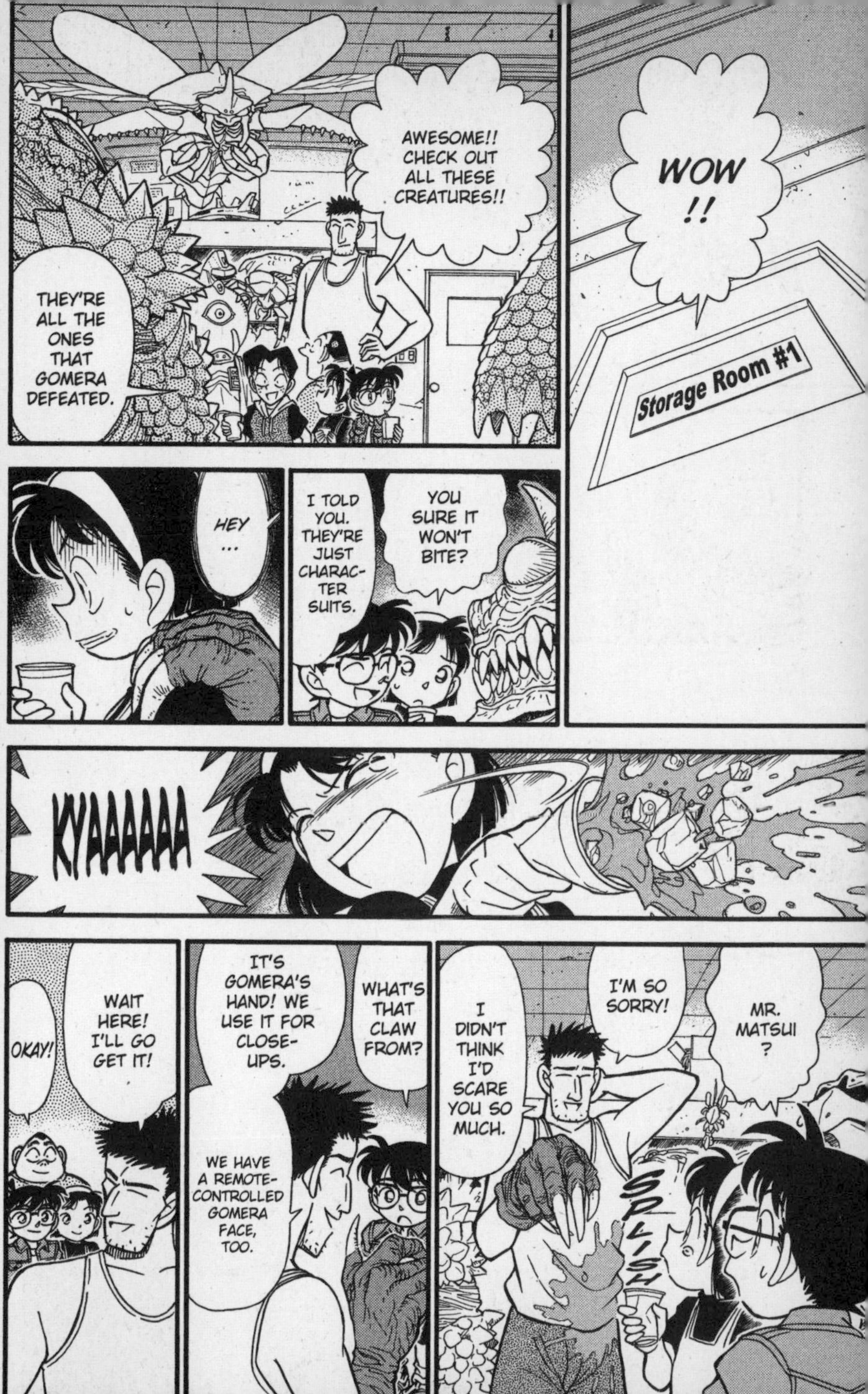
WOW !!
Storage Room #1
AWESOME!! CHECK OUT ALL THESE CREATURES!!
THEY'RE ALL THE ONES THAT GOMERA DEFEATED.
YOU SURE IT WON'T BITE?
I TOLD YOU. THEY'RE JUST CHARACTER SUITS.
HEY ...
KYAAAAAA
MR. MATSUI ?
I'M SO SORRY!
I DIDN'T THINK I'D SCARE YOU SO MUCH.
SPLISH
WHAT'S THAT CLAW FROM?
IT'S GOMERA'S HAND! WE USE IT FOR CLOSE-UPS.
WE HAVE A REMOTE-CONTROLLED GOMERA FACE, TOO.
WAIT HERE! I'LL GO GET IT!
OKAY!

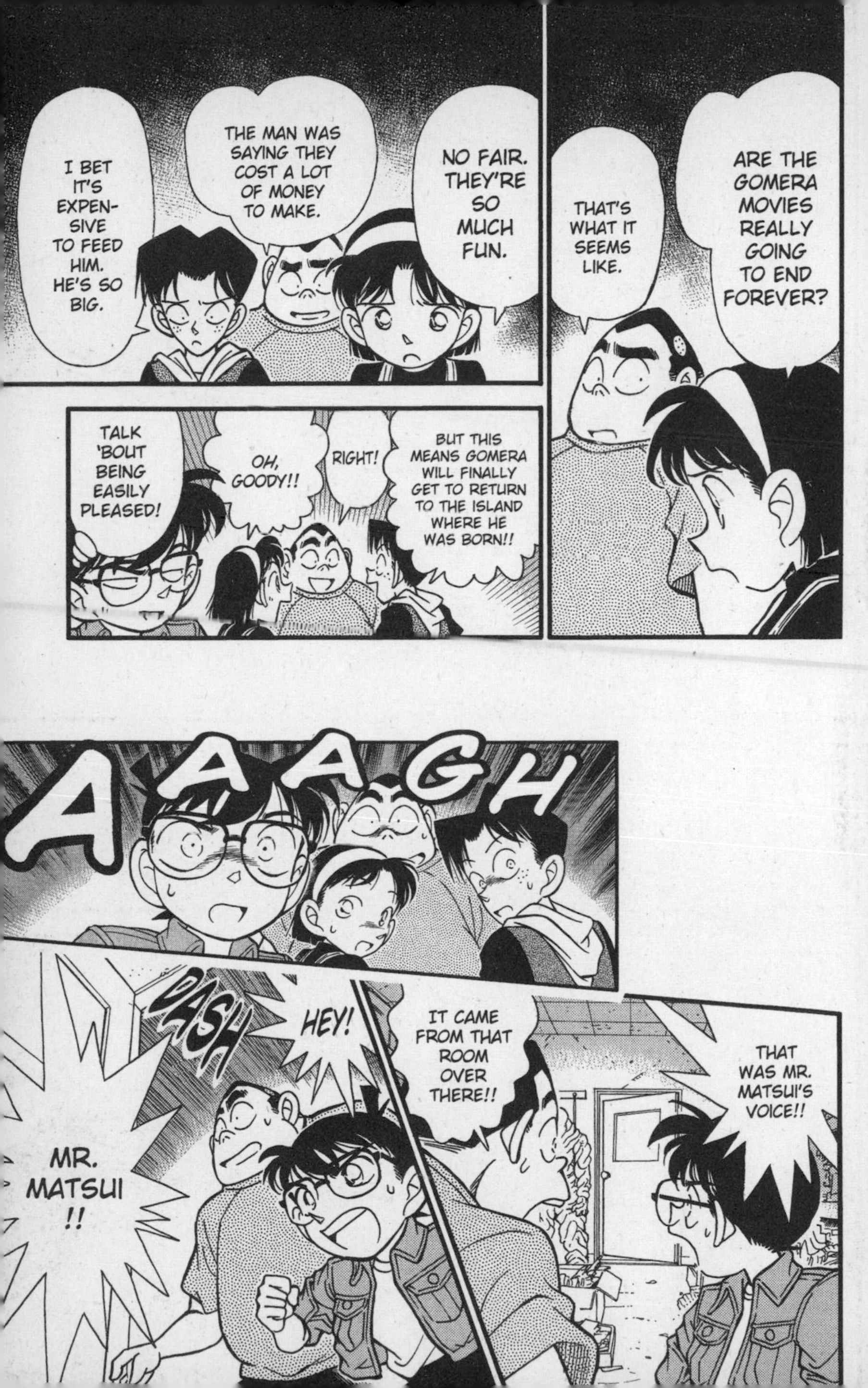
ARE THE GOMERA MOVIES REALLY GOING TO END FOREVER?
THAT'S WHAT IT SEEMS LIKE.
NO FAIR. THEY'RE SO MUCH FUN.
THE MAN WAS SAYING THEY COST A LOT OF MONEY TO MAKE.
I BET IT'S EXPEN-SIVE TO FEED HIM. HE'S SO BIG.
BUT THIS MEANS GOMERA WILL FINALLY GET TO RETURN TO THE ISLAND WHERE HE WAS BORN!!
RIGHT!
OH, GOODY!!
TALK 'BOUT BEING EASILY PLEASED!
AAAGH
THAT WAS MR. MATSUI'S VOICE!!
IT CAME FROM THAT ROOM OVER THERE!!
HEY!
DASH
MR. MATSUI !!

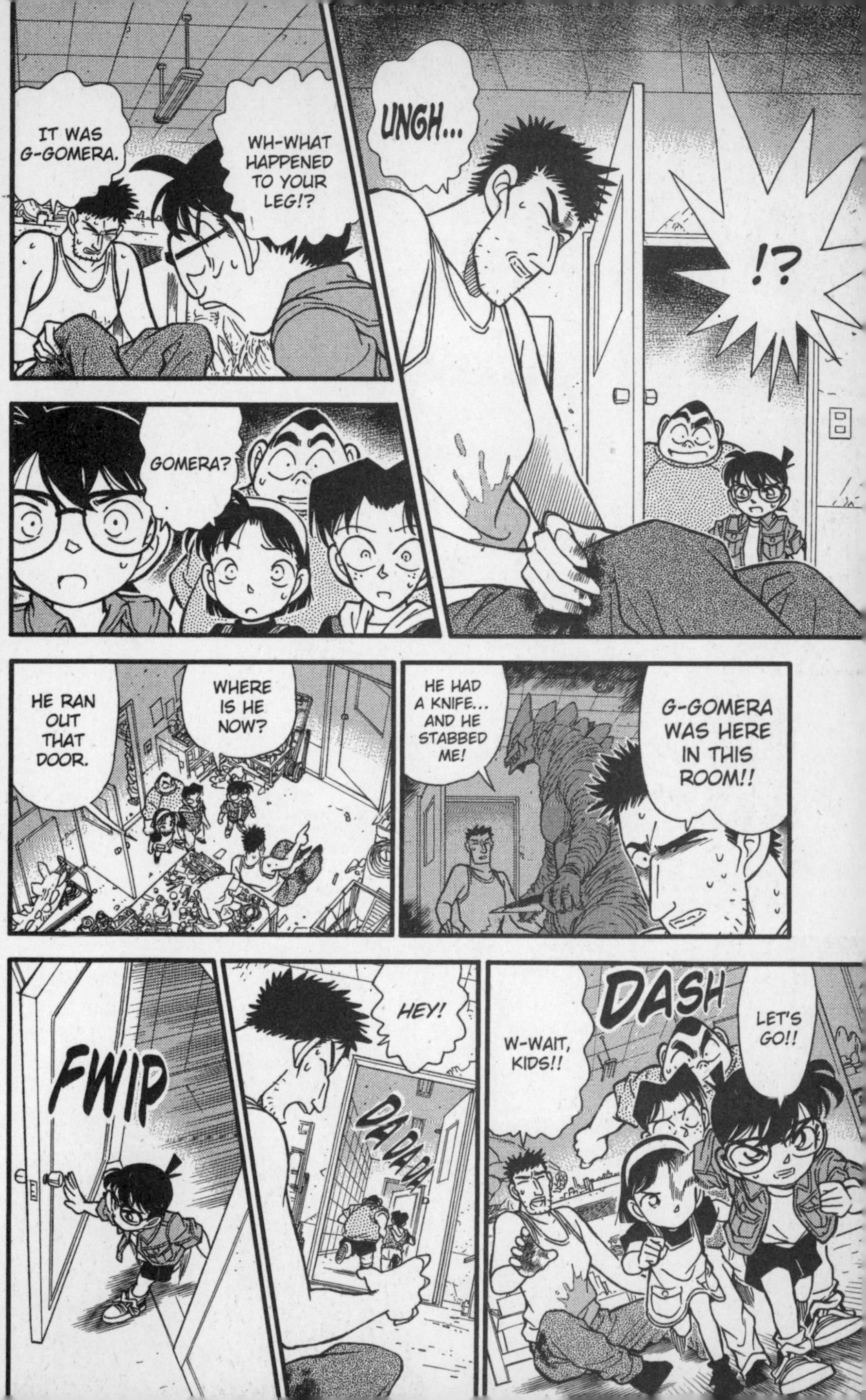
UNGH...
!?
WH-WHAT HAPPENED TO YOUR LEG!?
IT WAS G-GOMERA.
GOMERA?
G-GOMERA WAS HERE IN THIS ROOM!!
HE HAD A KNIFE... AND HE STABBED ME!
WHERE IS HE NOW?
HE RAN OUT THAT DOOR.
DASH
LET'S GO!!
W-WAIT, KIDS!!
HEY!
DA DA DA
FWIP

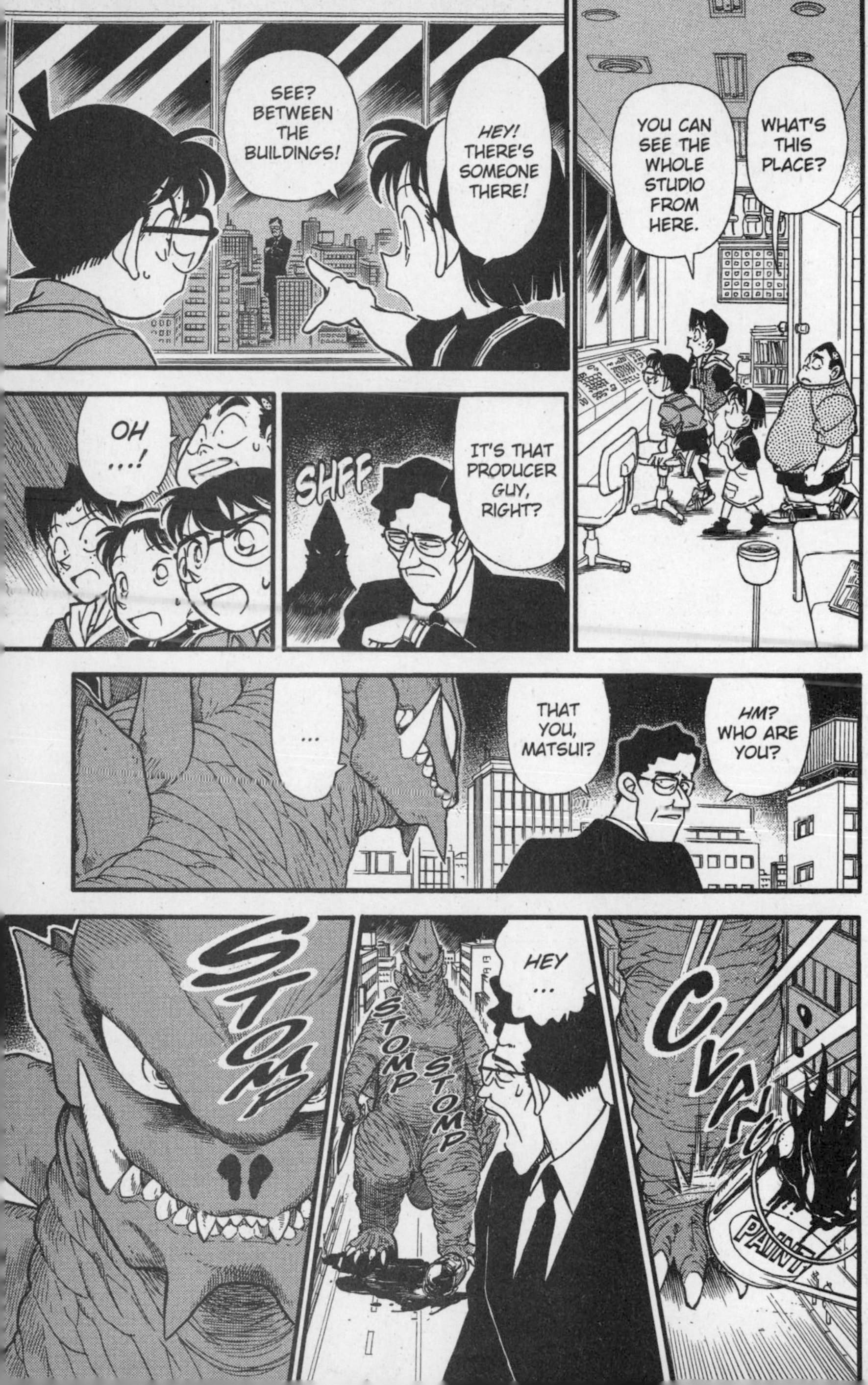
WHAT'S THIS PLACE?
YOU CAN SEE THE WHOLE STUDIO FROM HERE.
HEY! THERE'S SOMEONE THERE!
SEE? BETWEEN THE BUILDINGS!
IT'S THAT PRODUCER GUY, RIGHT?
SHFF
OH ...!
HM? WHO ARE YOU?
THAT YOU, MATSUI?
...
CVANG
PAINT
HEY ...
STOMP
STOMP
STOMP

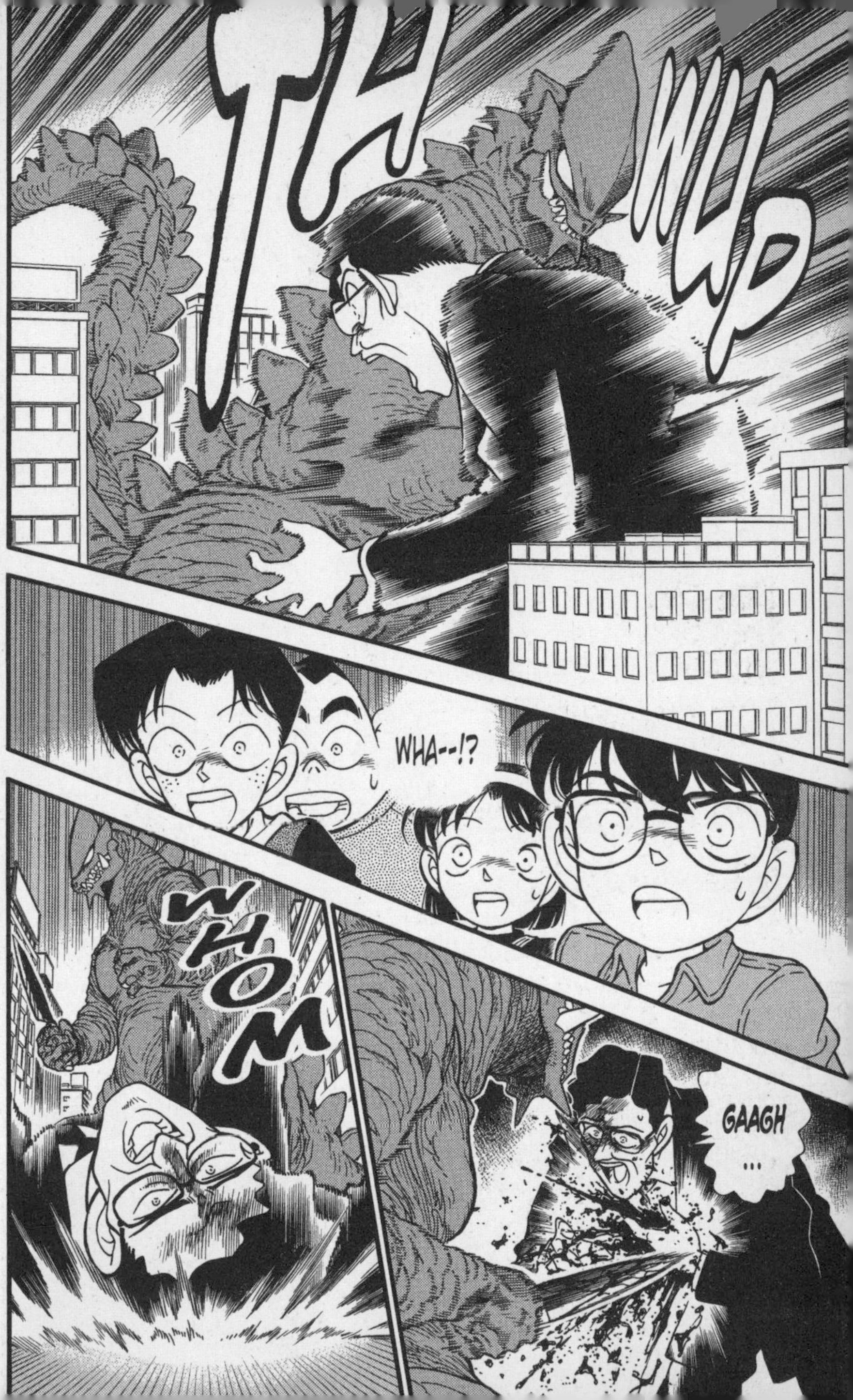
WHUP
THWHUP
WHA--!?
GAAGH
...
WHOM

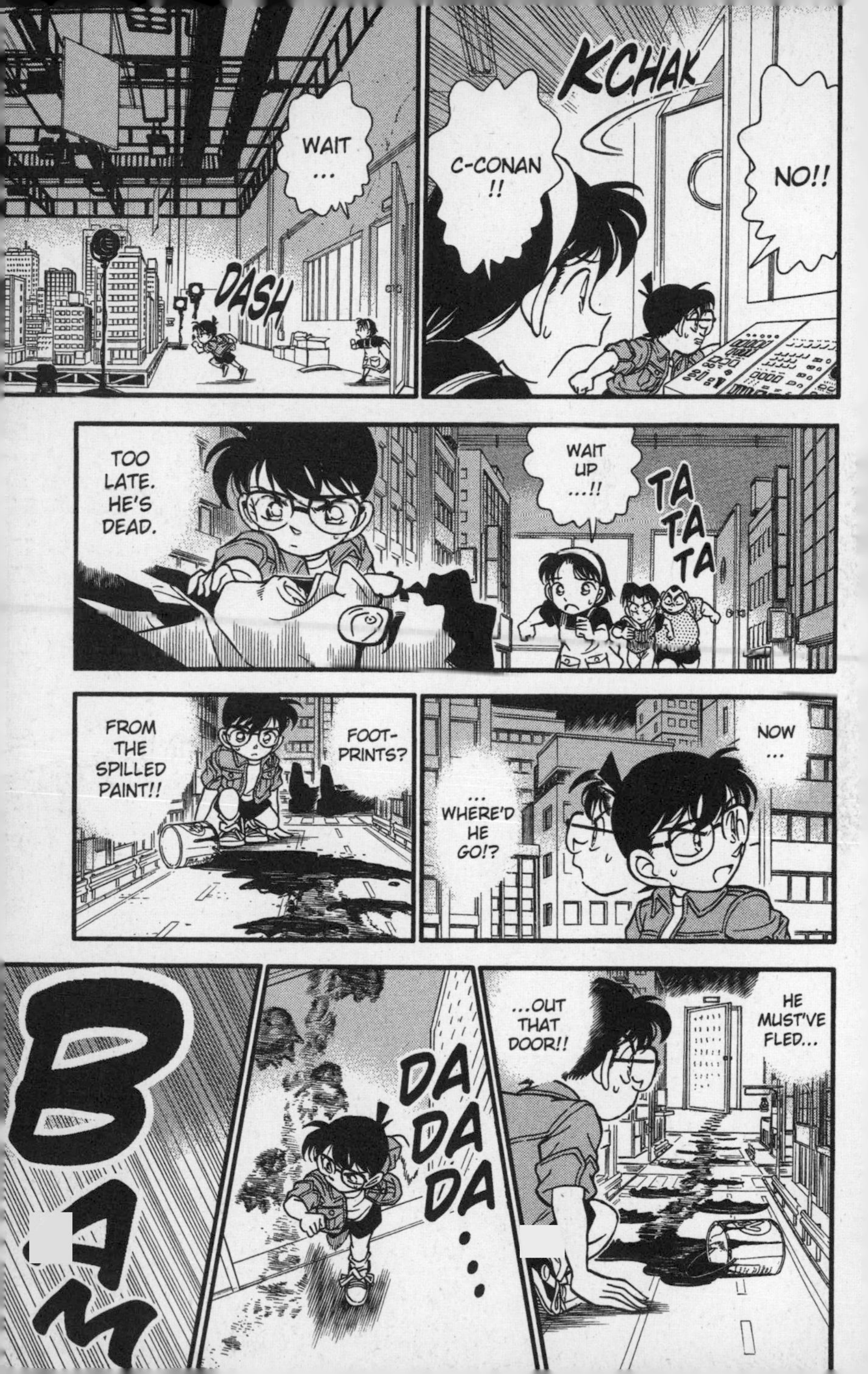
NO!!
KCHAK
C-CONAN !!
WAIT ...
DASH
TA TA TA
WAIT UP ...!!
TOO LATE. HE'S DEAD.
NOW ...
... WHERE'D HE GO!?
FOOT-PRINTS?
FROM THE SPILLED PAINT!!
HE MUST'VE FLED...
...OUT THAT DOOR!!
DA DA DA ...
BAM

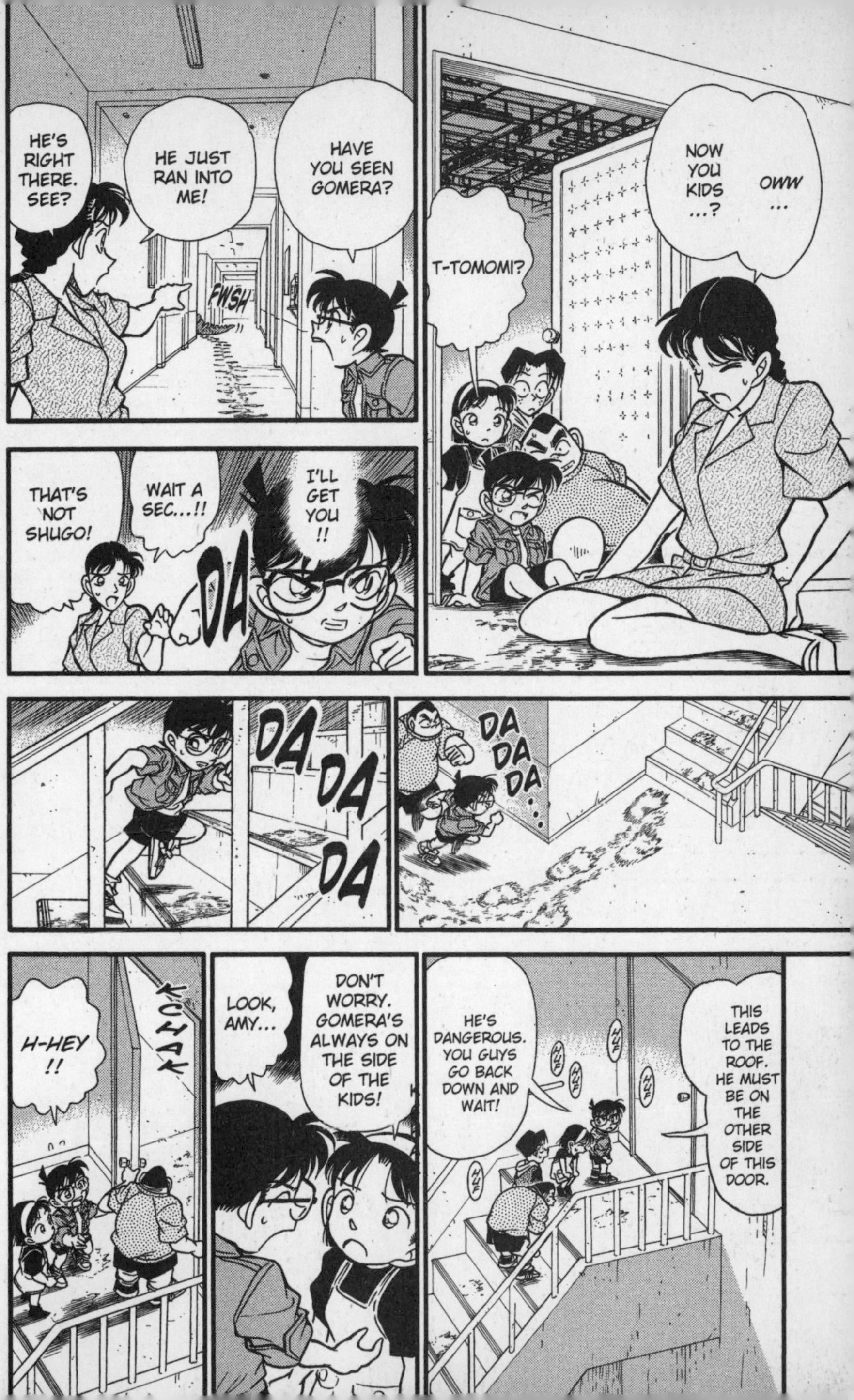
OWW ...
NOW YOU KIDS ...?
T-TOMOMI?
HAVE YOU SEEN GOMERA?
HE JUST RAN INTO ME!
HE'S RIGHT THERE. SEE?
FWSH
I'LL GET YOU !!
WAIT A SEC...!!
THAT'S NOT SHUGO!
DA
DA DA DA ...
DA DA DA
THIS LEADS TO THE ROOF. HE MUST BE ON THE OTHER SIDE OF THIS DOOR.
HUF
HE'S DANGEROUS. YOU GUYS GO BACK DOWN AND WAIT!
DON'T WORRY. GOMERA'S ALWAYS ON THE SIDE OF THE KIDS!
LOOK, AMY...
KCHAK
H-HEY !!

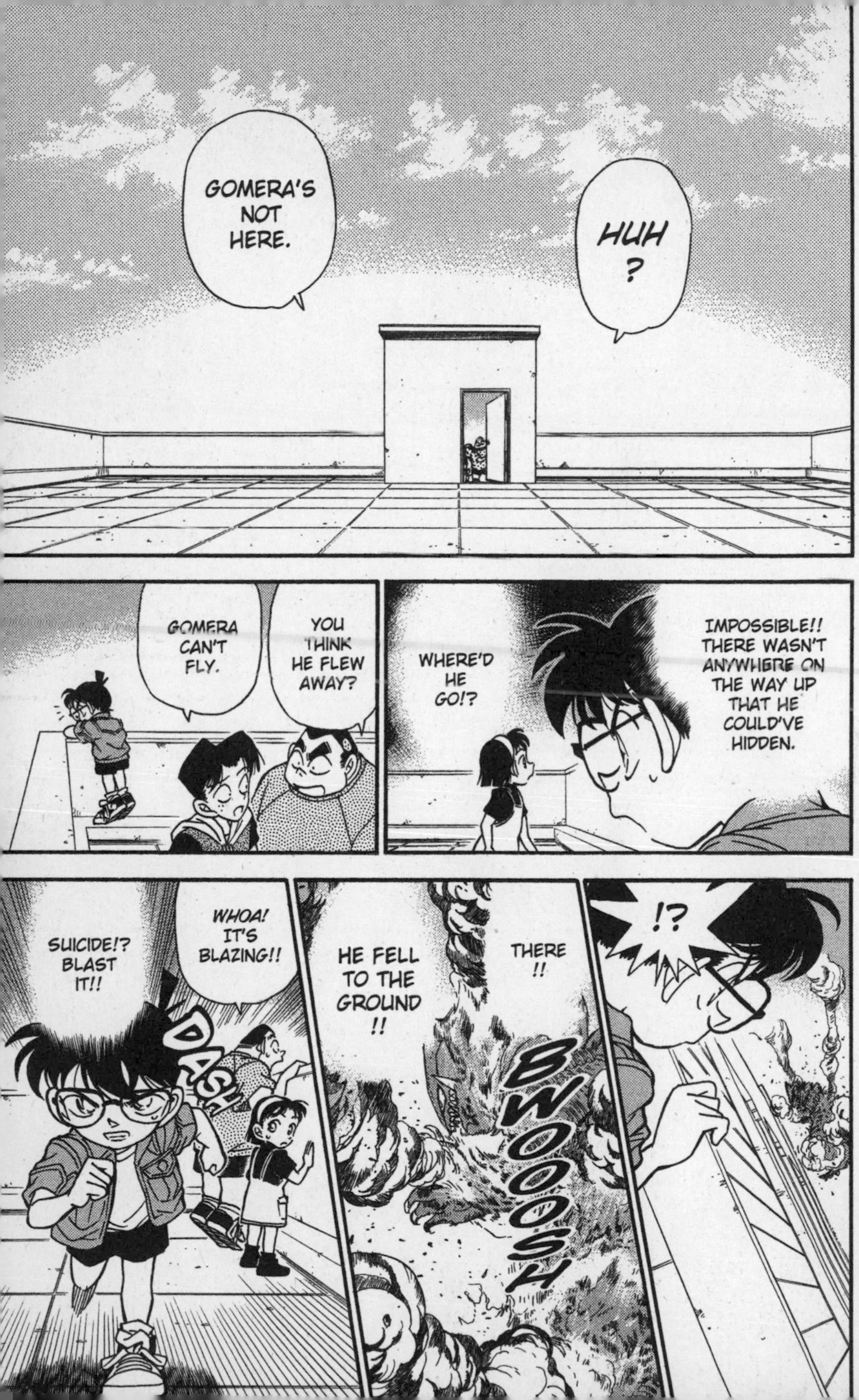
HUH?
GOMERA'S NOT HERE.
IMPOSSIBLE!! THERE WASN'T ANYWHERE ON THE WAY UP THAT HE COULD'VE HIDDEN.
WHERE'D HE GO!?
YOU THINK HE FLEW AWAY?
GOMERA CAN'T FLY.
!?
BWOOOOSH
THERE!!
HE FELL TO THE GROUND!!
WHOA! IT'S BLAZING!!
SUICIDE!? BLAST IT!!
DASH

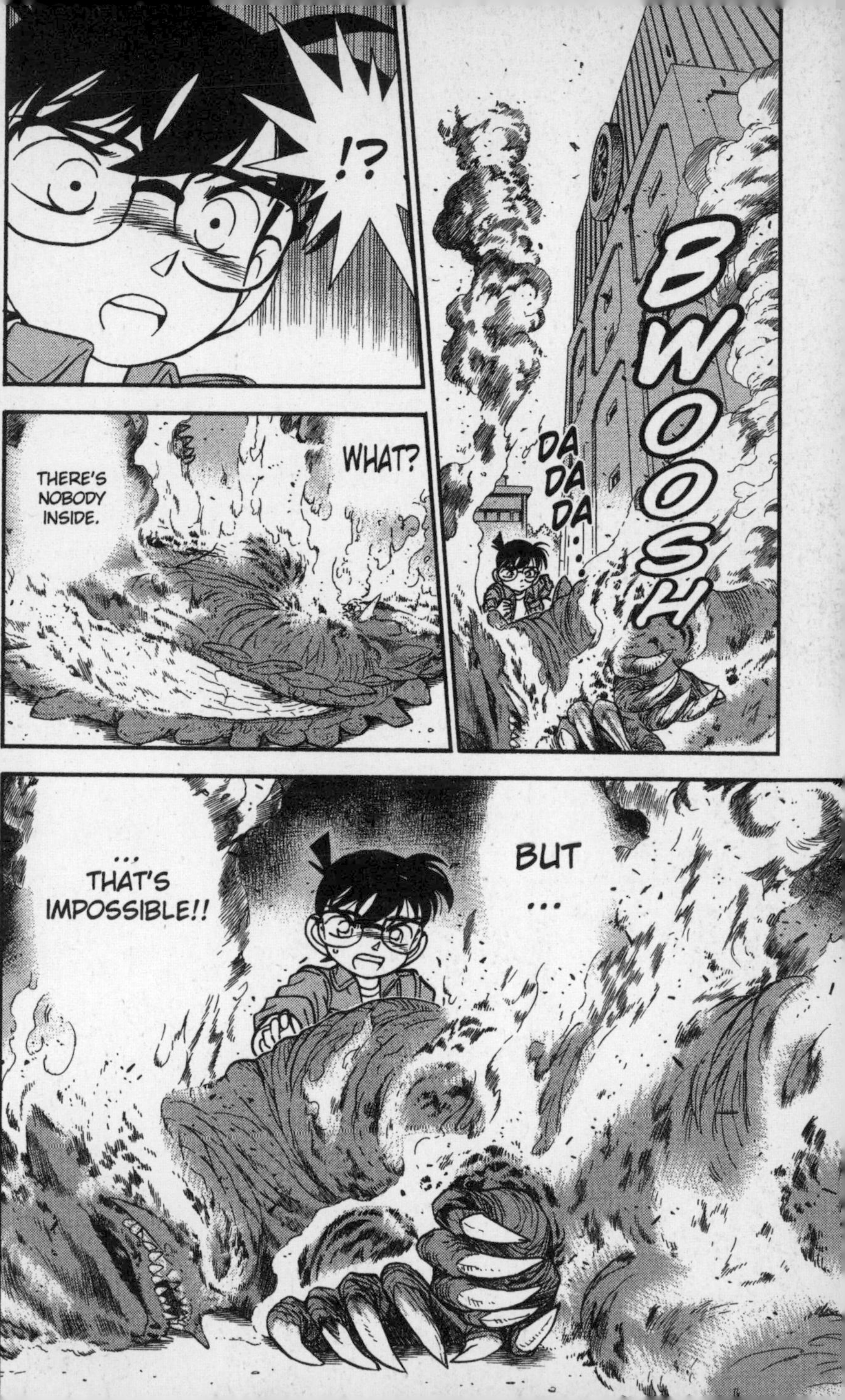
BWOOSH
DA DA DA...
!?
WHAT?
THERE'S NOBODY INSIDE.
BUT ...
... THAT'S IMPOSSIBLE!!

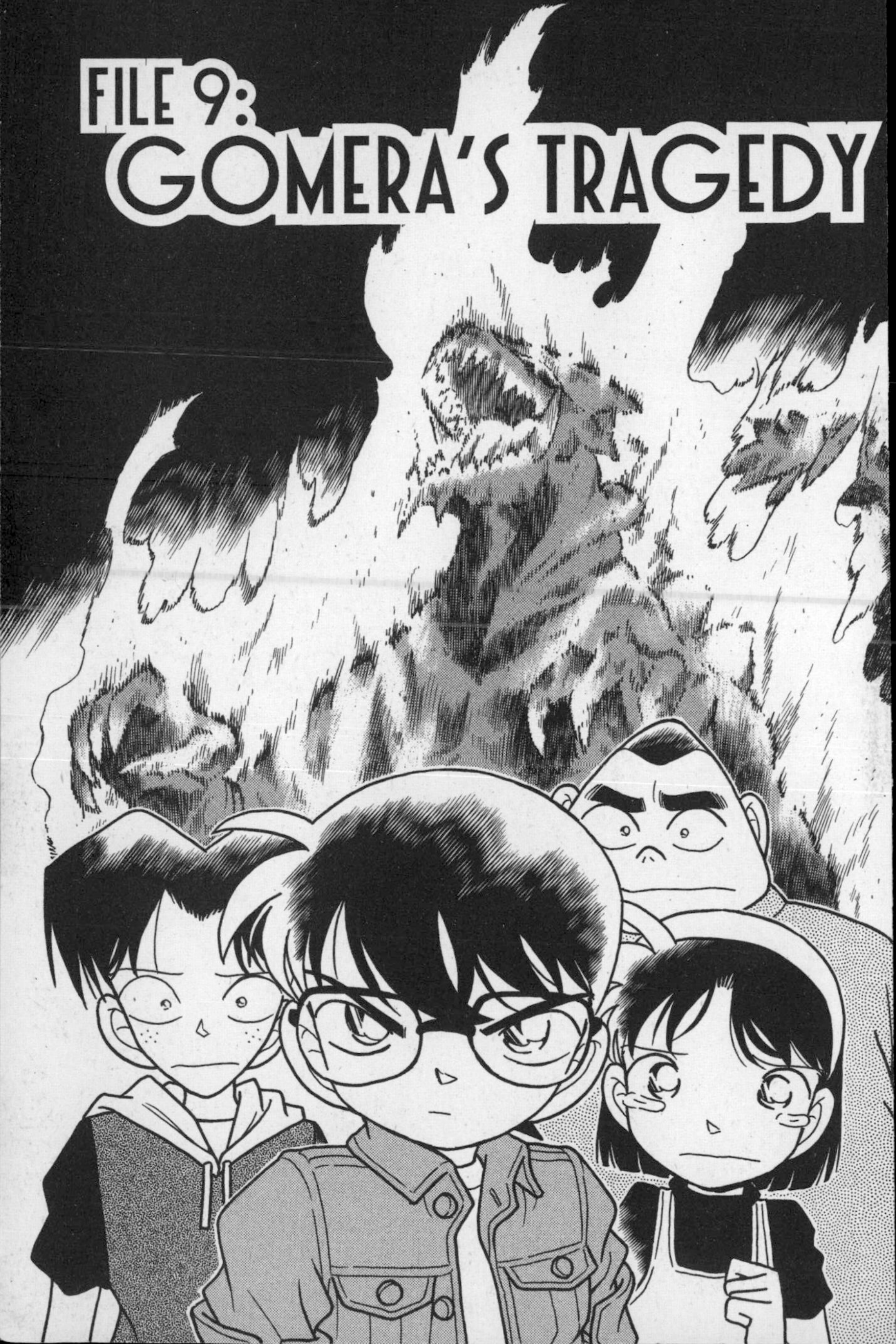
FILE 9:
GOMERA'S TRAGEDY

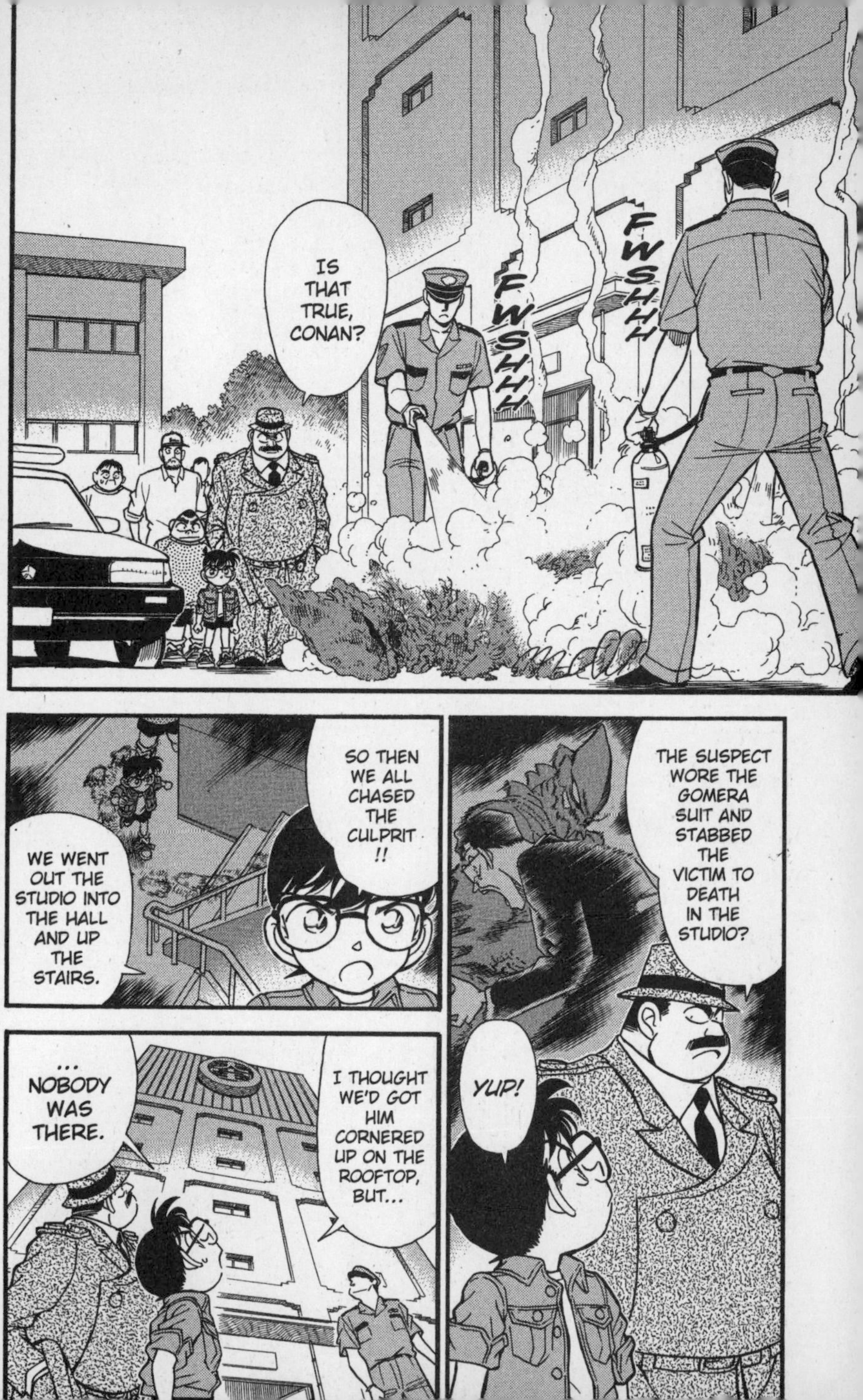
FWSHHH
FWSHHH
IS THAT TRUE, CONAN?
THE SUSPECT WORE THE GOMERA SUIT AND STABBED THE VICTIM TO DEATH IN THE STUDIO?
YUP!
SO THEN WE ALL CHASED THE CULPRIT!!
WE WENT OUT THE STUDIO INTO THE HALL AND UP THE STAIRS.
I THOUGHT WE'D GOT HIM CORNERED UP ON THE ROOFTOP, BUT...
... NOBODY WAS THERE.

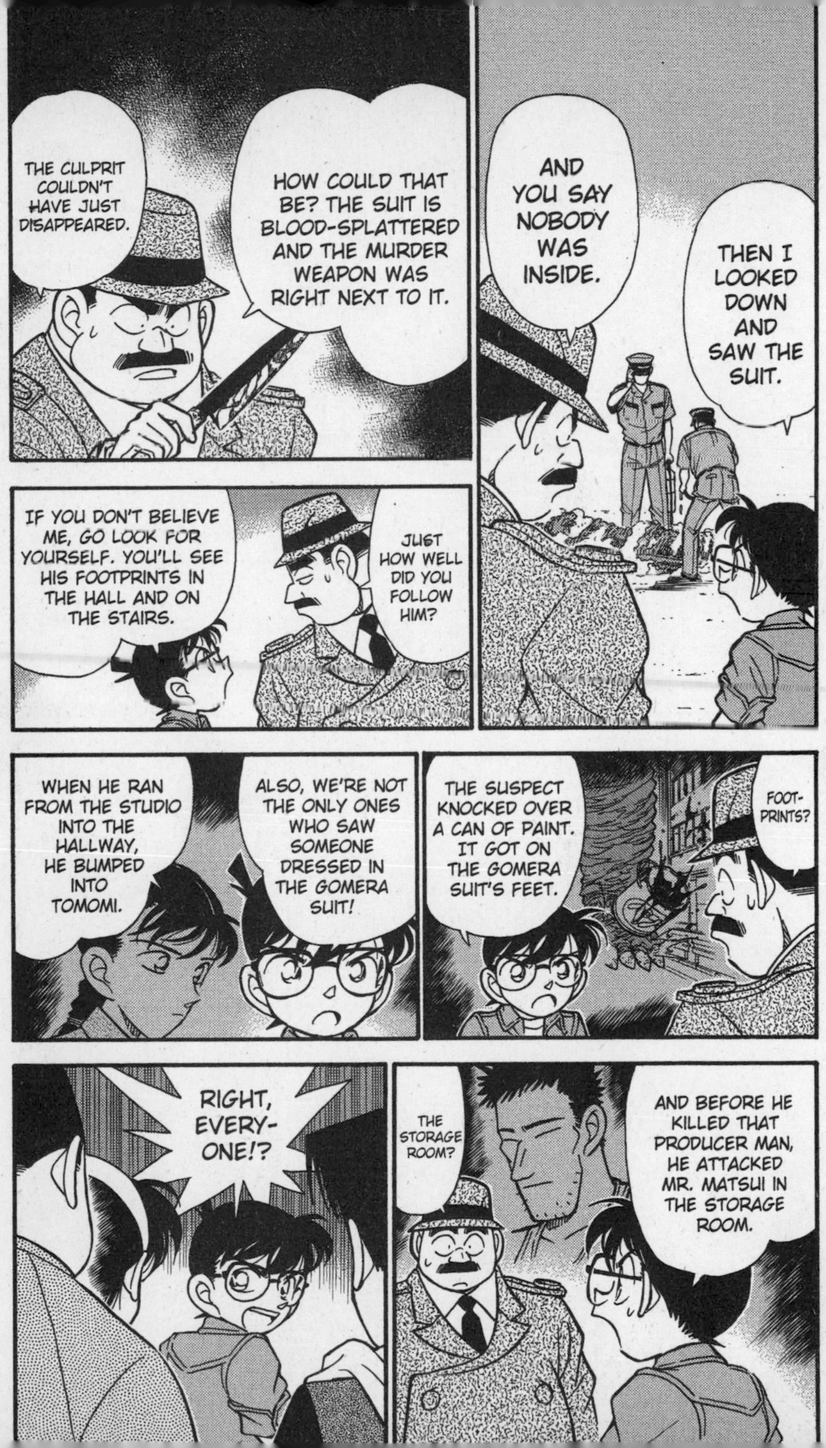
THEN I LOOKED DOWN AND SAW THE SUIT.
AND YOU SAY NOBODY WAS INSIDE.
HOW COULD THAT BE? THE SUIT IS BLOOD-SPLATTERED AND THE MURDER WEAPON WAS RIGHT NEXT TO IT.
THE CULPRIT COULDN'T HAVE JUST DISAPPEARED.
JUST HOW WELL DID YOU FOLLOW HIM?
IF YOU DON'T BELIEVE ME, GO LOOK FOR YOURSELF. YOU'LL SEE HIS FOOTPRINTS IN THE HALL AND ON THE STAIRS.
FOOT-PRINTS?
THE SUSPECT KNOCKED OVER A CAN OF PAINT. IT GOT ON THE GOMERA SUIT'S FEET.
ALSO, WE'RE NOT THE ONLY ONES WHO SAW SOMEONE DRESSED IN THE GOMERA SUIT!
WHEN HE RAN FROM THE STUDIO INTO THE HALLWAY, HE BUMPED INTO TOMOMI.
AND BEFORE HE KILLED THAT PRODUCER MAN, HE ATTACKED MR. MATSUI IN THE STORAGE ROOM.
THE STORAGE ROOM?
RIGHT, EVERY-ONE!?

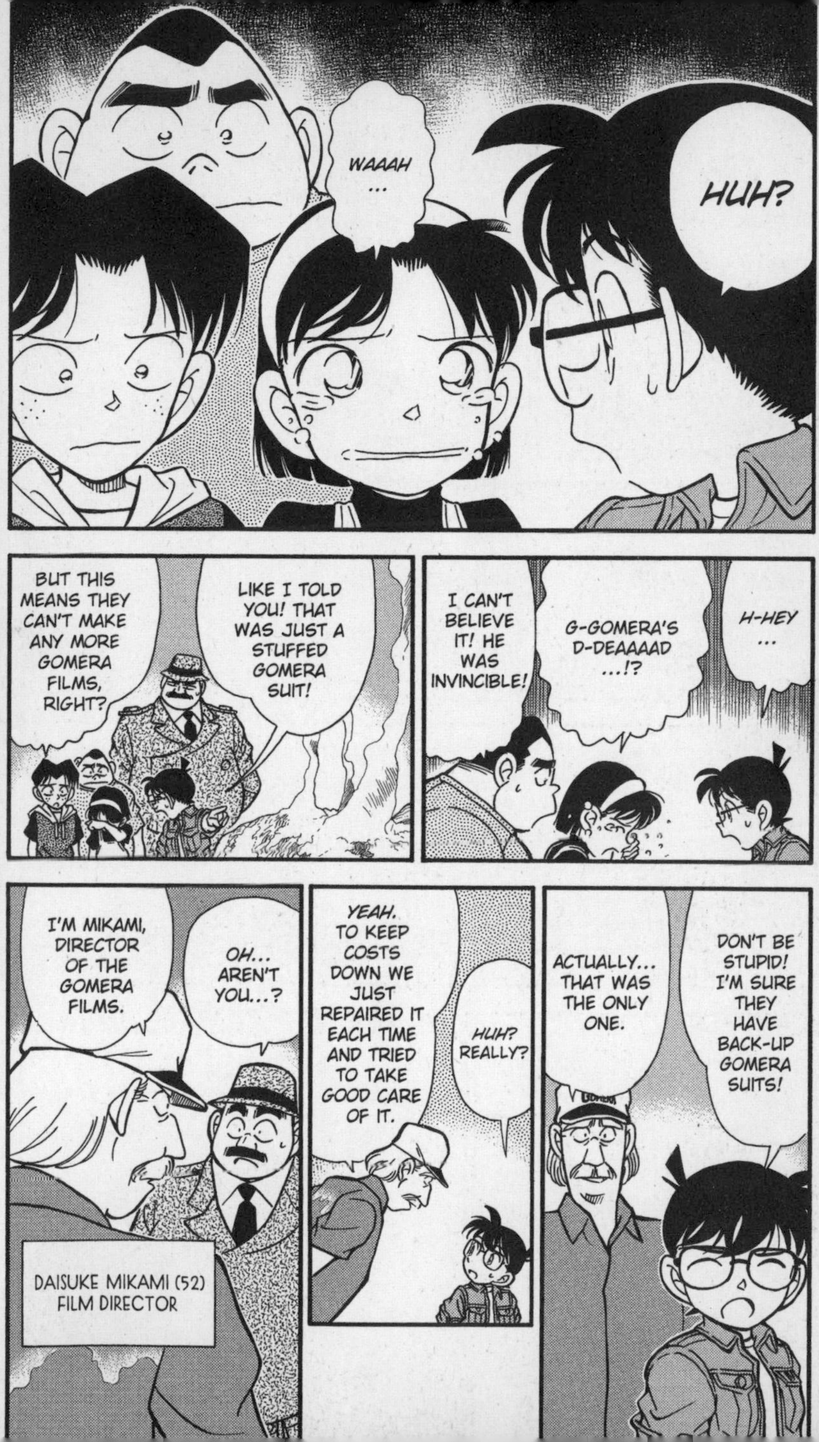
HUH?
WAAAH ...
H-HEY ...
G-GOMERA'S D-DEAAAAD ...!?
I CAN'T BELIEVE IT! HE WAS INVINCIBLE!
LIKE I TOLD YOU! THAT WAS JUST A STUFFED GOMERA SUIT!
BUT THIS MEANS THEY CAN'T MAKE ANY MORE GOMERA FILMS, RIGHT?
DON'T BE STUPID! I'M SURE THEY HAVE BACK-UP GOMERA SUITS!
ACTUALLY... THAT WAS THE ONLY ONE.
HUH? REALLY?
YEAH. TO KEEP COSTS DOWN WE JUST REPAIRED IT EACH TIME AND TRIED TO TAKE GOOD CARE OF IT.
OH... AREN'T YOU...?
I'M MIKAMI, DIRECTOR OF THE GOMERA FILMS.
DAISUKE MIKAMI (52) FILM DIRECTOR

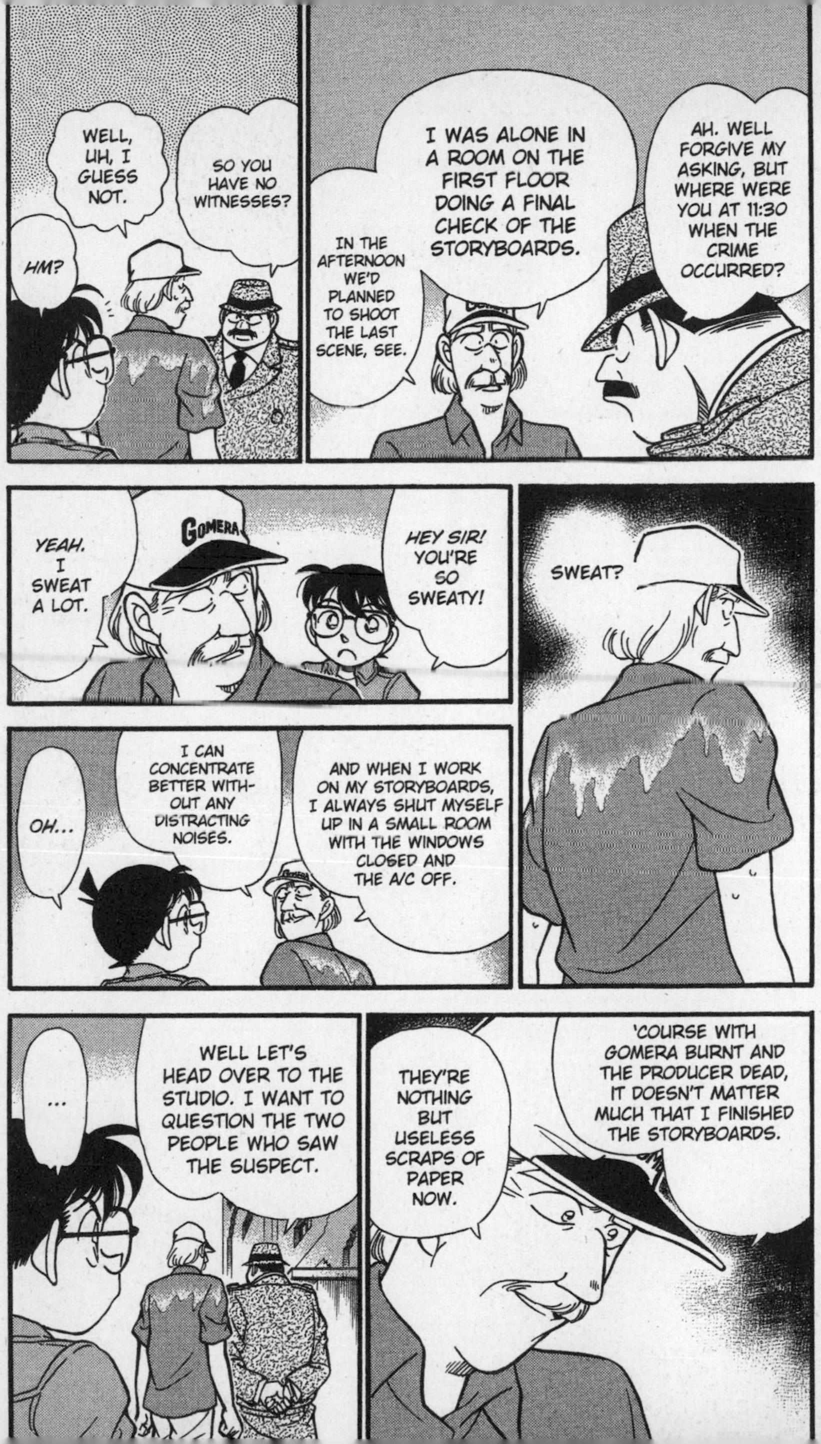
AH. WELL FORGIVE MY ASKING, BUT WHERE WERE YOU AT 11:30 WHEN THE CRIME OCCURRED?
I WAS ALONE IN A ROOM ON THE FIRST FLOOR DOING A FINAL CHECK OF THE STORYBOARDS.
IN THE AFTERNOON WE'D PLANNED TO SHOOT THE LAST SCENE, SEE.
SO YOU HAVE NO WITNESSES?
WELL, UH, I GUESS NOT.
HM?
SWEAT?
HEY SIR! YOU'RE SO SWEATY!
GOMERA
YEAH. I SWEAT A LOT.
AND WHEN I WORK ON MY STORYBOARDS, I ALWAYS SHUT MYSELF UP IN A SMALL ROOM WITH THE WINDOWS CLOSED AND THE A/C OFF.
I CAN CONCENTRATE BETTER WITH-OUT ANY DISTRACTING NOISES.
OH...
'COURSE WITH GOMERA BURNT AND THE PRODUCER DEAD, IT DOESN'T MATTER MUCH THAT I FINISHED THE STORYBOARDS.
THEY'RE NOTHING BUT USELESS SCRAPS OF PAPER NOW.
WELL LET'S HEAD OVER TO THE STUDIO. I WANT TO QUESTION THE TWO PEOPLE WHO SAW THE SUSPECT.
...

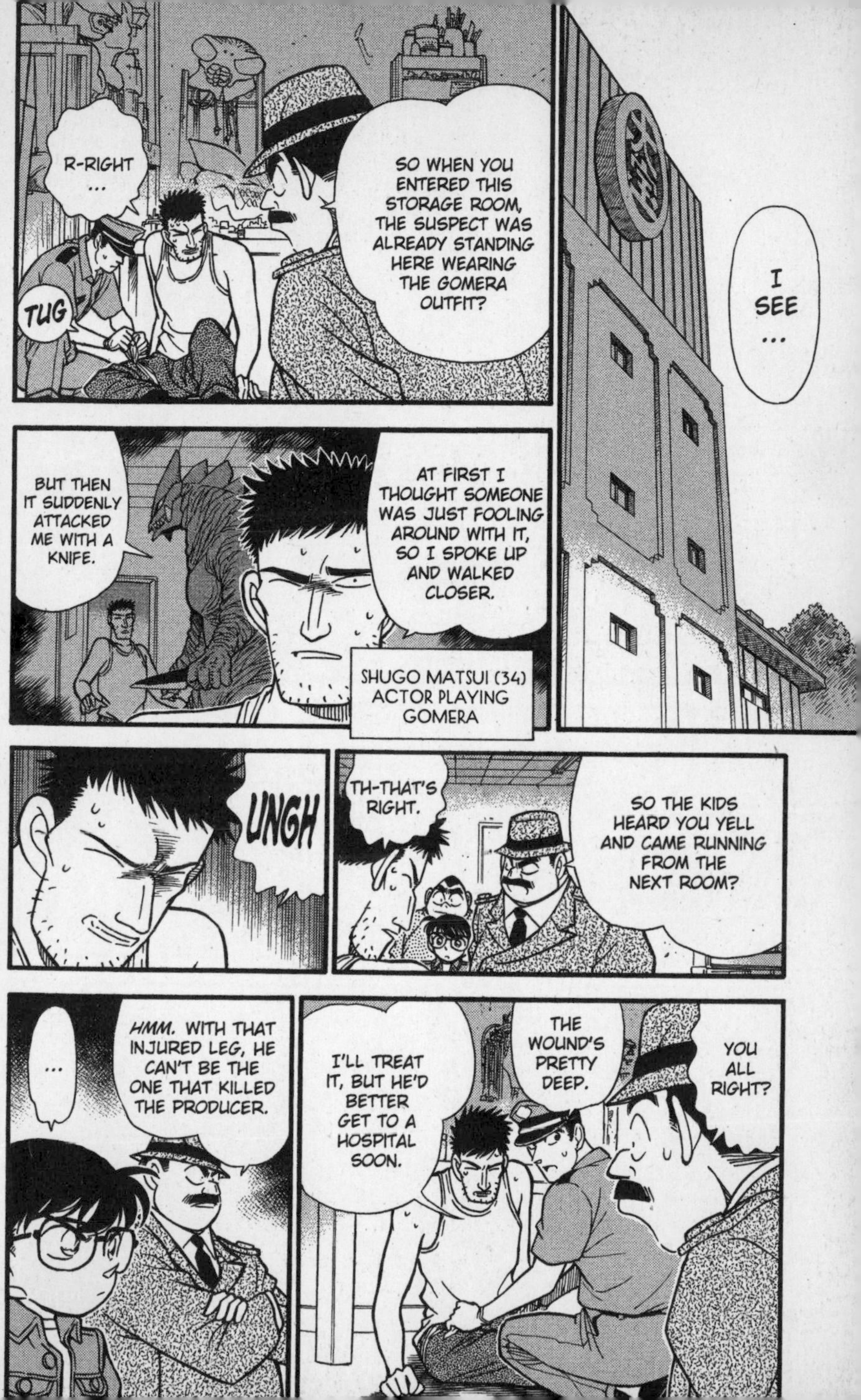
I SEE ...
SO WHEN YOU ENTERED THIS STORAGE ROOM, THE SUSPECT WAS ALREADY STANDING HERE WEARING THE GOMERA OUTFIT?
R-RIGHT ...
TUG
AT FIRST I THOUGHT SOMEONE WAS JUST FOOLING AROUND WITH IT, SO I SPOKE UP AND WALKED CLOSER.
BUT THEN IT SUDDENLY ATTACKED ME WITH A KNIFE.
SHUGO MATSUI (34) ACTOR PLAYING GOMERA
SO THE KIDS HEARD YOU YELL AND CAME RUNNING FROM THE NEXT ROOM?
TH-THAT'S RIGHT.
UNGH
YOU ALL RIGHT?
THE WOUND'S PRETTY DEEP.
I'LL TREAT IT, BUT HE'D BETTER GET TO A HOSPITAL SOON.
HMM. WITH THAT INJURED LEG, HE CAN'T BE THE ONE THAT KILLED THE PRODUCER.
...

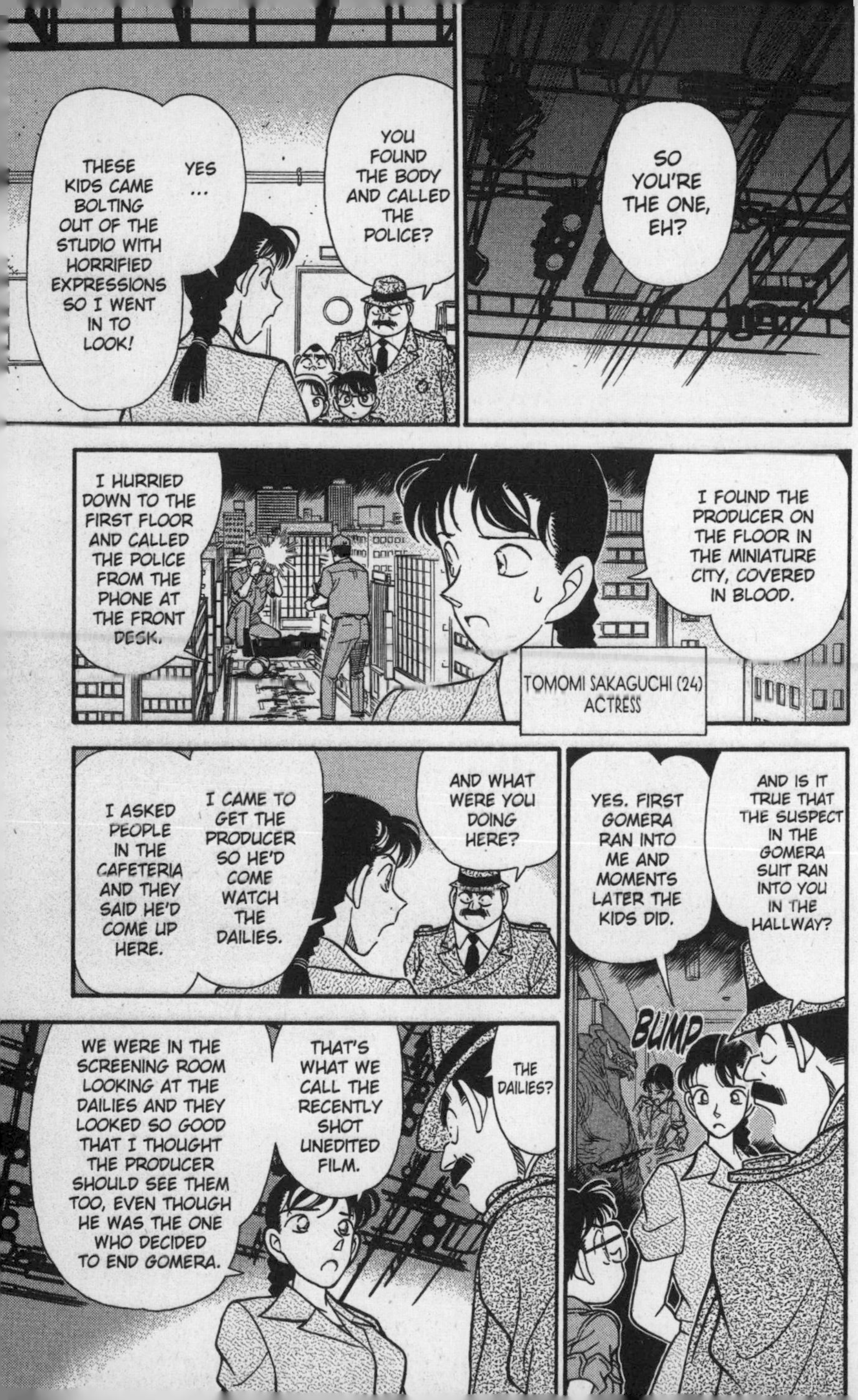
SO YOU'RE THE ONE, EH?
YOU FOUND THE BODY AND CALLED THE POLICE?
YES ...
THESE KIDS CAME BOLTING OUT OF THE STUDIO WITH HORRIFIED EXPRESSIONS SO I WENT IN TO LOOK!
I FOUND THE PRODUCER ON THE FLOOR IN THE MINIATURE CITY, COVERED IN BLOOD.
TOMOMI SAKAGUCHI (24) ACTRESS
I HURRIED DOWN TO THE FIRST FLOOR AND CALLED THE POLICE FROM THE PHONE AT THE FRONT DESK.
AND IS IT TRUE THAT THE SUSPECT IN THE GOMERA SUIT RAN INTO YOU IN THE HALLWAY?
YES. FIRST GOMERA RAN INTO ME AND MOMENTS LATER THE KIDS DID.
BUMP
AND WHAT WERE YOU DOING HERE?
I CAME TO GET THE PRODUCER SO HE'D COME WATCH THE DAILIES.
I ASKED PEOPLE IN THE CAFETERIA AND THEY SAID HE'D COME UP HERE.
THE DAILIES?
THAT'S WHAT WE CALL THE RECENTLY SHOT UNEDITED FILM.
WE WERE IN THE SCREENING ROOM LOOKING AT THE DAILIES AND THEY LOOKED SO GOOD THAT I THOUGHT THE PRODUCER SHOULD SEE THEM TOO, EVEN THOUGH HE WAS THE ONE WHO DECIDED TO END GOMERA.

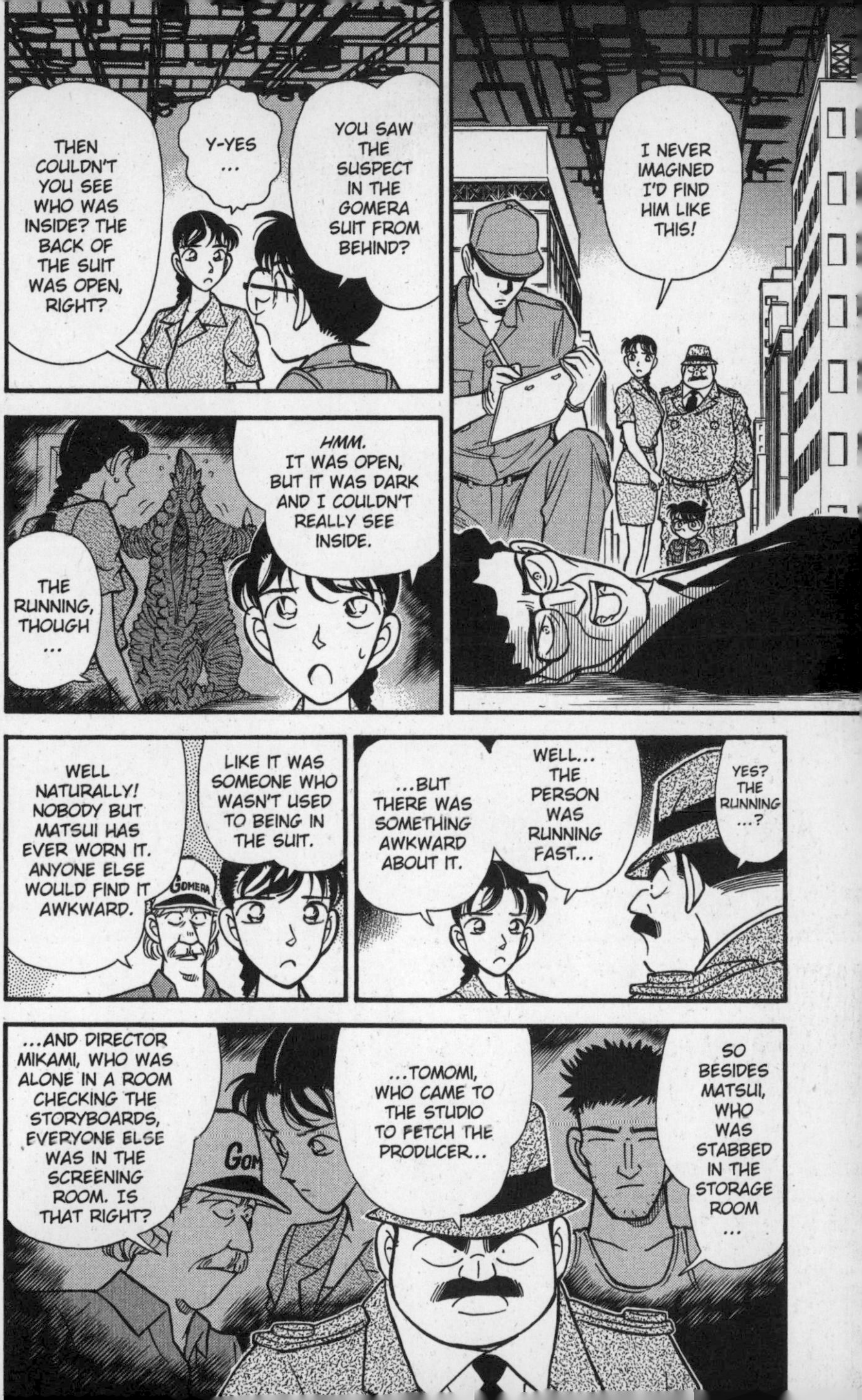

I NEVER IMAGINED I'D FIND HIM LIKE THIS!
YOU SAW THE SUSPECT IN THE GOMERA SUIT FROM BEHIND?
Y-YES ...
THEN COULDN'T YOU SEE WHO WAS INSIDE? THE BACK OF THE SUIT WAS OPEN, RIGHT?
HMM. IT WAS OPEN, BUT IT WAS DARK AND I COULDN'T REALLY SEE INSIDE.
THE RUNNING, THOUGH ...
YES? THE RUNNING ...?
WELL... THE PERSON WAS RUNNING FAST...
...BUT THERE WAS SOMETHING AWKWARD ABOUT IT.
LIKE IT WAS SOMEONE WHO WASN'T USED TO BEING IN THE SUIT.
GOMERA
WELL NATURALLY! NOBODY BUT MATSUI HAS EVER WORN IT. ANYONE ELSE WOULD FIND IT AWKWARD.
SO BESIDES MATSUI, WHO WAS STABBED IN THE STORAGE ROOM ...
...TOMOMI, WHO CAME TO THE STUDIO TO FETCH THE PRODUCER...
...AND DIRECTOR MIKAMI, WHO WAS ALONE IN A ROOM CHECKING THE STORYBOARDS, EVERYONE ELSE WAS IN THE SCREENING ROOM. IS THAT RIGHT?

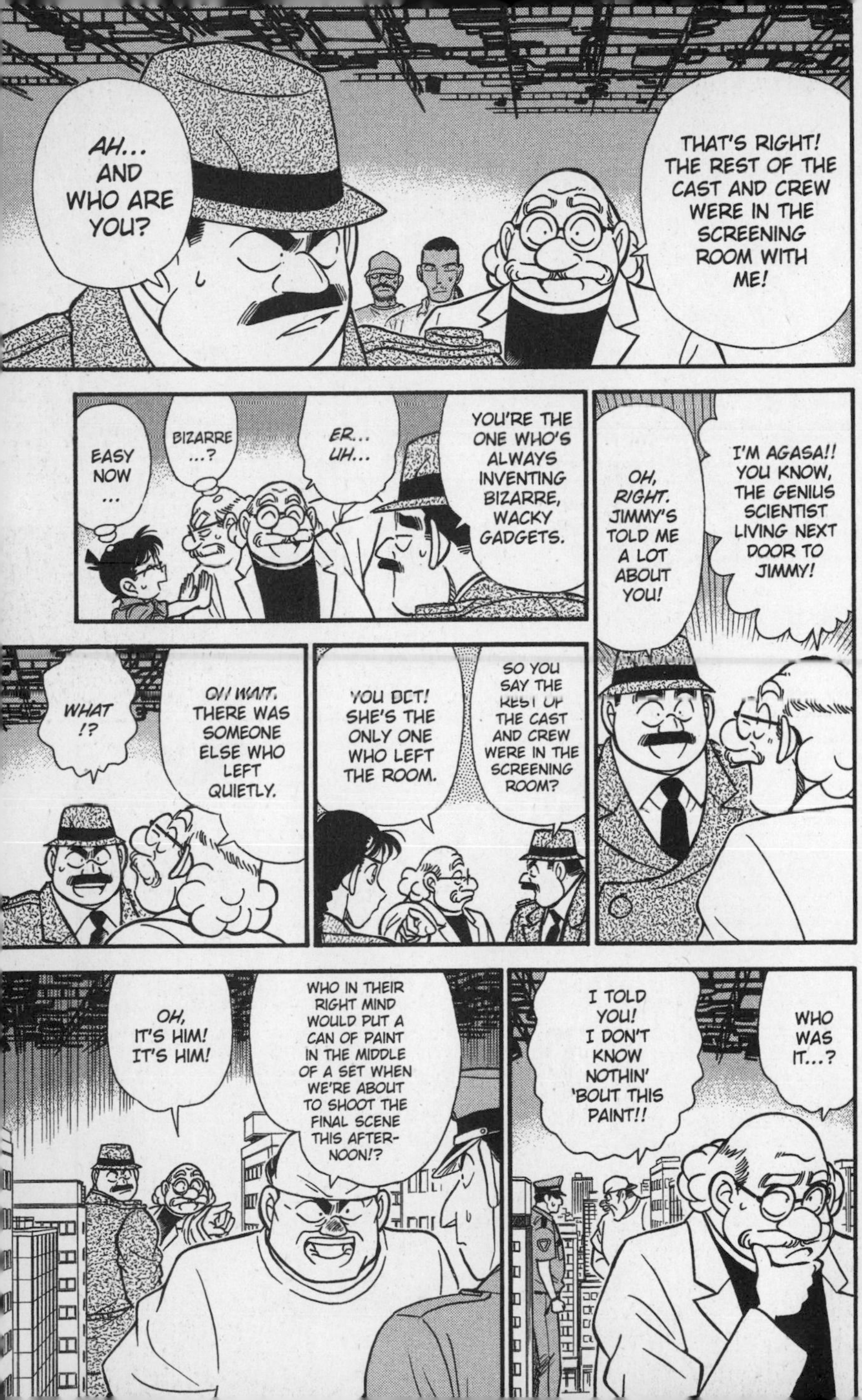
THAT'S RIGHT! THE REST OF THE CAST AND CREW WERE IN THE SCREENING ROOM WITH ME!
AH... AND WHO ARE YOU?
I'M AGASA!! YOU KNOW, THE GENIUS SCIENTIST LIVING NEXT DOOR TO JIMMY!
OH, RIGHT. JIMMY'S TOLD ME A LOT ABOUT YOU!
YOU'RE THE ONE WHO'S ALWAYS INVENTING BIZARRE, WACKY GADGETS.
ER... UH...
BIZARRE ...?
EASY NOW ...
SO YOU SAY THE REST OF THE CAST AND CREW WERE IN THE SCREENING ROOM?
YOU BET! SHE'S THE ONLY ONE WHO LEFT THE ROOM.
OH WAIT. THERE WAS SOMEONE ELSE WHO LEFT QUIETLY.
WHAT !?
WHO WAS IT...?
I TOLD YOU! I DON'T KNOW NOTHIN' 'BOUT THIS PAINT!!
WHO IN THEIR RIGHT MIND WOULD PUT A CAN OF PAINT IN THE MIDDLE OF A SET WHEN WE'RE ABOUT TO SHOOT THE FINAL SCENE THIS AFTER-NOON!?
OH, IT'S HIM! IT'S HIM!

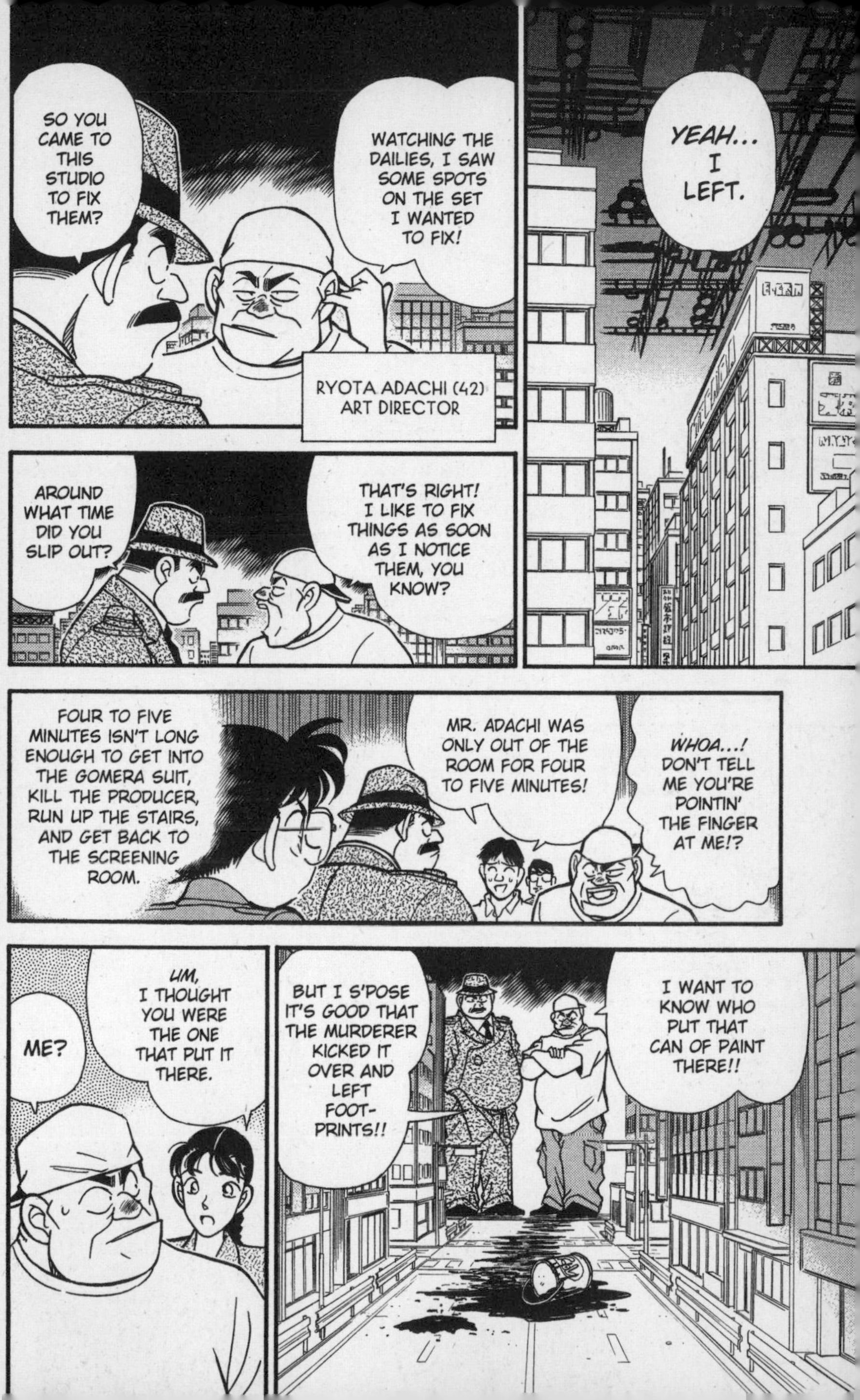
YEAH... I LEFT.
WATCHING THE DAILIES, I SAW SOME SPOTS ON THE SET I WANTED TO FIX!
SO YOU CAME TO THIS STUDIO TO FIX THEM?
RYOTA ADACHI (42) ART DIRECTOR
THAT'S RIGHT! I LIKE TO FIX THINGS AS SOON AS I NOTICE THEM, YOU KNOW?
AROUND WHAT TIME DID YOU SLIP OUT?
WHOA...! DON'T TELL ME YOU'RE POINTIN' THE FINGER AT ME!?
MR. ADACHI WAS ONLY OUT OF THE ROOM FOR FOUR TO FIVE MINUTES!
FOUR TO FIVE MINUTES ISN'T LONG ENOUGH TO GET INTO THE GOMERA SUIT, KILL THE PRODUCER, RUN UP THE STAIRS, AND GET BACK TO THE SCREENING ROOM.
I WANT TO KNOW WHO PUT THAT CAN OF PAINT THERE!!
BUT I S'POSE IT'S GOOD THAT THE MURDERER KICKED IT OVER AND LEFT FOOT-PRINTS!!
UM, I THOUGHT YOU WERE THE ONE THAT PUT IT THERE.
ME?

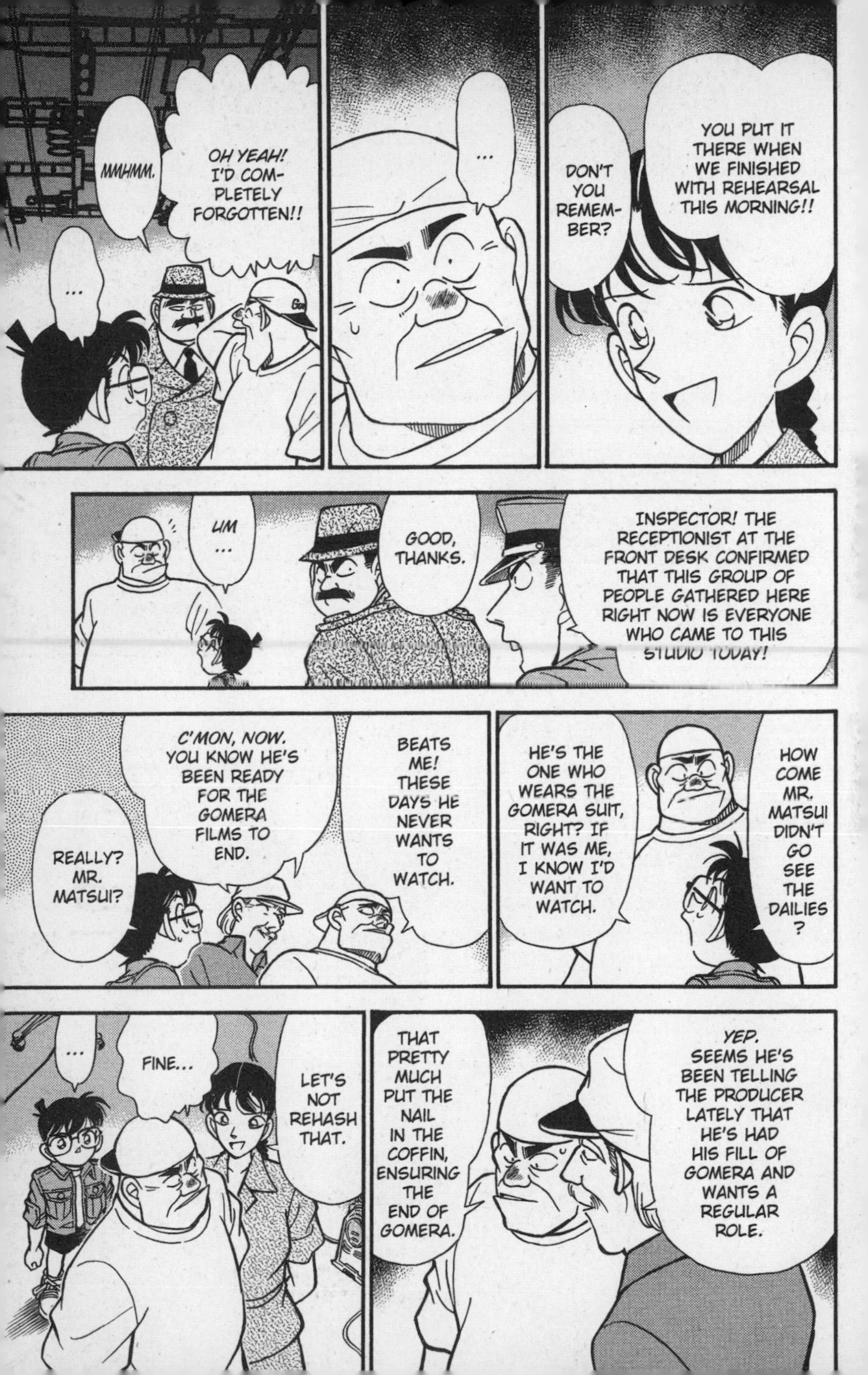
YOU PUT IT THERE WHEN WE FINISHED WITH REHEARSAL THIS MORNING!!
DON'T YOU REMEM-BER?
...
OH YEAH! I'D COM-PLETELY FORGOTTEN!!
MMHMM.
...
INSPECTOR! THE RECEPTIONIST AT THE FRONT DESK CONFIRMED THAT THIS GROUP OF PEOPLE GATHERED HERE RIGHT NOW IS EVERYONE WHO CAME TO THIS STUDIO TODAY!
GOOD, THANKS.
UM ...
HOW COME MR. MATSUI DIDN'T GO SEE THE DAILIES ?
HE'S THE ONE WHO WEARS THE GOMERA SUIT, RIGHT? IF IT WAS ME, I KNOW I'D WANT TO WATCH.
BEATS ME! THESE DAYS HE NEVER WANTS TO WATCH.
C'MON, NOW. YOU KNOW HE'S BEEN READY FOR THE GOMERA FILMS TO END.
REALLY? MR. MATSUI?
YEP. SEEMS HE'S BEEN TELLING THE PRODUCER LATELY THAT HE'S HAD HIS FILL OF GOMERA AND WANTS A REGULAR ROLE.
THAT PRETTY MUCH PUT THE NAIL IN THE COFFIN, ENSURING THE END OF GOMERA.
LET'S NOT REHASH THAT.
FINE...
...

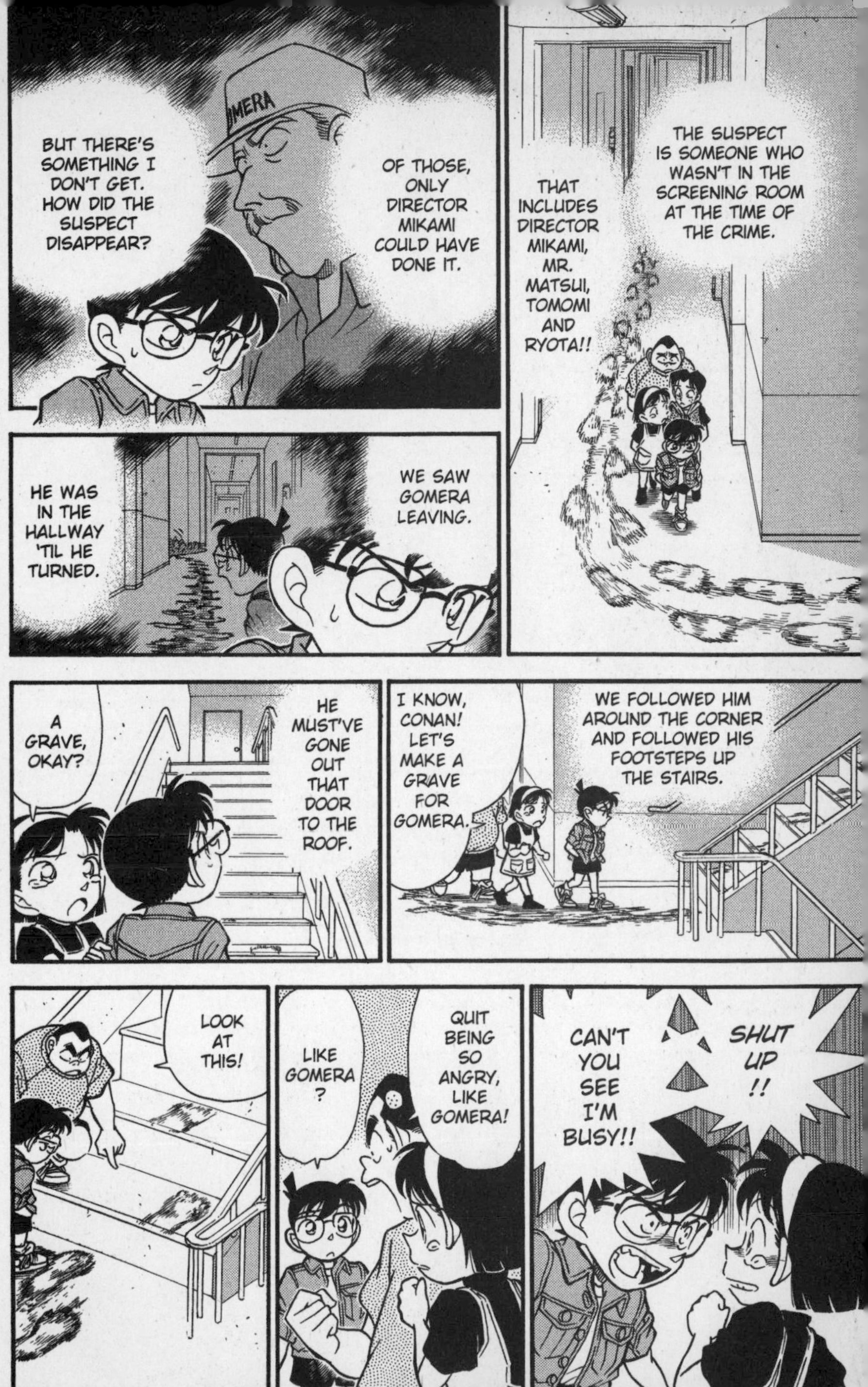
THE SUSPECT IS SOMEONE WHO WASN'T IN THE SCREENING ROOM AT THE TIME OF THE CRIME.
THAT INCLUDES DIRECTOR MIKAMI, MR. MATSUI, TOMOMI AND RYOTA!!
OF THOSE, ONLY DIRECTOR MIKAMI COULD HAVE DONE IT.
BUT THERE'S SOMETHING I DON'T GET. HOW DID THE SUSPECT DISAPPEAR?
WE SAW GOMERA LEAVING.
HE WAS IN THE HALLWAY 'TIL HE TURNED.
WE FOLLOWED HIM AROUND THE CORNER AND FOLLOWED HIS FOOTSTEPS UP THE STAIRS.
I KNOW, CONAN! LET'S MAKE A GRAVE FOR GOMERA.
HE MUST'VE GONE OUT THAT DOOR TO THE ROOF.
A GRAVE, OKAY?
SHUT UP!!
CAN'T YOU SEE I'M BUSY!!
QUIT BEING SO ANGRY, LIKE GOMERA!
LIKE GOMERA?
LOOK AT THIS!

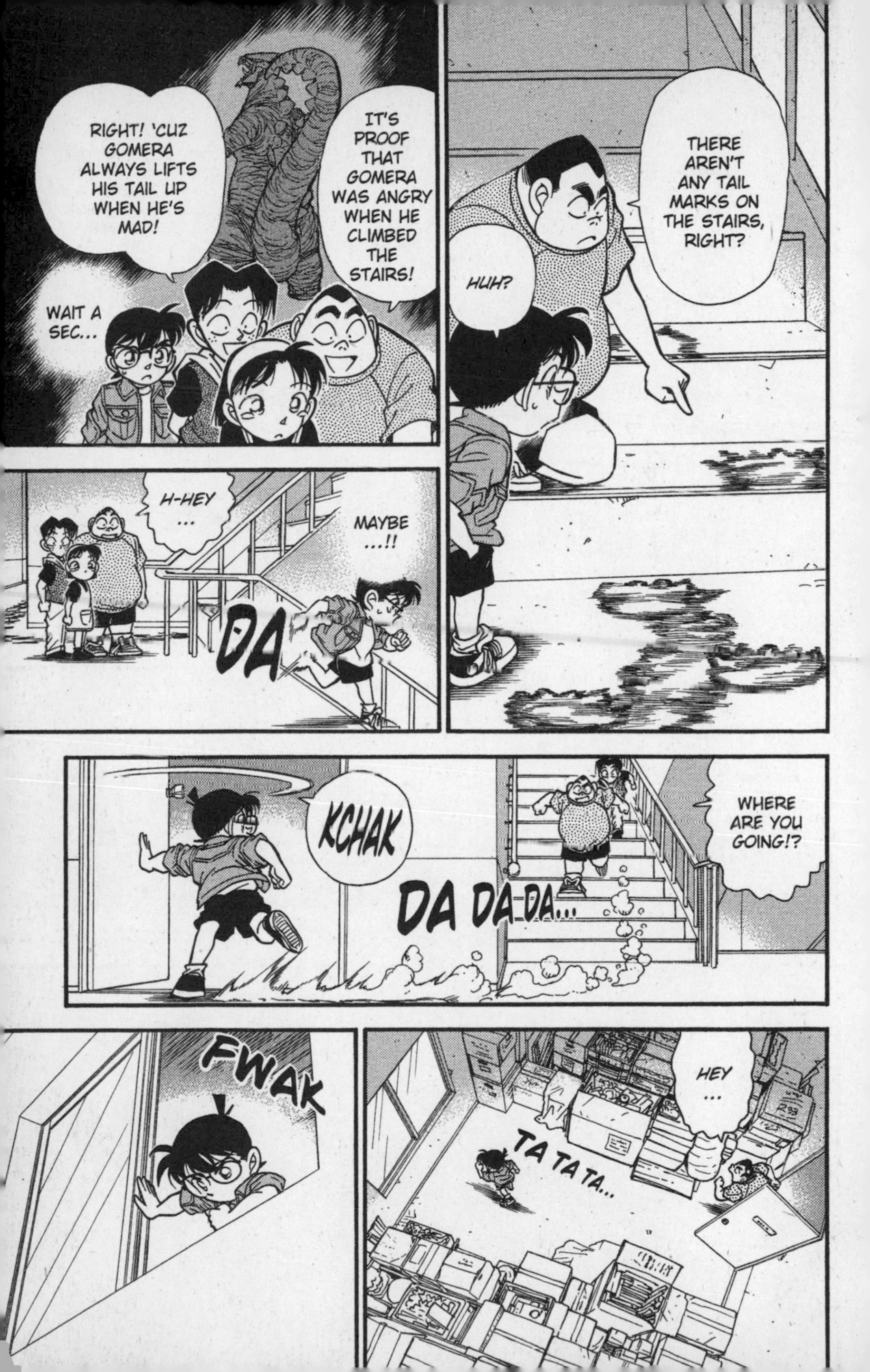
THERE AREN'T ANY TAIL MARKS ON THE STAIRS, RIGHT?
HUH?
IT'S PROOF THAT GOMERA WAS ANGRY WHEN HE CLIMBED THE STAIRS!
RIGHT! 'CUZ GOMERA ALWAYS LIFTS HIS TAIL UP WHEN HE'S MAD!
WAIT A SEC...
MAYBE ...!!
H-HEY ...
DA
WHERE ARE YOU GOING!?
DA DA DA...
KCHAK
HEY ...
TA TA TA...
FWAK

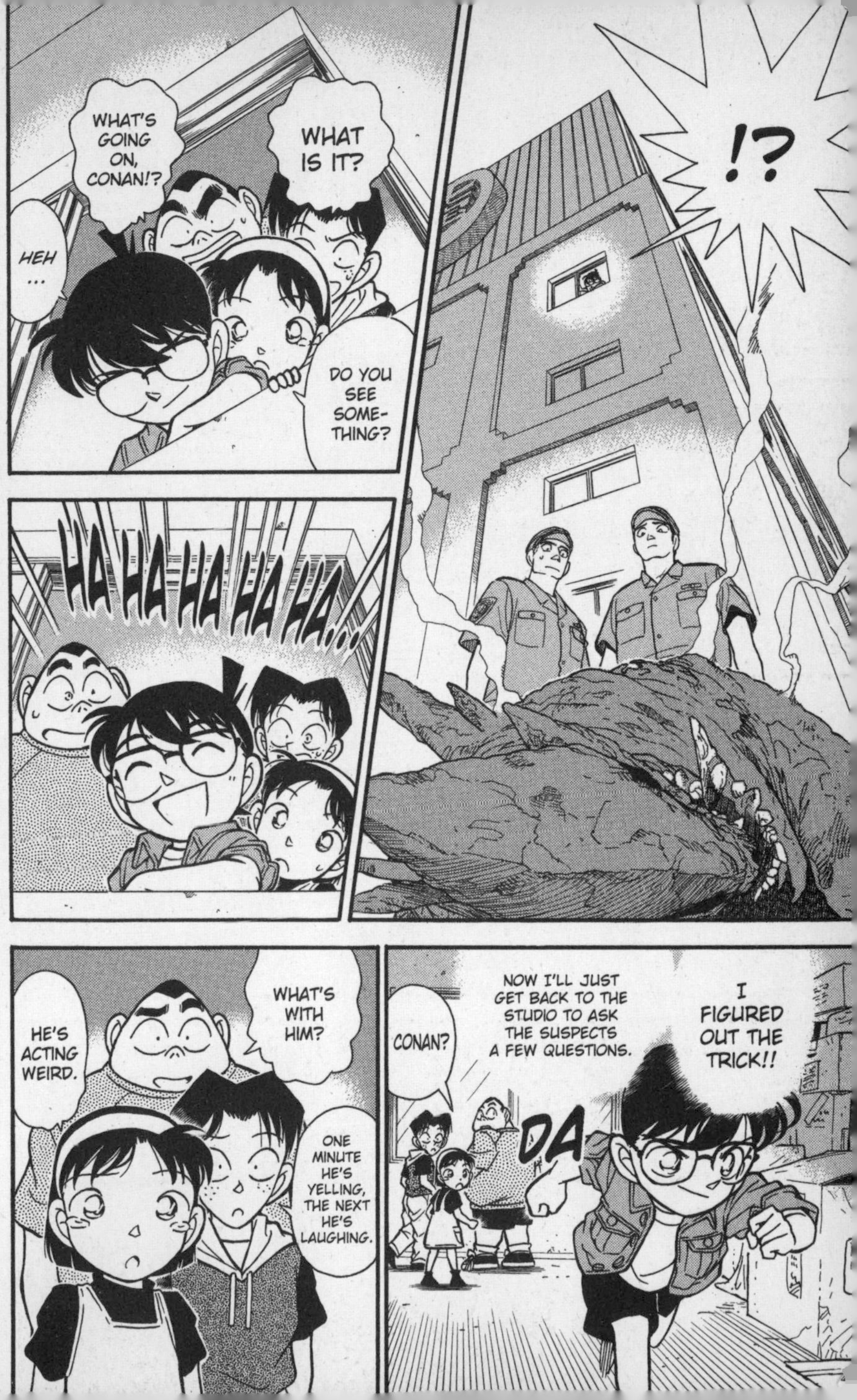
!?
WHAT IS IT?
WHAT'S GOING ON, CONAN!?
HEH ...
DO YOU SEE SOME-THING?
HA HA HA HA HA HA...
I FIGURED OUT THE TRICK!!
NOW I'LL JUST GET BACK TO THE STUDIO TO ASK THE SUSPECTS A FEW QUESTIONS.
CONAN?
DA
WHAT'S WITH HIM?
HE'S ACTING WEIRD.
ONE MINUTE HE'S YELLING, THE NEXT HE'S LAUGHING.

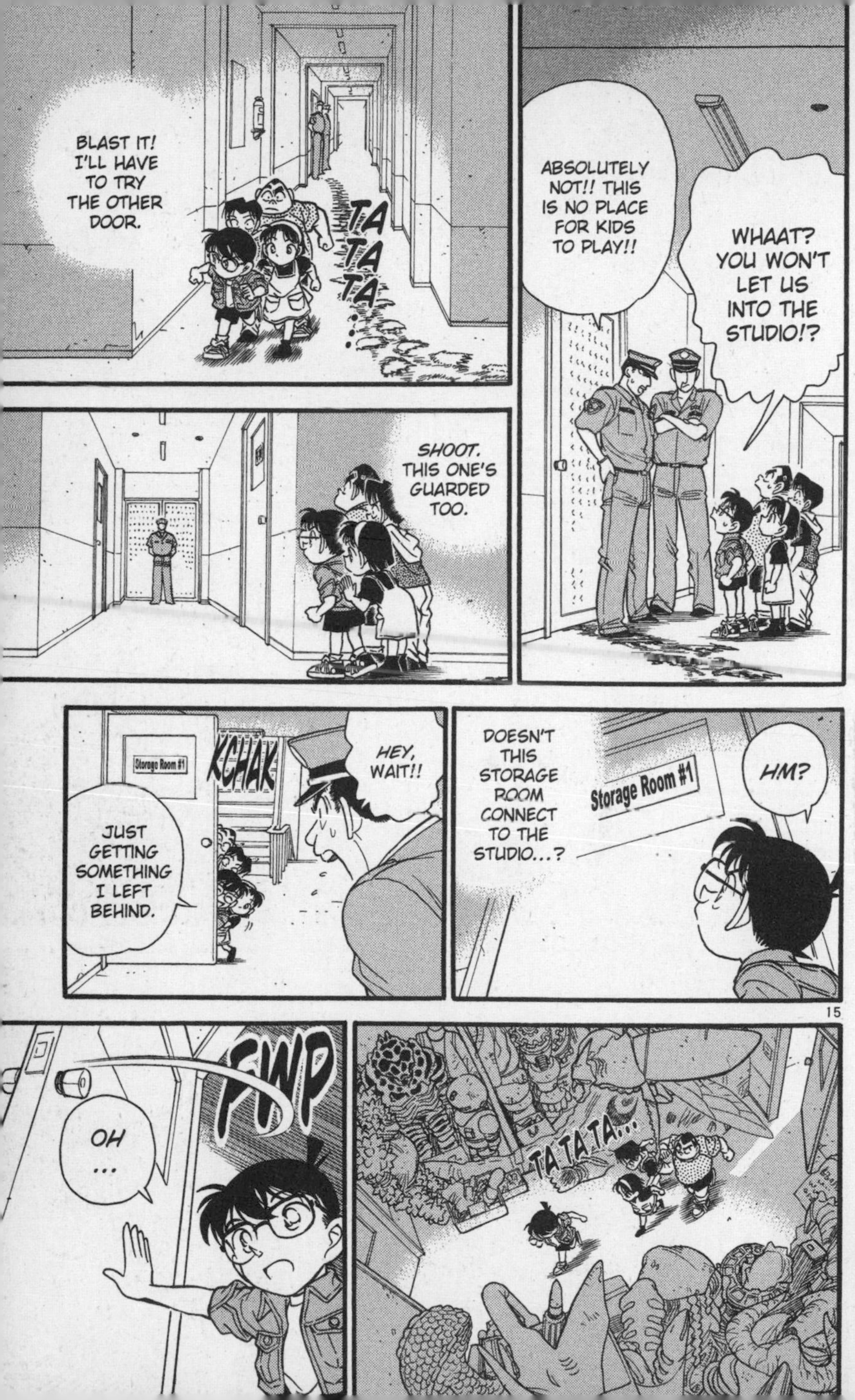

ABSOLUTELY NOT!! THIS IS NO PLACE FOR KIDS TO PLAY!!
WHAAT? YOU WON'T LET US INTO THE STUDIO!?
BLAST IT! I'LL HAVE TO TRY THE OTHER DOOR.
TA TA TA...
SHOOT. THIS ONE'S GUARDED TOO.
HM?
Storage Room #1
DOESN'T THIS STORAGE ROOM CONNECT TO THE STUDIO...?
HEY, WAIT!!
KCHAK
Storage Room #1
JUST GETTING SOMETHING I LEFT BEHIND.
TA TA TA...
FWP
OH ...

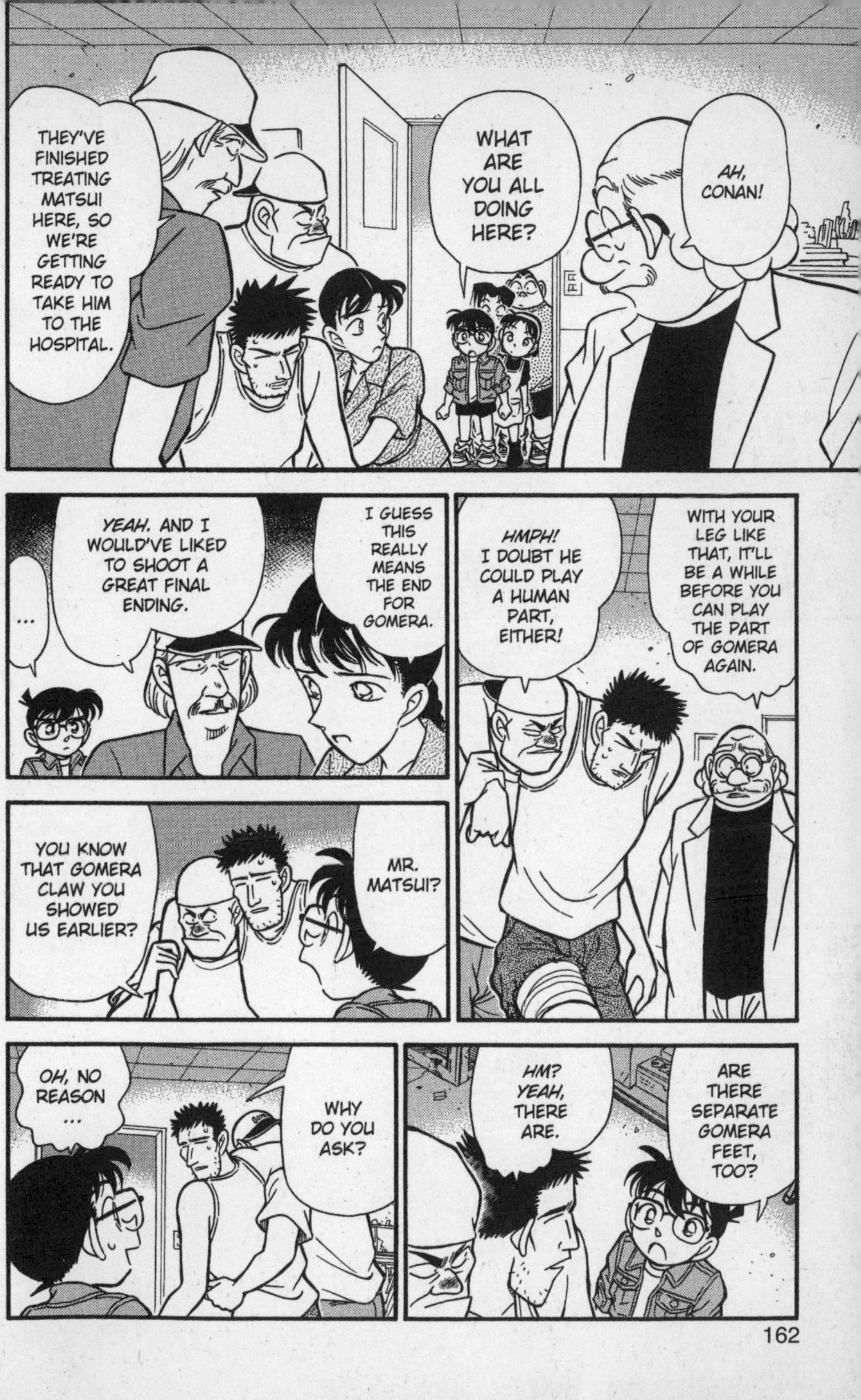
AH, CONAN!
WHAT ARE YOU ALL DOING HERE?
THEY'VE FINISHED TREATING MATSUI HERE, SO WE'RE GETTING READY TO TAKE HIM TO THE HOSPITAL.
WITH YOUR LEG LIKE THAT, IT'LL BE A WHILE BEFORE YOU CAN PLAY THE PART OF GOMERA AGAIN.
HMPH! I DOUBT HE COULD PLAY A HUMAN PART, EITHER!
I GUESS THIS REALLY MEANS THE END FOR GOMERA.
YEAH. AND I WOULD'VE LIKED TO SHOOT A GREAT FINAL ENDING.
...
MR. MATSUI?
YOU KNOW THAT GOMERA CLAW YOU SHOWED US EARLIER?
ARE THERE SEPARATE GOMERA FEET, TOO?
HM? YEAH, THERE ARE.
WHY DO YOU ASK?
OH, NO REASON ...

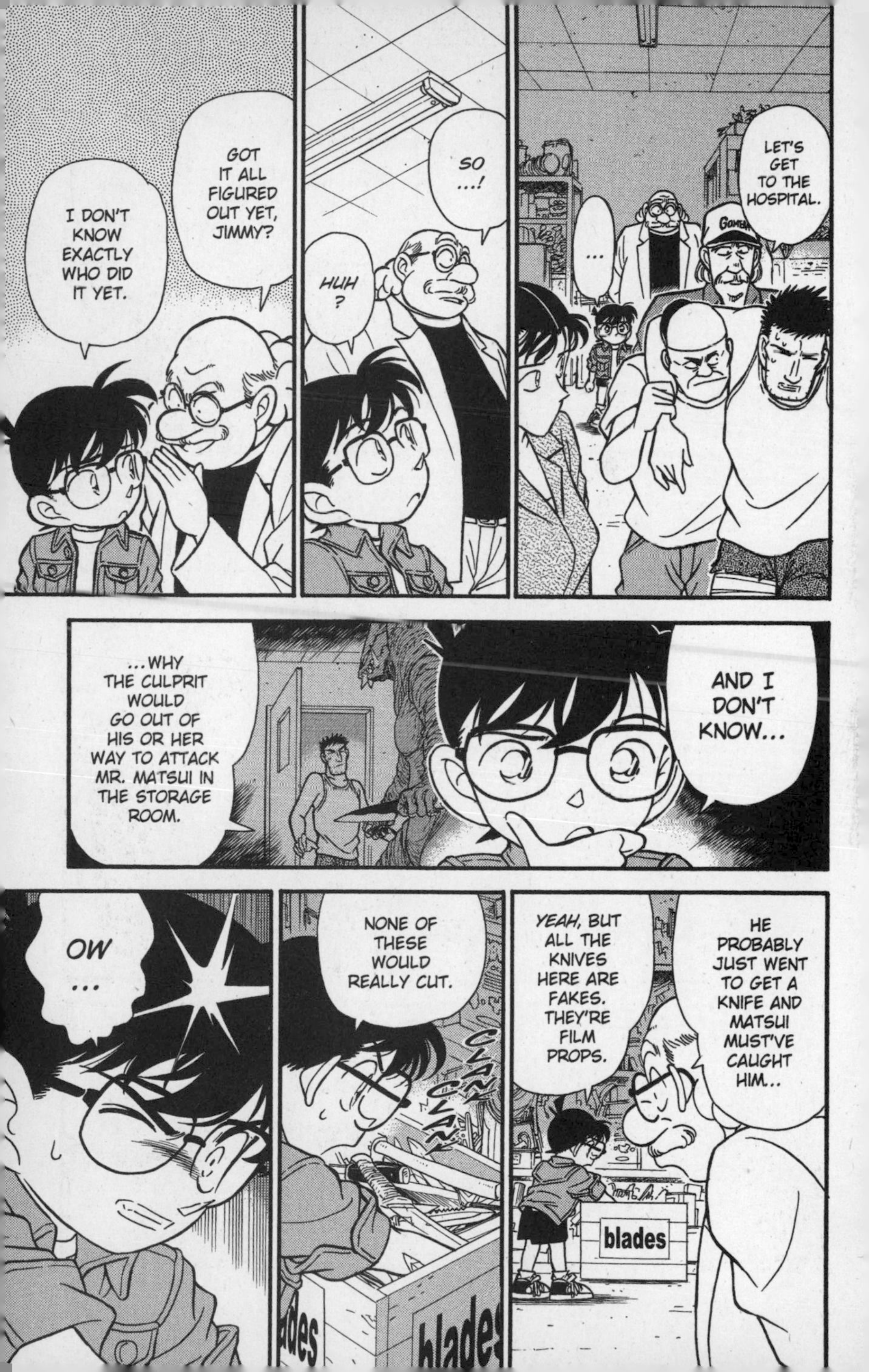
LET'S GET TO THE HOSPITAL.
...
SO ...!
HUH ?
GOT IT ALL FIGURED OUT YET, JIMMY?
I DON'T KNOW EXACTLY WHO DID IT YET.
AND I DON'T KNOW...
...WHY THE CULPRIT WOULD GO OUT OF HIS OR HER WAY TO ATTACK MR. MATSUI IN THE STORAGE ROOM.
HE PROBABLY JUST WENT TO GET A KNIFE AND MATSUI MUST'VE CAUGHT HIM..
YEAH, BUT ALL THE KNIVES HERE ARE FAKES. THEY'RE FILM PROPS.
blades
NONE OF THESE WOULD REALLY CUT.
CLANK
CLANK
blades
blades
OW ...

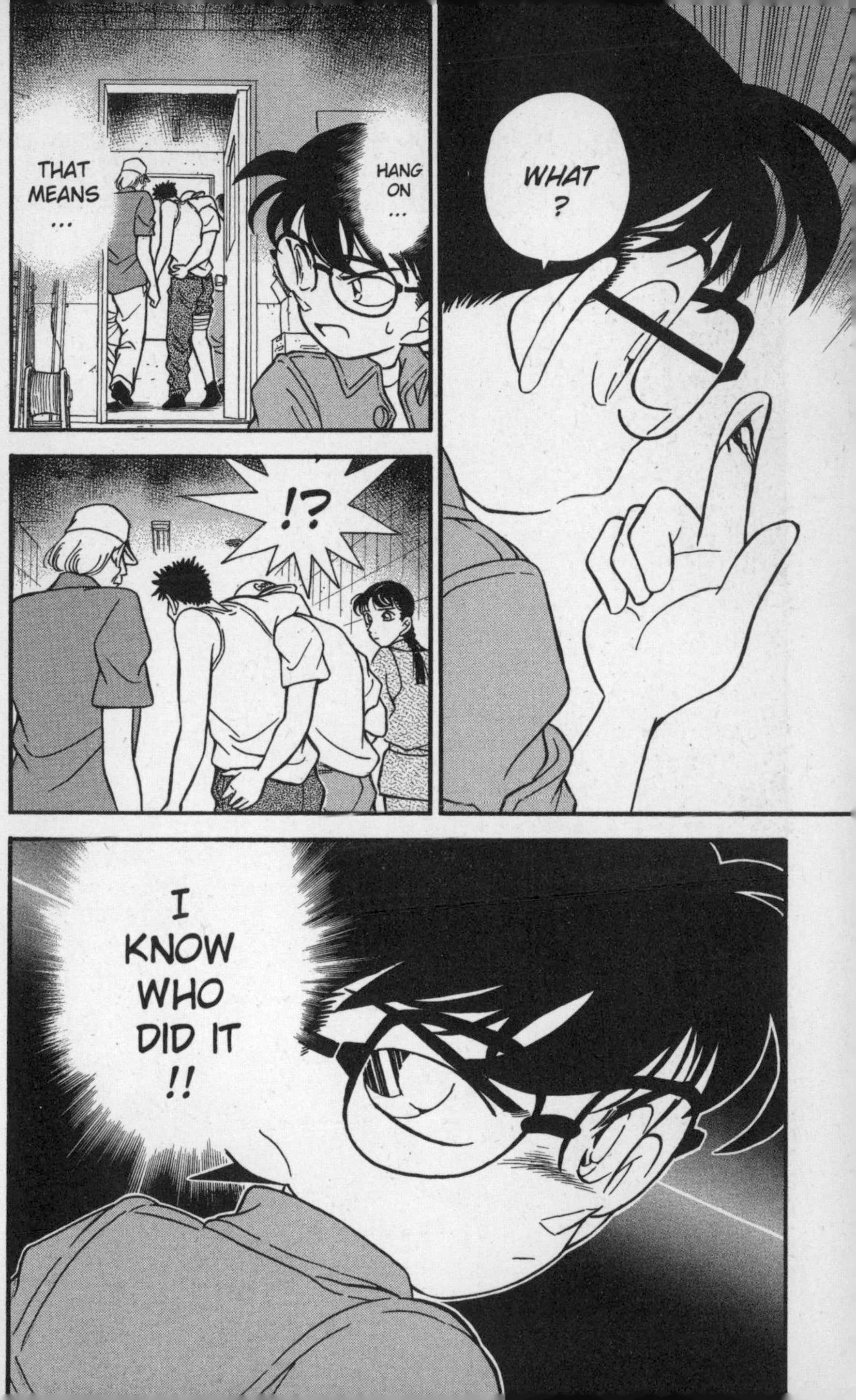
WHAT ?
HANG ON ...
THAT MEANS ...
!?
I KNOW WHO DID IT !!

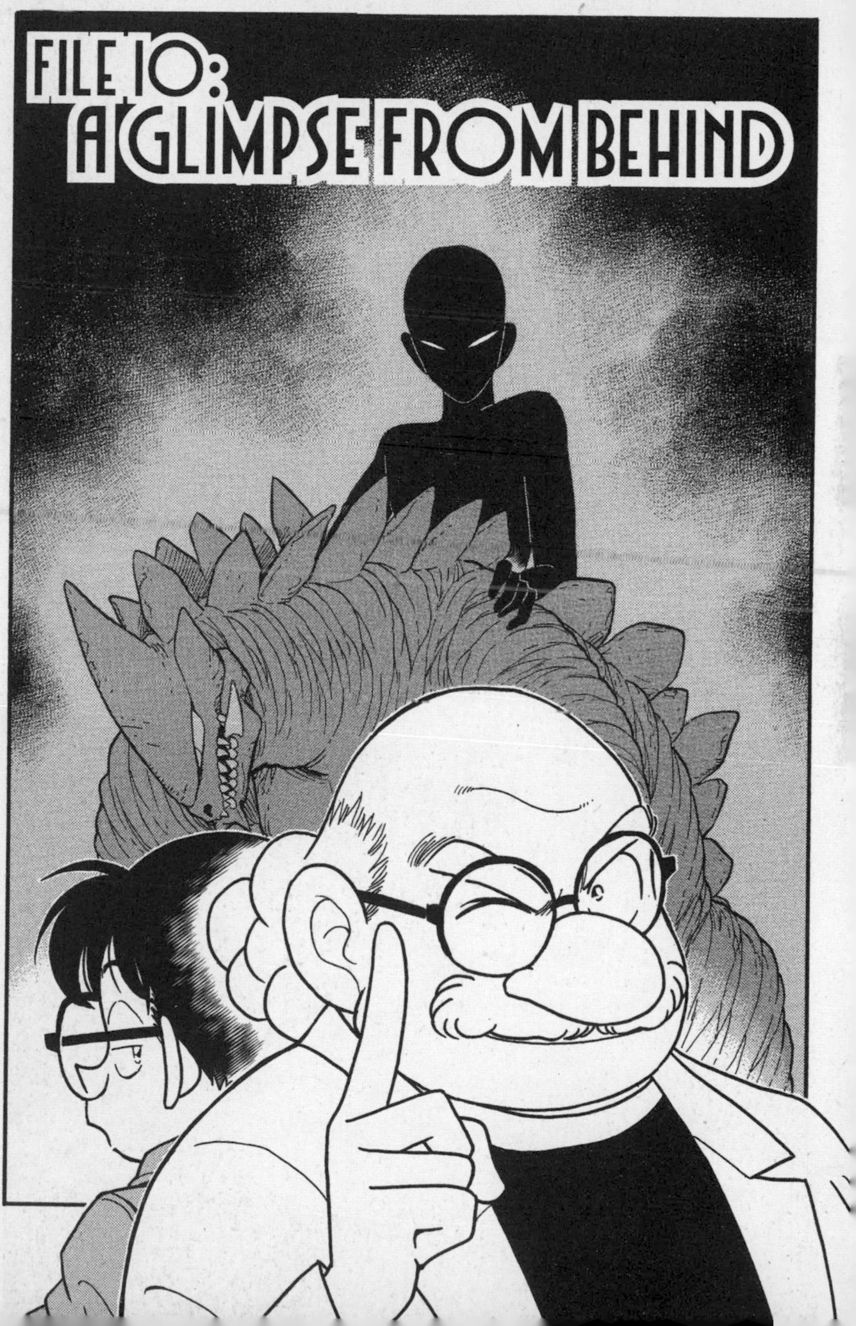
FILE 10:
A GLIMPSE FROM BEHIND

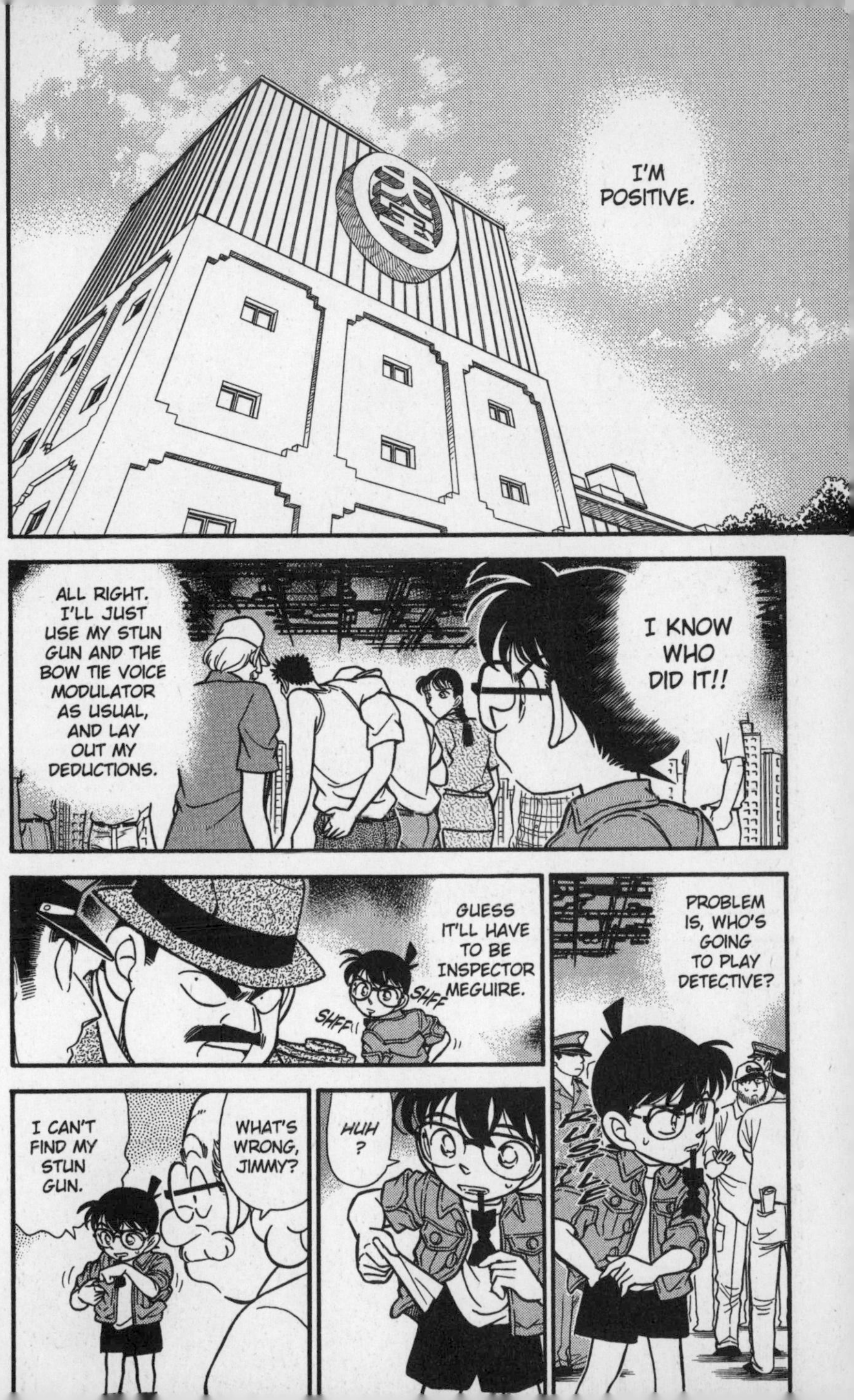
I'M POSITIVE.
I KNOW WHO DID IT!!
ALL RIGHT. I'LL JUST USE MY STUN GUN AND THE BOW TIE VOICE MODULATOR AS USUAL, AND LAY OUT MY DEDUCTIONS.
PROBLEM IS, WHO'S GOING TO PLAY DETECTIVE?
GUESS IT'LL HAVE TO BE INSPECTOR MEGUIRE.
SHFF
SHFF
HUH?
WHAT'S WRONG, JIMMY?
I CAN'T FIND MY STUN GUN.

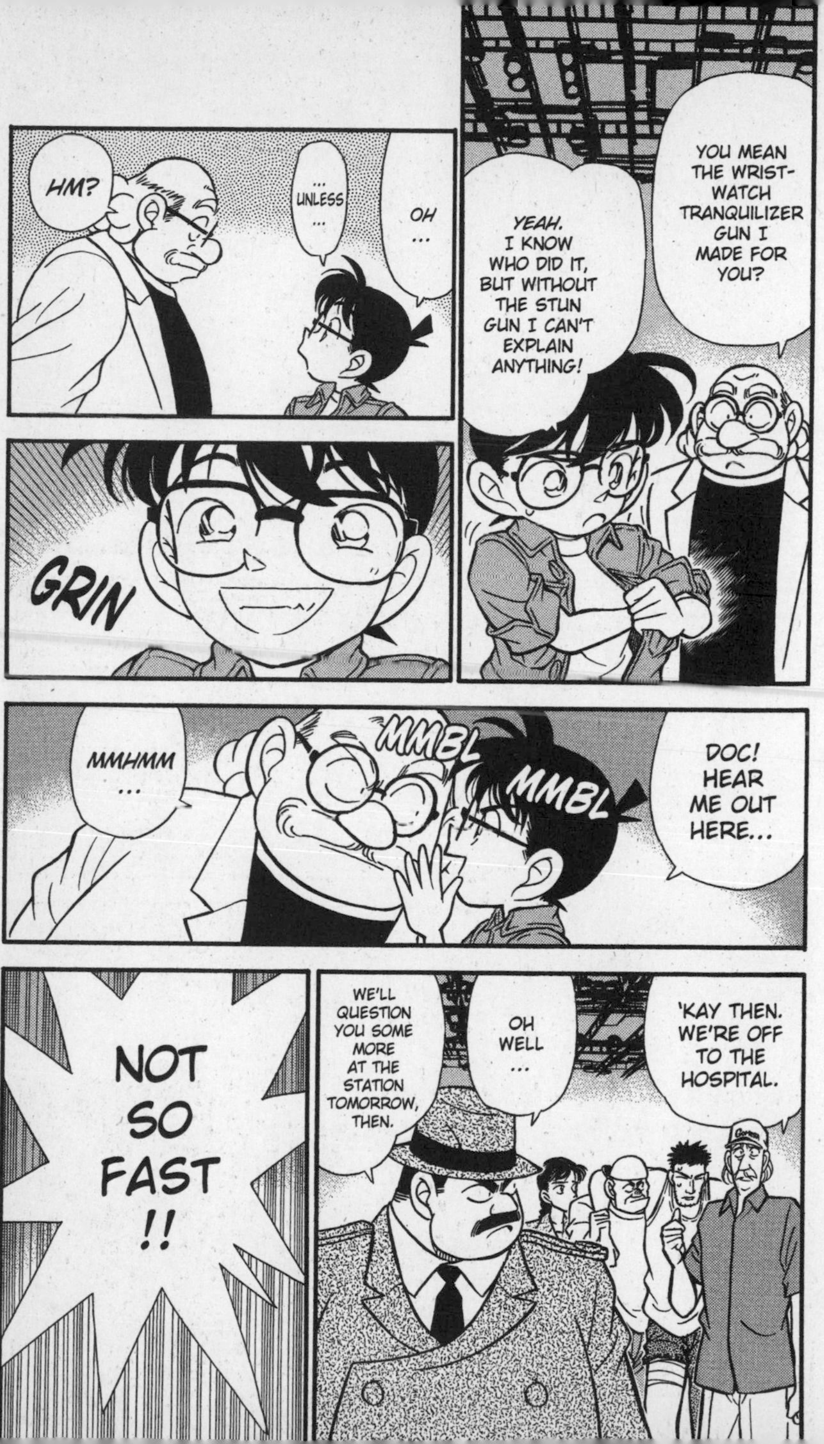
YOU MEAN THE WRIST-WATCH TRANQUILIZER GUN I MADE FOR YOU?
YEAH. I KNOW WHO DID IT, BUT WITHOUT THE STUN GUN I CAN'T EXPLAIN ANYTHING!
OH ...
... UNLESS ...
HM?
GRIN
DOC! HEAR ME OUT HERE...
MMBL
MMBL
MMHMM ...
'KAY THEN. WE'RE OFF TO THE HOSPITAL.
OH WELL ...
WE'LL QUESTION YOU SOME MORE AT THE STATION TOMORROW, THEN.
NOT SO FAST !!

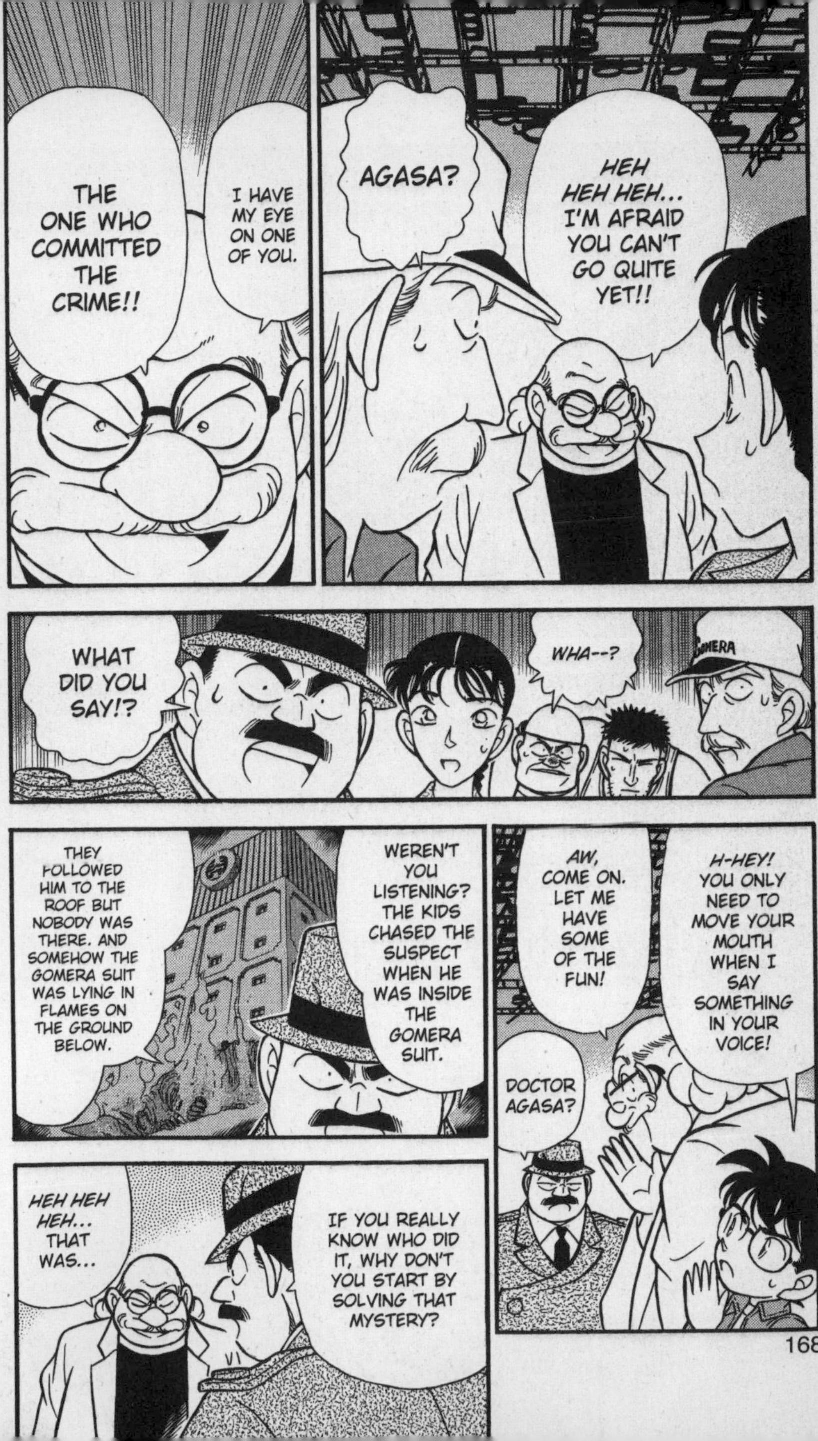
HEH HEH HEH... I'M AFRAID YOU CAN'T GO QUITE YET!!
AGASA?
I HAVE MY EYE ON ONE OF YOU.
THE ONE WHO COMMITTED THE CRIME!!
WHA--?
GOMERA
WHAT DID YOU SAY!?
H-HEY! YOU ONLY NEED TO MOVE YOUR MOUTH WHEN I SAY SOMETHING IN YOUR VOICE!
AW, COME ON. LET ME HAVE SOME OF THE FUN!
DOCTOR AGASA?
WEREN'T YOU LISTENING? THE KIDS CHASED THE SUSPECT WHEN HE WAS INSIDE THE GOMERA SUIT.
THEY FOLLOWED HIM TO THE ROOF BUT NOBODY WAS THERE. AND SOMEHOW THE GOMERA SUIT WAS LYING IN FLAMES ON THE GROUND BELOW.
IF YOU REALLY KNOW WHO DID IT, WHY DON'T YOU START BY SOLVING THAT MYSTERY?
HEH HEH HEH... THAT WAS...

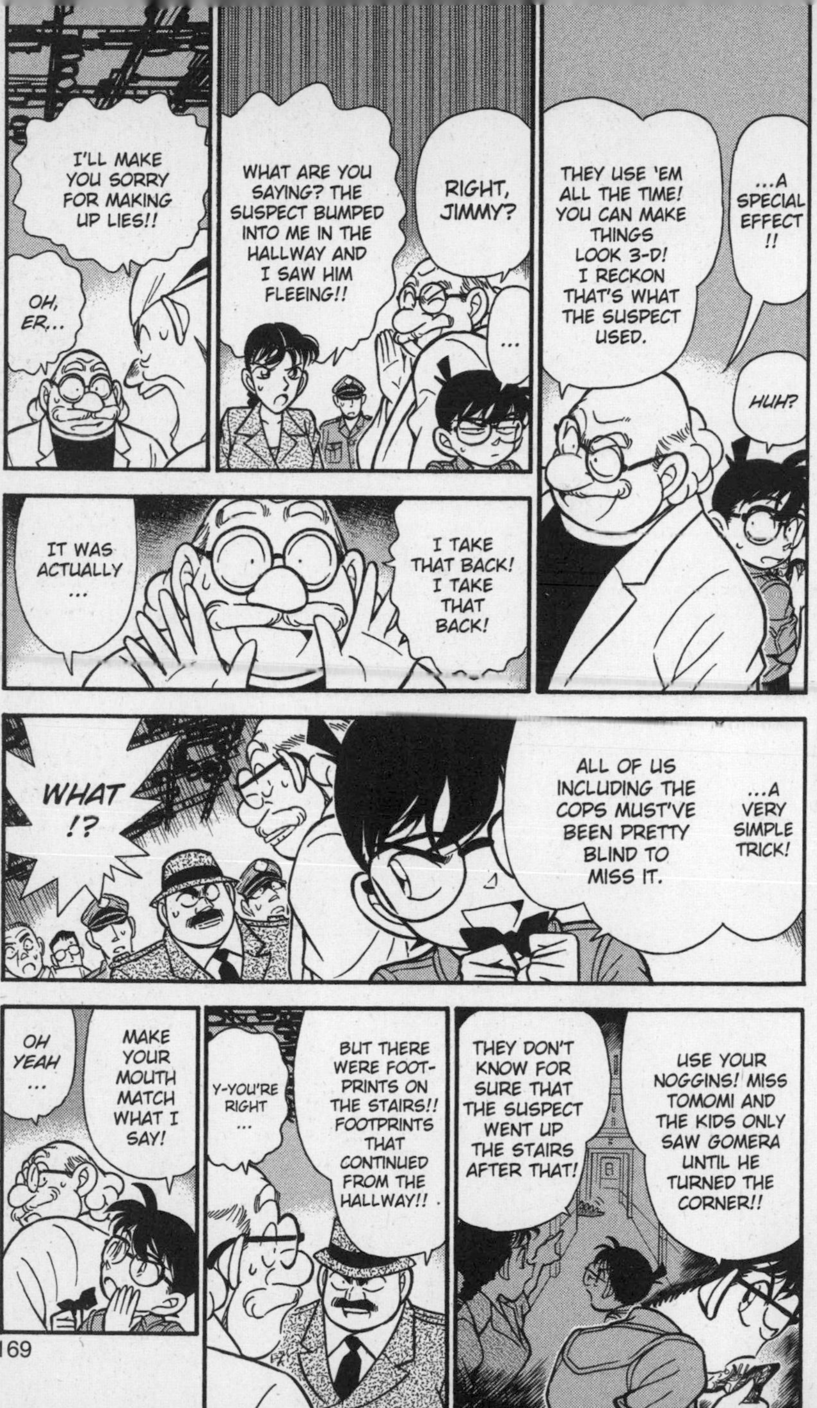
...A SPECIAL EFFECT!!
HUH?
THEY USE 'EM ALL THE TIME! YOU CAN MAKE THINGS LOOK 3-D! I RECKON THAT'S WHAT THE SUSPECT USED.
RIGHT, JIMMY?
...
WHAT ARE YOU SAYING? THE SUSPECT BUMPED INTO ME IN THE HALLWAY AND I SAW HIM FLEEING!!
I'LL MAKE YOU SORRY FOR MAKING UP LIES!!
OH, ER...
I TAKE THAT BACK! I TAKE THAT BACK!
IT WAS ACTUALLY ...
...A VERY SIMPLE TRICK!
ALL OF US INCLUDING THE COPS MUST'VE BEEN PRETTY BLIND TO MISS IT.
WHAT !?
USE YOUR NOGGINS! MISS TOMOMI AND THE KIDS ONLY SAW GOMERA UNTIL HE TURNED THE CORNER!!
THEY DON'T KNOW FOR SURE THAT THE SUSPECT WENT UP THE STAIRS AFTER THAT!
BUT THERE WERE FOOT-PRINTS ON THE STAIRS!! FOOTPRINTS THAT CONTINUED FROM THE HALLWAY!!
Y-YOU'RE RIGHT ...
MAKE YOUR MOUTH MATCH WHAT I SAY!
OH YEAH ...

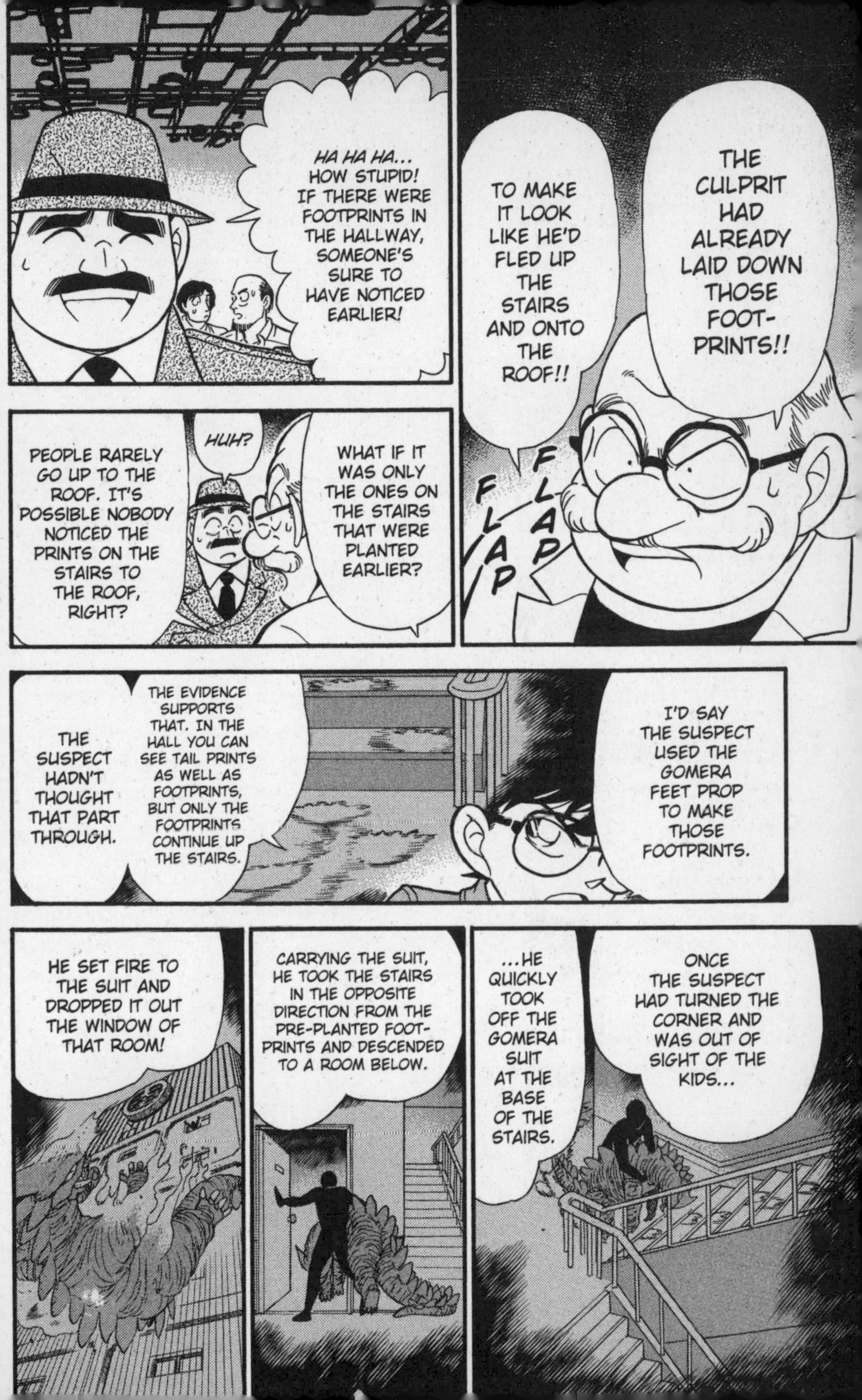
THE CULPRIT HAD ALREADY LAID DOWN THOSE FOOT-PRINTS!!
TO MAKE IT LOOK LIKE HE'D FLED UP THE STAIRS AND ONTO THE ROOF!!
FLAP
FLAP
HA HA HA... HOW STUPID! IF THERE WERE FOOTPRINTS IN THE HALLWAY, SOMEONE'S SURE TO HAVE NOTICED EARLIER!
WHAT IF IT WAS ONLY THE ONES ON THE STAIRS THAT WERE PLANTED EARLIER?
HUH?
PEOPLE RARELY GO UP TO THE ROOF. IT'S POSSIBLE NOBODY NOTICED THE PRINTS ON THE STAIRS TO THE ROOF, RIGHT?
I'D SAY THE SUSPECT USED THE GOMERA FEET PROP TO MAKE THOSE FOOTPRINTS.
THE EVIDENCE SUPPORTS THAT. IN THE HALL YOU CAN SEE TAIL PRINTS AS WELL AS FOOTPRINTS, BUT ONLY THE FOOTPRINTS CONTINUE UP THE STAIRS.
THE SUSPECT HADN'T THOUGHT THAT PART THROUGH.
ONCE THE SUSPECT HAD TURNED THE CORNER AND WAS OUT OF SIGHT OF THE KIDS...
...HE QUICKLY TOOK OFF THE GOMERA SUIT AT THE BASE OF THE STAIRS.
CARRYING THE SUIT, HE TOOK THE STAIRS IN THE OPPOSITE DIRECTION FROM THE PRE-PLANTED FOOT-PRINTS AND DESCENDED TO A ROOM BELOW.
HE SET FIRE TO THE SUIT AND DROPPED IT OUT THE WINDOW OF THAT ROOM!

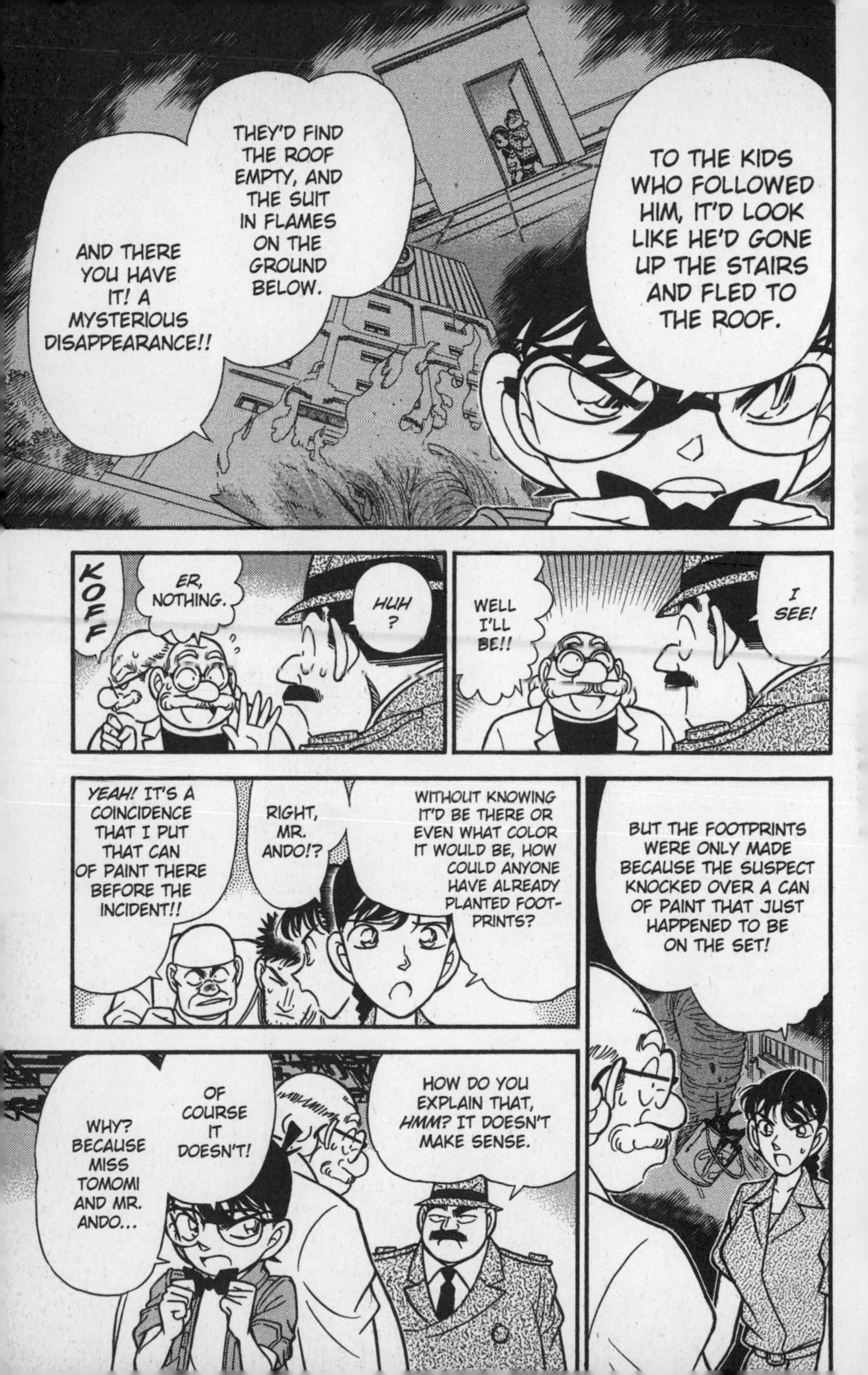
TO THE KIDS WHO FOLLOWED HIM, IT'D LOOK LIKE HE'D GONE UP THE STAIRS AND FLED TO THE ROOF.
THEY'D FIND THE ROOF EMPTY, AND THE SUIT IN FLAMES ON THE GROUND BELOW.
AND THERE YOU HAVE IT! A MYSTERIOUS DISAPPEARANCE!!
I SEE!
WELL I'LL BE!!
HUH?
ER, NOTHING.
KOFF
BUT THE FOOTPRINTS WERE ONLY MADE BECAUSE THE SUSPECT KNOCKED OVER A CAN OF PAINT THAT JUST HAPPENED TO BE ON THE SET!
WITHOUT KNOWING IT'D BE THERE OR EVEN WHAT COLOR IT WOULD BE, HOW COULD ANYONE HAVE ALREADY PLANTED FOOT-PRINTS?
RIGHT, MR. ANDO!?
YEAH! IT'S A COINCIDENCE THAT I PUT THAT CAN OF PAINT THERE BEFORE THE INCIDENT!!
HOW DO YOU EXPLAIN THAT, *HMM?* IT DOESN'T MAKE SENSE.
OF COURSE IT DOESN'T!
WHY? BECAUSE MISS TOMOMI AND MR. ANDO...

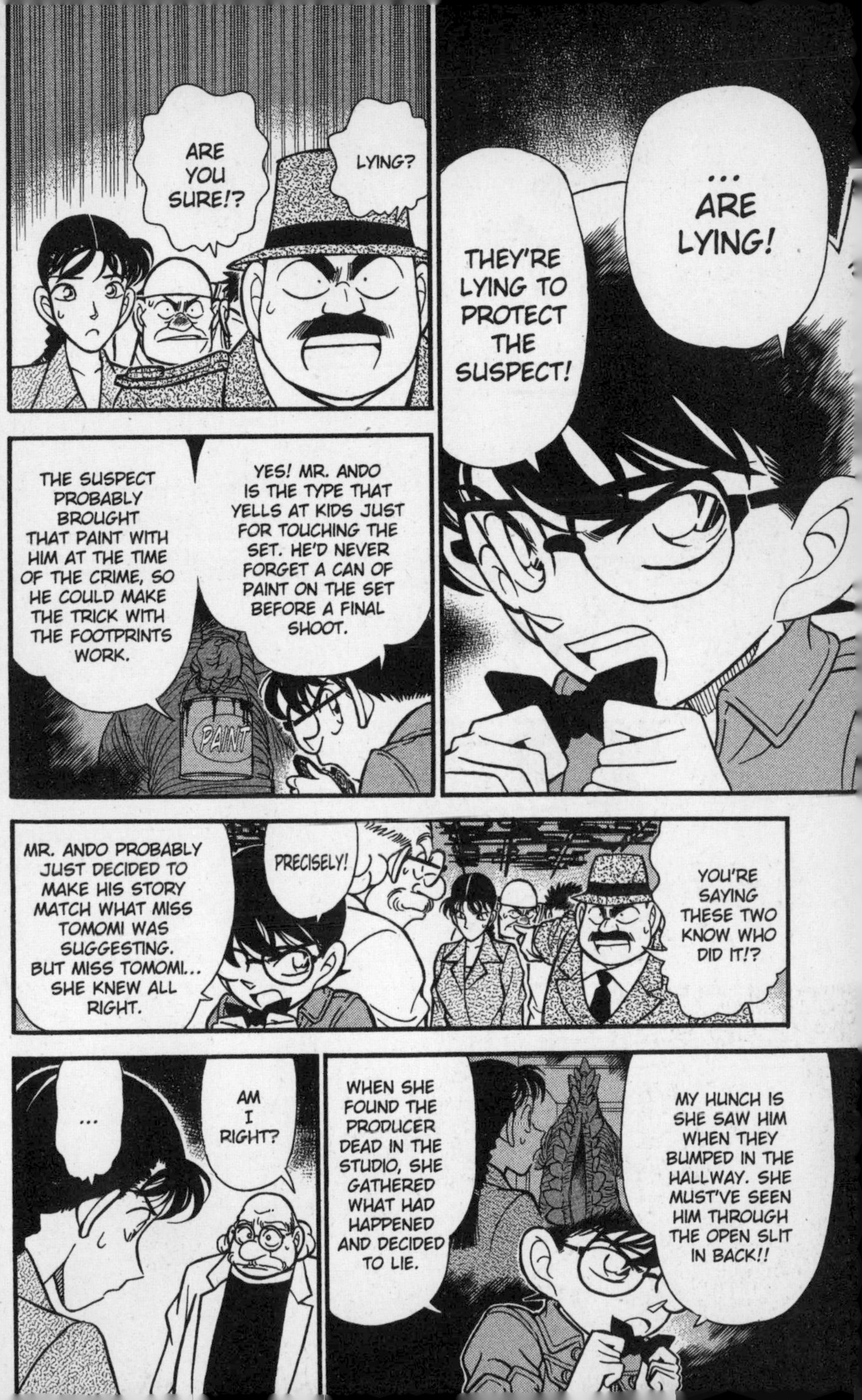
... ARE LYING!
THEY'RE LYING TO PROTECT THE SUSPECT!
LYING?
ARE YOU SURE!?
YES! MR. ANDO IS THE TYPE THAT YELLS AT KIDS JUST FOR TOUCHING THE SET. HE'D NEVER FORGET A CAN OF PAINT ON THE SET BEFORE A FINAL SHOOT.
THE SUSPECT PROBABLY BROUGHT THAT PAINT WITH HIM AT THE TIME OF THE CRIME, SO HE COULD MAKE THE TRICK WITH THE FOOTPRINTS WORK.
PAINT
YOU'RE SAYING THESE TWO KNOW WHO DID IT!?
PRECISELY!
MR. ANDO PROBABLY JUST DECIDED TO MAKE HIS STORY MATCH WHAT MISS TOMOMI WAS SUGGESTING. BUT MISS TOMOMI... SHE KNEW ALL RIGHT.
MY HUNCH IS SHE SAW HIM WHEN THEY BUMPED IN THE HALLWAY. SHE MUST'VE SEEN HIM THROUGH THE OPEN SLIT IN BACK!!
WHEN SHE FOUND THE PRODUCER DEAD IN THE STUDIO, SHE GATHERED WHAT HAD HAPPENED AND DECIDED TO LIE.
AM I RIGHT?
...

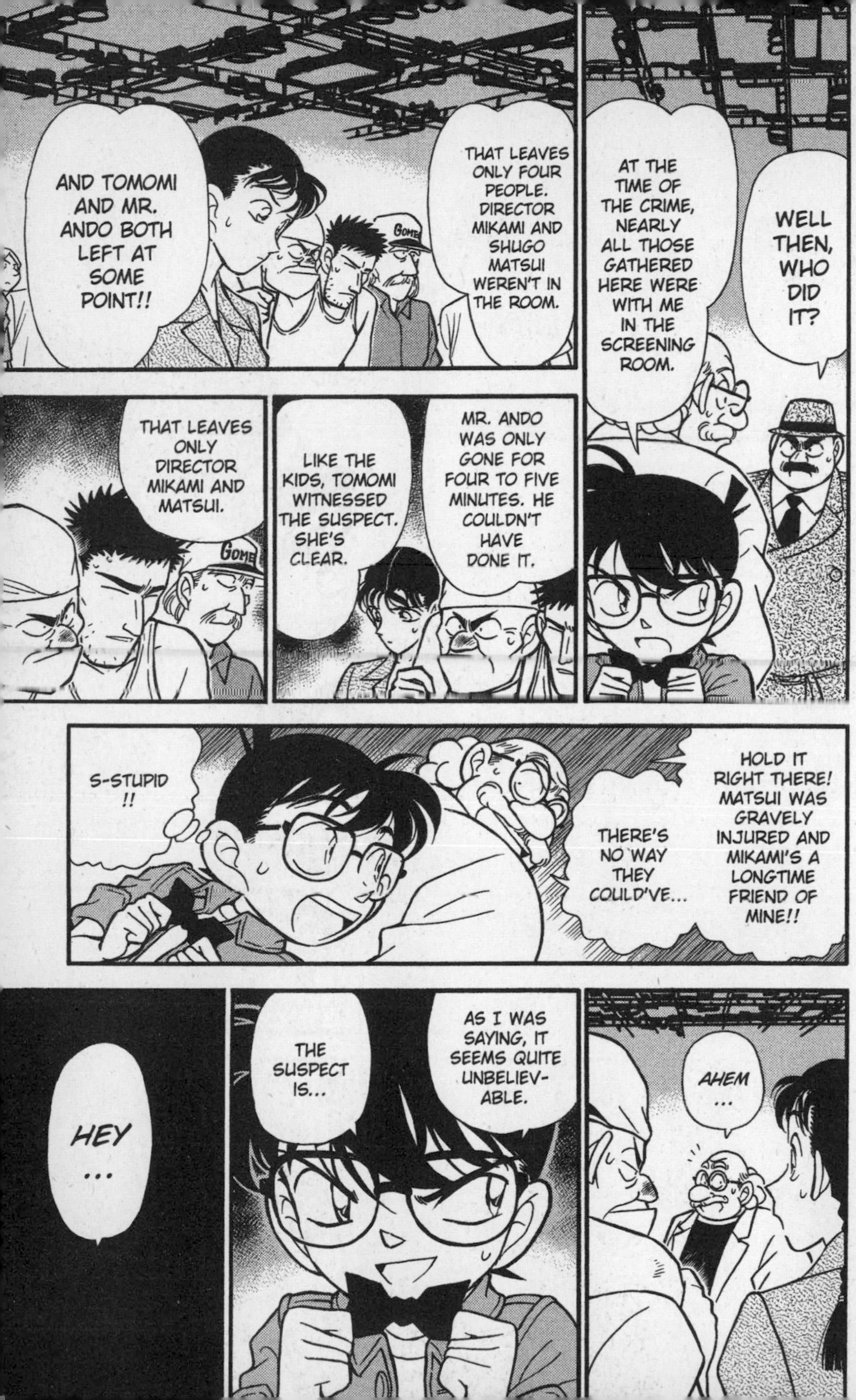
WELL THEN, WHO DID IT?
AT THE TIME OF THE CRIME, NEARLY ALL THOSE GATHERED HERE WERE WITH ME IN THE SCREENING ROOM.
THAT LEAVES ONLY FOUR PEOPLE. DIRECTOR MIKAMI AND SHUGO MATSUI WEREN'T IN THE ROOM.
AND TOMOMI AND MR. ANDO BOTH LEFT AT SOME POINT!!
MR. ANDO WAS ONLY GONE FOR FOUR TO FIVE MINUTES. HE COULDN'T HAVE DONE IT.
LIKE THE KIDS, TOMOMI WITNESSED THE SUSPECT. SHE'S CLEAR.
THAT LEAVES ONLY DIRECTOR MIKAMI AND MATSUI.
HOLD IT RIGHT THERE! MATSUI WAS GRAVELY INJURED AND MIKAMI'S A LONGTIME FRIEND OF MINE!!
THERE'S NO WAY THEY COULD'VE...
S-STUPID !!
AHEM ...
AS I WAS SAYING, IT SEEMS QUITE UNBELIEV-ABLE.
THE SUSPECT IS...
HEY ...

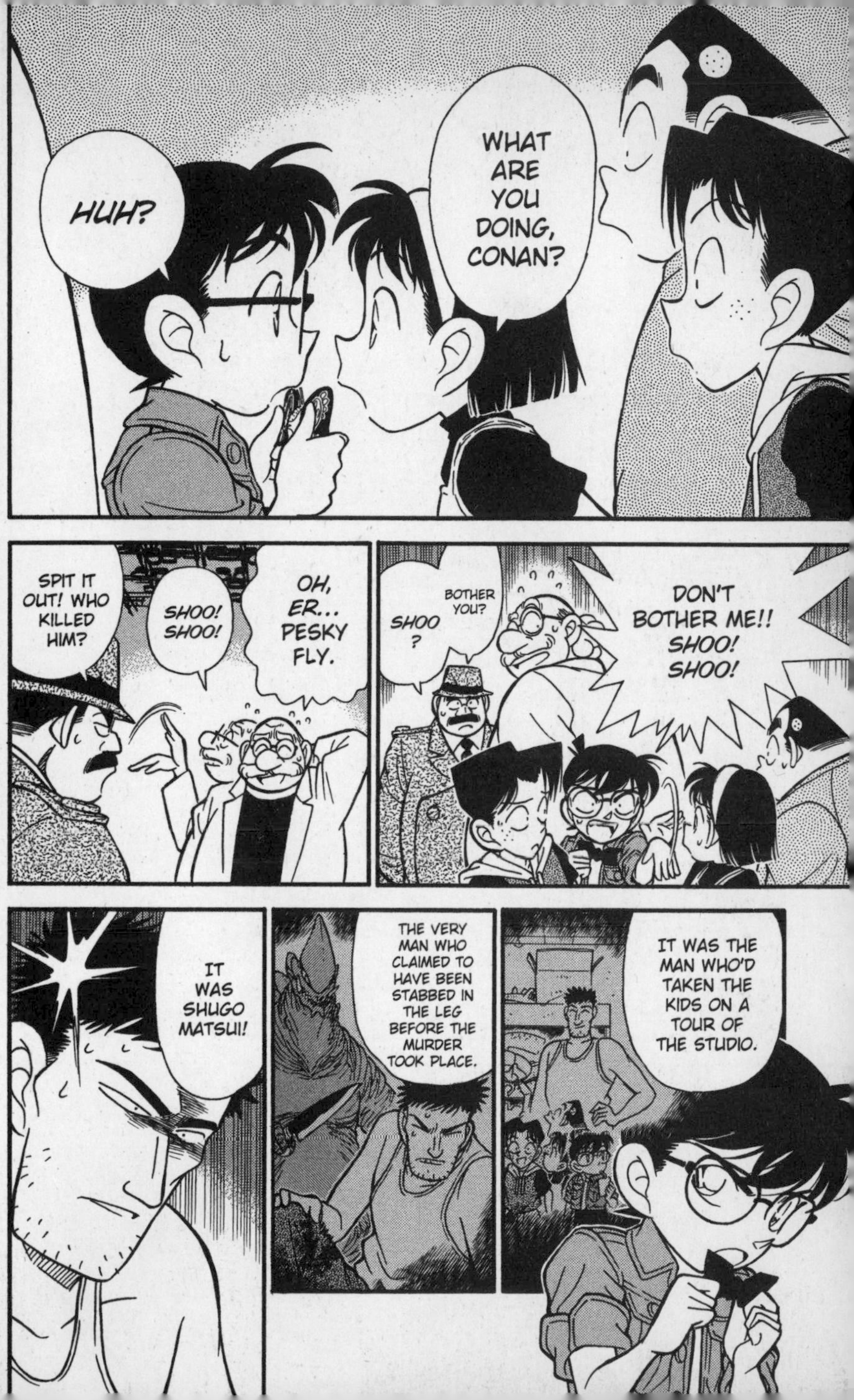
WHAT ARE YOU DOING, CONAN?
HUH?
DON'T BOTHER ME!! SHOO! SHOO!
BOTHER YOU?
SHOO ?
OH, ER... PESKY FLY.
SHOO! SHOO!
SPIT IT OUT! WHO KILLED HIM?
IT WAS THE MAN WHO'D TAKEN THE KIDS ON A TOUR OF THE STUDIO.
THE VERY MAN WHO CLAIMED TO HAVE BEEN STABBED IN THE LEG BEFORE THE MURDER TOOK PLACE.
IT WAS SHUGO MATSUI!

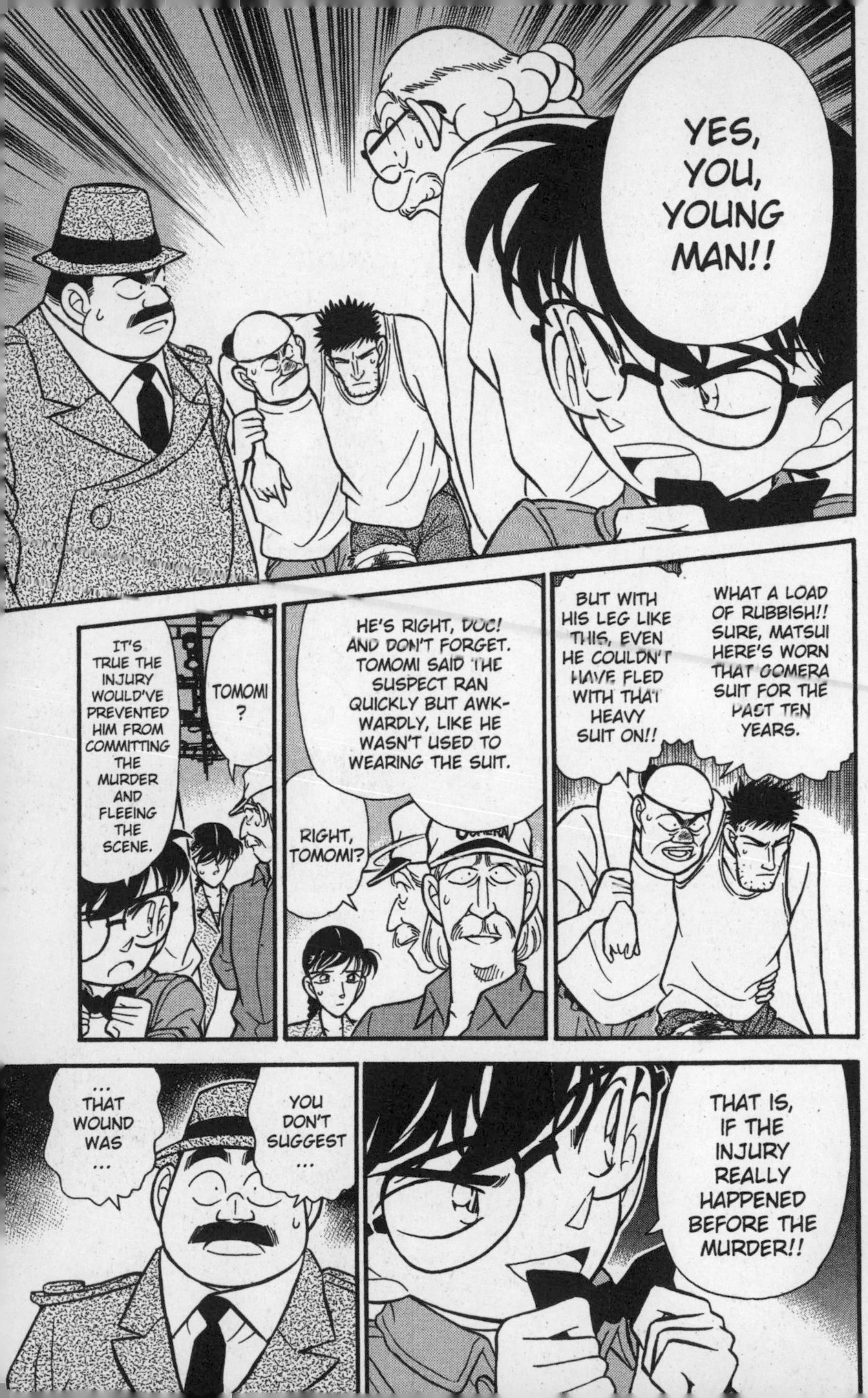
YES, YOU, YOUNG MAN!!
WHAT A LOAD OF RUBBISH!! SURE, MATSUI HERE'S WORN THAT GOMERA SUIT FOR THE PAST TEN YEARS.
BUT WITH HIS LEG LIKE THIS, EVEN HE COULDN'T HAVE FLED WITH THAT HEAVY SUIT ON!!
HE'S RIGHT, DOC! AND DON'T FORGET. TOMOMI SAID THE SUSPECT RAN QUICKLY BUT AWK-WARDLY, LIKE HE WASN'T USED TO WEARING THE SUIT.
RIGHT, TOMOMI?
TOMOMI ?
IT'S TRUE THE INJURY WOULD'VE PREVENTED HIM FROM COMMITTING THE MURDER AND FLEEING THE SCENE.
THAT IS, IF THE INJURY REALLY HAPPENED BEFORE THE MURDER!!
YOU DON'T SUGGEST ...
... THAT WOUND WAS ...

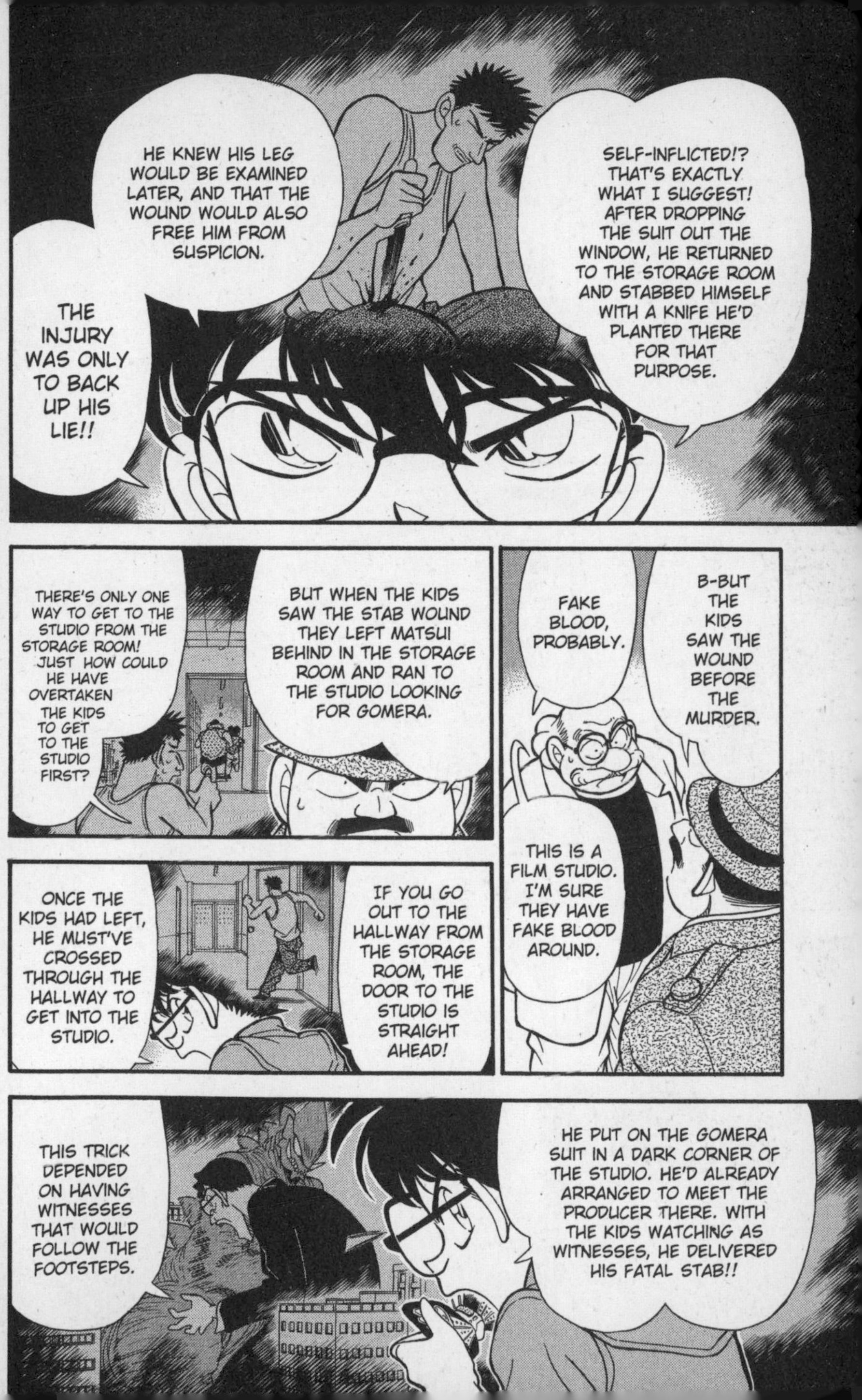
SELF-INFLICTED!? THAT'S EXACTLY WHAT I SUGGEST! AFTER DROPPING THE SUIT OUT THE WINDOW, HE RETURNED TO THE STORAGE ROOM AND STABBED HIMSELF WITH A KNIFE HE'D PLANTED THERE FOR THAT PURPOSE.
HE KNEW HIS LEG WOULD BE EXAMINED LATER, AND THAT THE WOUND WOULD ALSO FREE HIM FROM SUSPICION.
THE INJURY WAS ONLY TO BACK UP HIS LIE!!
B-BUT THE KIDS SAW THE WOUND BEFORE THE MURDER.
FAKE BLOOD, PROBABLY.
THIS IS A FILM STUDIO. I'M SURE THEY HAVE FAKE BLOOD AROUND.
BUT WHEN THE KIDS SAW THE STAB WOUND THEY LEFT MATSUI BEHIND IN THE STORAGE ROOM AND RAN TO THE STUDIO LOOKING FOR GOMERA.
THERE'S ONLY ONE WAY TO GET TO THE STUDIO FROM THE STORAGE ROOM! JUST HOW COULD HE HAVE OVERTAKEN THE KIDS TO GET TO THE STUDIO FIRST?
IF YOU GO OUT TO THE HALLWAY FROM THE STORAGE ROOM, THE DOOR TO THE STUDIO IS STRAIGHT AHEAD!
ONCE THE KIDS HAD LEFT, HE MUST'VE CROSSED THROUGH THE HALLWAY TO GET INTO THE STUDIO.
HE PUT ON THE GOMERA SUIT IN A DARK CORNER OF THE STUDIO. HE'D ALREADY ARRANGED TO MEET THE PRODUCER THERE. WITH THE KIDS WATCHING AS WITNESSES, HE DELIVERED HIS FATAL STAB!!
THIS TRICK DEPENDED ON HAVING WITNESSES THAT WOULD FOLLOW THE FOOTSTEPS.

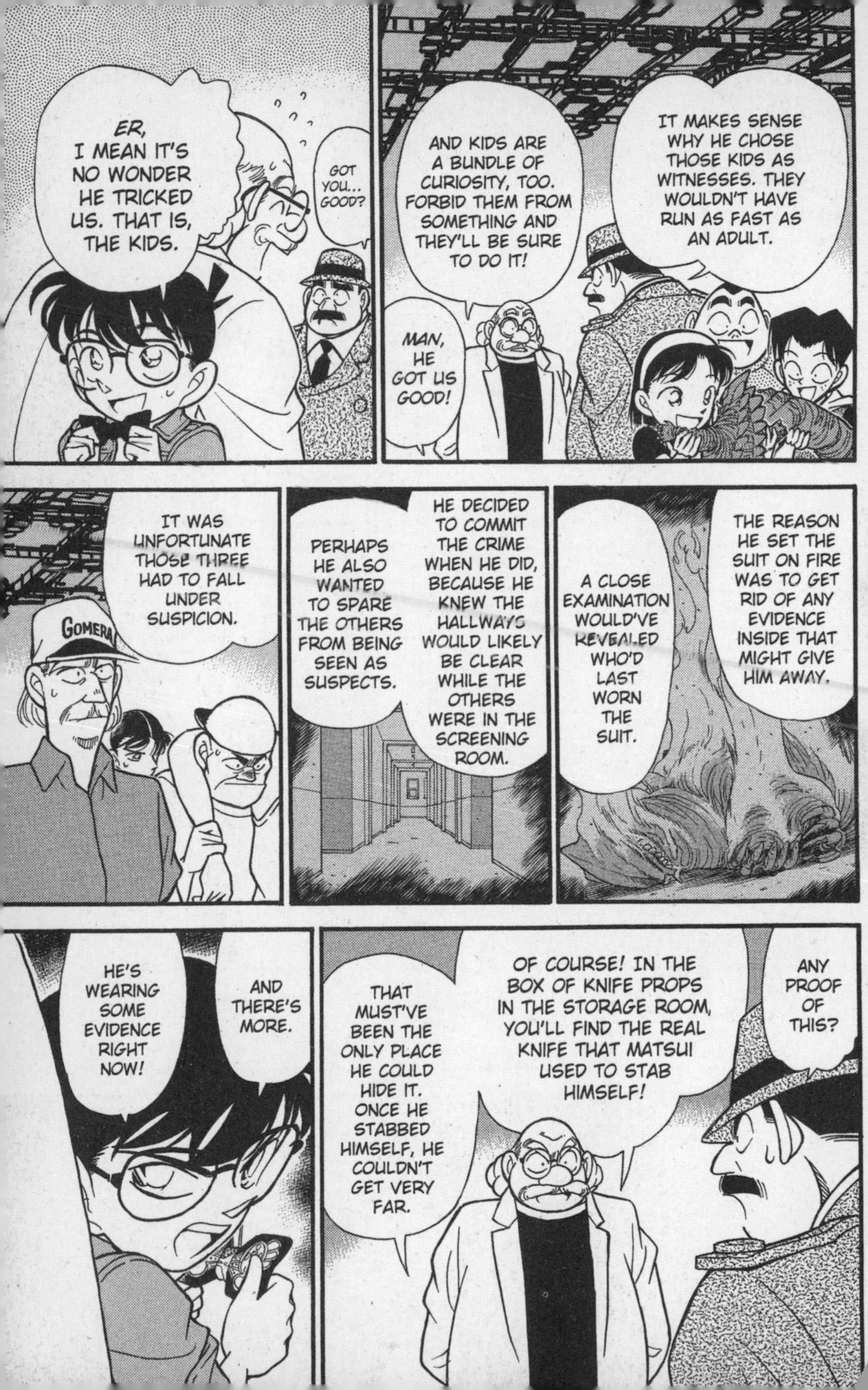
IT MAKES SENSE WHY HE CHOSE THOSE KIDS AS WITNESSES. THEY WOULDN'T HAVE RUN AS FAST AS AN ADULT.
AND KIDS ARE A BUNDLE OF CURIOSITY, TOO. FORBID THEM FROM SOMETHING AND THEY'LL BE SURE TO DO IT!
MAN, HE GOT US GOOD!
GOT YOU... GOOD?
ER, I MEAN IT'S NO WONDER HE TRICKED US. THAT IS, THE KIDS.
THE REASON HE SET THE SUIT ON FIRE WAS TO GET RID OF ANY EVIDENCE INSIDE THAT MIGHT GIVE HIM AWAY.
A CLOSE EXAMINATION WOULD'VE REVEALED WHO'D LAST WORN THE SUIT.
HE DECIDED TO COMMIT THE CRIME WHEN HE DID, BECAUSE HE KNEW THE HALLWAYS WOULD LIKELY BE CLEAR WHILE THE OTHERS WERE IN THE SCREENING ROOM.
PERHAPS HE ALSO WANTED TO SPARE THE OTHERS FROM BEING SEEN AS SUSPECTS.
IT WAS UNFORTUNATE THOSE THREE HAD TO FALL UNDER SUSPICION.
GOMERA
ANY PROOF OF THIS?
OF COURSE! IN THE BOX OF KNIFE PROPS IN THE STORAGE ROOM, YOU'LL FIND THE REAL KNIFE THAT MATSUI USED TO STAB HIMSELF!
THAT MUST'VE BEEN THE ONLY PLACE HE COULD HIDE IT. ONCE HE STABBED HIMSELF, HE COULDN'T GET VERY FAR.
AND THERE'S MORE.
HE'S WEARING SOME EVIDENCE RIGHT NOW!

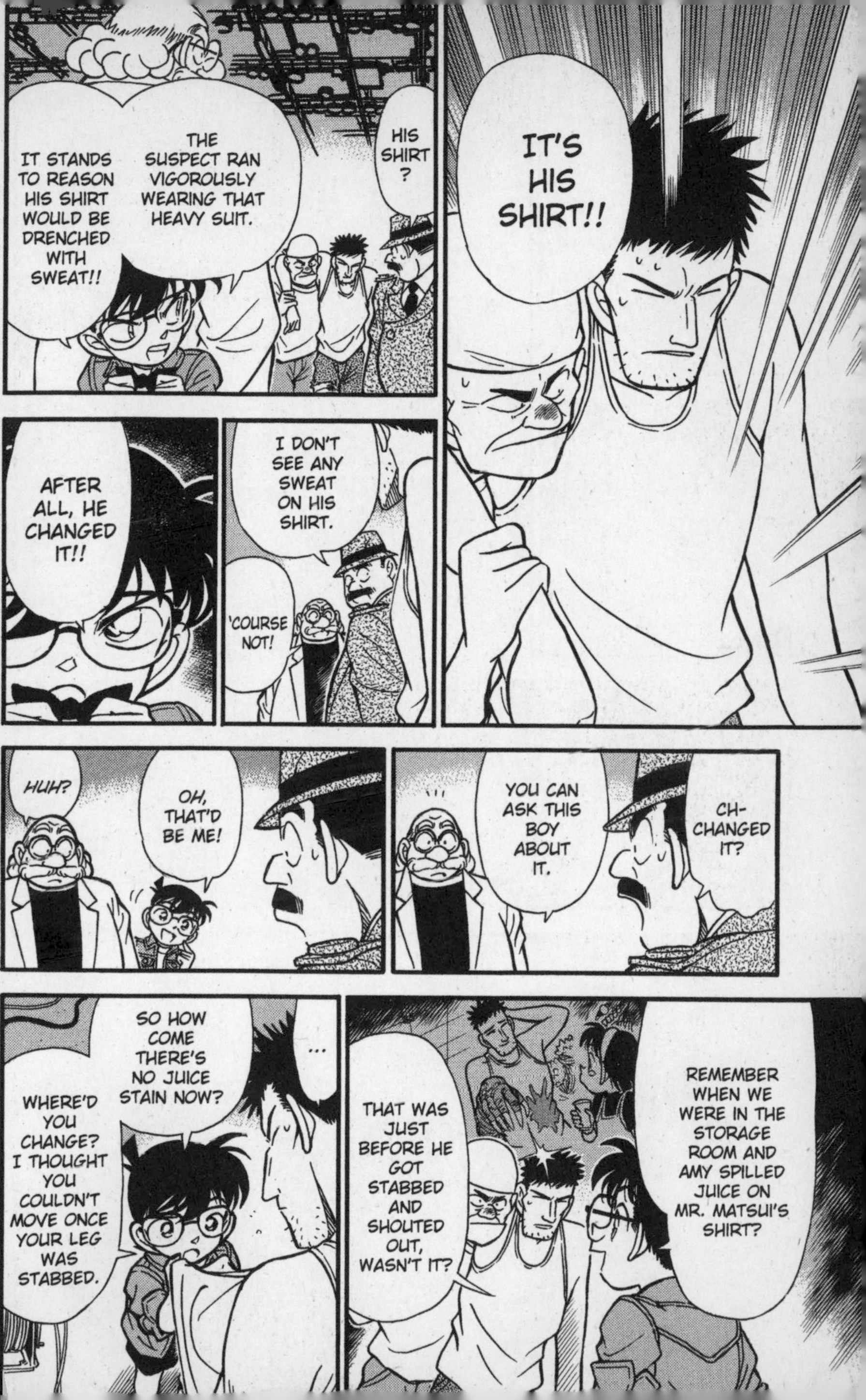
IT'S HIS SHIRT!!
HIS SHIRT?
THE SUSPECT RAN VIGOROUSLY WEARING THAT HEAVY SUIT.
IT STANDS TO REASON HIS SHIRT WOULD BE DRENCHED WITH SWEAT!!
I DON'T SEE ANY SWEAT ON HIS SHIRT.
'COURSE NOT!
AFTER ALL, HE CHANGED IT!!
CH-CHANGED IT?
YOU CAN ASK THIS BOY ABOUT IT.
OH, THAT'D BE ME!
HUH?
REMEMBER WHEN WE WERE IN THE STORAGE ROOM AND AMY SPILLED JUICE ON MR. MATSUI'S SHIRT?
THAT WAS JUST BEFORE HE GOT STABBED AND SHOUTED OUT, WASN'T IT?
...
SO HOW COME THERE'S NO JUICE STAIN NOW?
WHERE'D YOU CHANGE? I THOUGHT YOU COULDN'T MOVE ONCE YOUR LEG WAS STABBED.

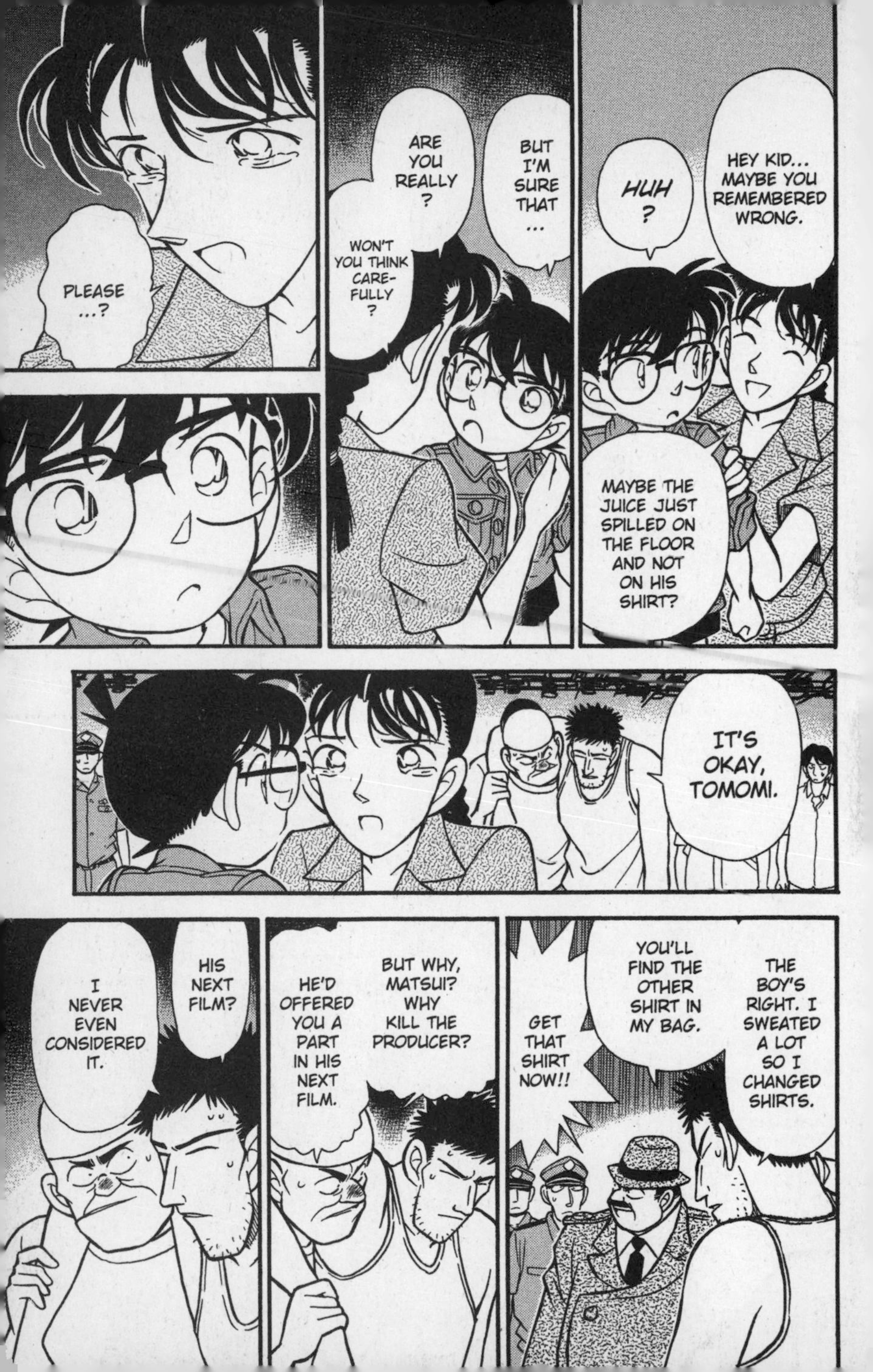
HEY KID... MAYBE YOU REMEMBERED WRONG.
HUH?
MAYBE THE JUICE JUST SPILLED ON THE FLOOR AND NOT ON HIS SHIRT?
BUT I'M SURE THAT...
ARE YOU REALLY?
WON'T YOU THINK CARE-FULLY?
PLEASE...?
IT'S OKAY, TOMOMI.
THE BOY'S RIGHT. I SWEATED A LOT SO I CHANGED SHIRTS.
YOU'LL FIND THE OTHER SHIRT IN MY BAG.
GET THAT SHIRT NOW!!
BUT WHY, MATSUI? WHY KILL THE PRODUCER?
HE'D OFFERED YOU A PART IN HIS NEXT FILM.
HIS NEXT FILM?
I NEVER EVEN CONSIDERED IT.

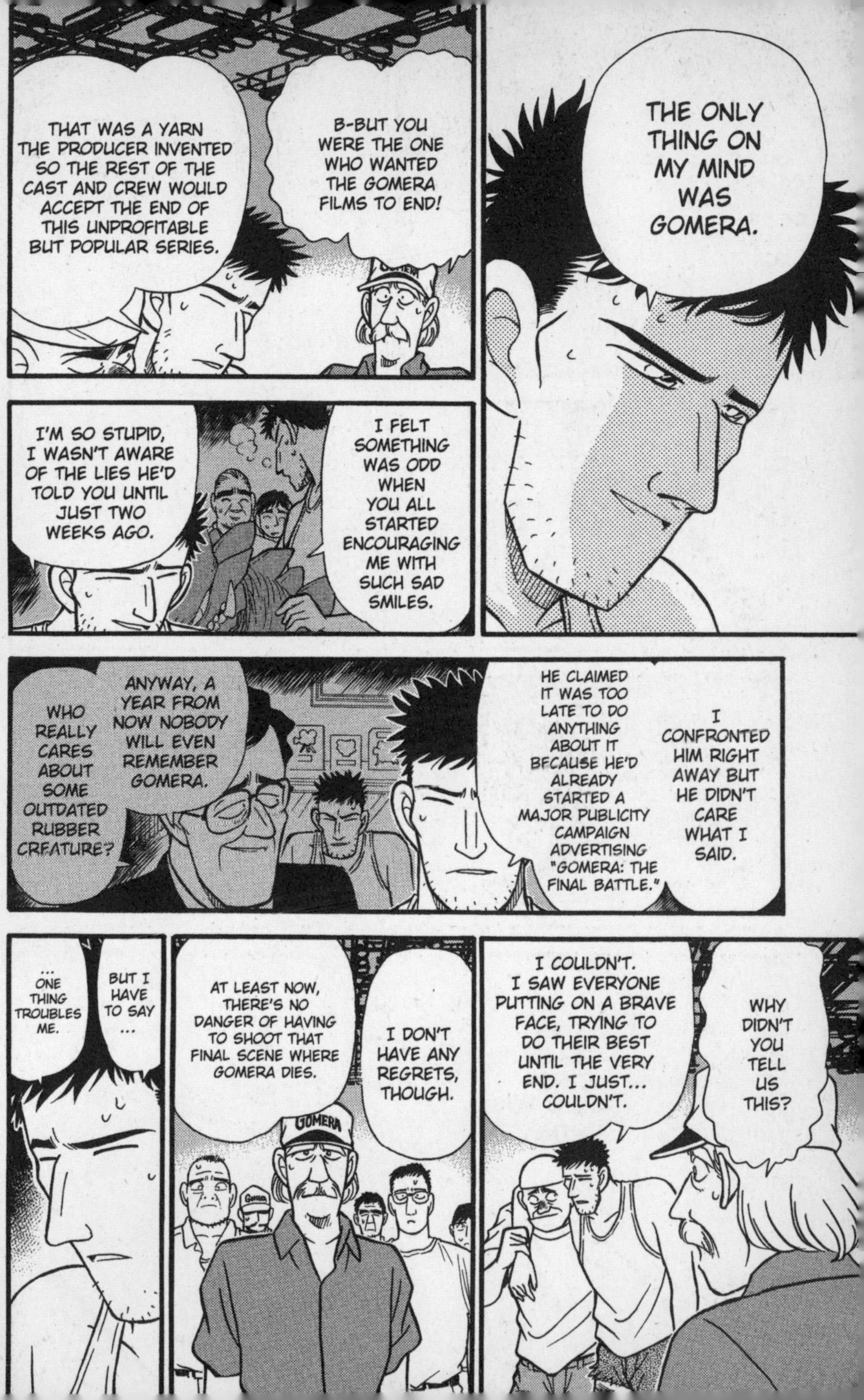
THE ONLY THING ON MY MIND WAS GOMERA.
B-BUT YOU WERE THE ONE WHO WANTED THE GOMERA FILMS TO END!
THAT WAS A YARN THE PRODUCER INVENTED SO THE REST OF THE CAST AND CREW WOULD ACCEPT THE END OF THIS UNPROFITABLE BUT POPULAR SERIES.
I FELT SOMETHING WAS ODD WHEN YOU ALL STARTED ENCOURAGING ME WITH SUCH SAD SMILES.
I'M SO STUPID, I WASN'T AWARE OF THE LIES HE'D TOLD YOU UNTIL JUST TWO WEEKS AGO.
I CONFRONTED HIM RIGHT AWAY BUT HE DIDN'T CARE WHAT I SAID.
HE CLAIMED IT WAS TOO LATE TO DO ANYTHING ABOUT IT BECAUSE HE'D ALREADY STARTED A MAJOR PUBLICITY CAMPAIGN ADVERTISING "GOMERA: THE FINAL BATTLE."
ANYWAY, A YEAR FROM NOW NOBODY WILL EVEN REMEMBER GOMERA.
WHO REALLY CARES ABOUT SOME OUTDATED RUBBER CREATURE?
WHY DIDN'T YOU TELL US THIS?
I COULDN'T. I SAW EVERYONE PUTTING ON A BRAVE FACE, TRYING TO DO THEIR BEST UNTIL THE VERY END. I JUST... COULDN'T.
I DON'T HAVE ANY REGRETS, THOUGH.
AT LEAST NOW, THERE'S NO DANGER OF HAVING TO SHOOT THAT FINAL SCENE WHERE GOMERA DIES.
BUT I HAVE TO SAY ...
... ONE THING TROUBLES ME.

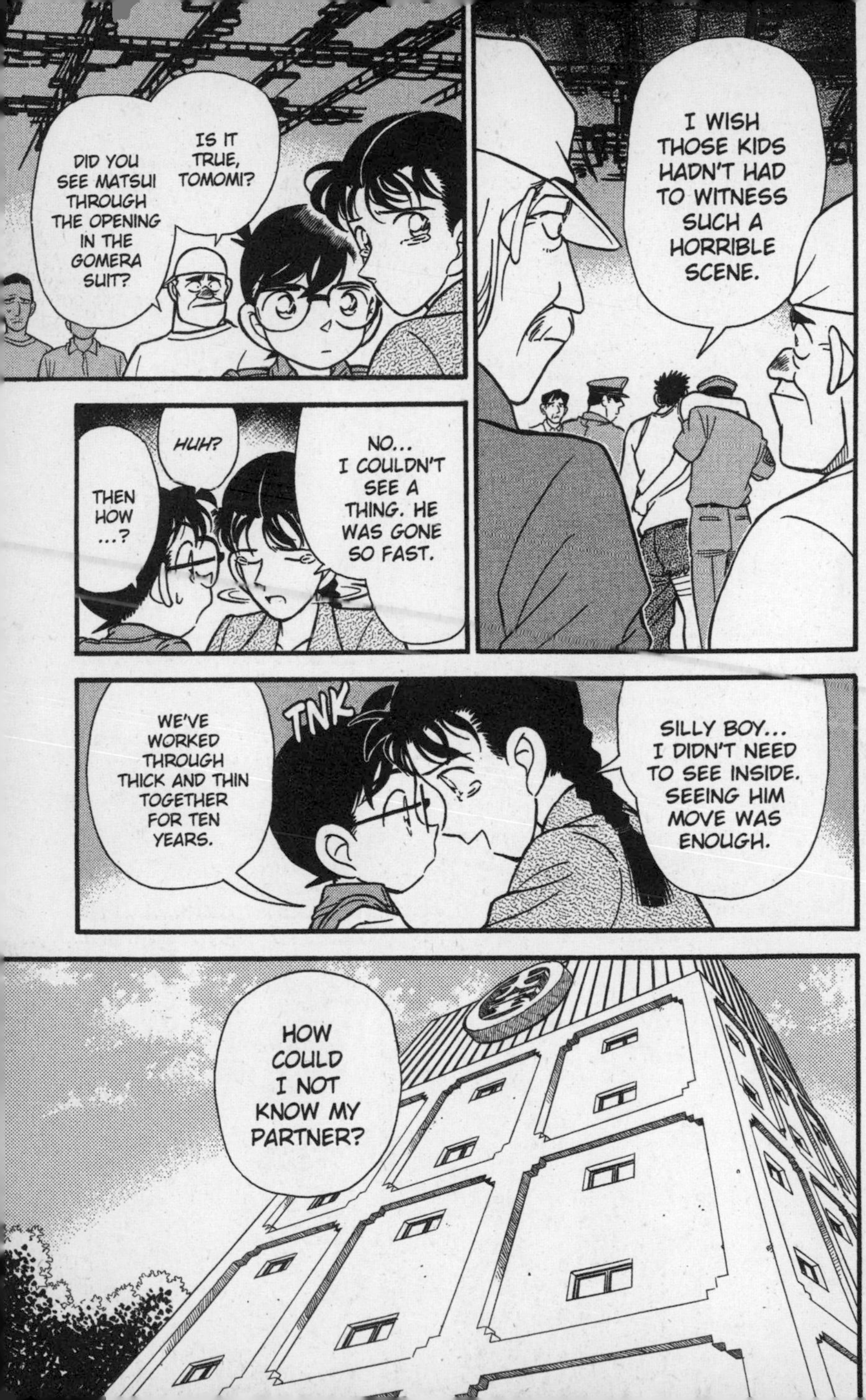
I WISH THOSE KIDS HADN'T HAD TO WITNESS SUCH A HORRIBLE SCENE.
IS IT TRUE, TOMOMI?
DID YOU SEE MATSUI THROUGH THE OPENING IN THE GOMERA SUIT?
NO... I COULDN'T SEE A THING. HE WAS GONE SO FAST.
HUH?
THEN HOW ...?
SILLY BOY... I DIDN'T NEED TO SEE INSIDE. SEEING HIM MOVE WAS ENOUGH.
TNK
WE'VE WORKED THROUGH THICK AND THIN TOGETHER FOR TEN YEARS.
HOW COULD I NOT KNOW MY PARTNER?

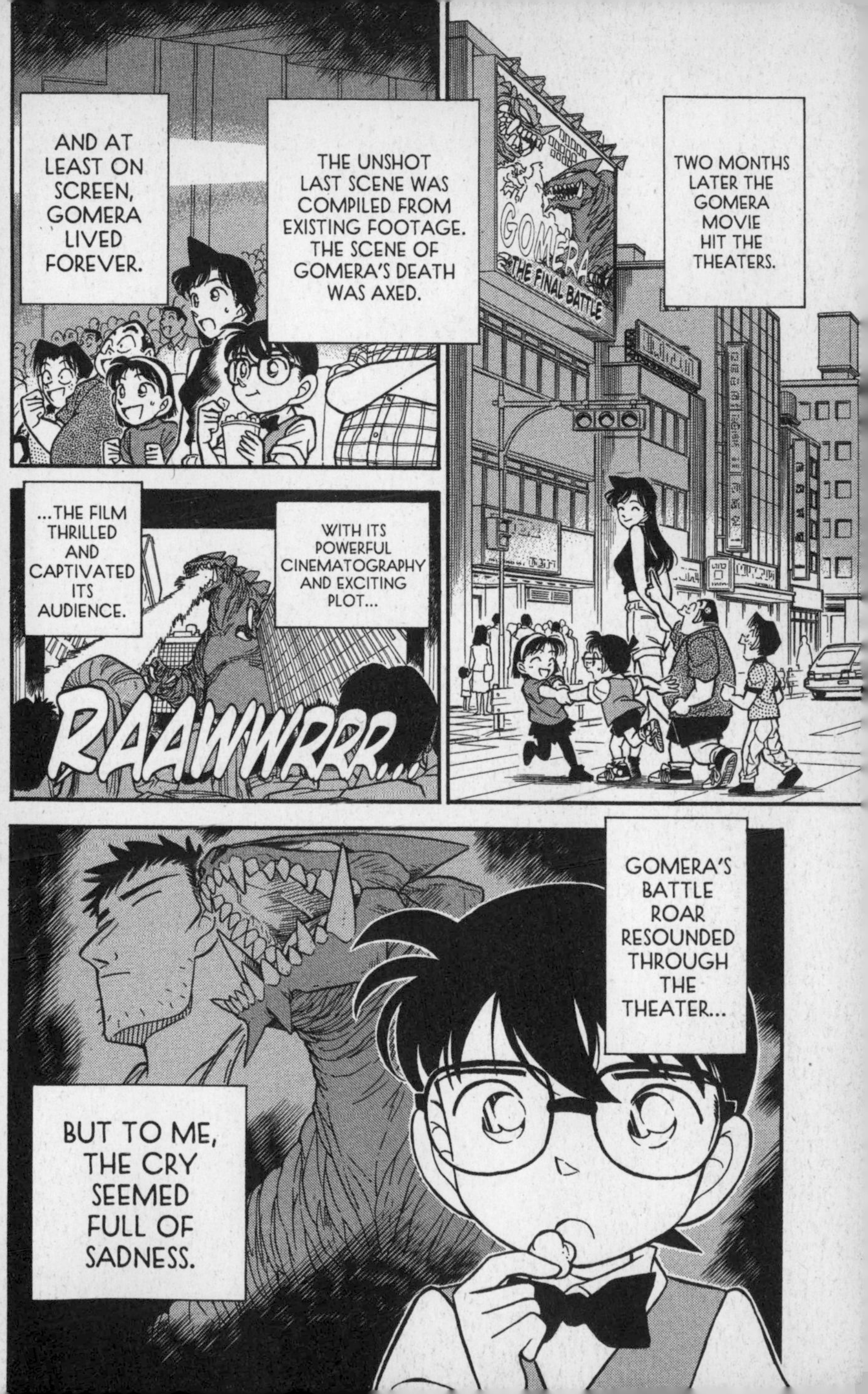
TWO MONTHS LATER THE GOMERA MOVIE HIT THE THEATERS.
GOMERA THE FINAL BATTLE
THE UNSHOT LAST SCENE WAS COMPILED FROM EXISTING FOOTAGE. THE SCENE OF GOMERA'S DEATH WAS AXED.
AND AT LEAST ON SCREEN, GOMERA LIVED FOREVER.
WITH ITS POWERFUL CINEMATOGRAPHY AND EXCITING PLOT...
...THE FILM THRILLED AND CAPTIVATED ITS AUDIENCE.
RAAWWRRR...
GOMERA'S BATTLE ROAR RESOUNDED THROUGH THE THEATER...
BUT TO ME, THE CRY SEEMED FULL OF SADNESS.

Hello, Aoyama here.

Three years have flown by since I started Conan!
He's already been involved in about 30 cases!!
Brutal cases, sad cases, unlucky cases, and more...
Boy! Case after case, Conan sure has his hands full!
I'm happy I'm not a detective. ♥
Oh wait. I'm the one thinking these up. (Ha ha ha...)

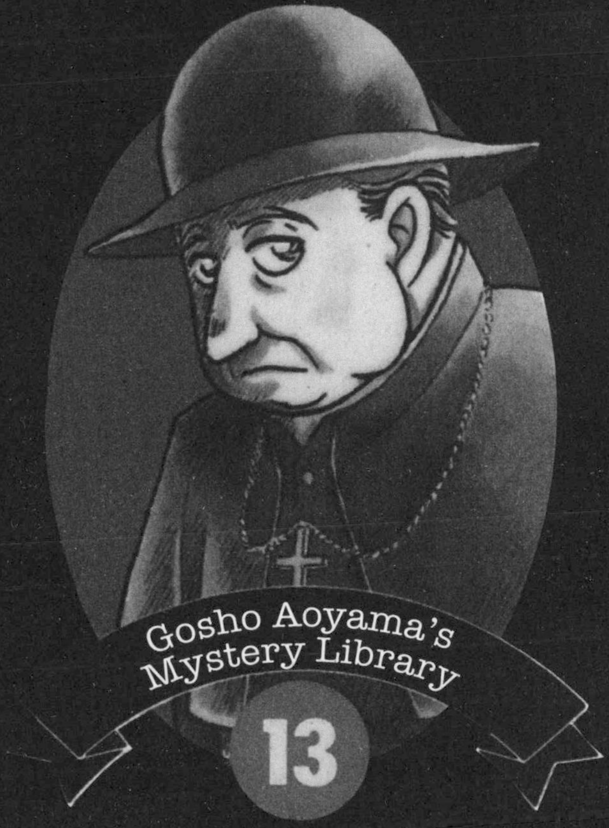
Gosho Aoyama's
Mystery Library
13

FATHER BROWN

There may be many great detectives, but the one whose outward appearance is most misleading is most certainly Father Brown! Created by G. K. Chesterton, this detective is short and pudgy. He has a round face with vacant, round eyes. He constantly forgets his trusty, worn umbrella, and looks like a doddering country priest. Yet as he meanders feebly through crime scenes, his keen observational skills help him understand the psychology of his criminal. He unravels even the most difficult cases with his unexpected yet brilliant deductions, dumbfounding those around him. But regretfully, his first job is that of a Catholic priest. Sometimes he gets the criminal to reform, then lets him go. One such criminal is Flambeau, who later assists him in some cases. Originally a jewel thief, after his reform he turns honest and becomes a private investigator. You could call yourself lucky to be a criminal who runs into Father Brown... (I recommend *The Queer Feet*.)